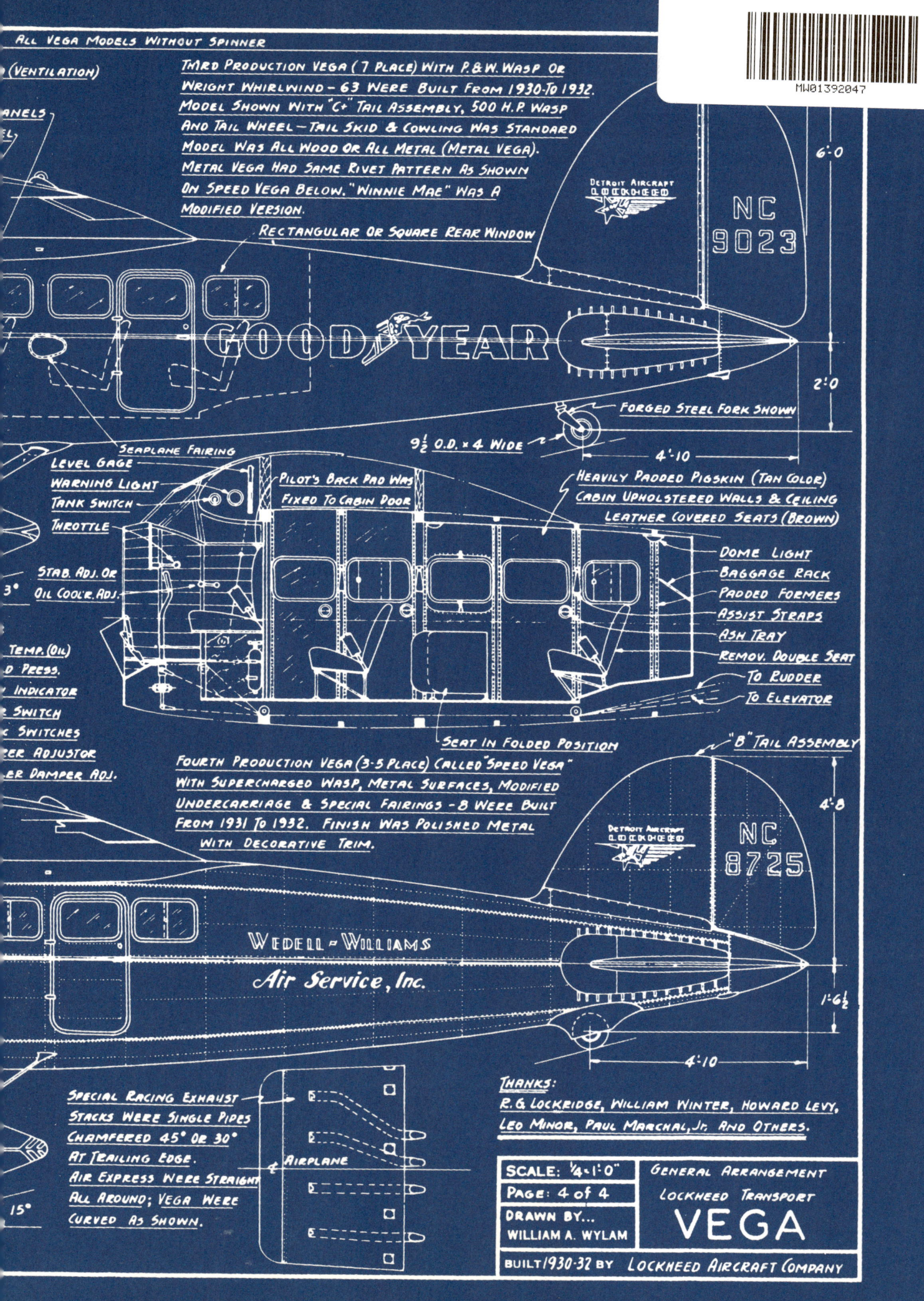

LOCKHEED

LOCKHEED

BILL YENNE

Crescent Books
A Division of Crown Publishers, Inc.
A Bison Book

Library of Congress Cataloging-in-Publication Data

Yenne, Bill, 1949–
   Lockheed.

   Includes index.
   1. Lockheed Aircraft Corporation.   2. Aircraft industry—United States.   3. Aerospace industries—United States.   I. Title
HD9711.U64L639 1987   338.7′6291334′0973   85-31368

Copyright © 1987 Bison Books Corp.

All rights reserved. No part of this publication may be reproduced, stored in a retrieval system or transmitted in any form by any means, electronic, mechanical, photocopying or otherwise, without first obtaining written permission of the copyright owner.

Published 1987 by
Cresent Books, distributed by
Crown Publishers Inc.

Produced by Bison Books Corp.
15 Sherwood Place
Greenwich, CT 06830, USA

Printed in Hong Kong

ISBN 0-517-60471-X
h g f e d c b a

Page 1: Like Rosie the Riveter, this young lady was one of thousands of women who worked on Lockheed's assembly line for the P-38 Lightning as part of the United States World War II production effort.

Pages 2-3: A Lockheed Model 649 Constellation plies the passenger skies for Pan American Airlines. 'Connies' were among the most important passenger liners of the postwar forties and fifties.

Pages 4-5: Above: One of the premier pursuit planes of World War II, the P-38 Lightning showed the 'machine guns bristling' aspect seen on these pages to many an enemy pilot.

CONTENTS

The Early Days
- The Brothers Loughead — 6
- Lockheed and the Vega — 13
- Detroit Lockheed — 18
- Lockheed's First Fighter — 23

Twin Engines and Twin Tails
- A New Start — 24
- The Electra — 24
- The Electra Junior — 28
- The Super Electra — 30
- The Hudson — 32
- The Ventura — 37
- A Summary of Lockheed's Twin-Engined, Twin-Tailed Aircraft — 40

The Constellation
- A Germ of an Idea — 44
- The Connie Becomes a Military Transport — 44
- The Connie Flies At Last — 45
- Into Airline Service — 46
- The Super Constellation — 48
- The Last Constellations — 52
- The Starliner — 56

The Fork-Tailed Devil
- Ahead of Its Time — 60
- The Lightning at War — 68

Lockheed Patrol Planes
- The Neptune — 78
- The Electra and the Orion — 82
- The Viking — 92

Lockheed Jet Fighters
- The Shooting Star — 96
- The T-Bird and SeaStar — 103
- The Starfire — 106
- The XF-90 Project — 108
- The Pogo — 112
- The Starfighter — 114

The Skunk Works Projects
- A Place So Secret — 124
- The U-2 Project — 124
- The TR-1 Project — 127
- Liquid Hydrogen Powered Aircraft — 129
- The A-12/YF-12 Project — 132
- The Blackbird — 136
- The Skunk Works after Kelly Johnson — 144

Lockheed Helicopters
- The Model 475 — 146
- The Model 186/286 Series — 146
- The Cheyenne — 147

Lockheed of Georgia
- Going South — 150
- The Hercules — 150
- The Jetstar — 166
- The Starlifter — 167
- The Galaxy — 171

The L-1011 Tristar
- Planning a Jumbo Jet — 182
- Early Development — 186
- Competition and Crisis — 186
- The TriStar in Service — 193

Lockheed Missiles & Space
- New Frontiers, New Programs — 204
- The Polaris — 206
- The Poseidon — 208
- The Trident — 209
- Other LMSC Programs — 212
- LMSC Aircraft — 220
- The Hubble Space Telescope — 223

Reaching for the Stars
- A Portrait of Lockheed — 226
- The Aeronautical Systems Group — 231
- The Missiles & Space Systems Group — 233
- The Information Systems Group — 233
- The Marine Systems Group — 233
- The Electronic Systems Group — 235
- Corporate Components Not Assigned to Groups — 235
- A Concise Financial History of Lockheed — 235
- The Birth of the F-22 Program — 244
- Reaching for the Stars — 247

THE EARLY DAYS

THE BROTHERS LOUGHEAD

In San Francisco aviation circles they still talk about that foggy June morning in 1913 when Allan and Malcolm Loughead (pronounced *Lockheed*) trucked their Model G Float plane down to the foot of Laguna street. The fog that almost always greets San Franciscans on summer mornings is more like a low overcast—not good flying weather at higher altitudes, but better for takeoffs and landings than in the afternoon when the fog burns off and the wind picks up.

Allan Loughead climbed into the cockpit and coaxed the 80 hp Curtiss V-8 engine to life. Slowly at first, Allan taxied across the cold waters of San Francisco Bay. When he was sure that the Curtiss was running smoothly, he accelerated and then pulled back on the stick. As Malcolm Loughead and Bob Coleman cheered from the shore, Allan lifted the Model G into the air and into the annals of American aviation history. For 15 minutes Allan flew high above the Bay and the city. He rounded Alcatraz and swept around the city's waterfront. He flew over the San Francisco Ferry Building and looked down on Market Street where thousands of workmen were still rebuilding the city's financial district in the wake of the great earthquake seven years before.

The second flight of the Model G immediately followed the first after the enthusiastic Allan returned to Laguna to collect his brother. It was ten years since those other brothers named Wright had first flown a heavier-than-air craft and just two years since Glenn Curtiss had become the first American to take off in a float plane, but still the historic event gathered little notice in the local press; the San Francisco papers were more concerned with the upcoming lightweight title bout between champion Willie Ritchie and challenger Joe Rivers. As far as the Bay was concerned, more attention was being given the five schooners from the San Francisco and Sausalito yacht clubs and their big race than was given to the little float plane scampering about. For the Loughead brothers, however, it was a milestone.

As young boys in San Francisco, and later in their teens after the family moved south to the Santa Clara Valley, both Allan and Malcolm had shown a great deal of interest in things mechanical. In 1904, at age 17, Malcolm moved back to San Francisco to work as a mechanic for the White Steam Car Company. Two years later he was joined by his younger brother, who worked for White for two years before he took a job driving Corbin automobiles in hill climbing exhibitions.

Allan Loughead's entree into the world of aviation came by way of his and Malcolm's older half-brother, Victor Loughead. Victor was an aeronautical engineer by avocation and was the author of two books on aircraft theory. Victor shared his interest in aviation with his employer, James Plew, who was the Chicago distributor for White Steam Car. In 1910 Victor came to California to enlist Allan's help in buying a Montgomery glider for Plew. In the course of the negotiations, Allan accepted a job with Plew and returned to Chicago with Victor, where he was to work as a mechanic on Plew's Curtiss and his motorized Montgomery glider.

Once he got his Curtiss to Chicago, Plew had it taken out to snow-covered Hawthorne race track for its first flight. Two pilots already had tried unsuccessfully to get it airborne when 23 year old Allan Loughead stepped forward.

'Help me turn it around. I know it will fly,' he said. 'All it needs is a little adjustment. I've got a $20 gold piece that says I'll make it fly. Any takers?'

There were none. Allan set to work and within minutes the engine was throbbing and the Curtiss began to taxi across the snow. Suddenly it lifted into the air and Allan Loughead was airborne. After a couple of turns around the field, he returned to earth, having become a pilot.

Allan Loughead remained as one of James Plew's pilots until the latter gave up on aviation in 1911. Allan then worked for a time as a flying instructor for International Aviation of Chicago. In 1912 he made four appearances as a barnstormer at Illinois county fairs, but the last of these ended with he and his airplane hanging from a telegraph pole on the outskirts of Hoopeston, Illinois.

Allan Loughead walked away from the Hoopeston wreck with a few scratches and a determination to build a better flying machine. He rejoined Malcolm in San Francisco where they pooled $1800 of their own money with $1200 invested by Max Mamlock of the Alco Taxicab Company to start the Alco Hydro-Aeroplane Company. The Loughead brothers took regular jobs, but worked nights and weekends at their garage on Pacific Avenue. Over the course of the next 18 months the Model G gradually took shape and on 15 June 1913 their hard work finally paid off.

The Model G was the first successful tractor seaplane (front-mounted propeller) in the United States, and it came just two years after Glenn Curtiss pioneered America's first seaplane and just three years after Henri Fabre of France flew the first seaplane.

Two years later San Francisco's northern waterfront was the scene of the Panama-Pacific Exposition, a grand world's fair designed to celebrate the completion of the Panama Canal and San Francisco's successful recovery from the disastrous 1906 earthquake. Visitors by the thousands came to the Exposition, and more than 600 lined up to pay $10 apiece for a ride in the Loughead Model G. In just fifty days Allan and Malcolm Loughead recouped not only their own initial investment but Max Mamlock's as well.

By 1916 the Panama-Pacific Exposition had come to an end and the Alco Hydro-Aeroplane Company was dissolved. The Loughead brothers headed south to sunnier climes and established themselves in a garage on State Street in Santa Barbara, where they hung out the shingle of the Loughead Aircraft Manufacturing Company. With the backing of financier Berton Rodman, a machine shop owner, the Lougheads expanded the new firm beyond their own personal capability. They brought aircraft designer Anthony Stadlman, an old friend of Allan's, out from Chicago as plant superintendent and they hired as a draftsman a 20 year old high school graduate named John K

Above: Shown returning to shore with two thrilled and satisfied customers—the Loughead Model G on San Francisco Bay during the Panama Pacific Exhibition. *Below:* Allan Loughead explains the Model G to interested passenger Audrey Munson.

At left, left to right: Norman Hall, Anthony Stadlman, Berton Rodman, Allan Loughead and John Northrop pose *in front* of the Loughead-built Curtiss HS-2L flying boat. Manning this US Navy warplane's turret is Malcolm Loughead. This gathering represented the 'top brass' of Loughead Aircraft Manufacturing Company.

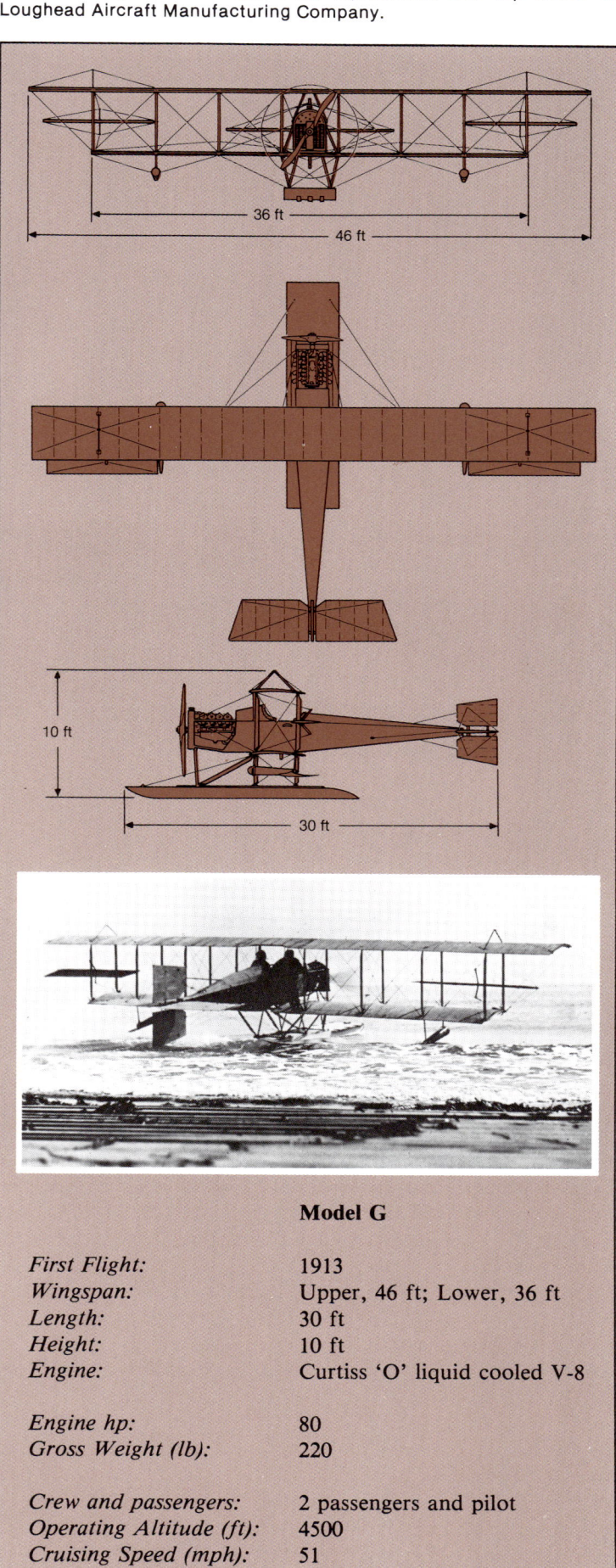

Model G

First Flight:	1913
Wingspan:	Upper, 46 ft; Lower, 36 ft
Length:	30 ft
Height:	10 ft
Engine:	Curtiss 'O' liquid cooled V-8
Engine hp:	80
Gross Weight (lb):	220
Crew and passengers:	2 passengers and pilot
Operating Altitude (ft):	4500
Cruising Speed (mph):	51

Northrop. Though no one would've predicted it at the time, young Northrop was to go on to achieve greatness as an aircraft designer with Douglas Aircraft and as founder of his own Northrop Aircraft Company.

The first aircraft designed and completed by the Loughead Aircraft Manufacturing Company was, however, a long time coming. It was not until March 1918, after the brothers had been in Santa Barbara for two years, that their twin-engined F-1 (aka FB-1) flying boat made its first flight. The United States had been embroiled in World War I for 11 months and the Lougheads harbored some optimism that they might be able to land a Navy contract for their big ship. It was one of the biggest flying boats then flying, with a 10-person passenger capacity, and it must have made an impressive display as it touched down at San Diego's North Island Navy Base. The Navy looked the F-1 up and down, and then allowed as how they were more in the market for patrol planes than transports. The Lougheads didn't go away empty handed, however. The Navy gave them a contract to build a pair of Curtiss-designed HS-2L patrol bombers. The $50,000 contract kept the 85 Loughead personnel busy until past the Armistice, but the two completed HS-2Ls were delivered too late to see service during the war.

In 1919 the Lougheads set about converting the F-1 to land plane configuration. A major obstacle to the range and speed needed for a planned flight to Washington, DC was aerodynamic drag. During the conversion process a crude wind tunnel was built in which cigar smoke was blown into a glass tube so that Jack Northrop could study airflow. The modifications undertaken as a result of the cigar smoke wind tunnel tests resulted in an airspeed increase to nearly 100 mph. The transcontinental demonstration flight, however, ended in failure when one of the Hall-Scott engines failed on takeoff from Gila Bend, Arizona and the plane, redesignated F-1A, crashed into a dry creek bed. The F-1 was hauled back to Santa Barbara where it was rebuilt as a flying boat again and put into service flying excursion flights. In October 1919 when King Albert and Queen Elizabeth of Belgium were in California, the Loughead F-1 was chartered to fly them from Santa Barbara to the Channel Islands. The King had such a good time that he awarded Allan and Malcolm Loughead the Belgian Order of the Golden Crown. However, there were no orders for F-1s forthcoming from the Belgian air force.

The Loughead brothers sold their F-1 and turned their attention to a dream that fascinated, and ultimately frustrated, a

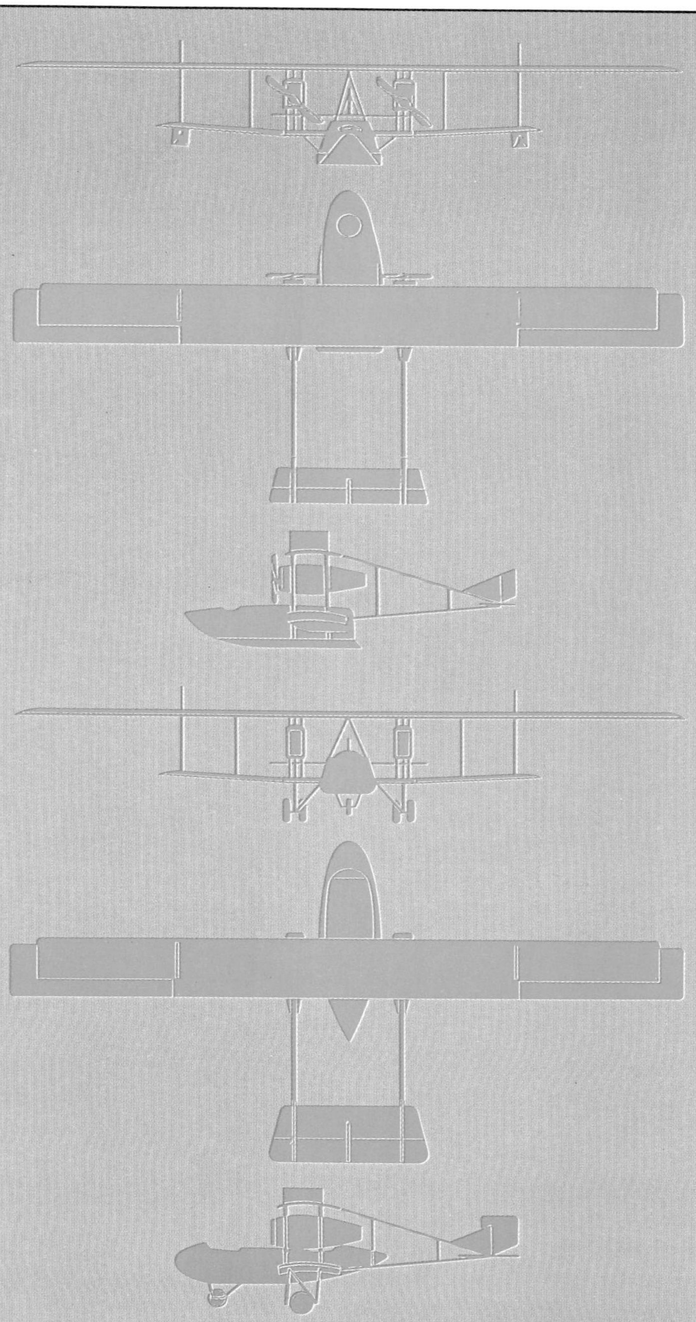

Model FB-1 (F-1) Seaplane

First Flight:	1918
Wingspan:	Upper, 74 ft; Lower, 48 ft
Length:	35 ft
Height:	12 ft
Engine:	Liquid cooled Hall-Scott
Engine hp:	150
Gross Weight (lb):	7300 (useful load: 3100)
Crew and passengers:	10
Operating Altitude (ft):	9700
Cruising Speed (mph):	74

Above left: The Loughead Model F-1 first saw completion in 1918. This photo shows the FB-1 flying boat ('FB') configuration—on the 'skids' in Loughead's Santa Barbara days. The F-1 also was built as a landplane (the F-1A; for comparison, *see* the illustrations *above*). *Left:* The King (*center*) and Queen (*right*) of Belgium just before their FB-1 day trip from Santa Barbara to the Channel Islands in October of 1919.

Above: The S-1 in front of San Francisco City Hall during the 1919 San Francisco air show, which was held at nearby Brooks Hall. *Left:* The S-1 featured folding wings. *Right above:* A decade later, an early Vega sans NACA (National Advisory Committee for Aeronautics) engine cowling, which was designed for streamlining. The Models 1 and 2 Vega preceded the Model 3 Air Express which was the first commercial aircraft to have the NACA engine cowling.

Model S-1 Sport Biplane

First Flight:	1920
Wingspan:	Upper, 28 ft; Lower, 24 ft
Length:	21 ft
Height:	7 ft, 3 in
Engine:	Loughead XL-1
Engine hp:	25
Gross Weight (lb):	825
Max Payload (lb):	225
Crew and passenger:	2
Operating Altitude (ft):	12,000
Cruising Speed (mph):	68

good many American aircraft designers in the 1920s—that of a personal sport airplane that everyone would want and could afford.

The new plane, which Allan Loughead designated S-1 for *Sportplane, Model One,* was sleek and modern. The overall design of this single-seat biplane was reminiscent of the wartime aircraft built in Germany by the Albatros Werke, but there were a number of special features that made the S-1 unique. First, there was the Tony Stadlman-designed Loughead 25 hp water-cooled, two-cylinder horizontally opposed XL-1 engine that was contained entirely within the bullet-shaped, aerodynamically optimized fuselage. Second, there was the fact that its wings folded so that it could be wheeled into a garage and the fact that the lower wing could be folded vertically for use as brakes. Most of all, however, the S-1 was important for the sake of the method of construction that Loughead pioneered.

The S-1 is said to have had the first successful monocoque fuselage, in which its strength came from the skin rather than a heavy internal structural bracing. The fuselage skin was constructed of Casein glued plywood veneer strips molded in halves

using a concrete mold. This process not only produced a lighter, sleeker aircraft, it required a great deal less time and labor.

The maroon and cream-colored S-1 was the rage of the 1919 San Francisco Air Show and was later exhibited in 1920 at Redwood City. The S-1 was a grand success as an airplane but a dismal failure as a commercial product. It had cost Loughead $29,800 to develop the S-1 and by the time it was ready to go into production, the US government had dumped thousands of unused surplus aircraft on the commercial market for a tiny fraction of their original cost. Against this backdrop, not a single S-1 was sold. Competing against the flood of war surplus airplanes, a great many fledgling aircraft companies went out of business and Loughead Aircraft Company was one of them.

LOCKHEED AND THE VEGA

Malcolm Loughead had left the Loughead Aircraft Manufacturing Company in 1919 to found the Lockheed Hydraulic Brake Company, but his brother Allan, along with Jack Northrop, stayed until the final bankruptcy. After they turned out the lights for the last time in Santa Barbara, Northrop headed south to work in the burgeoning aircraft industry in the Los Angeles area. Allan Loughead drifted in and out of real estate sales and took a job for a while with the brake company founded by Malcolm that used the phonetic spelling of their last name. In 1926, however, the two men got back together around a design that Northrop had worked up in his spare time while employed by Donald Douglas in Santa Monica. A new company was formed with financier Fred Keeler assuming the presidency and Allan Loughead the vice presidency. Northrop quit Douglas to become chief engineer and Tony Stadlman was hired to oversee production. Incorporated in December 1926, the new Company was called Lockheed Aircraft Company, using the phonetic spelling of its vice president's name. The Lockheed factory at the corner of Sycamore and Romaine in Los Angeles immediately began work on Jack Northrop's brainchild, a single-engined monoplane, constructed with the same type of laminated plywood fuselage that had been pioneered on the S-1. Beginning a tradition that Lockheed still follows, the new aircraft was named for celestial phenomena. In this case it was named 'Vega', for a star of the 0.1 magnitude in the constellation Lyra.

Less than five months later, on 21 May 1927, Charles Lindbergh successfully completed the first nonstop solo flight across the Atlantic, causing a massive outpouring of public interest in aviation. Four days after Lindbergh landed in Paris, James D Dole, of the Hawaiian pineapple Doles, put up $35,000 in prize money for first and second place in a nonstop San Francisco to Honolulu air race. George Hearst Jr, publisher of the then-influential *San Francisco Examiner*, was himself caught up in the enthusiasm and decided to personally take part in the Dole Race. His aircraft in the 'pineapple derby', he announced, would be the first Lockheed Vega.

Left: A late model Vega doing airmail and passenger service for Varney Speed Lanes. *Above, left to right:* Allan Loughead, Frank Hawkes, Malcolm Loughead and Ben Hunter. Allan and Malcolm seem to covet Frank's coat, but Ben is all business. Hawkes, sponsored by Texaco, was a customer for the Model 3.

The first bright orange Vega rolled out of the shop at Sycamore and Romaine on 4 July 1927 to make her first flight from Bennett's Farm on the site of present-day Los Angeles International Airport. This first flight came less than six weeks after the Lindbergh flight and less than six weeks before the Dole Race. On 16 August, Hearst's pilot took off from Oakland in his Vega, which he'd christened *Golden Eagle*. The favorite in a field of four, Hearst's pilot roared over downtown San Francisco and headed out toward the lonely Pacific. He was never heard from again.

The loss of the first Vega, especially in the midst of such a high-publicity event as the Dole Race, might have been a disaster for Lockheed were it not for Australian adventurer Captain George Hubert Wilkins who had already seen the *Golden Eagle* and liked what he saw. Wilkins traveled to Hollywood, where the second and third Vegas were nearing completion. He bought the fourth for his planned transarctic flight from Alaska to Europe.

The Wilkins plane, christened *Los Angeles,* was specially modified for operations in the harsh arctic climate and designed so that he could exchange the wheels for skis when he arrived in Alaska. In mid-March 1928 Wilkins and his pilot, Ben Eilson, flew the *Los Angeles* into Point Barrow and prepared for the 2200 mile flight across the roof of the world to Norway's Spitzbergen. On 15 April the blue and orange Vega roared down the 5000 × 14 foot runway that had been carved out of the frozen muskeg by Inuit tribesmen.

The two adventurers and their trusty craft braved high winds and minus 50 degrees F weather to become the first men to fly across the arctic. They arrived over Spitzbergen 20 hours after their takeoff from Alaska only to find it impossible to land because of a blizzard. They were forced to divert to a landing on uninhabited Dead Man's Island where they spent most of a week waiting for clear weather and their triumphant five mile flight to Spitzbergen.

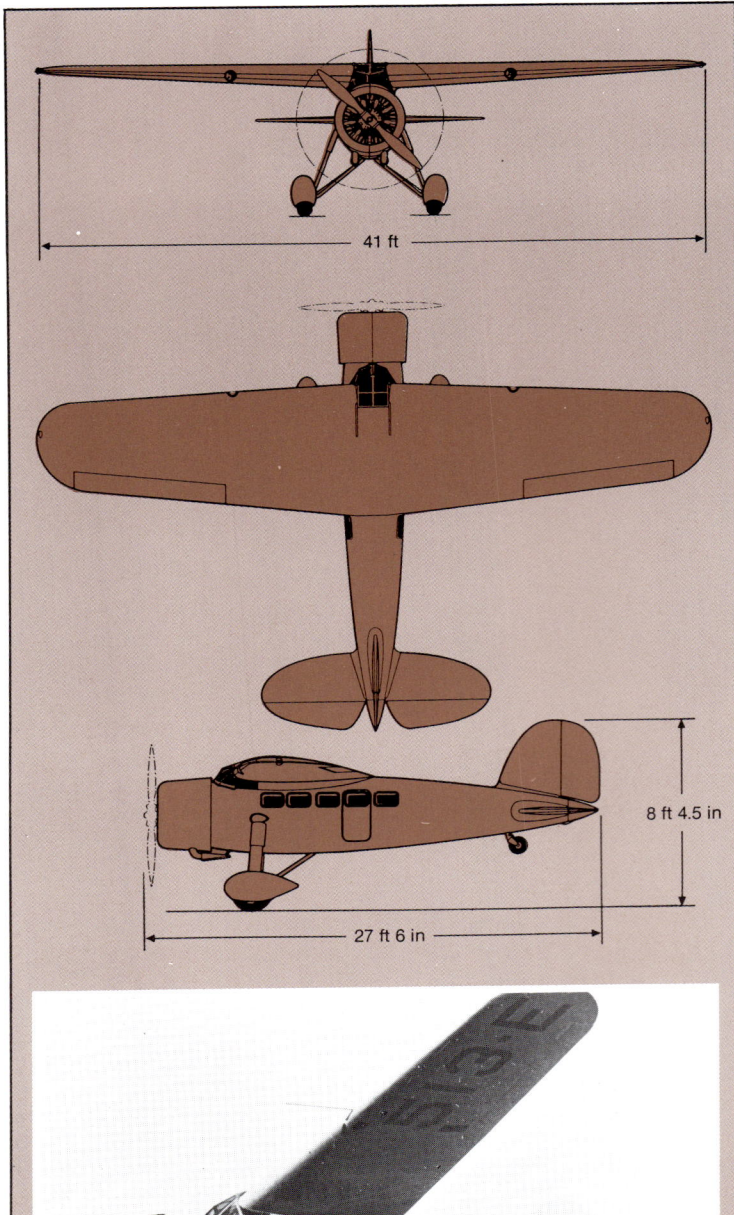

Model 1 and 2 Vega

First Flight:	1927
Wingspan:	41 ft
Length:	27 ft, 6 in
Height:	8 ft, 2 in
Engine:	Wright J-5
Engine hp:	225
Gross Weight (lb):	3470 (Model 1) 3853 (Model 2)
Empty Weight (lb):	1650 (Model 1) 2140 (Model 2)
Crew and passengers:	6
Operating Altitude (ft):	159,000 (Model 1) 160,000 (Model 2)
Cruising Speed (mph):	115 (Model 1) 135 (Model 2)
Top Speed (mph):	135
Max Range (miles):	725 (Model 1) 900 (Model 2)

Wilkins went on to use his Vega to become the first man to fly over both the North *and* South polar regions, and the Vega became hugely successful for the new Lockheed Company. Their decision to name the first airplane after a star was auspicious because the Vega was truly a star performer.

There were 180 Vegas built under Lockheed model numbers 1, 2 and 5. Another seven aircraft (some sources say ten) were built as the Model 3 Air Express, with parasol wing, open cockpit and wheel 'pants.' The Air Express was marketed under the slogan 'It takes a Lockheed to beat a Lockheed.' Two Vega derivatives called Explorer were built under the Model numbers 4 and 7. Also known as 'Low Wing Specials' because their wings were positioned differently from the standard Vega, the two Explorers were distinguishable by the fact that Model 4 was a land plane, while Model 7 was a float plane.

Hubert Wilkins was knighted by King George V for the arctic flight, Eilson received the Distinguished Flying Cross and Lockheed's Vega became one of the most popular planes in America. The US Army and seven airlines including Western, TWA and Pan American, purchased the Vega. Because it was the fastest airplane of its era, many of the great aviators of the late 1920s and early 1930s flew Vegas. Arthur Goebel set a transcontinental speed record (23 hours, 45 minutes) with his Vega, the *Yankee Doodle*, in April 1928 and Amelia Earhart set a woman's speed record of 184.17 mph in November 1929. Ruth Nichols made the first transcontinental flight by a woman in December 1930. Amelia Earhart flew her Vega on numerous record-breaking flights, becoming the first woman to fly the Atlantic solo in May 1932 and the first woman to make a nonstop transcontinental flight three months later.

Using the Model 3 Air Express derivative of the Vega, Captain Frank Hawkes broke Goebel's transcontinental speed record twice during 1929 and Colonel Roscoe Turner became the first man to win the Bendix, Harmon and Thompson trophies.

The most famous Vega, however, was probably the *Winnie Mae*. Wealthy oilman F C Hall had actually owned two Vegas named *Winnie Mae* after his daughter, but it was the second of these that became a legend.

Having won the National Air Races in 1930 with the *Winnie Mae*, Hall's pilot, Wiley Post, came up with the idea of a record-breaking, round-the-world flight. The first-ever flight around the world had been achieved in 1924 by a pair of Douglas World Cruisers flown by US Army pilots—but it had taken them 174 days, including stopovers. Nellie Bly of the *New York World* had made the same trip in just 72 days by land in 1889 when she took up the challenge of Jules Verne's fictional *Around the*

Upper left: Frank Hawkes in 1939 with his Texaco-sponsored Model 3 Air Express, which was complete with NACA cowling and wheel pants. *Above:* The legendary Wiley Post stands beside his Vega Model 5B, the *Winnie Mae,* upon whose fuselage are recorded some of his many records. In 1935, Post flew the *Winnie Mae* to an altitude of 55,000 feet.

World in Eighty Days. Then, in 1929, the German air ship *Graf Zeppelin* accomplished the feat entirely by air in an incredible 21 days.

The *Graf Zeppelin* had cut 153 days off the time of the Douglas World Cruisers and Wiley Post was certain that the *Winnie Mae* could bury that record. With his navigator, Harold Gatty, Post took off from Roosevelt Field, Long Island on 23 June 1931, just four years after Charles Lindbergh had left the same field on *his* historic flight. The *Winnie Mae* set a new record in the crossing to Liverpool, then pressed onward across Europe to Russia and on to Alaska. In Edmonton, Alberta the airstrip was flooded in a rainstorm, so Post had to take off from Portage Avenue on the final leg to New York City. When they arrived back in New York, Post, Gatty and the *Winnie Mae* had established a new round-the-world record of 8 days and 16 hours. Two years later, in July 1933, Wiley Post did himself one better. Flying the *Winnie Mae* over the same course, except for the substitution of a single nonstop New York-to-Berlin leg, Post made a *solo* flight around the world in just seven days, 19 hours.

Wiley Post didn't rest with the notion of using his Vega solely for capturing speed and distance records. In 1935 he flew the *Winnie Mae* to an unofficial record altitude of 55,000 feet, more than three miles higher than the service ceiling of modern jetliners! At this altitude he became the first pilot to encounter the high altitude winds known as jet streams.

	Model 3 Air Express	Model 4 low-wing monoplane	Model 5 Vega
First Flight:	1928	1928	1928
Wingspan:	43 ft	48 ft, 5 in	41 ft
Length:	27 ft, 6 in	27 ft, 6 in	27 ft, 6 in
Height:	9 ft, 8 in	9 ft, 8 in	8 ft, 2 in
Engine:	Pratt & Whitney R1350	Pratt & Whitney Wasp	Pratt & Whitney Wasp R1340C, CS, SC1
Gross Weight (lb):	4375	9008	4375
Empty Weight (lb):	2533	3075	2595
Crew and passengers:	4	6	6
Operating Altitude (ft):	25,000	20,000	20,000
Cruising Speed (mph):	150	150	155
Top Speed (mph):	180	165	185
Range (miles):	250	250	250

The Lockheed Sirius Model 8 (*upper opposite*) took Charles Lindberg and his wife, Anne Morrow Lindberg (*lower opposite*), on many of their famous exploits of the early thirties. The Lockheed Altair (*above*) was designed as a low-wing 'Special Sirius,' and was the first plane purchased by both the US Army Air Corps and the US Navy to have fully retractable landing gear.

	Model 8 Sirius (Lindbergh's plane had several variations in fuel capacity and engines)	**Model 8D Altair**
First Flight:	1929	1930
Wingspan:	42 ft, 9¼ in	42 ft, 9 in
Length:	27 ft, 1 in	27 ft, 1 in
Height:	9 ft, 3 in	9 ft, 3 in
Engine:	Pratt & Whitney Wasp R-1340 (original land plane version); Wright Cyclone SR-1820 (later seaplane version)	Pratt & Whitney Wasp SR-1340
Engine hp:	450; 710	625
Gross Weight (lb):	4600	4600
Empty Weight (lb):	2978	3000
Crew and passengers:	2	2 or 3
Operating Altitude (ft):	20,000	23,200
Cruising Speed (mph):	150	200
Top Speed (mph):	185	227
Max Range (miles):	975	950

DETROIT LOCKHEED

The magnificent Vega and its derivatives were the only aircraft to be built by the original independent Lockheed Aircraft Company. In early 1929, with Vega orders flooding in, the Lockheed board decided to accept an offer of a buyout by the Detroit Aircraft Company. Allan Loughead voted against the idea of Lockheed becoming part of Detroit Aircraft's scheme to form a 'General Motors of the Air,' but his associates on the board carried the day.

In July 1929, three months before the stock market crash and the onset of the Great Depression, Lockheed became a division of Detroit Aircraft Corporation.

A bitter Allan Loughead resigned from Lockheed to form his third aircraft company, the Loughead Brothers Aircraft Corporation. The new venture, which included Malcolm Loughead on the board, developed the Olympic Duo-Four, a twin-engine high wing monoplane. Only one prototype was built and the company folded when this aircraft crashed. Allan Loughead went on to start a fourth venture, the Alcor Aircraft Corporation, which again succeeded in building just a single prototype before it went out of business. The Alcor adventure was Allan Loughead's swan song in the aircraft industry. Although he kept his hand in and served as a consultant to Lockheed in the 1960s prior to his death in 1969, Loughead never formed another aircraft company and never masterminded another great airplane.

The Explorer (Lockheed Model 7) was designed by Jack Northrop in 1928 to specifications set out by Sir Hubert Wilkins. Shortly after Lockheed began work on the first Explorer, Wilkins ran out of cash and Northrop left Lockheed to help form the Avion Corporation, which later became the Northrop Corporation.

In 1930 another pilot, Harold Bromley, expressed an interest in the partially completed aircraft. Work on the Explorer resumed and she first flew in late 1929. Bromley intended to fly the plane, which he called *City of Tacoma*, to Tokyo but he ground looped on takeoff for the race and the plane was destroyed. A second Explorer, which Bromley called *City of Tacoma II*, was ordered but it crashed during an early flight when a Lockheed test pilot was trying to demonstrate a flutter that he'd discovered in the noncounterbalanced rudder.

The first new aircraft project undertaken by Lockheed after becoming part of the 'General Motors of the Air' was a plane named Sirius (Lockheed Model 8) after the 'Dog Star,' brightest of all the stars. The customer this time was the world's most famous aviator, Charles Lindbergh. When it was announced that the 'Lone Eagle' would be a Sirius customer, Lockheed found itself with a half dozen additional orders for the low wing monoplane.

Lindbergh and his wife, Anne Morrow Lindbergh, took delivery of their Sirius on 20 April 1930 and promptly flew it to New York in 14 hours, 23 minutes, unofficially breaking the transcontinental speed record. In July 1931 the Lindberghs undertook a survey flight across the North Pacific at the behest of Pan American Airways. For this flight the black and red monoplane was retrofitted with floats. Their flight across Canada, down the Aleutian chain and on to Tokyo and Hankow, was chronicled in Anne Morrow Lindbergh's best-selling book *North to the Orient*. Damaged while being lowered into the Yangtze River from the *HMS Hermes*, the Lindbergh Sirius was returned to the Lockheed factories to be repaired and fitted with a 710 horsepower Wright Cyclone engine.

On 9 July 1933 the daring couple took off on another survey flight, this time over the chilly North Atlantic. They departed New York for Greenland, where they discovered two hitherto unknown mountain ranges during two overflights. During a stopover at Angmagssalik, Greenland, the Sirius was christened *Tingmissartog*, meaning 'one who flies like a big bird', by a young Greenlander.

The *Tingmissartog* then continued on to Europe and to Moscow where Lindbergh landed the plane between the bridges over the Moscow River. From Moscow they flew to Africa. The *Tingmissartog* crossed the Atlantic between Gambia and Brazil and returned triumphantly to New York on 19 December 1933. Later sold by Lindbergh, this famous Sirius is today preserved in the collection of the Smithsonian's National Air and Space Museum in Washington, DC.

While Charles Lindbergh and his young wife were capturing headlines in their Sirius, Lockheed engineers were at work on a 'Special Sirius,' a low wing monoplane with retractable landing gear. Named Altair and given the Lockheed Model number 8D, it first flew in September 1930. The new plane attracted the

attention of US Army Air Corps General Ira Eaker, who recommended that the Air Corps purchase some Altairs. In 1931 a single Altair was delivered to the Air Corps under the service-test designation Y1C-25. The US Navy followed suit the same year with the purchase of a single Altair for use by the Assistant Secretary of the Navy. These two Altairs were the first aircraft of any type with *fully retractable* landing gear to be purchased by their respective services.

The most reknowned of the Altairs, however, was the *Lady Southern Cross* purchased by Sir Charles Kingsford-Smith for his own use in the 1934 London-to-Melbourne race. As it turned out, Sir Charles had to withdraw from the race, but he made up for this with a 55 hour flight from Brisbane, Australia to Oakland, California in the first east-to-west aerial crossing of the Pacific.

Left: Laura Ingalls, Amelia Earhart (*center*) and Roscoe Turner pose, with a Lockheed Sirius as their stage. Ingalls piloted her Lockheed Air Express for a 17,000 mile solo flight around South America in 1934; Amelia Earhart set many records and became the first woman to 'solo' across the Atlantic Ocean non-stop, flying a specially-equipped Vega in 1932; and famous racing pilot Roscoe Turner remarked of the Vega that 'All you have to do is point it at a distant destination and there's another new record...'

Right: The name Wiley Post is synonymous with the early, adventuresome days of flying. Among his other feats, Post invented his own early pressure suit for high-altitude flying. He is shown *in this photograph* in Alaska, while standing on the landing float of his seaplane—which he had built, using an Orion fuselage and Sirius wings. Post was warned of the plane's probable instability, but insisted on flying it. He and Will Rogers were killed in this plane in 1935. *Below:* Jimmy Doolittle was in the air from the early days to the advent of the jet age. *Here* he is shown with the orange and red Lockheed Orion that he piloted for the Shell Oil Company. As well as his other piloting adventures, Doolittle is celebrated for his World War II feats: he led the only Army Air Forces bomber squadron to make their attack from an aircraft carrier; led the famous Tokyo raid (for which he was promoted to general); and commanded the 'Mighty' Eighth Air Force in England. He retired at the end of the war.

After the Sirius/Altair series, the next logical step for Lockheed was the development of a low wing *airliner* with retractable landing gear for the commercial market. Roughly the same size as the Vega, Sirius and Altair, the new airliner incorporated many of the design features that had proven successful on these aircraft, featuring an enclosed cockpit and passenger cabin. It first flew in April 1931 and was called Orion, after one of the most identifiable constellations in the sky, and given the Lockheed Model number 9.

The new Lockheed quickly became one of the most identifiable aircraft at American airports. The biggest-selling Lockheed product since the Vega, the Orion was purchased by such major airlines as TWA, American and Northwest. A California carrier, Varney Speed Lanes, put Orions into service between Los Angeles and San Francisco. The flights between the Golden state's two largest cities regularly took just 86 minutes, and one flight saw an Orion covering the distance in an incredible 65 minutes! The commuter jetliners of the 1980s frequently take longer to cover the distance than Varney did in the 1930s with its Orions. In Europe, the newly formed Swissair purchased Orions

Above left, a casualty of the 1929 Depression, the YP-24 was Lockheed's first fighter plane. The last of Lockheed's wooden planes, the Orion (*left*) was certainly the fastest of the early 'airliners.' *Below right:* In a photo that could be called the 'Loughead Hall of Fame,' we have, *left to right,* an Orion, a Vega Air Express and an Altair. *Note* the name—*Lady Southern Cross*—on the Altair, identifying it as Sir Charles Kingsford-Smith's famous plane, in which he made the first east to west aerial crossing of the Pacific Ocean. From the first, the brothers Loughead produced customer-satisfying planes.

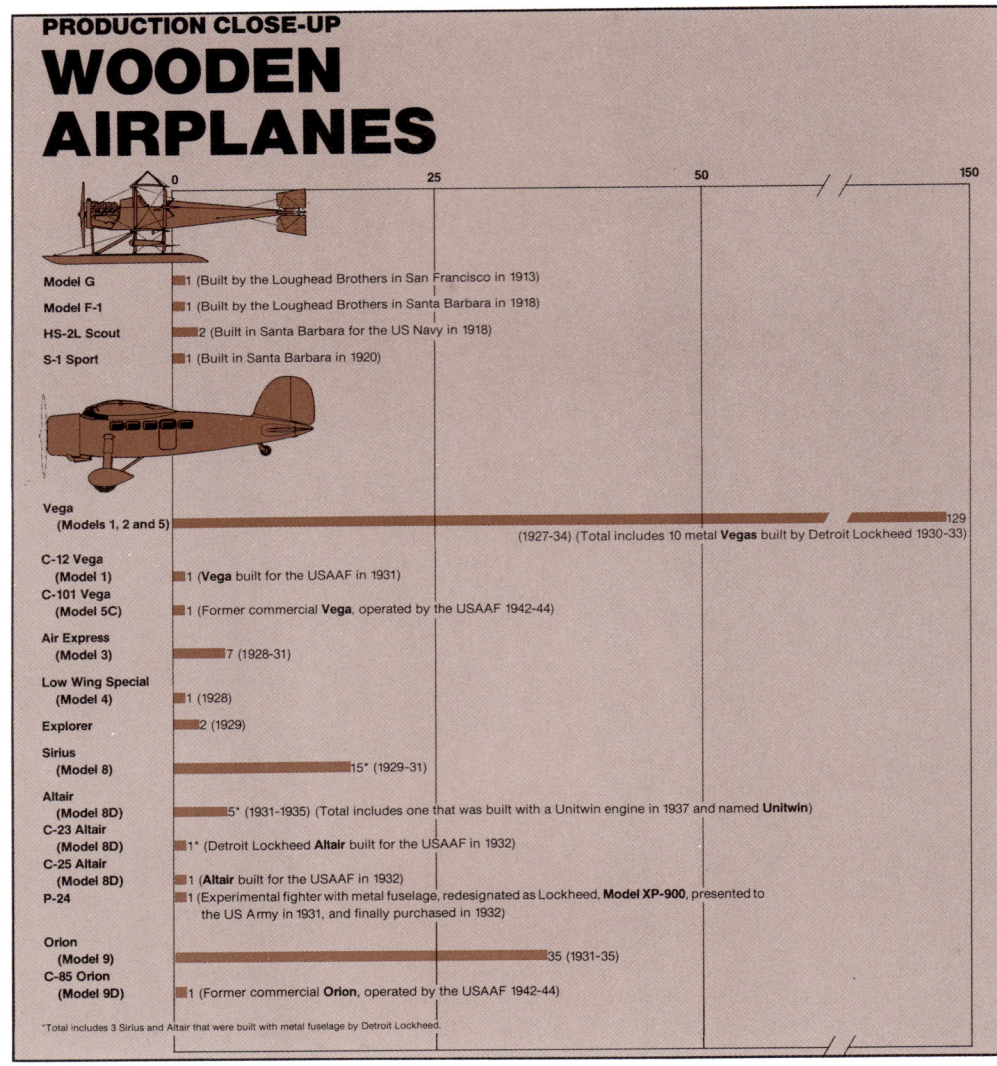

for high-speed express route flights between Vienna and Munich, as well as other routes.

During the Detroit Lockheed period from 1929 to 1931, all of the Lockheed aircraft built in the Burbank, California plant had wooden fuselages using the process pioneered in 1927 on the first Vega. There were, however, ten Vegas built in Detroit with metal fuselages under the Detroit Lockheed designation DL-1, DL-2, DL-2A, etc. These went to US Army Air Corps under the military service designation Y1C-12. These metal Vegas were followed by a handful of metal Sirius/Altair types designated DL-2.

LOCKHEED'S FIRST FIGHTER

Also produced in Detroit was the first Lockheed combat aircraft. She was given the Lockheed designation XP-900 for 'Experimental Pursuit, Model 9 derivative', because she was designed around an all-metal Altair (Model 9) airframe. The major difference between the Altair and the XP-900 was that the latter had a 600 hp Curtiss Conqueror liquid-cooled engine, while the Altair and all the preceding Lockheed monoplanes from the Vega through the Altair and Orion had air-cooled engines. The two-place XP-900 also was fitted with bomb racks, provision for a fuel tank that could be dropped and three .30 caliber machine guns—two forward-firing, and one rear-firing gun in the aft cockpit.

Lockheed built the prototype XP-900 hoping to interest the US Army Air Corps in purchasing it as a replacement for the then-obsolescent P-16. The Air Corps inspection team arrived in Detroit in March 1931 to view the XP-900 mock-up, liked what they saw and ordered four fighter versions under the Air Corps service test designations YP-24 and Y1P-24. There was also interest in an additional four ground-attack versions which would have been designated Y1A-g. Lockheed built one prototype Y1A-g under the company designation XA-938, but the other three were never ordered.

The first YP-24 was completed and delivered to Wright Field, Ohio for Air Corps testing on 29 September 1931. With a top speed of 214 mph, it soon proved to be the fastest fighter that the Air Corps had ever considered. On 19 October, however, the landing gear failed to operate and the pilot had to bail out.

Eight days after the YP-24 crashed into the Ohio countryside, the Detroit Aircraft Company, the 'General Motors of the Air,' collapsed. The strain of the Great Depression, combined with the softness in the new airplane market, was too much. In the wake of the 27 October bankruptcy, the Army canceled its orders for P-24 pursuit planes and A-g attack planes. The money that had been appropriated for the P-24 project was transferred to Consolidated Aircraft of Buffalo, New York to continue development of a similar aircraft type. Robert Wood, the Lockheed engineer who had masterminded the XP-900 program, went to Consolidated and began work on the new aircraft, which prototype was given the Air Corps service designation Y1P-25. Eventually the Y1P-25 prototype was followed by 54 Consolidated P-30 fighters (later redesignated PB-2 for Pursuit, Biplace) and five Consolidated A-11 attack planes, all of which were remarkably similar to the Lockheed XP-900.

TWIN ENGINES AND TWIN TAILS

A NEW START

Following the 27 October 1931 bankruptcy of the Detroit Aircraft Corporation, the Title Insurance & Trust Company of Los Angeles was named receiver for the Lockheed division in Burbank. Greatly reduced operations continued at the Burbank plant under the receivers and were geared only toward completion of the few remaining orders for Vegas and Orions. Meanwhile, a group of investors—including Lockheed's Burbank plant manager Carl Squier, aircraft designer Lloyd Stearman and investment banker Robert Gross—were scraping together the cash to get Lockheed out of hock. Finally, on 6 June 1932 they went into federal court in Los Angeles and handed Judge Harry Holzer a cashier's check for $40,000. Holzer looked down at the three men, rapped his gavel and said, 'I hope you know what you're doing.'

They were sure at the time that they did and, as it turned out, they were right: 6 June 1932 was the birthdate of the present Lockheed Corporation, which was known as Lockheed Aircraft Corporation until 1977 when the middle word was dropped in deference to the company's varied non-aircraft activities.

When the new company opened on 7 June 1932 for its first full day in business, Gross was installed as treasurer, Stearman as president and general manager, and Squier as vice president and sales manager. Sales during their first year amounted to only $23,000, but in 1933 the company managed to sell sixteen aircraft, most of them Orions.

THE ELECTRA

By the end of 1932 the newly constituted Lockheed began development of the Model 10, the first twin-engined aircraft to bear the name since the Loughead F-1 more than a decade before. The decision to develop a twin-engined plane was based largely on an impending federal safety regulation that would forbid the use of single-engined aircraft for scheduled commercial airline flights after 1934. The idea of multiengined airliners also made good sense commercially because they could carry more passengers and could fly longer distances. Both Boeing and Douglas were known to be working on twin-engined designs and Lockheed would have to follow suit in order to stay in the commercial market.

The Model 10 was given the name Electra after a star in the constellation Pleiades.

In March 1933 a wind tunnel model of the Electra was sent to the tunnel at the University of Michigan for tests. At Michigan, the model was handed to a 23 year old university student and wind tunnel staffer named Clarence Leonard Johnson, who found the plane to have some serious failings. These problems, which involved longitudinal stability and directional control, were not considered unusual considering the state of the art in aircraft design, and the Electra passed its initial wind tunnel test.

Six weeks later Johnson arrived on Lockheed's Burbank doorstep, armed with a Master of Science degree, looking for a job. He arrived on the heels of his own report on the Electra, and the first thing he did upon being hired was to tell the company that the plane on which they were pinning their future was dangerously unstable. Johnson went on to tell his new employer that he could fix the problem. Not only did he fix the Electra but Clarence Leonard 'Kelly' Johnson went on to become Lockheed's greatest designer, and one of the greatest designers in the history of American aviation.

Though his parents were from Sweden, his classmates in elementary school had given him what he later described as a 'fighting Irish nickname.' As a result, Clarence Johnson would be known for the rest of his life as Kelly Johnson.

When the Electra first flew on 23 February 1934, she joined the Boeing 247 and the Douglas DC-1 (prototype of the DC-2 and DC-3 series) as part of a new generation of American twin-engined transports that had all made their debut in the space of twelve months.

In late spring of 1934, after it had been certified by the Civil Aeronautics Authority for commercial sale, the Electra prototype was on a routine test flight out of Mines Field in Los Angeles when one of the main landing gear failed to extend. Landing at Lockheed's Burbank airfield could have been a disaster. The crippled Electra would need a longer airstrip to attempt a crash landing, and Burbank had no firefighting equipment in case the fuel exploded. There was no radio communication with the plane, so people on the ground had to wave the Electra away when pilot Marshall Headle came in for a landing. Among the spectators on the ground was famed aviator Jimmy Doolittle, who quickly scrawled 'Try landing at Union, Good Luck' on the side of his orange Shell Oil Company Orion and scrambled up into the air to warn Headle. Headle knew that Union Air Terminal had a longer strip as well as firefighting equipment and his landing there was textbook perfect. He landed on one wheel and kept the plane perfectly balanced until it had rolled practically to a stop. Damage was minor and Kelly Johnson was able to find the cause of the gear failure and issue corrective instructions.

In June 1934 the first commercial deliveries were made to Northwest and Pan Am, and by the end of the year sales had reached $562,000, with over a million dollars in orders.

Above: Kelly Johnson with the Model 10 wind tunnel mockup. *Below:* A Northwest Model 10 landing in the Twin Cities. *Note* the concave windshield which was characteristic of the first Model 10s. *Facing page:* An Electra of Eastern Airlines' Great Silver Fleet on the wing.

Facing page: Model 10s in the assembly shop in 1935. *Above:* Seen *here* at Wright Field in the 1930s, the Air Corps XC-35 (Model 10) was the first fully pressurized airplane. *Note* the supercharger on the engine. *Below:* A Northwest Airlines Model 10 Electra at rest.

The Electra went on to become the most successful airplane that Lockheed had yet built, outselling even the great Vega. Between June 1934 and July 1941 there were 149 Model 10s delivered to commercial customers in the United States and abroad, as well as to the US Army Air Corps (C-36 and C-37), The US Navy (XJO-3 and R2O-1) and the US Coast Guard (R3O-1). In June 1936 the Air Corps contracted with Lockheed to build what would be the first airplane with a fully pressurized passenger cabin. Given the military experimental designation XC-35, this modified Model 10 first flew in August 1936 and won the 1937 Collier Trophy for having made the most valuable contribution to aircraft development for that year.

The most famous of the Model 10s was the one in which Amelia Earhart attempted what she hoped would be the first round-the-world flight by a woman. She took off on 1 June 1937, flying a west to east course across Africa that was closer to the equator than previous round-the-world flights. On 1 July she took off with her navigator, Fred Noonan, from Lae, New Guinea en route to Howland Island 2556 miles away in the Pacific. They were never seen again, and the mystery surrounding their disappearance has been debated with a great deal of interest ever since. While it is generally accepted that the plane crashed into the vast Pacific, the theory (some would say 'rumor') still persists that Earhart and Noonan were carrying out secret aerial reconnaissance of Japanese-owned Pacific islands and that they were shot down. There were subsequent reports of Amelia Earhart having been seen later in Japanese custody in the Pacific, but no conclusive proof has ever been presented.

THE ELECTRA JUNIOR

Carl Squier had to mortgage his house to meet Lockheed's December 1932 payroll, but three years later the Electra had put the company firmly in the black. With the profits from the Electra rolling in, Squier and Gross began looking at other markets for a follow-on aircraft. Their decision was to develop a scaled-down version of the Model 10 which could be used as an executive transport and sold to smaller feeder airlines. The new plane became known as the Electra Junior and was designated Lockheed Model 12.

Looking like its older sister except for size, the Electra Junior made its first flight on 27 June 1936. Over the next six years there were 114 Electra Juniors put into service with a wide variety of customers that ranged from South American governments to Indian Maharajahs. An additional 16 were built with bomb racks and a gun turret for the Netherlands air force under the Lockheed Model 212 designation and delivered to the Netherlands East Indies on the eve of World War II.

The Electra Junior also served with the US Army Air Corps under the C-40 designation and the US Navy under the designation series JO-1 through JO-3.

Two of the latter were experimentally fitted with tricycle landing gear. During August 1939 one of these XJO-3s was operated from the deck of the USS *Lexington*, becoming one of the first twin-engined airplanes to take off from, and land on, an aircraft carrier.

The most important military use of the Electra Junior, however, came *prior* to World War II and involved Model 12s in the *civilian* registry. By 1938, despite British Prime Minister Neville Chamberlain's optimistic prediction of 'peace in our time', it was clear that England and France were headed toward war with Germany. The intelligence services of all three nations were already gearing up for the inevitable. Part of the focus was the task of obtaining up-to-date reconnaissance photographs of opposition territory. The Germans, in fact, had secretly attached cameras to Lufthansa airliners making commercial flights to London and Paris.

The British and French intelligence services, meanwhile, each ordered a Model 12 from Lockheed. Given civilian registration and commercial markings, the planes made a number of reconnaissance flights over Germany, Italy and North Africa during

Clockwise from left: Amelia Earhart and her Model 10 Electra, one of the Model 212s that were built for the Netherlands Air Force, and a Model 12 Electra Junior over the Wright Brothers Monument at Kitty Hawk, North Carolina.

	Model 10 Electra	XC-35 (Model 10)	Model 12 Electra Junior	Model 212
First Flight:	1934	1937	1935	1936
Wingspan:	55 ft	55 ft	49 ft, 6 in	55
Length:	38 ft, 7 in	38 ft, 7 in	36 ft, 4 in	38 ft, 7 in
Height:	10 ft, 1 in	10 ft, 1 in	9 ft, 11 in	10 ft, 1 in
Engines:	two Pratt & Whitney R985-SB	two Pratt & Whitney R1350-S3H1	two Pratt & Whitney R985-SB	two Pratt & Whitney Wasp Junior R985-SB*
Engine hp:	450	550	450	459
Gross Weight (lb):	10,500	10,500	8650	9200
Empty Weight (lb):	6454	7940	5960	5400
Crew and passengers:	14	3	10	4
Operating Altitude (ft):	19,400	31,500	22,300	21,000
Cruising Speed (mph):	190	214	202	200
Top Speed (mph):	202	236	226	216
Max Range (miles):	950	950	1100	1100

*One Model 212 was built with Wright Whirlwind R975 engines

Bottom of this page: A cutaway view of the Model 14 Super Electra. *Opposite page, at top:* A Model 14 doing service for the Netherlands' KLM airlines. The Model 14 was the direct predecessor of WWII's Hudson bomber. *Opposite page, middle:* This is a view of Howard Hughes and crewmembers in the pilot's control room of a Model 14. Flying a Model 14 named *World's Fair 1939* in 1938, Hughes set the record of three days, 19 hours and 14 minutes for a round-the-world flight: In a specially prepared Model 14 with extra fuel capacity, Hughes made refueling stops at Paris, Moscow, Omsk, Takutsk, Fairbanks and Minneapolis, and is shown *below* returning to his starting point, New York's Floyd Bennett Field.

Model 14	
First Flight:	1937
Wingspan:	65 ft, 6 in
Length:	44 ft, 4 in
Height:	11 ft, 10½ in
Engines:	two Wright GR 1820-G3B, (Pratt & Whitney Hornet and higher horsepower Wrights optional)
Engine hp:	620
Gross Weight (lb):	15,650
Empty Weight (lb):	10,700
Passengers:	14
Operating Altitude (ft):	24,700
Cruising Speed (mph):	227
Top Speed (mph):	246
Max Range (miles):	2060

the early part of 1939. The principal pilot of the British Model 12 was Australian native Sidney Cotton, who had made a number of flights throughout Europe promoting Dufay color film. His promotional flights proved to be a perfect cover for the 'spy plane' flights.

In May 1939 a third Model 12 was delivered to the British and given the civilian registration G-AFTL. It was modified with extra fuselage fuel tanks that more than doubled its range. There were three cameras mounted beneath the floor and two were concealed within the wings. Once again Sidney Cotton was the pilot and his flights took him throughout the Middle East and repeatedly to Germany. He even made flights to Berlin and, in fact, took several unsuspecting German officials for a ride in the plane!

THE SUPER ELECTRA

The next step after having developed the Electra Junior to *complement* the Electra, was to develop a plane which would *improve* upon it. Developed by Kelly Johnson, the Lockheed Model 14 Super Electra first flew on 29 July 1937 and entered service with Northwest Airlines in October. The major purchases of Model 14 Super Electras, however, came not from American, but rather from overseas airlines. International customers included Ireland's Aer Lingus, Poland's LOT, Trans-Canada and British Airways. KLM in the Netherlands bought Model 14s for its own use and for that of KNILM, its subsidiary in the Netherlands East Indies.

The most famous exploit by a commercial Model 14 was the 1938 record-breaking, round-the-world flight undertaken by the eccentric millionaire pilot Howard Hughes. Accompanied by a crew of four, Hughes took off from Floyd Bennett Field, New

York en route to Paris on 10 July 1938, in a specially modified Model 14 with long-range fuel tanks named *World's Fair 1939*. With refueling stops in Moscow, Omsk, Yakutsk, Fairbanks and Minneapolis, Hughes and his crew accomplished the flight in a record three days, 19 hours and 14 minutes. Even with the stops factored in, the Super Electra averaged a respectable 165 mph.

Given the fact that the United States was less than five years away from going to war with Japan, it is interesting to note that Japan was one of the leading customers for the commercial Model 14. Not only were 30 Burbank-built Super Electras exported to Japan, but an additional 119 were built by Tachikawa and Kawasaki in Japan and fitted with Mitsubishi engines. Kawasaki, in fact, went on to develop a longer derivative (similar to Lockheed's own Model 18) of the Super Electra under the Kawasaki designation Ki-56. All of these types were destined to cause confusion for troops on both sides when they were encountered in combat during World War II.

In light of the impending World War and the fact that British intelligence was about to start using a Lockheed Electra Junior as a spy plane, it is a point of interest that a Super Electra played a role in the efforts to prevent the War. One of the British Airways Model 14s, G-AFGN, had the distinction of being the aircraft that carried British Prime Minister Neville Chamberlain to the last two of his infamous series of summit conferences with German Chancellor Adolf Hitler in September 1938. He had flown to the first of the series in a British Airways Lockheed Model 10. It was on 29 September that G-AFGN returned Chamberlain to England from Munich after he had agreed to dismember Czechoslovakia in order to achieve 'peace in our time.' Within a year Britain and Germany were at war and military derivatives of the Model 14, the great Hudson bombers, were in combat.

THE HUDSON

The Hudson was essentially the bomber version of the Model 14 Electra, but it was more than that. Given the company model number series 214/314 and 414 to distinguish it from the commercial Super Electras, the Hudson served the air forces of the United States and the British Empire throughout World War II and became the biggest-selling plane Lockheed had yet built. There were, in fact, *six times* as many Hudsons built by Lockheed than *all* of the company's earlier efforts *combined*! In all of Lockheed's history, only two aircraft (the P-38 and T-33) have been built in larger quantities than the Hudson.

The Hudson project began almost by accident and was a classic case of seizing an opportunity. By 1938 the winds of war already were blowing strongly over Europe. Despite Neville Chamberlain's public optimism, the British government had recognized that war was inevitable and was moving to prepare for Britain's defense. One aspect of those preparations, prompted by memories of the crippling U-boat warfare of World War I, was the planned acquisition of a coastal patrol bomber. In April 1938 a British purchasing commission came to the United States to find an American planemaker that could produce several hundred such patrol bombers. If such a large block of planes could be purchased abroad their production would not interfere with the production capacity of British factories, which was already heavily in demand.

Lockheed found out about the arrival of the commission just five days before they landed in California. It seemed an impossible task but a full-scale mock-up of an anti-submarine variant of the Model 14 was completed in time for their arrival. The British were impressed and invited Lockheed to send representatives to London to submit a formal proposal. The Lockheed team, which included Courtlandt Gross (younger brother of Lockheed president Robert Gross), Carl Squier and Kelly Johnson, promptly sailed on the *Queen Mary*, and when they arrived in London set up shop in a flat in Mayfair Court. The British Air Ministry asked for numerous changes in the basic Model 14 design and the Model 214 Hudson was literally created in the Mayfair Court flat in a series of all-night drafting sessions. Finally, on 23 June 1938 the Air Ministry issued an order for 200 Hudsons and told Lockheed that they would take 250, or as many as could be produced and sent to England by December 1939.

The German government also showed an interest in the Hudson. Shortly after the Lockheed team sailed for New York aboard the German liner *Bremen*, they found their staterooms ransacked. The plans for the Model 214, however, had already sailed for the United States—in a diplomatic pouch in the safe of the *Queen Mary*.

The British Air Ministry's $25 million order for Hudsons was the largest order of any kind that had yet been placed with an American aircraft manufacturer. Lockheed fulfilled the contract with flying colors, delivering the 250th Hudson seven weeks ahead of schedule just after World War II began. In the meantime, however, there had been a good deal of scrambling in Burbank to prepare for construction of so many aircraft in so short a time. A quarter of a million square feet of floor space was added, the Lockheed work force more than tripled, and Lockheed issued a public stock offering.

The first Model 214 flew on 10 December 1938, and as soon as three were completed, Kelly Johnson went to England with them to supervise service testing. Between December 1938 and June 1939, only 50 Hudsons had been built, but by December 1939 all 250 of the original block of 214s were completed. In September 1939, when Britain went to war with Germany and the US Neutrality Act prohibited delivery of any warplanes to a belligerent, the Hudsons were flown to Pembina, North Dakota, where mules towed them across the border into Manitoba and the British Empire.

More than a hundred additional Model 214 Hudsons were added to the original order and these were followed by Model

The Hudson bomber (*upper left and upper right* — in the factory), which saw much action early in World War II, was essentially a military version of the Lockheed Super Electra.

	Hudson I (Model 214)	Hudson III (Model 414-56)
First Flight:	1938	1939
Wingspan:	65 ft, 6 in	65 ft, 6 in
Length:	44 ft, 4 in	44 ft, 4 in
Height:	11 ft, 10 in	11 ft, 10 in
Engines:	two Wright R-1829-G102A	two Wright R-1820-G205A
Engine hp:	1100 takeoff; 900 at 6700 ft	1200 at takeoff; 900 at 15,200 ft
Gross Weight (lb):	17,500	18,500
Operating Altitude (ft):	27,200	26,500
Cruising Speed (mph):	220	223
Max Range (miles):	1960	2160

	Hudson IIIA (A-29/Model 414-56)	**Hudson V** (Model 414-13)	**Hudson VI** (Model 414-17)
First Flight:	1941	1941	1941
Wingspan:	65 ft, 6 in	65 ft, 6 in	65 ft, 6 in
Length:	44 ft, 4 in	44 ft, 4 in	44 ft, 4 in
Height:	11 ft, 11 in	11 ft, 11 in	11 ft, 11 in
Engines:	two Wright R1820-87	two Pratt & Whitney R1830-45	two Pratt & Whitney R1830-67
Engine hp:	1200	1050	1200
Gross Weight (lb):	20,500	18,500	18,500
Operating Altitude (ft):	26,500	26,000	27,000
Cruising Speed (mph):	205	206	224
Max Range (miles):	2800	1800	2160

Above: The Hudson military Model 414 is shown *above* in USAAF colors as a US military-designated A-28, but was soon to be turned over to the Royal Air Force, and then to be christened as a 'Hudson.' *Below:* This civilian Electra sports the distinctive Hudson bomber nose that was not standard on commercial Model 14s.

314 Hudsons for the Royal Australian Air Force. The Model 314s were virtually identical to the Model 214, except for the substitution of Pratt & Whitney Twin Wasp engines for the Wright Cyclones that had been standard on the earlier Hudson. The Twin Wasp engines became the standard engine on the Model 414, which in turn became the standard Hudsons, serving the air forces of the British Empire as Hudson Marks II, III, IV and V; the US Army Air Forces as A-28 and A-29; and the US Navy as PBO-1. By the time production of the Hudson ended at Burbank, 2941 had been built.

In wartime service with the Royal Air Force, the Hudson quickly earned a reputation for being an extremely durable aircraft. They could sustain tremendous battle damage and still return to base. For this reason the Hudson came to be known as 'Old Boomerang'—the planes that went out nearly always came back.

On 3 September 1939 in the first Anglo-German air-to-air combat of the war, a Hudson gunner shot down a Dornier flying boat. In May 1940 Hudsons were used to provide air cover for the evacuation of British troops from Dunkirk. They flew over the German positions in waves of a dozen planes every fifteen minutes.

Of the 259 German U-boats sunk by aircraft of the Royal Air Force Coastal Command, most died at the hands of Hudsons. It was a Hudson, in fact, that was the only airplane ever to *capture* a submarine. On 27 August 1941 a Hudson, piloted by Sq Ldr James Thompson of 269 Squadron, was on patrol out of Kaldadarnes, Iceland. Thompson's Hudson was cruising at 300 feet when suddenly it broke through a patch of clouds and found the U-570, a brand new German Type VIIC submarine that was out on its first patrol, surfacing dead ahead. The RAF crew dropped a string of four depth charges which, among other things, damaged the sub's batteries, creating a serious chlorine gas leak. The German crew scrambled out onto the deck to escape the deadly gas only to face the machine guns of Thompson's circling

Above: This Model 18 Lodestar was christened *Starliner Anchorage* by Alaska Star Airlines. The Model 18 was similar in many ways to the Model 14/414 series. *Below:* The Lodestar's interior shows plush accoutrements, including the Model 18's standard leather seats.

Hudson. Other aircraft arrived, and soon the Royal Navy was on the scene to take the German crew into custody and tow the U-570 to Iceland. Aboard the U-boat was a new type of electric torpedo, as well as an example of the top secret *Enigma* code machine.

Royal Air Force Hudsons were also used during World War II by 161 Squadron under the direction of the Special Operations Executive (SOE) for clandestine flights into occupied Europe prior to the Norway Invasion in June 1944. These dangerous missions, designed to aid and equip resistance organizations, were considered 'most secret' and were not made public for over forty years.

THE LODESTAR

Lockheed's Model 18 Lodestar bore the same relationship to the Model 14 Super Electra that the Model 14 bore to the Model 10 Electra: each was a larger version of an earlier aircraft. The idea for an enlarged Model 14 probably surfaced even before the first flight of the Model 14, and design work was going on while production was underway on the Model 14 and its Hudson derivatives. The first flight of the Model 18 came on 2 February 1940, and the name came from Geoffry Chaucer's 'Loade Sterre', a reference to the navigator's star—Polaris, the 'north star'.

Mid-Continent Airlines bought three Lodestars for $270,000 before the first one was completed, and by the end of 1940 there had been 54 Model 18s built for such diverse customers as Regie Air Afrique, Alaskan Star Airlines and the Netherlands East Indies. The latter aircraft played a big role in the evacuation of civilians from the Dutch colony in advance of the Japanese invasion in 1941-42.

The US Army Air Corps (US Army Air Forces after 1941) and the US Navy each bought Lodestars for use as transports under the designations C-57 through C-60 and R5O-1.

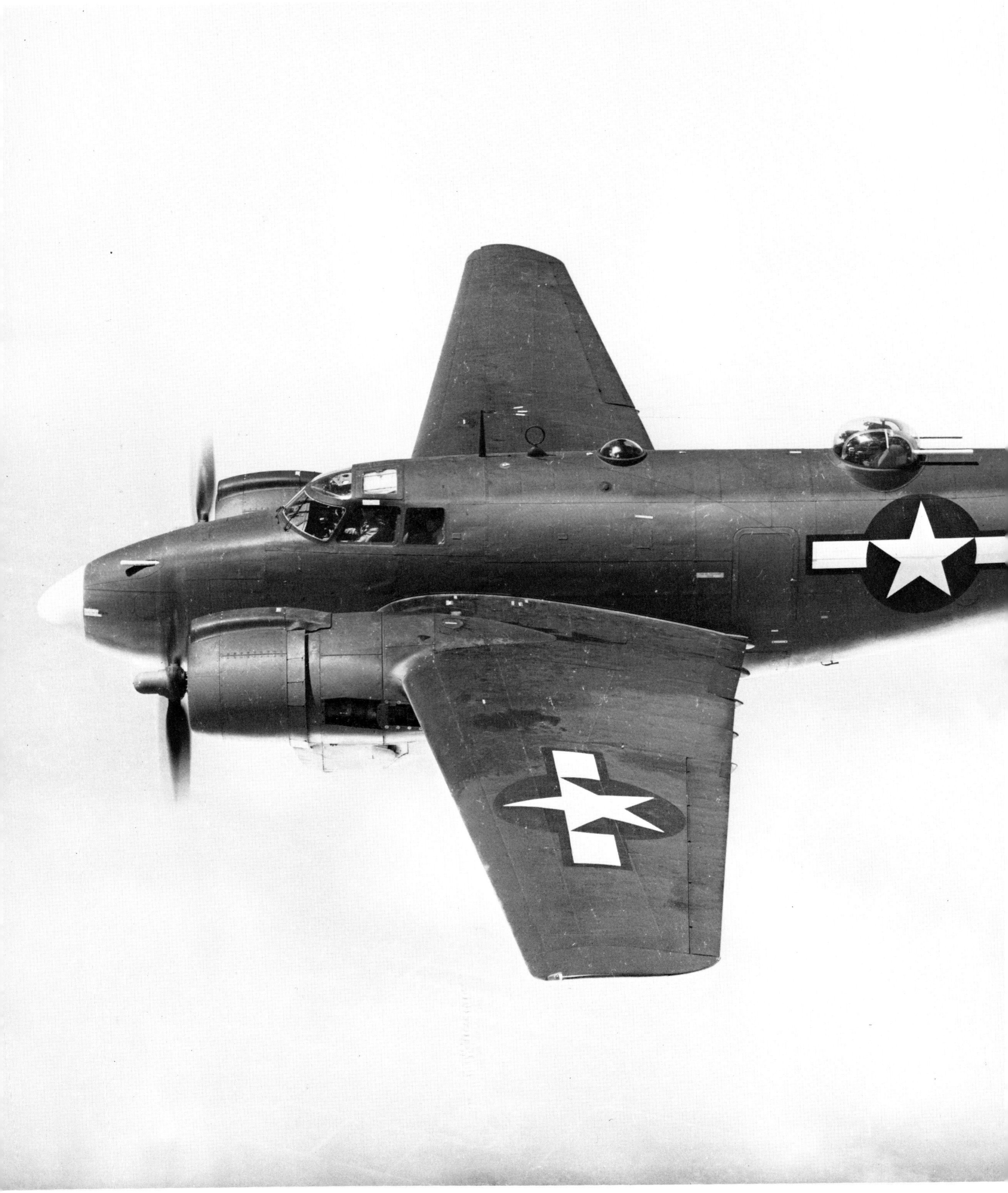

Compared to the PV-1 (*overleaf*), which was essentially a 'super' Model 37, the PV-2 Harpoon (*at left*) had greater range, wider wings and a tail that was redesigned for better stability. The PV-2 Harpoon was the ultimate of the twin-tailed, twin-engined Lockheeds.

In all there were a total of 625 Model 18 Lodestar transports built for military and civilian customers before the production lines were given over to Model 37 series being built by Lockheed's Vega subsidiary, the bomber version of the Model 18.

THE VENTURA

It had been an admirable selling job on the part of Carl Squier, Courtlandt Gross and Kelly Johnson to convince the British Royal Air Force to take a version of the Model 14 Super Electra airliner as a maritime patrol bomber, but as soon as the Hudson went into RAF service, it sold itself. Then Lockheed developed its Model 18 Lodestar, which was, in effect, a *super* Super Electra. There was little wonder, against the backdrop of the Hudson's success, that the RAF should be interested in a bomber version of the Model 18.

Ordered by the RAF in February 1940, this new bomber was developed by Lockheed's Vega subsidiary and designated as Lockheed Model 37. In keeping with the British custom of assigning place names to their bomber types, the Model 37 was named Ventura after the California county north of Los Angeles, and because 'Vega Ventura' is translated as 'Lucky Star.'

The first Ventura I flew on 31 July 1941, and the initial RAF order for 25 aircraft quickly expanded to a total of 188 Ventura Is, which in turn was followed by an order for 487 more heavily armed Ventura IIs for the RAF and 200 Ventura IIAs (Lockheed Model 137) for the Royal New Zealand Air Force. The latter were actually procured for lend-lease purposes by the US Army Air Forces under the designation B-34, but ironically a number of former RAF and RNZAF Venturas later served with the USAAF as B-34 Lexingtons.

The USAAF ordered an enhanced Wright Cyclone-powered armed observation version (Lockheed Model 437) under the designation O-56. The initial order called for 550 of the O-56s, but only 18 were built, and they were delivered as B-37s. After 1942, however, the entire production run of 1600 additional Model 37 series aircraft went to the US Navy as antisubmarine patrol bombers under the designation PV-1.

In 1943 Lockheed's Vega subsidiary introduced a *super* PV-1 Ventura. In effect, it was super Model 37 (a *super, super* Model 14 Super Electra) and it carried the company designation Model 15. In US Navy service it was designated PV-2 and named Harpoon.

The Harpoon had a greater wingspan (75 feet) than the Ventura, a redesigned tail for greater stability, and more fuel capacity which provided greater range. First delivered in March 1944, the Harpoon served with 14 Navy squadrons and remained in production until December 1945. A PV-2 squadron based on Attu in the Aleutian Islands attacked the Japanese-held Kurile Islands with bombs and rockets in April 1945; two other squadrons also were based in the Pacific. In addition to overseas service in both the Atlantic and Pacific, the PV-1 and PV-2 provided the backbone of American coastal defense during World War II and PV-2s served with the US Navy until 1948.

The Lockheed/Vega Venturas and Harpoons were succeeded in US Navy antisubmarine patrol service by the Lockheed Neptune and later by the Lockheed Orion, which will continue in that role to the end of the century.

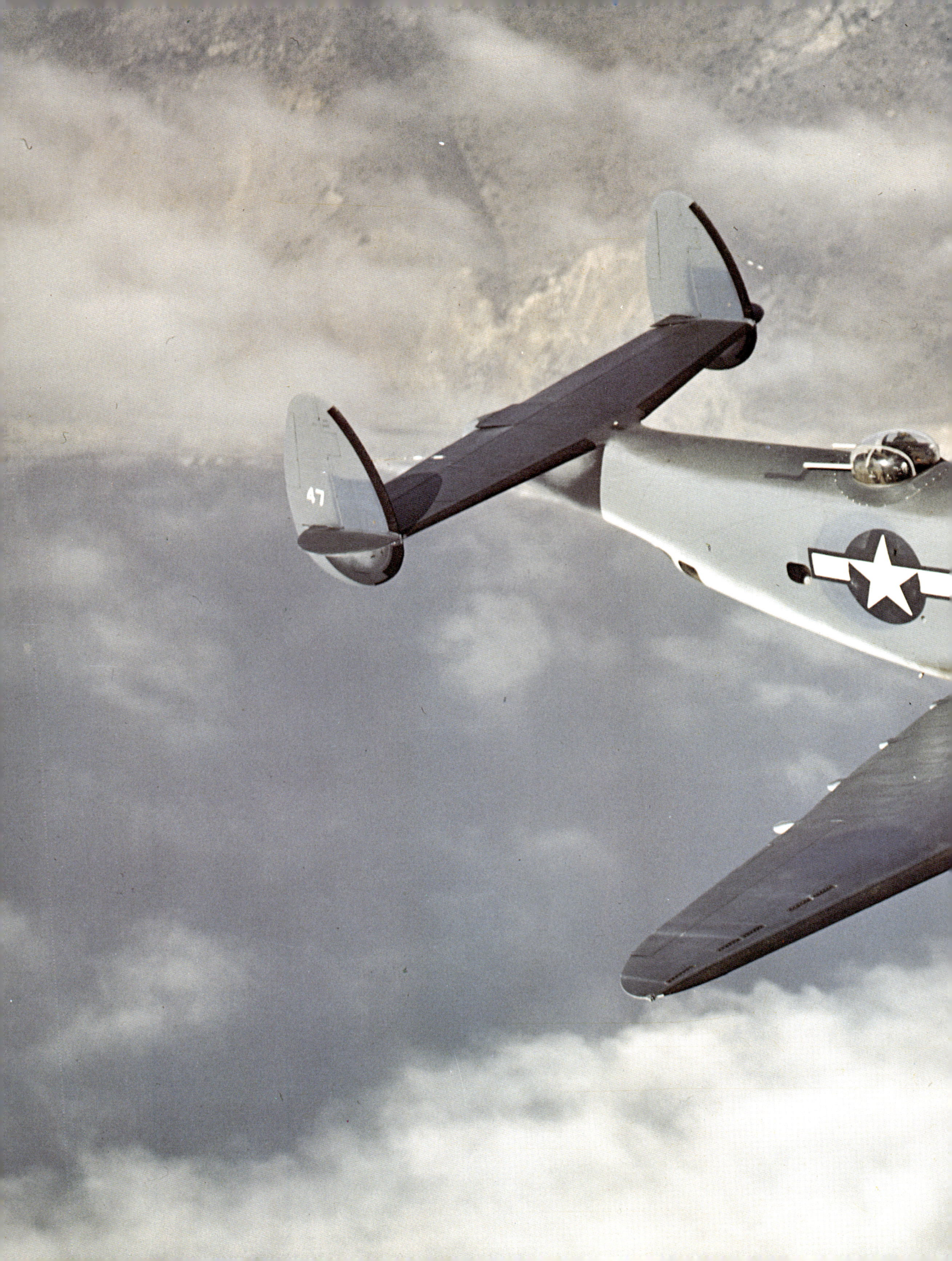
47

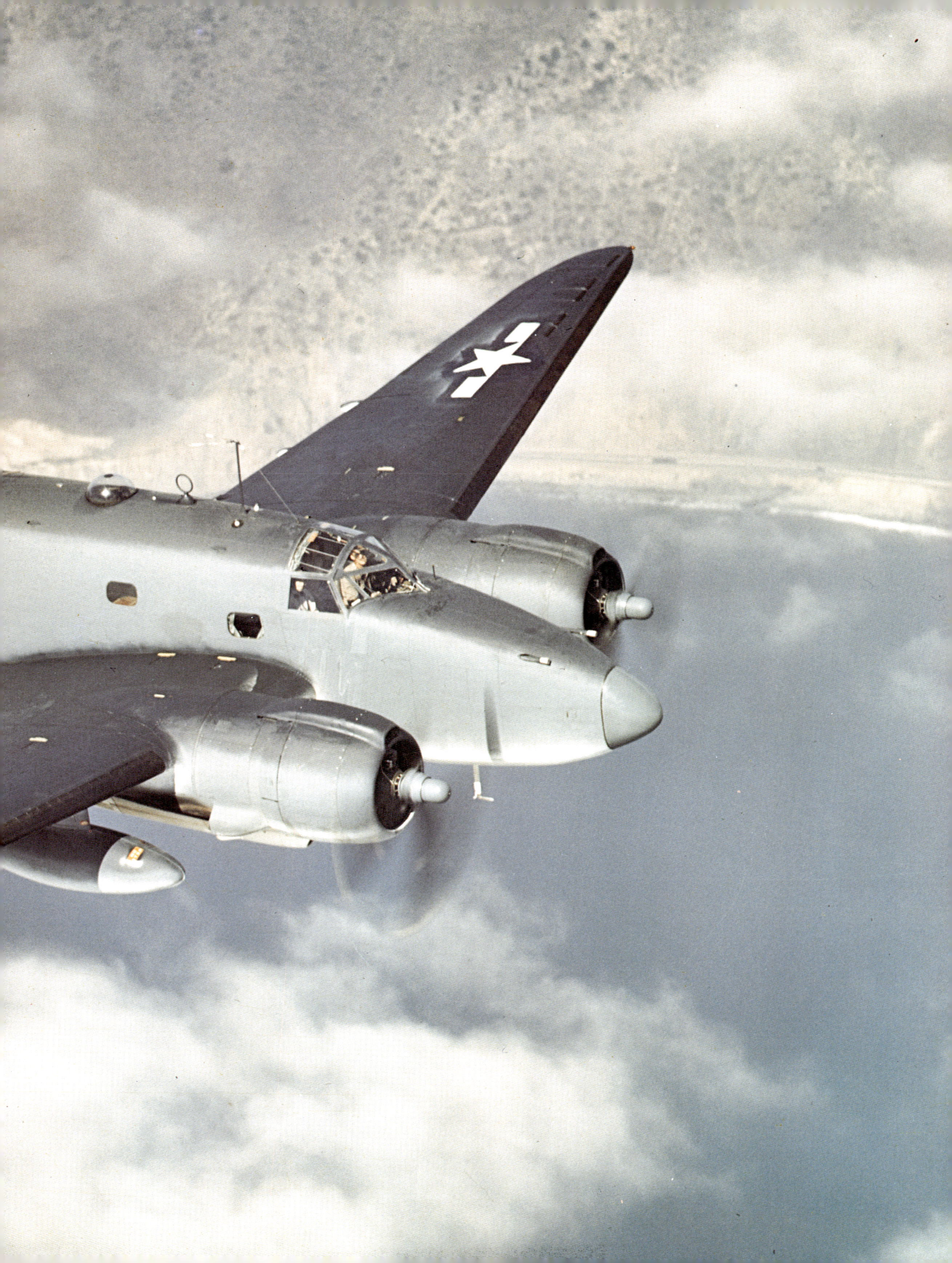

PRODUCTION CLOSE-UP (MODEL 10/12/14 SERIES)
ELECTRA SERIES

Commercial Transports

Model	Qty	Notes
Model 10 Electra	144	(1934-41) (Total includes those which later became C-36A, C-36B, and C-36C)
Model 12 Electra Junior	100	(1936-42) (Total includes those which later became C-40C)
Model 12 Starliner	1	(Model 12 built in 1939 with Unitwin engine)
Model 14 Super Electra	111	(1937-40)

Military Transports

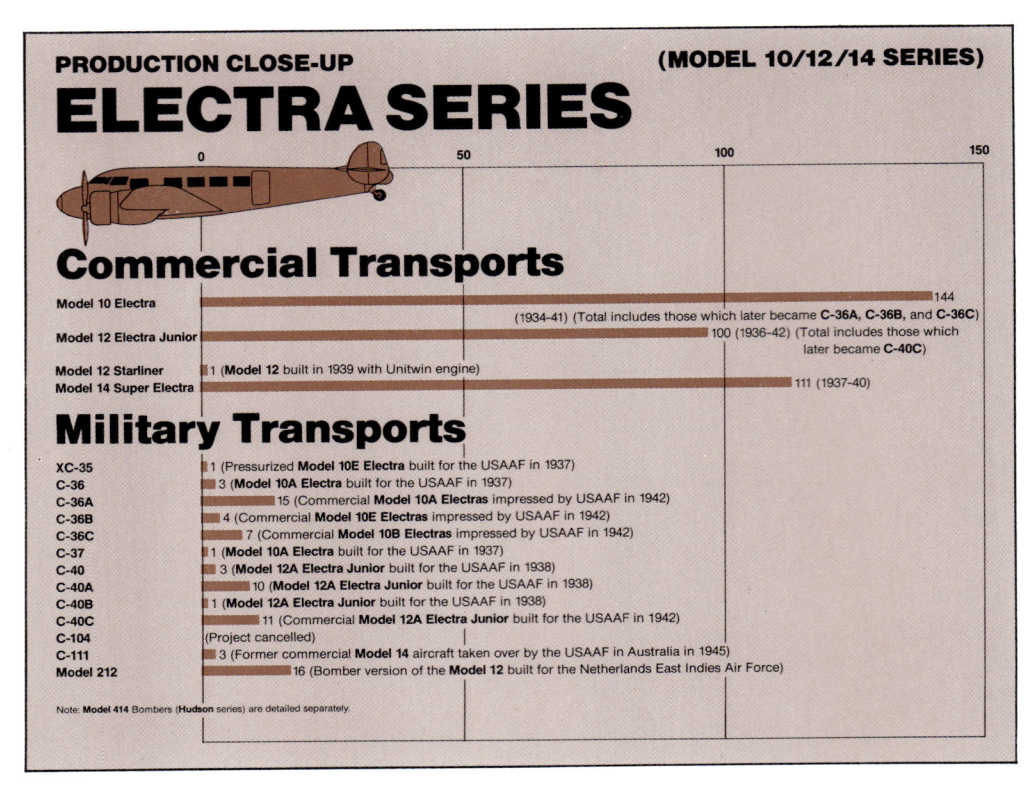

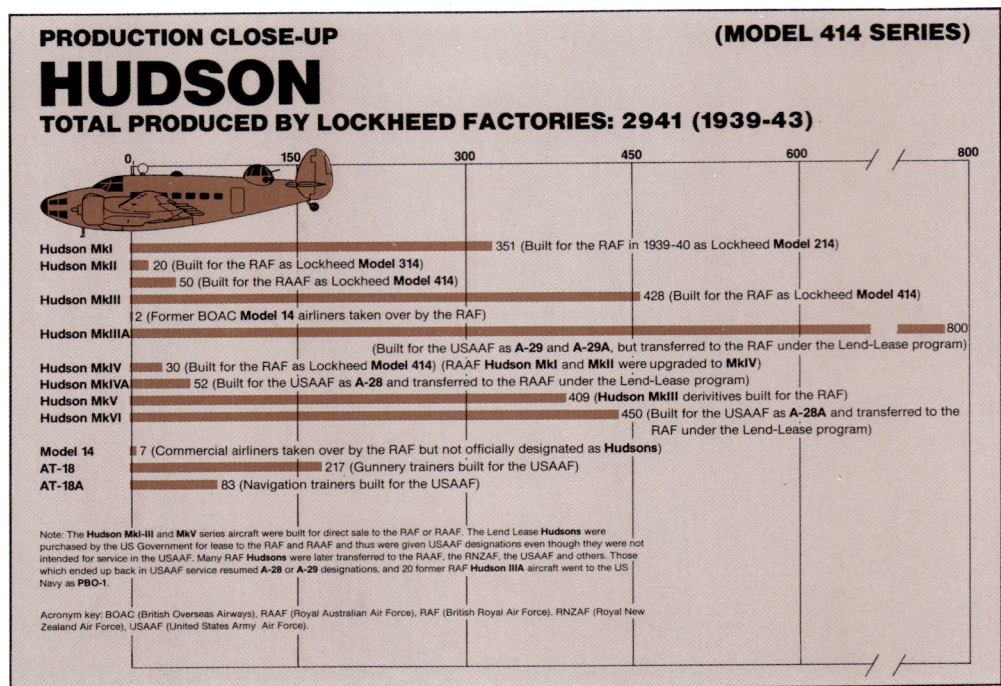

Model	Qty	Notes
XC-35	1	(Pressurized Model 10E Electra built for the USAAF in 1937)
C-36	3	(Model 10A Electra built for the USAAF in 1937)
C-36A	15	(Commercial Model 10A Electras impressed by USAAF in 1942)
C-36B	4	(Commercial Model 10E Electras impressed by USAAF in 1942)
C-36C	7	(Commercial Model 10B Electras impressed by USAAF in 1942)
C-37	1	(Model 10A Electra built for the USAAF in 1937)
C-40	3	(Model 12A Electra Junior built for the USAAF in 1938)
C-40A	10	(Model 12A Electra Junior built for the USAAF in 1938)
C-40B	1	(Model 12A Electra Junior built for the USAAF in 1938)
C-40C	11	(Commercial Model 12A Electra Junior built for the USAAF in 1942)
C-104	—	(Project cancelled)
C-111	3	(Former commercial Model 14 aircraft taken over by the USAAF in Australia in 1945)
Model 212	16	(Bomber version of the Model 12 built for the Netherlands East Indies Air Force)

Note: **Model 414** Bombers (**Hudson** series) are detailed separately.

PRODUCTION CLOSE-UP (MODEL 414 SERIES)
HUDSON
TOTAL PRODUCED BY LOCKHEED FACTORIES: 2941 (1939-43)

Model	Qty	Notes
Hudson MkI	351	(Built for the RAF in 1939-40 as Lockheed Model 214)
Hudson MkII	20	(Built for the RAF as Lockheed Model 314)
	50	(Built for the RAAF as Lockheed Model 414)
Hudson MkIII	428	(Built for the RAF as Lockheed Model 414)
	2	(Former BOAC Model 14 airliners taken over by the RAF)
Hudson MkIIIA	800	(Built for the USAAF as A-29 and A-29A, but transferred to the RAF under the Lend-Lease program)
Hudson MkIV	30	(Built for the RAF as Lockheed Model 414) (RAAF Hudson MkI and MkII were upgraded to MkIV)
Hudson MkIVA	52	(Built for the USAAF as A-28 and transferred to the RAAF under the Lend-Lease program)
Hudson MkV	409	(Hudson MkIII derivitives built for the RAF)
Hudson MkVI	450	(Built for the USAAF as A-28A and transferred to the RAF under the Lend-Lease program)
Model 14	7	(Commercial airliners taken over by the RAF but not officially designated as Hudsons)
AT-18	217	(Gunnery trainers built for the USAAF)
AT-18A	83	(Navigation trainers built for the USAAF)

Note: The **Hudson MkI-III** and **MkV** series aircraft were built for direct sale to the RAF or RAAF. The Lend Lease **Hudsons** were purchased by the US Government for lease to the RAF and RAAF and thus were given USAAF designations even though they were not intended for service in the USAAF. Many RAF **Hudsons** were later transferred to the RAAF, the RNZAF, the USAAF and others. Those which ended up back in USAAF service resumed **A-28** or **A-29** designations, and 20 former RAF **Hudson IIIA** aircraft went to the US Navy as **PBO-1**.

Acronym key: BOAC (British Overseas Airways), RAAF (Royal Australian Air Force), RAF (British Royal Air Force), RNZAF (Royal New Zealand Air Force), USAAF (United States Army Air Force).

Above: A US Navy PV-1 Ventura patrol bomber, Lockheed Vega Model 37. *Right:* This diagram is illustrative of the evolution of Lockheed twin-engine, twin-tailed aircraft. *From left* they are the Model 10 Electra; the Model 414 Hudson bomber (which is representative of the Model 14 Super Electra upon which it is based); and the Model 37 Ventura, which served the US Navy as PV-1 (*as above*).

A SUMMARY OF LOCKHEED'S TWIN-ENGINED, TWIN-TAILED AIRCRAFT

Between 1934 and 1945 Lockheed and its Vega subsidiary produced almost seven thousand related twin-engined, twin-tailed aircraft of five basic model types and numerous sub-types. The five basic Model types were (in chronological order): The Model 10 Electra, the Model 12 Electra Junior, the Model 14 Super Electra, the Model 18 Lodestar, and the Model 15 Harpoon. With the exception of the Model 12, which was a downscaled Model 10, each succeeding model type was a larger, more powerful aircraft than its predecessor, while at the same time following the same basic overall design.

Each of the basic model types, except the Model 15, began as a commercial airliner. Each of the basic model types, except the Model 10, begat a series of bombers that sold in greater numbers than the commercial version. The biggest sellers were the Hudson series (Models 214, 314 and 414), which was based on the Model 14 Super Electra; and the Ventura series (Models 37, 137, 237, 337 and 437), which was based on the Model 18 Lodestar. There were 2941 Hudsons and 2493 Venturas built.

A final postscript to this highly successful series was the Model 44 Excalibur project. The Excalibur was conceived as early as the summer of 1937 as a four-engined version of the Model 18 Lodestar. It was to have been 73 feet long, with a wingspan of 95 feet, and a passenger capacity of 32. Pan American expressed interest and Lockheed went so far as to begin construction on a series of full-size wooden mock-ups before World War II intervened. By this time, however, Lockheed's long-range planning for the development of larger airliners had already turned to the Model 69 project, which would evolve as the Constellation, one of Lockheed's greatest achievements.

PRODUCTION CLOSE-UP (MODEL 18 SERIES)
LODESTAR
TOTAL PRODUCED BY LOCKHEED FACTORIES: 625 (1939-43)

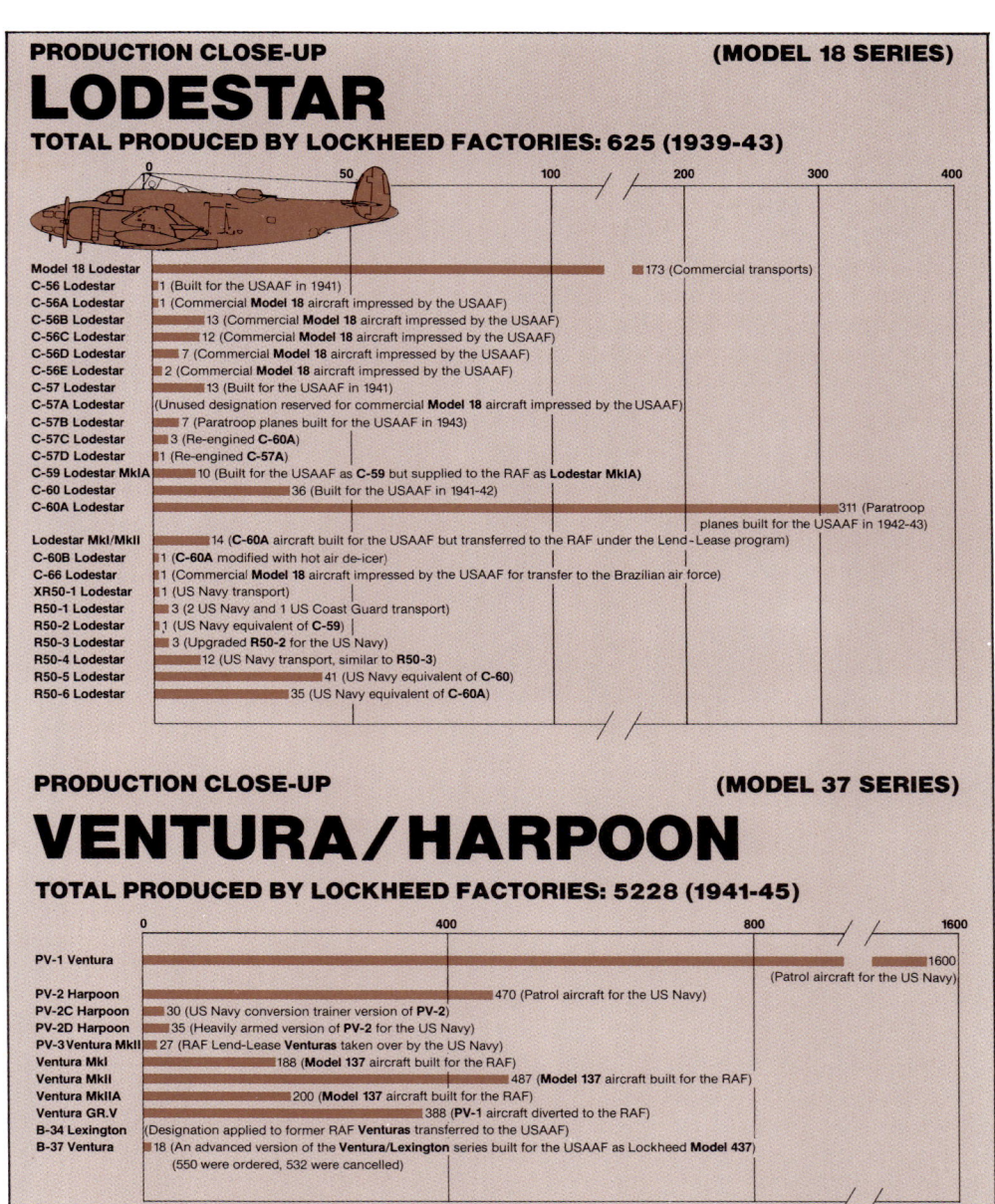

Variant	Count	Notes
Model 18 Lodestar	173	(Commercial transports)
C-56 Lodestar	1	(Built for the USAAF in 1941)
C-56A Lodestar	1	(Commercial Model 18 aircraft impressed by the USAAF)
C-56B Lodestar	13	(Commercial Model 18 aircraft impressed by the USAAF)
C-56C Lodestar	12	(Commercial Model 18 aircraft impressed by the USAAF)
C-56D Lodestar	7	(Commercial Model 18 aircraft impressed by the USAAF)
C-56E Lodestar	2	(Commercial Model 18 aircraft impressed by the USAAF)
C-57 Lodestar	13	(Built for the USAAF in 1941)
C-57A Lodestar		(Unused designation reserved for commercial Model 18 aircraft impressed by the USAAF)
C-57B Lodestar	7	(Paratroop planes built for the USAAF in 1943)
C-57C Lodestar	3	(Re-engined C-60A)
C-57D Lodestar	1	(Re-engined C-57A)
C-59 Lodestar MkIA	10	(Built for the USAAF as C-59 but supplied to the RAF as Lodestar MkIA)
C-60 Lodestar	36	(Built for the USAAF in 1941-42)
C-60A Lodestar	311	(Paratroop planes built for the USAAF in 1942-43)
Lodestar MkI/MkII	14	(C-60A aircraft built for the USAAF but transferred to the RAF under the Lend-Lease program)
C-60B Lodestar	1	(C-60A modified with hot air de-icer)
C-66 Lodestar	1	(Commercial Model 18 aircraft impressed by the USAAF for transfer to the Brazilian air force)
XR50-1 Lodestar	1	(US Navy transport)
R50-1 Lodestar	3	(2 US Navy and 1 US Coast Guard transport)
R50-2 Lodestar	1	(US Navy equivalent of C-59)
R50-3 Lodestar	3	(Upgraded R50-2 for the US Navy)
R50-4 Lodestar	12	(US Navy transport, similar to R50-3)
R50-5 Lodestar	41	(US Navy equivalent of C-60)
R50-6 Lodestar	35	(US Navy equivalent of C-60A)

PRODUCTION CLOSE-UP (MODEL 37 SERIES)
VENTURA/HARPOON
TOTAL PRODUCED BY LOCKHEED FACTORIES: 5228 (1941-45)

Variant	Count	Notes
PV-1 Ventura	1600	(Patrol aircraft for the US Navy)
PV-2 Harpoon	470	(Patrol aircraft for the US Navy)
PV-2C Harpoon	30	(US Navy conversion trainer version of PV-2)
PV-2D Harpoon	35	(Heavily armed version of PV-2 for the US Navy)
PV-3 Ventura MkII	27	(RAF Lend-Lease Venturas taken over by the US Navy)
Ventura MkI	188	(Model 137 aircraft built for the RAF)
Ventura MkII	487	(Model 137 aircraft built for the RAF)
Ventura MkIIA	200	(Model 137 aircraft built for the RAF)
Ventura GR.V	388	(PV-1 aircraft diverted to the RAF)
B-34 Lexington		(Designation applied to former RAF Venturas transferred to the USAAF)
B-37 Ventura	18	(An advanced version of the Ventura/Lexington series built for the USAAF as Lockheed Model 437) (550 were ordered, 532 were cancelled)

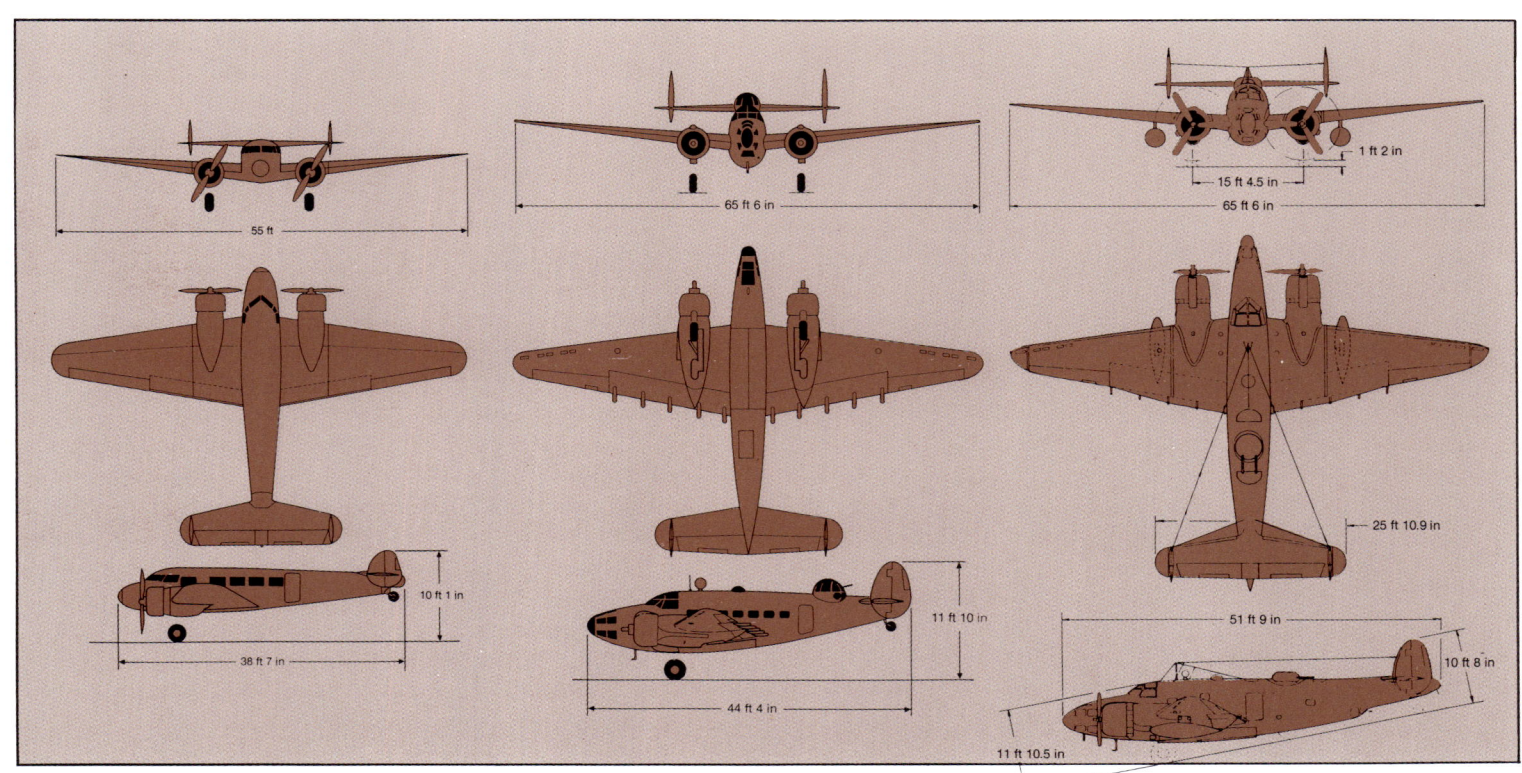

THE VEGA AIRPLANE COMPANY
1937–1943

In August 1937 Lockheed created a wholly-owned subsidiary called the AiRover Company for the purpose of developing light aircraft for the general aviation market. Mac Short, a well-known light plane designer, was named president. The cornerstone of the AiRover Company was the Unitwin engine, which was developed by engine designer Al Menasco. The Unitwin involved two of Menasco's six-cylinder engines linked to a single three-bladed Hamilton standard propeller. The AiRover Model 1 was actually a single Lockheed Model 9 Altair equipped with a Unitwin engine that itself was known officially as the 'Flying Test Stand', and familiarly as the *Unitwin*.

The AiRover Model 2 was an all-new light plane, with a Unitwin engine and tricycle landing gear, which was christened Starliner. By the time that the Starliner made its first flight in December 1937, the AiRover name had been dropped and the fledgling Lockheed subsidiary was renamed Vega Airplane Company, a reference to Lockheed's heretofore most famous airplane. Only a single Starliner was produced, but it was later retrofitted with an Electra-like twin tail.

The third aircraft developed by the subsidiary was designated as Lockheed Model 40. Built under an Air Corps contract issued in 1939, the Model 40 was an 848-pound, remote-controlled aerial target drone with a 23-foot wingspan. Only five Model 40s were built by the time the project was canceled in 1940, and all were apparently shot down as intended, during Air Corps gunnery tests.

In 1941 the Vega subsidiary purchased the rights to produce a fixed-gear monoplane trainer designed by the North American Aviation Company, but only five were actually built by Vega. Originally designated as North American's Model NA-35, the Vega-built trainers conveniently became the Lockheed/Vega Model 35. At the same time, the Vega subsidiary had received a contract from its parent company to produce a large number of Lockheed Hudsons.

In 1940, with World War II already raging in Europe, the notion of Vega continuing as a developer of light planes was abandoned and Courtlandt Gross, brother of Lockheed president Robert Gross, succeeded Mac Short as Vega president. At the same time the British Royal Air Force had expressed an interest in a bomber version of Lockheed's Model 18 Lodestar airliner. The RAF was more than satisfied with its Hudson bombers, which were the bomber derivative of the Model 14 airliner, so when the Model 18 (which was an improved Model 14) was introduced, the idea of a bomber derivative of the Model 18 seemed logical. Lockheed turned the whole project of creating such a plane over to the Vega subsidiary, and the result was the Vega Ventura (Lockheed Model 37). The Ventura *(see text)* not only served the air forces of the British Empire, but the US Army Air Forces and the US Navy as well. In the USAAF the Model 37 served as the B-34 and B-37 Lexington. In the US Navy the Model 37 was the PV-1 Ventura, which in turn begat the similar but larger PV-2 Harpoon (Lockheed Model 15). In all, there were 2493 Model 37s produced, followed by 535 Model 15s.

In April 1941 the US Army Air Corps (US Army Air Forces after June 1941) asked Lockheed to join in a three-company effort to produce a massive number of four-engine heavy bombers. Lockheed turned its part of the production contract over to its Vega subsidiary. The particular design in question was the Boeing Model 299, better known by its military designation as the B-17 Flying Fortress. Before World War II was over, Boeing, Douglas and Vega produced over 12,000 of the historic bombers, with 2752 coming off the Vega assembly line under the Lockheed designation Model 17.

During this period, Vega built two specialized Flying Fortress variants that, while they didn't go into mass production, provide an important footnote to the Flying Fortress story. The first of these was the XB-38 (Vega model 134), which was an off-the-shelf B-17E equipped with Allison 12-cylinder, liquid-cooled engines in place of the B-17's standard Wright Cyclone air-cooled engines. The idea was that the B-38 series could be put into production if a shortage of the more powerful Cyclones should occur. The shortage never befell the B-17 program so the B-38 project ended in 1943 with a single prototype.

The second Flying Fortress variant developed by Vega was the B-40 series (Vega Model 139). They took the basic B-17E airframe and equipped it with turrets containing up to 30 machine guns and 20mm cannons, thus more than tripling the defensive armament of a conventional B-17E. This true 'flying fortress' was intended to serve not as a bomber but as a flying gun platform to escort bombers. The XB-40 prototype was a formidable weapon, and twenty YB-40 service test aircraft were built. The type first went into combat in May 1943, but the weight of the guns and ammunition prevented it from being able to keep up with the lighter B-17s after the bombers had dropped their bombs. The project was abandoned and the surviving YB-40s became TB-40 gunnery trainers.

The Vega subsidiary, which was now the Vega Aircraft Corporation, did not survive 1943. By this time Lockheed was ready to absorb its enormous offspring, which had evolved far beyond its intended purpose. In the six years of Vega's existence—although it built only six copies of its two indigenous designs (the Starliner and Model 40)—as a contract producer of designs that originated elsewhere, it produced 5785 Model 35s, Model 37s, Model 15s and (Model 17) Flying Fortresses. From its humble start, Vega had racked up an outstanding box score.

Opposite page: The Lockheed Starliner, shelved to make way for military production in 1939, featured side by side 'Unitwin' engines and boasted 210mph-plus speeds.

Working away in the nose of a Vega-built B-17G bomber (Vega Model 17), Rosie the Riveter's sister (*above*) polishes the glass bubble for some lucky 'Joe' of a bombardier.

THE CONSTELLATION

THE GERM OF AN IDEA

Lockheed made the Model 44 Excalibur project public in April 1939. The world was not yet at war and for many airlines the concept of a four-engined transport held a great deal of interest. Aircraft manufacturers were already beginning to answer the call. Boeing had already produced the Model 307 Stratoliner and Model 314 Clipper, while Douglas had flight tested its prototype DC-4E and was ready to go into production. For Lockheed, the development of a four-engined airliner was considered an essential step in order to stay in the commercial aircraft business.

The flamboyant millionaire Howard Hughes, who had just flown around the world in a Lockheed Lodestar, took an immediate interest in the Lockheed Excalibur. He was also the majority stockholder in TWA and wanted that airline to be able to offer nonstop transcontinental service and, all things being equal, he'd just as soon see TWA be able to do it with Lockheed aircraft. Hughes and TWA president Jack Frye sat down with Lockheed in June 1939 to go over the Excalibur's specifications, but the plane was just too small for the job. The Lockheed engineers, including Kelly Johnson and Hall Hibbard, went back to their drawing boards and in the third week of June they were able to hand Hughes the initial design concept for the Lockheed Model 49 Constellation. On 10 July 1939 the contract was signed for 40 Lockheed Model 49s and work began on what would become the greatest four-engined, propeller-driven airliner in American history. Though she was officially named Constellation, her legion of admirers would come to know her simply as 'Connie'.

The passion for secrecy that Howard Hughes would develop to absurd proportions later in his life had already begun to manifest itself. He insisted that the Constellation remain secret and that the development contract be between Lockheed and Hughes Tool Company so that it would not be known that TWA was to be the ultimate customer. The project was further disguised by the aircraft's being publicly called Excalibur A, rather than Constellation. By early 1940, however, Pan American had found out about the project and expressed an interest in buying some Constellations of its own. At that time TWA and Pan American did not have a competitive route structure, and since the cat was already out of the bag, Hughes consented to Lockheed's acceptance of an order from Pan American for 22 Model 49s. Because of its long transoceanic routes, Pan American also went so far as to commission Lockheed to retrofit 18 Model 49s into a *longer* range Constellation configuration, which became Lockheed's Model 149.

The Model 44 Excalibur (*above*) was a pre-World War II four engine transport concept. Out of it grew the passenger-carrying Model 49 Constellation (*right*), designed at the behest of Howard Hughes.

THE CONNIE BECOMES A MILITARY TRANSPORT

By mid-1941 much of the world was at war and the United States, while not yet directly involved, was gearing up for national defense. A Commercial Aircraft Priority Committee was formed to control production. On 4 May 1941 the Committee announced that Lockheed would be permitted to proceed with only three Constellation prototypes, and only if this didn't conflict with military aircraft production.

On 20 December 1941, less than two weeks after the United States entered World War II, the US Army Air Forces undertook an evaluation of the American four-engined transports currently in production or under development, with an eye toward the gargantuan airlift capability that would be required to win the war. The Douglas DC-4 and its military counterpart, the C-54, were the largest and best of what was in production, but the Constellation was even larger and promised longer range and greater capability when it did reach production, so the USAAF became Lockheed's third customer. The USAAF Constellation would be similar to the commercial Model 49, but with a larger cargo door and reinforced flooring to accommodate not only troops, but 105mm howitzers, small trucks and other heavy equipment as well. The USAAF would buy 180 planes built as Lockheed Model 349 under the USAAF designation C-69. The Model 249 was to have been a long-range bomber version. The USAAF showed some interest in the project and went so far as to reserve the designation B-30 for the Model 249, but no Constellation bombers were ever built.

In March 1942 Lockheed sat down with representatives of TWA, Pan American, the USAAF's Air Transport Command and the War Production Board to plan the production of the Constellation. It was decided that Lockheed would go ahead with the 80 Constellations that were then under contract from the airlines, but they would be *sold* to the USAAF. Jack Frye of TWA objected to this idea because of the investment that TWA and Pan American had already made in the Constellation project. At last a compromise was reached by which the planes would be delivered to the airlines *then* transferred to the USAAF under the designation C-69. The airlines would provide crews to operate the planes. Under this plan the USAAF would own the aircraft and be able to operate them as its needs dictated, but the airlines would save face. To quote Jack Frye:

'In view of the large expenditure of time and money, much of which is intangible and for which we cannot hope to be otherwise compensated, we must not *also* lose the recognition and prestige that will accrue to us through our continued association with the airplane in its final stages of production.'

By the end of August 1942 the project had been streamlined to include 50 Model 49s to be delivered as C-69 and C-69A, and 210 Model 349s to be delivered as C-69B. The Constellation prototype, now designated XC-69 by the USAAF, was scheduled to have made its first flight on 31 August, but it did not.

By the end of the year, however, the prototype was finally ready. Painted olive drab and marked with USAAF insignia, the XC-69 Constellation prototype (Lockheed serial number 1961) nevertheless was delivered for flight testing with the civilian registration NX25600, rather than with a military tail number.

THE CONNIE FLIES AT LAST

The cockpit crew for the XC-69's first flight was an all-star cast. In the pilot and copilot seats were Boeing's Eddie Allen, the nation's top multiengine aircraft test pilot, and Milo Burcham, who had limited experience with multiengine aircraft but who was Lockheed's top experimental test pilot with experience in the P-38 program. Rudy Thoren was the flight engineer and aircraft designer Kelly Johnson was also aboard.

The first Connie took off from Lockheed Air Terminal in Burbank on 9 January 1943 for a 50 minute flight to USAAF's experimental test facility at Muroc Dry Lake (now Edwards AFB) in the California desert. Although flight test programs

Above: A Trans World Airlines 'Connie' on the fly. *At right:* This Constellation flew in the service of Suid Afrikaanse Lugdiens—South African Airlines. *Note:* Connies up to Model 749 had portholes, as opposed to rectangular windows. *Opposite page, below:* The pilot's cabin of a Constellation.

usually take a number of flights to work the bugs out of a new aircraft, Eddie Allen pronounced the Constellation a success after the first flight.

On 17 April 1944 Howard Hughes and TWA president Jack Frye personally took the controls of the second C-69 Constellation for a flight from Burbank to Washington DC and set a new transcontinental speed record of six hours, 58 minutes, 51 seconds. On the return flight, they stopped over in Vandalia, Ohio, where they made a short flight with none other than Orville Wright in the copilot's seat. Wright, the coinventor of powered flight, was impressed with the Constellation and noted that its wingspan was greater than the whole *distance* of his historic first flight in 1903.

Constellation flight testing continued, but despite the huge plane's great promise, the program moved slowly and only 15 of the 260 planned C-69s were completed by the time World War II ended in 1945.

INTO AIRLINE SERVICE AT LAST

On 1 October 1945, less than a month after the end of World War II, TWA *finally* took delivery of its first commercial Constellation. For Lockheed the transition from C-69 to commercial Constellation was an easy one because the fabrication facilities and the C-69 subassemblies that were were in existence when the war ended could be used in production of commercial Model 49s.

Two serious accidents involving Constellations occurred in the summer of 1946, however. On 18 June the supercharger driveshaft on a Pan American plane broke loose and burned the engine completely off the wing. The plane landed safely, but on 11 July another Constellation was not so lucky. An electrical fire from the main generator circuit ignited some insulation material, resulting in a disastrous crash and the suspension of Lockheed's airworthiness certificate for the Model 49. When the Constellation resumed service it was a much safer aircraft.

Despite this setback, orders for the Connie came in from all over the world. By 1947 there were Model 49s in service not only with TWA and Pan American but American Overseas, British Overseas, Air France and the Netherlands' KLM as well. In May 1947 Eastern Air Lines' *Great Silver Fleet* became the first airline to take delivery of the first postwar improved version of the Constellation, the 'Gold Plate' Model 649. The Model 649, which first flew in July 1946, was outwardly identical to the Model 49 but had upgraded engines and a higher gross weight. *(See table.)* It was followed in 1949 with the similar, but slightly improved, Model 649A.

The Model 749, also introduced in 1947, was similar to the Model 649 but it was adapted for long-range transatlantic service. When the Model 649A was introduced in 1949, a parallel 749A was also made available.

The US Army Air Forces (which became the US Air Force) in 1947 also purchased the Model 749 Constellation to which they assigned the designation C-121. These aircraft were on hand

47

Facing page: This photo shows the Lockheed facility for building Model 1049 Super Constellations. *In the foreground* is the wing assembly area, and *in the background*, a row of Navy R7Vs are under construction. Excepting the military models built with a few porthole passenger windows, the Super Constellations had rectangular passenger compartment windows.

Below: This illustration shows three views of the configuration that characterized the earlier series Constellations with their circular porthole windows. The Connie's graceful sweeping lines were already clearly in evidence, though.

in time to serve during the 1948 Berlin airlift, making direct flights to Berlin's Tempelhof Airport from Westover AFB in Massachusetts.

The C-121 was also configured as a VIP transport. One of the more famous C-121 executive transports was *Bataan*, which was used by General Douglas MacArthur in his role as military governor of Japan, and later as commander of United Nations forces during the early part of the Korean War. *Columbine* was General Dwight Eisenhower's C-121 when he was Supreme Commander of Allied Forces in Europe, and the C-121 *Columbine II* served him after he became president of the United States.

The US Navy selected the Model 749 as their PO-1 (designated WV-1 in 1952), a long-range maritime patrol aircraft.

THE SUPER CONSTELLATION

During April 1948 and July 1949 Lockheed proposed its Model 849 and Model 949. They were successively improved versions of the Model 649 and Model 749, but potential customers turned thumbs down, so none were built. The new Constellations were better than the then-current Constellations, but they didn't go far enough. The only thing that could improve on the Constellation, it was decided, would be a *Super* Constellation. And thus it happened that the Model 1049 was born.

The prototype Model 1049 Super Constellation was actually the original Model 49 prototype, serial number 1961. She had been repurchased and was still on hand in Burbank after the earlier flight testing, so rather than building a new plane from the ground up, Lockheed took a torch to old 1961 and cut her into three pieces. The fuselage was cut just fore and aft of the wing and 'plugs', or fuselage sections, were inserted to lengthen the plane by 18.4 feet. Wright R-3350 engines were installed and the gross weight was increased by 30 percent over the Model 649. The cabin water system and the fuel system were revamped and enlarged, as was the cockpit. The round portholes of the earlier Constellations were later replaced by rectangular windows. The new plane first flew on 13 October 1950, and was cleared for airline service on 14 May 1952.

In the meantime, the US Air Force and the US Navy ordered their own share of Model 1049s. The Air Force series began with the C-121C designation, while the Navy ordered transports under the R7V series and patrol aircraft in the WV series.

	Original C-69 Constellation	Model 49 Constellation	Model 649 Constellation
First Flight:	1943	1945	1946
Wingspan:	123 ft	123 ft	123 ft
Length:	95 ft, 3 in	95 ft, 3 in	95 ft, 3 in
Height:	23 ft	23 ft	23 ft
Engines:	four Wright R3350 Cyclones (745C18BA1)	four Wright R3350 Cyclones (745C18BA3)	four Wright GR3350 Cyclones
Engine hp:	2200	2200	2500
Gross Weight (lb):	86,250	90,000	102,000
Empty Weight (lb):	49,392 to 50,372	52,156	56,797
Passengers:*	69	81	81
Operating Altitude (ft):	25,300	25,300	25,700
Cruising Speed (mph):	298	300	321
Top Speed (mph):	340	340	352
Max Range (miles):	2300	2300	3700

*High density seating. Standard configuration was 60-80 percent of high density.

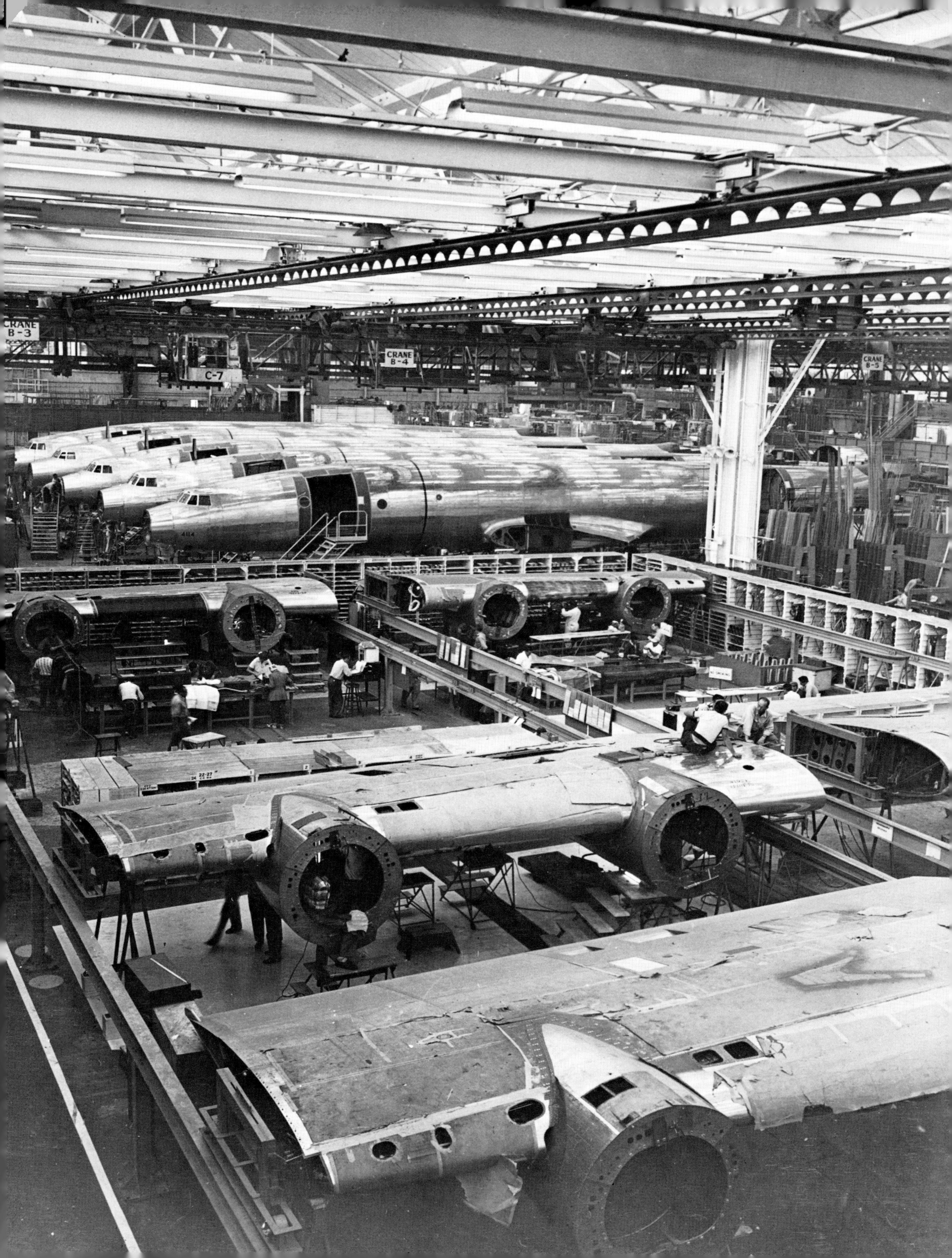
CRANE
B-3
C-7
CRANE
B-4
CRANE
B-5

Above: An Eastern Air Lines Super Constellation wings its way over scenic America. *Facing page:* This US Air Force C-121C Super Constellation, nicknamed *Columbine,* served as General Dwight D Eisenhower's executive transport. *Columbine III,* a VC-121E, was his 'Air Force One' after he became president. *Below:* This view of a Northwest Orient Super Constellation shows the Sky Lounge—one of many luxuries built into Lockheed Super Constellation airliners—which seated up to eight of the capacious plane's many passengers.

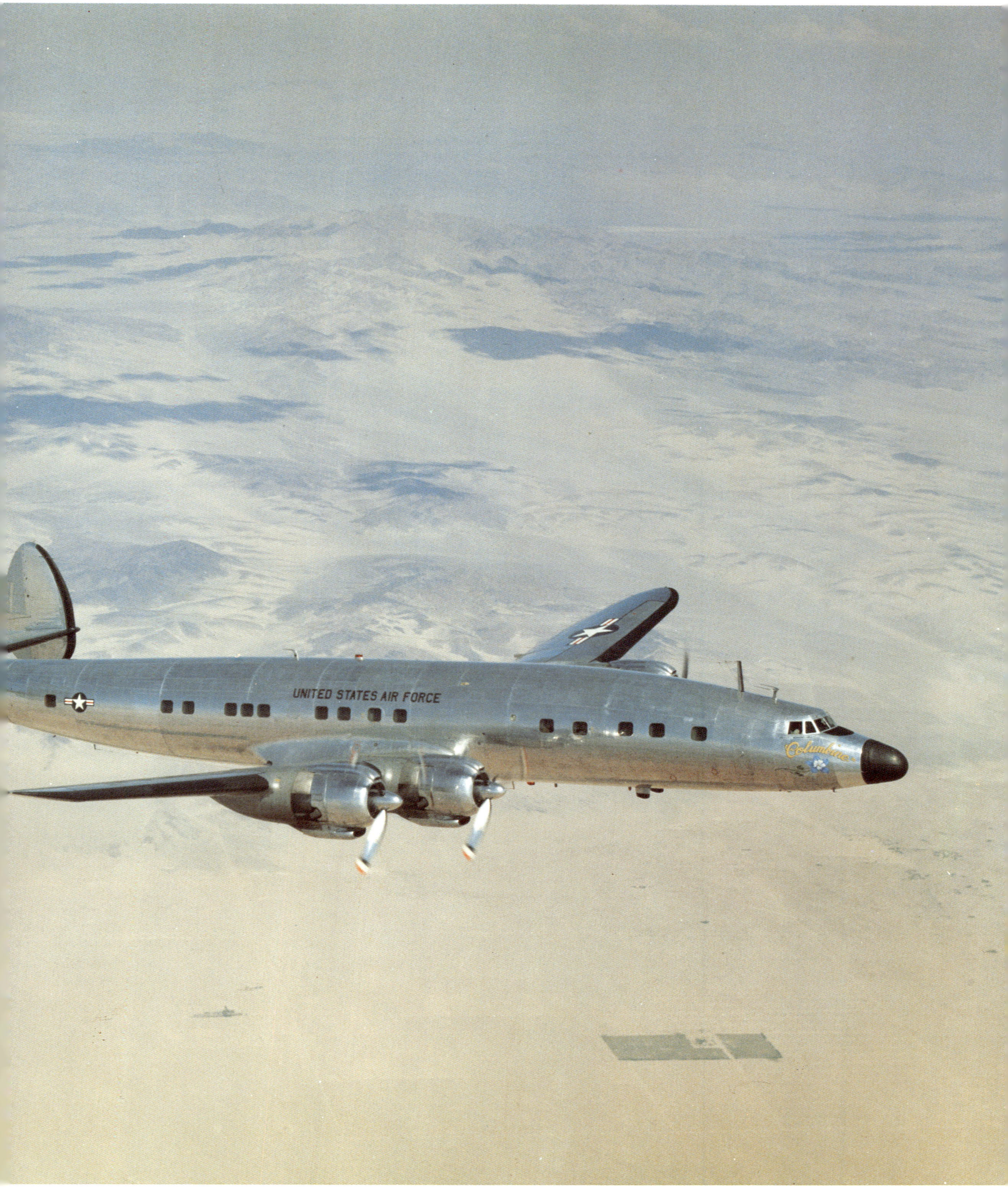
UNITED STATES AIR FORCE
Columbine

The C-121C served the US Air Force in a variety of ways. The basic transport version was used in the Military Air Transport Service's Atlantic Division, and the identical C-121G was used in the Pacific Division. The TC-121C served as a trainer, and a single VC-121E became President Eisenhower's *Columbine III*.

A number of military Model 1049s were modified for electronic warfare and reconnaissance purposes, and many of them went on to serve in Vietnam. These special versions included the US Air Force EC-121C, EC-121D, RC-121C and RC-121D, as well as the US Navy's WV-2 and WV-3, which were redesignated as EC-121K and WC-121N when the Air Force and Navy nomenclature systems were merged in 1962.

Commercial Model 1049s were delivered to a wide variety of customers including TWA, Lufthansa, Quantas, Air France, KLM and Air India. Of these the Model 1049G and Model 1049H were considered to be the top of the line.

THE LAST CONSTELLATIONS

The highly successful Model 1049 was followed by a series of follow-on proposals which were never produced. The Model 1149 was proposed as a turboprop-powered Model 1049 conversion. Four Model 1249As were the only Constellations that were ever actually built with turboprop engines. They were delivered to the US Air Force and US Navy as YC-121F and R7V-2 respectively, but the power provided by the Pratt & Whitney T-34s was much more than the Connie required. Aviation writer Louis Barr noted that with all that power 'they would have made excellent transports for gold bullion.'

The Model 1249B designation was reserved by Lockheed for a commercial turboprop plane, but the idea was abandoned.

	Model 1049 Constellation	Model 1649 Constellation (Starliner)
First Flight:	1950	1956
Wingspan:	123 ft	150 ft
Length:	113 ft, 9 in	116 ft
Height:	24 ft, 6 in	24 ft, 9 in
Engines:	four Wright R3350 Cyclones	Wright 988TC-18EA-2 Turbo Cyclones
Engine hp:	2700	3400
Gross Weight (lb):	120,000	156,000
Empty Weight (lb):	81,390	
Passengers*:	94	99
Operating Altitude (ft):	27,200	23,700
Cruising Speed (mph):	331	290
Top Speed (mph):	352	372
Max Range (miles):	4820	6180

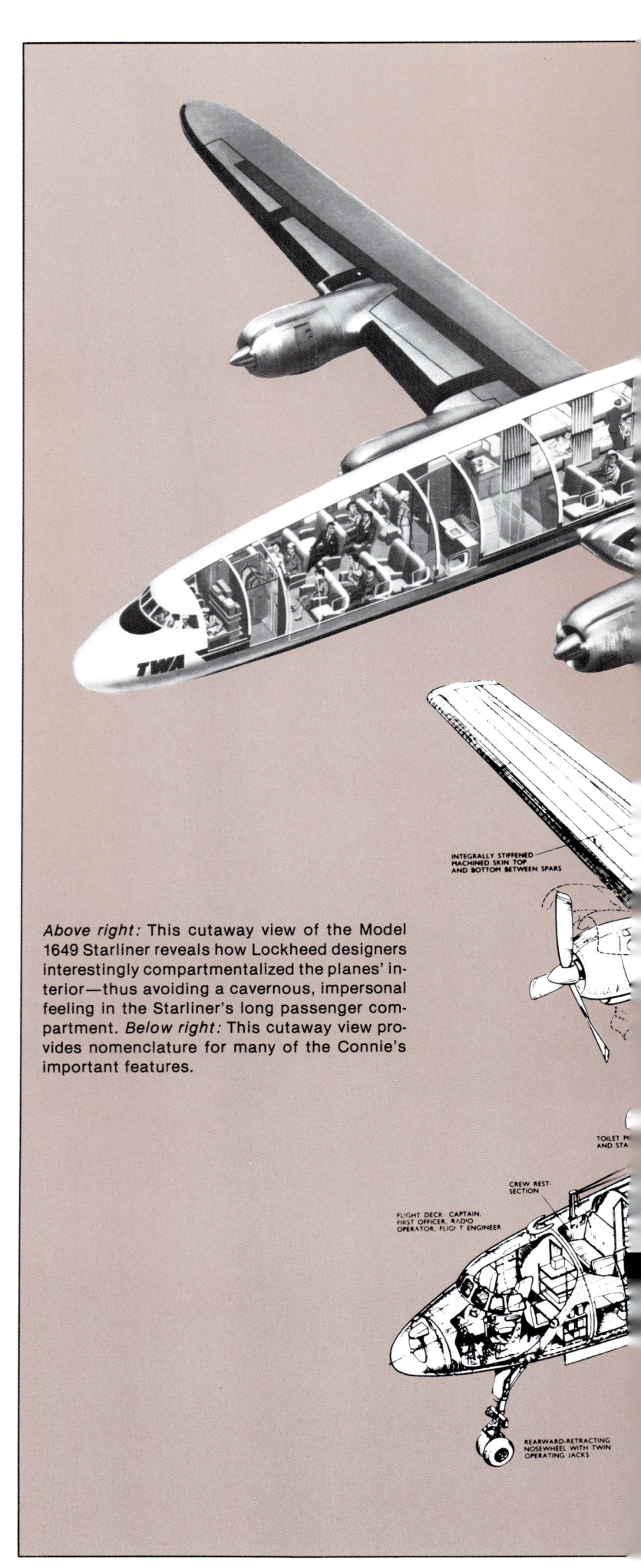

*High density seating. Standard configuration was 60-80 percent of high density.

Above right: This cutaway view of the Model 1649 Starliner reveals how Lockheed designers interestingly compartmentalized the planes' interior—thus avoiding a cavernous, impersonal feeling in the Starliner's long passenger compartment. *Below right:* This cutaway view provides nomenclature for many of the Connie's important features.

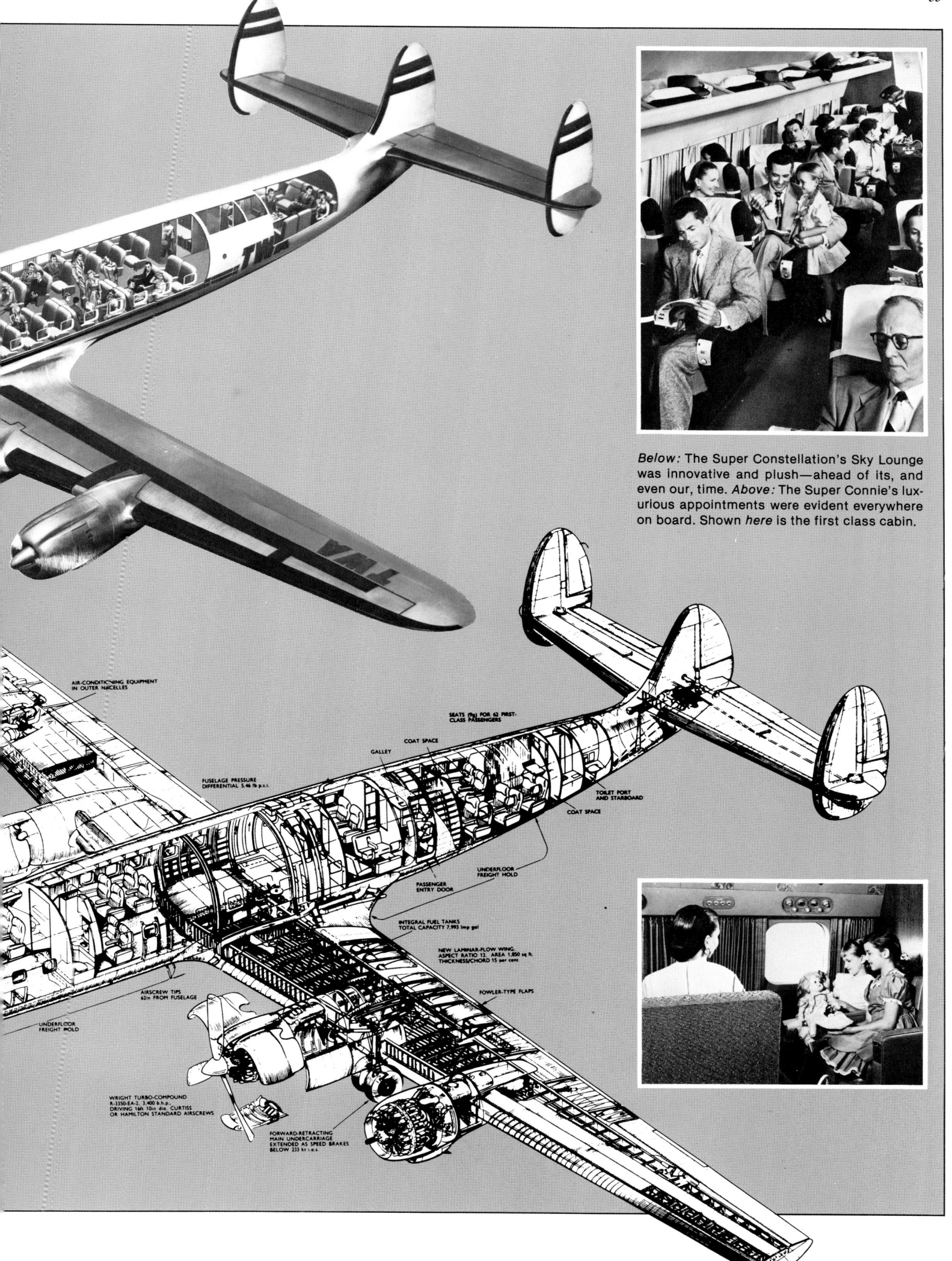

Below: The Super Constellation's Sky Lounge was innovative and plush—ahead of its, and even our, time. *Above:* The Super Connie's luxurious appointments were evident everywhere on board. Shown *here* is the first class cabin.

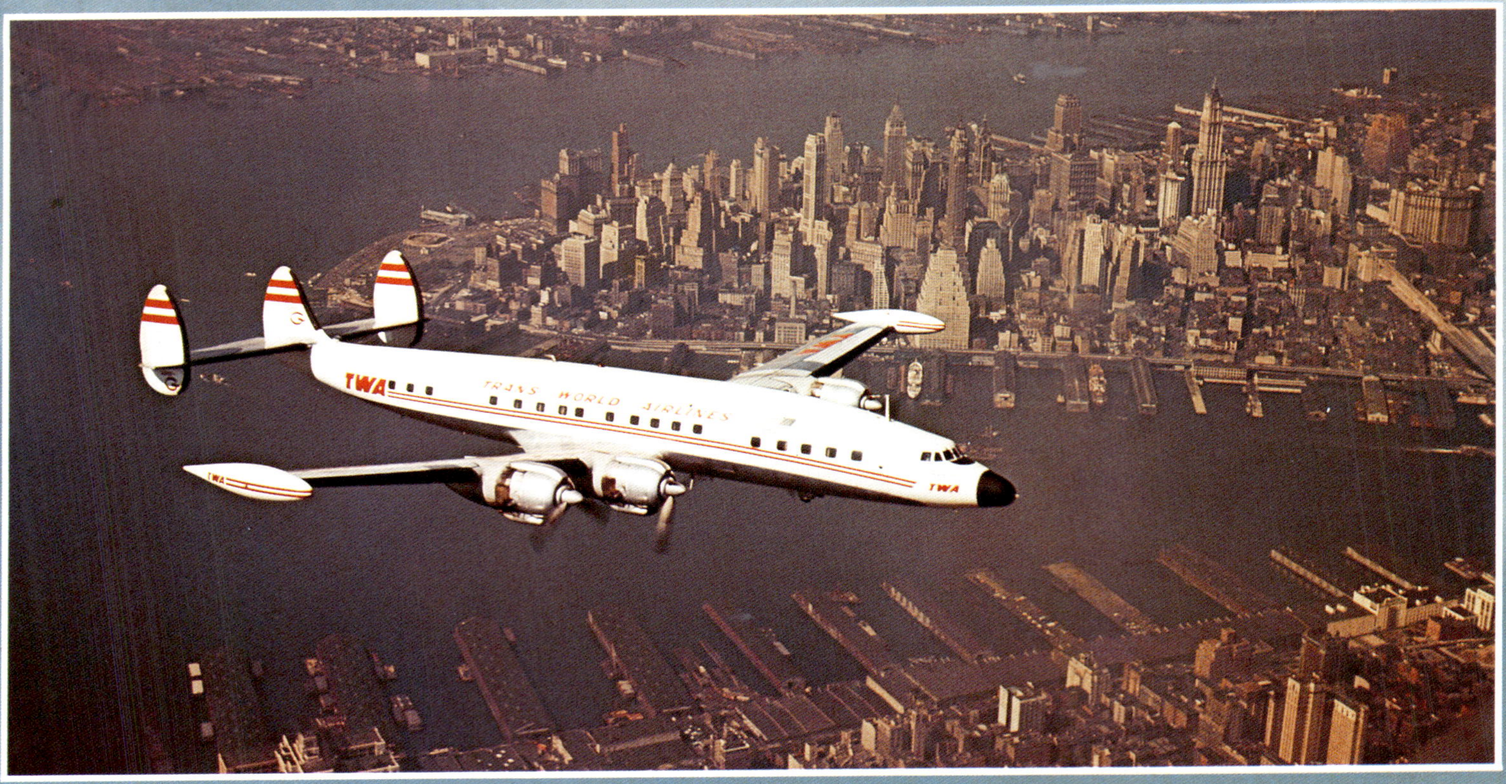
TWA
TRANS WORLD AIRLINES
TWA

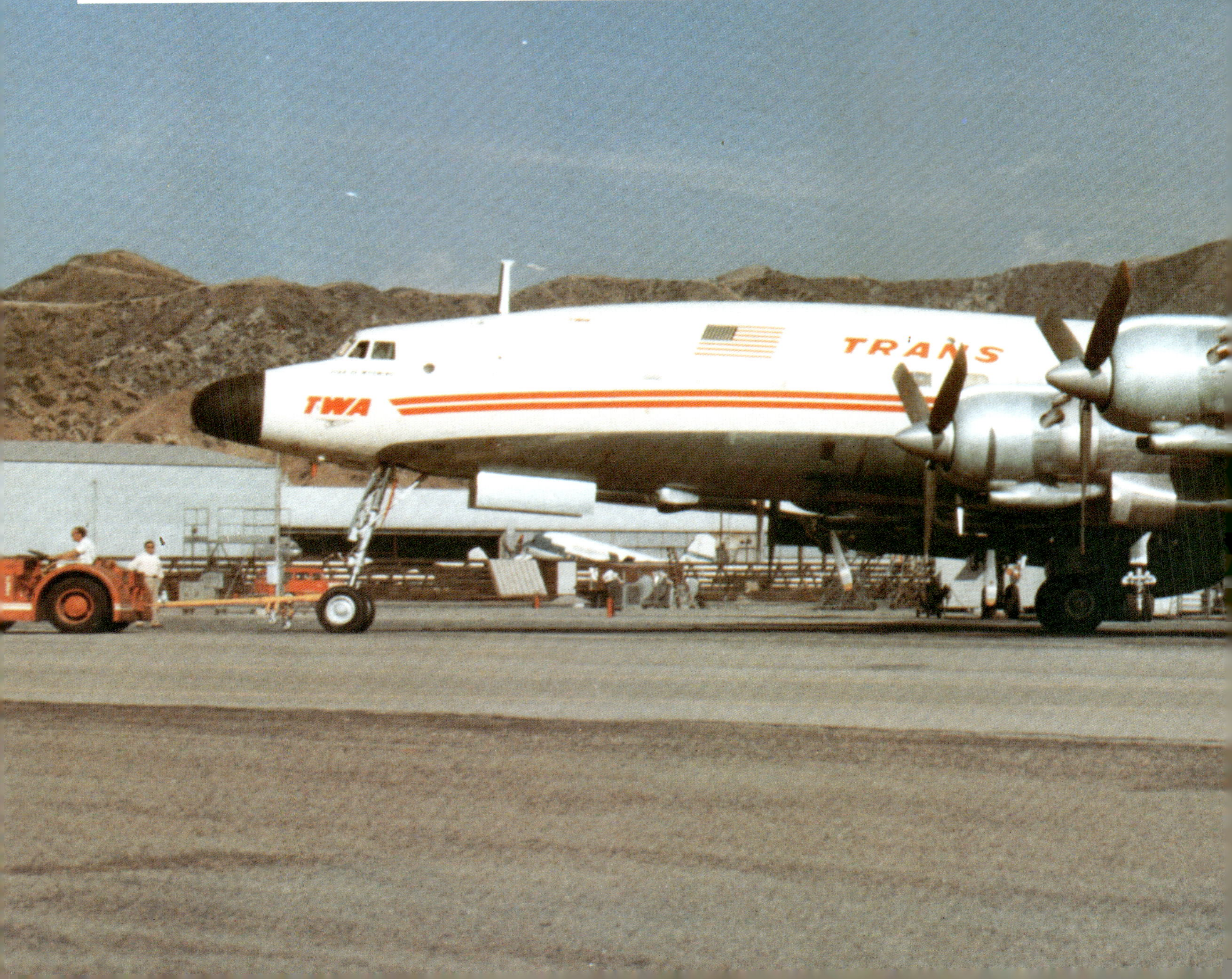
TWA
TRANS

Left: A TWA 1649 gives its passengers a breathtaking view of Manhattan. *Right:* The US Navy EC-121 radar surveillance plane—another version of the Model 1649 Starliner. *Below:* Lockheed's Burbank facility was the *background* for this photo of a Model 1649 freighter.

The Model 1449 and Model 1549 projects were intended to be larger and more capable derivatives of the Model 1049, with greater gross weights. Where the Model 1049 had a gross weight 30 percent greater than the Model 649, the gross weight of the Model 1449 would have been 86 percent greater than that of the Model 649 and the gross weight of the Model 1549 would have been double that of the Model 649. However, the Model 1449 and Model 1549 ideas bore the same relationship to the Model 1049 that the Model 849 and Model 949 had to the Model 649: they were better, but not better enough to elicit an investment from the airlines.

THE STARLINER

The last of the Constellations, the Lockheed Model 1649, nicknamed 'Starliner' after the Vega subsidiary's first airplane, made its maiden flight on 11 October 1956. It had been two years since Boeing had test flown the prototype of its Model 707 jetliner series and Douglas was already deeply engrossed in its own DC-8 jetliner program. Nobody was sure in 1956 whether jetliners would come to replace piston engine airliners on the major transcontinental and transoceanic routes, nor did anyone dare to predict that jets would render piston engine airliners obsolete within a decade.

In the postwar years Lockheed's Constellation and the big Douglas four-engined transports had practically monopolized the commercial airliner market worldwide, while Boeing's four-engined Stratocruiser didn't do nearly so well. Lockheed and Douglas were doing so well with piston-engined planes that there seemed little need to gamble on jetliners.

Douglas conceded the lead to Boeing before tentatively going ahead with its DC-8, but Lockheed chose to stay with propeller-driven airliners and not enter the marketplace with a first-generation jetliner, even though Lockheed had done a design study for a 40-passenger jetliner as far back as 1946.

Lockheed countered Boeing's jetliner with the best she could offer—the ultimate Constellation. The Model 1649 was a truly luxurious airplane. In terms of passenger comfort, her plush appointments surpassed not only all the earlier Constellations but today's jetliners as well.

TWA, the original Constellation customer, rushed to put the Model 1649 into service, but the proverbial handwriting was on the wall and the word that it was spelling read 'jetliners'. On 6 April 1967, TWA flew a Lockheed Constellation from New York to St Louis as it had many times during the preceding 20 years, but this time the big bird flew with the caveat that this would be the last TWA flight of a piston-engined aircraft. Henceforth, all TWA service would be in jets.

TWA was Lockheed's staunchest Connie customer, but on 6 April 1967, TWA fielded its last piston-engine flight, with a Model 1649 like the one *at right*. The 1649 has gone on to perform various duties well into the present day. *Below:* Thailand-based US Air Force EC-121Qs, such as this one photographed in November 1967, provided radar surveillance of North Vietnam during the Vietnam War.

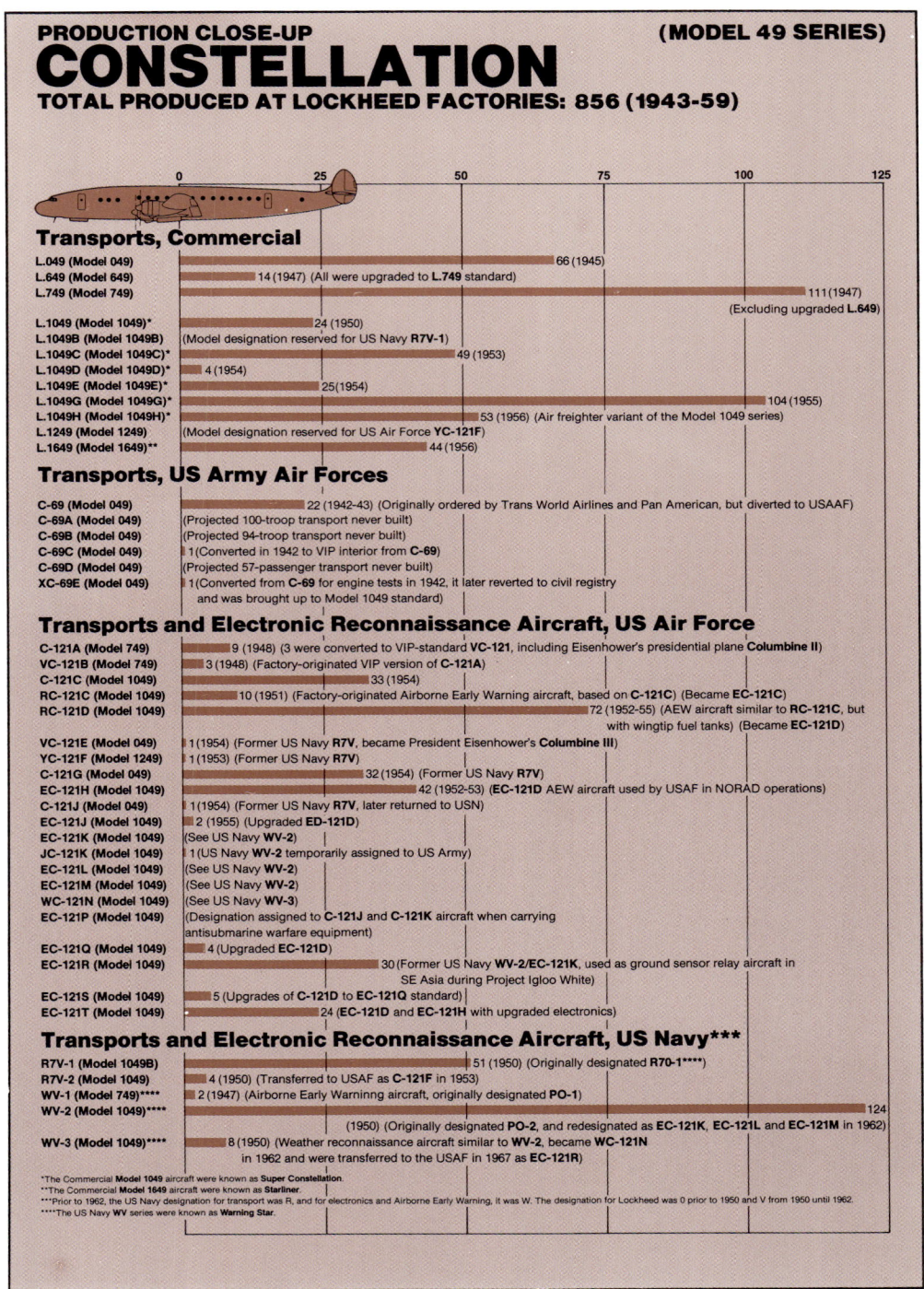

PRODUCTION CLOSE-UP (MODEL 49 SERIES)
CONSTELLATION
TOTAL PRODUCED AT LOCKHEED FACTORIES: 856 (1943-59)

Transports, Commercial

Designation	Count
L.049 (Model 049)	66 (1945)
L.649 (Model 649)	14 (1947) (All were upgraded to L.749 standard)
L.749 (Model 749)	111 (1947) (Excluding upgraded L.649)
L.1049 (Model 1049)*	24 (1950)
L.1049B (Model 1049B)	(Model designation reserved for US Navy R7V-1)
L.1049C (Model 1049C)*	49 (1953)
L.1049D (Model 1049D)*	4 (1954)
L.1049E (Model 1049E)*	25 (1954)
L.1049G (Model 1049G)*	104 (1955)
L.1049H (Model 1049H)*	53 (1956) (Air freighter variant of the Model 1049 series)
L.1249 (Model 1249)	(Model designation reserved for US Air Force YC-121F)
L.1649 (Model 1649)**	44 (1956)

Transports, US Army Air Forces

Designation	Count
C-69 (Model 049)	22 (1942-43) (Originally ordered by Trans World Airlines and Pan American, but diverted to USAAF)
C-69A (Model 049)	(Projected 100-troop transport never built)
C-69B (Model 049)	(Projected 94-troop transport never built)
C-69C (Model 049)	1 (Converted in 1942 to VIP interior from C-69)
C-69D (Model 049)	(Projected 57-passenger transport never built)
XC-69E (Model 049)	1 (Converted from C-69 for engine tests in 1942, it later reverted to civil registry and was brought up to Model 1049 standard)

Transports and Electronic Reconnaissance Aircraft, US Air Force

Designation	Count
C-121A (Model 749)	9 (1948) (3 were converted to VIP-standard VC-121, including Eisenhower's presidential plane Columbine II)
VC-121B (Model 749)	3 (1948) (Factory-originated VIP version of C-121A)
C-121C (Model 1049)	33 (1954)
RC-121C (Model 1049)	10 (1951) (Factory-originated Airborne Early Warning aircraft, based on C-121C) (Became EC-121C)
RC-121D (Model 1049)	72 (1952-55) (AEW aircraft similar to RC-121C, but with wingtip fuel tanks) (Became EC-121D)
VC-121E (Model 049)	1 (1954) (Former US Navy R7V, became President Eisenhower's Columbine III)
YC-121F (Model 1249)	1 (1953) (Former US Navy R7V)
C-121G (Model 049)	32 (1954) (Former US Navy R7V)
EC-121H (Model 1049)	42 (1952-53) (EC-121D AEW aircraft used by USAF in NORAD operations)
C-121J (Model 049)	1 (1954) (Former US Navy R7V, later returned to USN)
EC-121J (Model 1049)	2 (1955) (Upgraded ED-121D)
EC-121K (Model 1049)	(See US Navy WV-2)
JC-121K (Model 1049)	1 (US Navy WV-2 temporarily assigned to US Army)
EC-121L (Model 1049)	(See US Navy WV-2)
EC-121M (Model 1049)	(See US Navy WV-2)
WC-121N (Model 1049)	(See US Navy WV-3)
EC-121P (Model 1049)	(Designation assigned to C-121J and C-121K aircraft when carrying antisubmarine warfare equipment)
EC-121Q (Model 1049)	4 (Upgraded EC-121D)
EC-121R (Model 1049)	30 (Former US Navy WV-2/EC-121K, used as ground sensor relay aircraft in SE Asia during Project Igloo White)
EC-121S (Model 1049)	5 (Upgrades of C-121D to EC-121Q standard)
EC-121T (Model 1049)	24 (EC-121D and EC-121H with upgraded electronics)

Transports and Electronic Reconnaissance Aircraft, US Navy***

Designation	Count
R7V-1 (Model 1049B)	51 (1950) (Originally designated R70-1****)
R7V-2 (Model 1049)	4 (1950) (Transferred to USAF as C-121F in 1953)
WV-1 (Model 749)****	2 (1947) (Airborne Early Warning aircraft, originally designated PO-1)
WV-2 (Model 1049)****	124 (1950) (Originally designated PO-2, and redesignated as EC-121K, EC-121L and EC-121M in 1962)
WV-3 (Model 1049)****	8 (1950) (Weather reconnaissance aircraft similar to WV-2, became WC-121N in 1962 and were transferred to the USAF in 1967 as EC-121R)

*The Commercial **Model 1049** aircraft were known as **Super Constellation**.
The Commercial **Model 1649 aircraft were known as **Starliner**.
***Prior to 1962, the US Navy designation for transport was R, and for electronics and Airborne Early Warning, it was W. The designation for Lockheed was 0 prior to 1950 and V from 1950 until 1962.
****The US Navy WV series were known as **Warning Star**.

THE CONSTITUTION

Even before the Constellation had made its first flight, Lockheed engineers like Dick Pulver and Willis Hawkins were working on an enormous transport with a half-again greater wingspan and more than twice the fuselage volume. The project, which led to the Lockheed Model 89 Constitution, was begun at the behest of Pan American Airways in mid-1942. Pan Am had two ideas in mind for proposing a huge intercontinental cargo plane: first was the airline's wartime contract with the US Navy to conduct airlift operations in the vast reaches of the Pacific; the second notion was that such an airplane could find an important niche—for itself and Pan Am—in the postwar commercial market.

The airplane that evolved was the largest transport of the day, but it arrived too late for wartime service. The Navy contract was trimmed to just two airplanes, delivered under the Navy designation XR6V-1, and Pan Am lost interest.

The Constitution, named for the US Navy's historic Revolutionary War-era frigate, was an impressive plane with room for 168 people in her double-decked, pressurized passenger compartment and a galley designed to prepare meals for 180. Its first flight was from Burbank, California on 9 November 1946, with Joe Tonle and Tony LeVier at the controls. Nearly 10,000 people, including large numbers of Lockheed employees and their families, came out to watch the Saturday takeoff.

The first of the Constitutions were officially delivered to the Navy at Alameda Naval Air Station on 2 February 1949.

Designed for four 5000 hp turboprop engines which weren't yet available, the XR6V-1 Constitution had to settle for 3000 hp Pratt & Whitney Wasp Major piston engines instead. This lack of power combined with budgetary limitations to ensure that the two Constitution prototypes would not be followed by a fleet of production aircraft. The Navy nevertheless made good use of its R6V-1s. One of them was used on a 19-city recruiting tour in the early 1950s during which 546,000 people tramped through the big bird. Later, the Navy used both planes to ferry personnel between Moffett Naval Air Station near San Francisco and Pearl Harbor, Hawaii.

In late August 1955 the two Constitutions were flown to Litchfield Park, Arizona to be sold for scrap. Ten years later Lockheed engineers would be back at their drawing boards designing another giant—the C-5 Galaxy—the largest aircraft the world had ever seen!

Lockheed's huge Model 89 Constitution (*above and below*), never made it into full production. It was 43 feet longer, its wings were 66 feet wider and it weighed 33,000 pounds more than the average Connie (*in background below*).

XR6V-1 Constitution (Model 89)

First Flight:	1946
Wingspan:	189 ft, 1¼ in
Length:	156 ft, 1 in
Height:	50 ft, 4½ in
Engines:	Original version Pratt & Whitney Twin Wasp Majors, R4360-18
Engine hp:	3000
Gross Weight (lb):	184,000
Empty Weight (lb):	114,575
Passengers:	180
Operating Altitude (ft):	27,600
Cruising Speed (mph):	269
Top Speed (mph):	303
Max Range (miles):	4500

THE FORK-TAILED DEVIL

AHEAD OF ITS TIME

To the designers who conceived them, they were called Atalanta after the beautiful fleet-footed maiden of Greek legend. To the men who developed them and built them, they were the Lockheed Model 22 series. To the US Army Air Forces, who bought more than nine thousand of them, they were called P-38. To just about everyone they were the Lockheed Lightning. The nicknames ranged from 'three bullets on a knife' to 'Twin Boom Angel,' but to the Luftwaffe fighter pilots who fought against them, they were *der Gabelschwanz Teufel*—the fork-tailed devil.

Work on the Model 22 project began in June 1937 after Lockheed won the competition for a US Army Air Corps contract to build a high-speed, twin-engine air superiority fighter. Hall Hibbard and Kelly Johnson gave the Model 22 an unusual twin fuselage to accommodate its engine. Said Johnson:

'It was considered a radically different design—even funny looking, some said. It wasn't to me. There was a reason for everything that went into it, a logical evolution. The shape took care of itself. In design, you are forced to develop unusual solutions to unusual problems.

For the new fighter, we were required to use the liquid-cooled Allison engine. This meant that we had to have a Prestone radiator. We had a long engine so we had to use a General Electric turbo supercharger. And we had a landing gear that had to retract into the nacelle. By the time we had strung all of that together we were almost back to where the tail should be. So, we faired it back another five feet and added the tail. It was a twin-engine airplane, and that produced the characteristic twin-tailed airplane that would go through 18 versions in all theaters of action in World War II, set some records, and make some design contributions. The use of contra-rotating propellers on the P-38 was a new and important feature for fighters. It eliminated the torque effect, or pulling to one side.

With the first plane faster than 400 miles an hour, I knew we would be entering an unknown region of flight and possible trouble. It was the phenomenon of compressibility—the buildup of air ahead of the airplane at high speed. In 1937, in connection with our proposal, I had warned the Air Corps, ". . . as airplane speeds and altitudes (thinner air) increase, consideration must be given to the effect of compressibility."

When I first anticipated the trouble with compressibility, I went to the two best experts in the world on the subject, Dr Von Karman and Dr Milliken at Cal Tech. I told them what I proposed to do in design, how we intended to compute performance, and our concern about stability and control.

"We don't know anything different. Go ahead," they agreed.'

As such the Model 22, Lockheed's first serious fighter plane project, was the first aircraft to reach the fringes of the sound barrier. The unusual design of the Lightning offered many extra advantages, and it freed the space ahead of the cockpit for a nosewheel, extra armament and, in several later versions, specialized radar.

The first XP-38 prototype was secretly constructed between June and December 1938. On New Year's Eve the finished aircraft was disassembled, wrapped in white canvas, and loaded on three trucks for the March Army Air Field near Riverside. The plane arrived just before dawn on the first day of 1939, several hours after its highway travel permit had expired.

The flight test phase of the project got off to a bad start when the XP-38 rolled off the end of the runway during taxi tests. Lt Ben Kelsey tried so hard to stop the plane that his foot bent a brake pedal that had withstood a 500 pound static test. The problem, traced to grease on a brake shoe, was quickly corrected and the XP-38 made her first flight on 27 January 1939. On 11

Above: The Lockheed XP-38 design was born of practical considerations. *Facing page:* This cluster of battle-ready Lightnings stand by at a USAAF field, as the fighter pilots (*in the foreground*) study maps in preparation for a mission.

61

Facing page: Gleaming new Model 122 US Army Air Corps YP-38s on the Lockheed Burbank flightline in 1939. (Note the Hudsons in the background.) *Above:* A Model 222 P-38D in flight. The USAAF star's red center spot had been painted out following Pearl Harbor, to avoid confusion with the Japanese 'rising sun.'

February Kelsey took the prototype on a transcontinental flight, during which he attained a cruising speed of 420 mph. He reached Amarillo, Texas in two hours, 48 minutes and the leg to Dayton, Ohio took just three minutes less. He arrived at Mitchell Army Air Field on Long Island after seven hours, two minutes of flying time, but lost power on approach and wrecked the prototype when he crashlanded on a golf course.

Nevertheless, the Air Corps placed an order for 13 service test aircraft under the designation YP-38. These aircraft, which were factory-designated as Model 122, were different from the original Lightning prototype in that they had outward-turning rather than inward-turning propellers. The armament consisted of four .50 caliber machine guns and a 37mm cannon, rather than the two .50 caliber and two .30 caliber machine guns and 23mm cannon that had been provided for the XP-38. When World War II began in Europe in September 1939 the Air Corps ordered an additional 20 upgraded YP-38s under the simple designation P-38. Although the first YP-38 was not delivered until March 1941, the first P-38s (Lockheed Model 222) had arrived in service by the time the US Army Air Corps became the US Army Air Forces in June 1941. The armament of the Model 222 was the same as that of the Model 122, but armor protection for the pilot was added.

The only P-38A (actually designated XP-38A) was a P-38 converted by the addition of a pressurized cockpit. Given the Lockheed model number 622, it served as the prototype for future production series Lightnings with pressurized cockpits.

The USAAF designations P-38B and P-38C were reserved for further conversion projects that never reached fruition, so the P-38D (Model 222) was actually the first fully service-rated Lightning (although only 36 were built, with the first of these delivered in August 1941).

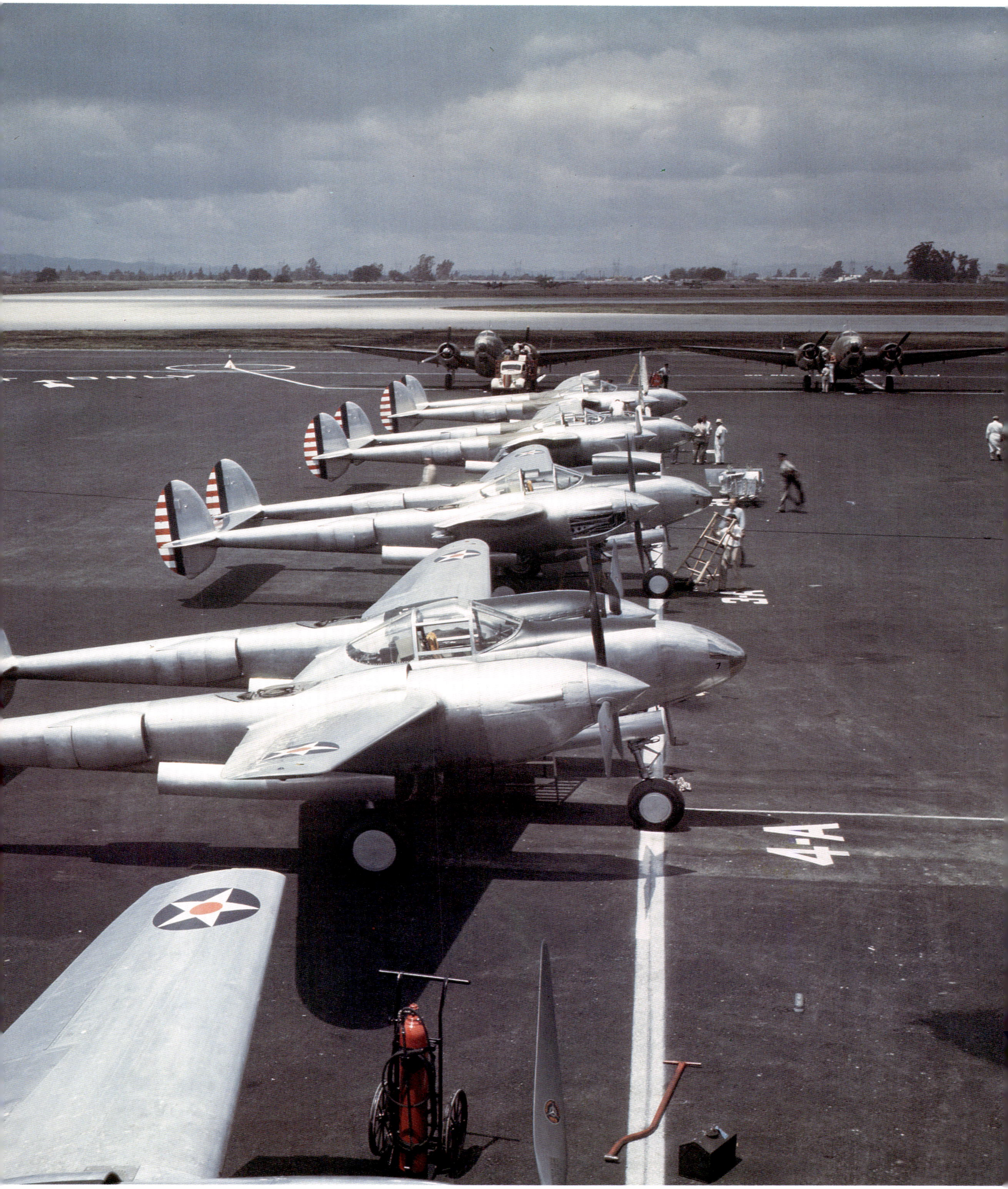

	XP-38 (Model 22)	**YP-38** (Model 122)	**P-38** (Model 222)	**P-38D** (Model 222)
First Flight:	1939	1940	1941	1941
Wingspan:	52 ft	52 ft	52 ft	52 ft
Length:	37 ft, 10 in	37 ft, 10 in	37 ft, 10 in	37 ft, 10 in
Height:	12 ft, 10 in	9 ft, 10 in	9 ft, 10 in	9 ft, 10 in
Engines:	Allison V-1710-11,-15	Allison V-1710-27,-29	Allison V-1710-27,-29	Allison V-1710-27,-29
Engine hp (at takeoff):	1150	1150	1150	1150
Gross Weight (lb):	13,500	13,500	14,178	14,456
Empty Weight (lb):	11,507	11,171	11,672	11,780
Crew:	1	1	1	1
Operating Altitude (ft):	39,100	38,000	38,000	39,000
Cruising Speed (mph):	393	338	310	390
Top Speed (mph):	417	420		
Max Range (miles):	400 (at max speed)	1150	1490 (at max speed)	975

In the meantime, the British Royal Air Force had expressed an interest in the Lightning. Since the Allison engine with its supercharger was not cleared for export, the RAF Lightnings were built with the less powerful C15 engine and noncontra-rotating propellers. They were designated Lockheed Model 322. The Model 322s were delivered in December 1941 under the RAF designation Lightning Mk I.

By the time the United States entered the war, the USAAF had taken delivery of the first P-38Es (Model 222) with improved propellers and avionics systems and 20mm Hispano cannon, which replaced the 37mm Oldsmobile cannon. There were a total of 1849 Model 222 Lightning fighters delivered to the USAAF under the designations P-38, P-38D, P-38E, P-38F and P-38G. These models were complemented by 300 Model 222 Lightning photo reconnaissance aircraft, delivered to the USAAF under the F-4 and F-5 designations.

By April 1943 the Lockheed Model 422, the 'ultimate Lightning,' was ready for mass production. Equipped with Allison F-15 engines delivering 1600 war-emergency hp, the Model 422 and the similar Model 522 were durable and powerful fighters that earned the Lightning a deserved reputation as one of the best combat aircraft of World War II. The USAAF took delivery of 4949 Lockheed Model 422s under the designations P-38H, P-38J, P-38K and P-38L; and 1960 Model 522s under the P-38T designation. The Vultee Aircraft Company also built 113 P-38Ls for the USAAF under license from Lockheed.

The Model 522, which went into production as part of the P-38J series, was an outgrowth of a secret project begun during 1940 to develop a pressurized high altitude interceptor version of the Lightning. Since the Lightning was still in its YP-38 (Model 122) service test phase, the Model 522 interceptor was ordered under the Air Corps designation XP-49. The XP-49 finally made its first flight in November 1942, but its performance was not significantly better than that of the Lightnings already in service. The Model 522 was then developed as part of the P-38J production run and the XP-49 project was abandoned. The single prototype went to the USAAF research and development center at Wright Army Air Field, where it served out the war years as a test bed for experiments with pressurized cockpits.

At left: The P-38's instrument panel featured, as part of its daunting array of instrumentation, a control wheel (*extreme foreground*)—as opposed to a control stick (the usual case for that era's fighters)—and throttle levers (*left*) for its engines.

The high altitude Lockheed XP-49 (*above*) carried out stratospheric research above 40,000 feet, and could fly at better than 450mph.

	P-38L (Model 422)	XP-49 (Model 522)
First Flight:	1943	1942
Wingspan:	52 ft	52 ft
Length:	37 ft, 10 in	40 ft, 15/16 in
Height:	9 ft, 10 in	10 ft, 5¼ in
Engines:	Allison V-1710-11, -173	Continental IV-1430-1
Engine hp:	1475 at takeoff, 1600 at 28,700	1500 at 3300 rpm
Gross Weight (lb):	17,500	18,750
Empty Weight (lb):	12,800	15,464
Crew:	1	1
Operating Altitude (ft):	44,000	37,000
Cruising Speed (mph):	350	262
Top Speed (mph):	414	458
Max Range (miles):	450	679

	P-38G (Model 222)	P-38H (Model 422)	P-38J (Model 422)
First Flight:	1942	1943	1943
Wingspan:	52 ft	52 ft	52 ft
Length:	37 ft, 10 in	37 ft, 10 in	37 ft, 10 in
Height:	9 ft, 10 in	9 ft, 10 in	9 ft, 10 in
Engines:	Allison V-1710-51,-55	Allison V-1710-89,-91	Allison V-1710-89,-91
Engine hp (at takeoff):	1325	1425	1425
Gross Weight (lb):	15,800	16,300	17,500
Empty Weight (lb):	12,200	12,380	12,780
Crew:	1	1	1
Operating Altitude (ft):	39,000	44,000	44,000
Cruising Speed (mph):	340	300	350
Top Speed (mph):	404	402	415
Max Range (miles):	2400	2400	2600

1. Opposite-turning propellers
2. Magazines for 4 (50-cal.) machine guns
3. Magazine for 20-mm. cannon
4. Bulletproof windshield
5. Reflector gun sight
6. Bulletproof fuel tanks
7. One 20-mm. shell-firing gun
8. New nose houses intercoolers
9. Allison V-type liquid-cooled engine
10. Cantilever engine mount
11. Two-way radio equipment
12. Retracting entrance ladder
13. Tool and baggage compartment
14. External elevator mass balances
15. Rudder mass balances
16. Fuselage empennage joint
17. Battery compartment
18. Coolant radiator shroud
19. Coolant radiator scoop
20. Exhaust driven supercharger
21. Navigation lights

DOUGLAS ROLFE

This transparent view (*above left*) of the P-38J is further elucidated by the nomenclature of its various features given in the illustration *at left*. *Right:* These Lockheed mechanics give one of the P-38J's Allison V-1710-89 engines a pre-flight maintenance preparation.

THE LIGHTNING AT WAR

Within hours of the United States declaration of war on Germany in December 1941, an Iceland-based Lightning shot down a German Fw-200 patrol bomber. From there the Lightning went on to serve with the USAAF on all of the world's battlefronts—from Alaska to the South Pacific, and from North Africa to Northern Europe.

Most of the Lightnings served as fighters: flying combat air patrols, engaging and intercepting enemy fighters, escorting bombers, supporting ground troops and strafing enemy positions behind the lines. Some were equipped with radar to serve as night fighters. Many P-38s also served as fighter-bombers and, of course, the F-4 and F-5 Lightnings operated as photo reconnaissance aircraft.

There were, however, many other roles for which the versatile twin-engined fighter was uniquely suited. Some Lightnings were used to tow gliders and some to carry torpedoes, while others were modified for use in laying smokescreens. Some were modified to carry a second person in the cramped cockpit for flight training. Others were modified with enlarged noses for radar aiming and navigation equipment so that they could serve as pathfinders for bomber formations. A special pod containing a stretcher was designed to be fitted to the Lightning's fuel tank so that the aircraft also could be used as a high-speed aerial ambulance.

The 'Droopsnoot' Lightning was a two-place P-38L built with a glassed nose to accommodate a Norden bombsight and a bombardier. They were used in Europe during 1944 to lead formations of other Lightnings that were armed with two tons of bombs each. By 1944 the Luftwaffe was using its dwindling interceptor fleet only against *bomber* formations. The formations of bomb-laden Lightnings led by 'Droopsnoot' P-38Ls appeared to be formations of *fighters,* so they caused a great deal of damage before the Germans discovered the ruse.

Because of its relatively long range, the Lightning was particularly suited for the great distances that characterized operations in the Pacific, and more Japanese aircraft were downed by Lightnings than by any other fighter. The most famous P-38 mission of the Pacific war came on 18 April 1943.

Admiral Isoroku Yamamoto of the Imperial Japanese Navy, the mastermind of Japan's fantastic successes in the early part of the war and the man who *planned* the infamous attack on Pearl Harbor, was on an inspection tour of Japanese bases in the South Pacific. A brilliant strategist, Yamamoto had developed a fanatical following and legendary reputation in Japan. For Americans, he was the arch villain.

Above right: This 1942 photo captures the US Army as it trucks a pair of P-38s through Noumea, the capital of New Caledonia, in the South Pacific. *Note* that the planes' wings have been removed from the engine nacelles outward for transporting. *Below:* Equipped with high velocity aerial rockets, this P-38J was ready for action.

69

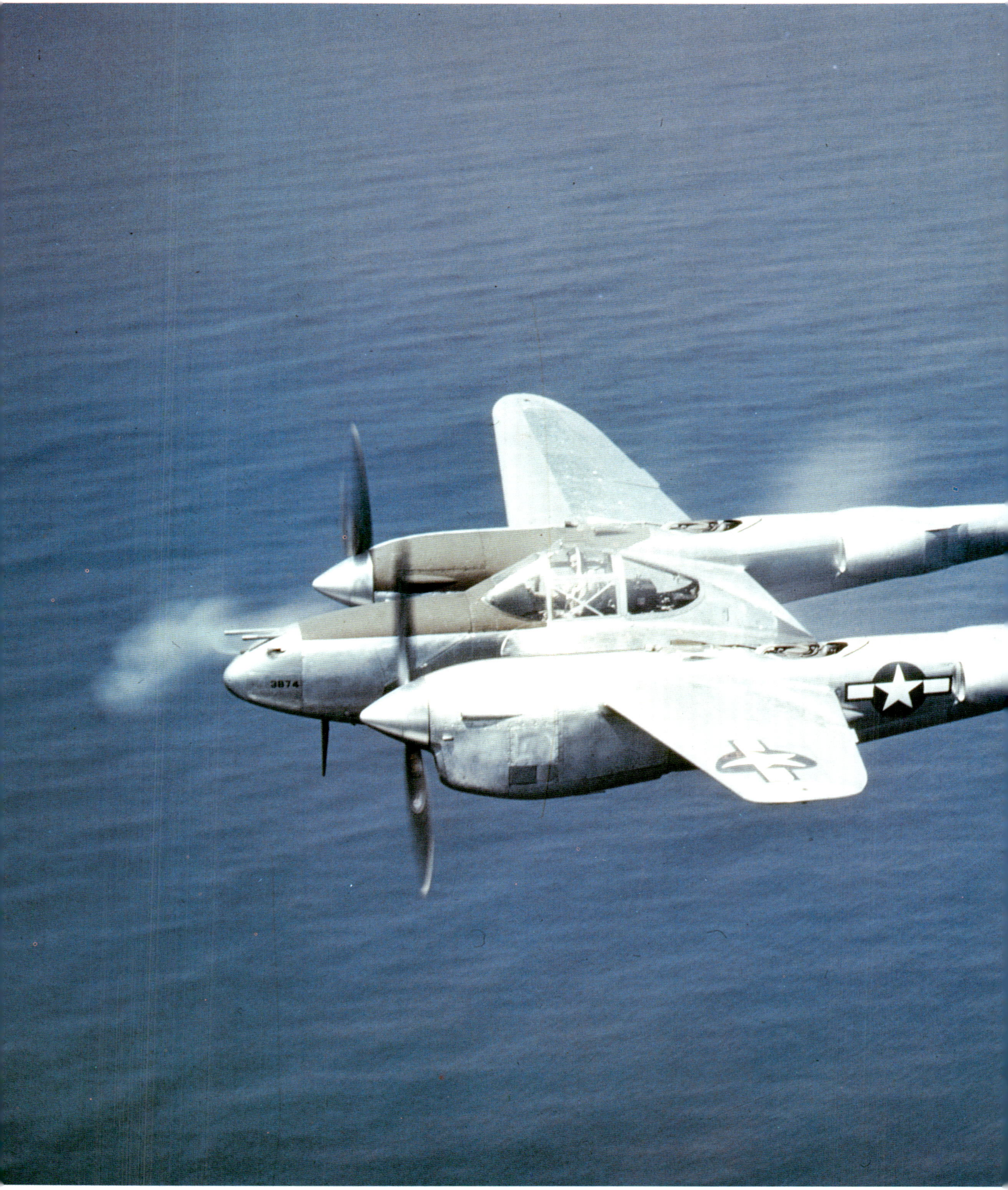
3874

Left: Smoke trails from this speeding P-38's guns as the pilot squeezes off a high-velocity burst. *Above:* Patrolling the vast expanses of the South Pacific, this wing of P-38s flies in a stack formation—above one another on a diagonal.

In early April a US Navy radio operator intercepted a Japanese code transmission outlining in great detail the itinerary of Yamamoto's inspection. The United States had secretly broken the Japanese code, and it was suddenly possible to see exactly where and when the Admiral would be: the decision was quickly made at the highest levels that Yamamoto should be eliminated. The task fell to P-38s of the Thirteenth US Army Air Force based at Henderson Army Air Field on Guadalcanal. It was decided that Lightnings of the 12th, 70th and 339th Fighter Squadrons, led by 339th FS Commander Major John Mitchell, would intercept Yamamoto's aircraft over the Japanese-held island of Bougainville. Special enlarged fuel tanks were rushed to Henderson Field to ensure that the Lightnings would be able to comfortably make the 870 mile return trip.

At 7:45 am, 18 Lightnings took off on the low-level intercept mission. Knowing that Yamamoto was passionately punctual and that he was scheduled to land in Ballale, Bougainville at 9:45 am, the Americans planned their intercept to take place exactly ten minutes before his planned arrival. Both the forces of the 16 P-38s (two were forced to turn back en route) and the Japanese arrived at the intercept point precisely on schedule. Admiral Yamamoto's party was traveling in a pair of Mitsubishi G4M1 'Betty' bombers, escorted by six A6M 'Zero' fighters. Dropping their fuel tanks for maximum maneuverability, 12 of the Lightnings broke off to engage the Zeros, while a force of four P-38s, led by Captain Thomas Lanphier of the 70th FS, went in after the bombers.

The Bettys quickly separated, one flying out to sea, while the other, which carried Yamamoto, dropped to treetop level and tried to evade the P-38s over the island. Though they didn't know at the time which Betty carried the infamous Admiral, it was Lanphier and his wing man Lt Rex Barber of the 339th FS who pursued the Betty over land. Lanphier was about to attack when a Zero got on his tail and he had to roll out to get away. Barber pressed the attack on the bomber from a distance of barely twenty yards and managed to shoot off part of the Betty's tail. The Betty slowed abruptly and Barber overshot it.

Meanwhile, Lanphier had shot down the Zero and rejoined the attack on Yamamoto's plane. As Lanphier himself described the action:

'I began firing a long steady burst across the bomber's line of flight, from approximately right angles. Long before I considered myself in range, the bomber's right engine, and then the right wing, began to burn. I had accomplished my part of the mission. (We had learned from experience that) once afire, no Japanese aircraft ever ceased burning short of blowing up.

Apparently, the only numbers up for liquidation that day were Japanese, for just as I moved into range of its cannon, the bomber's right wing came off, and it plunged into the jungle and exploded.'

In the other Japanese bomber, Vice Admiral Matome Ugaki, Chief of Staff of the Imperial Combined Fleet, watched the scene unfold over the jungle. He was later to record in his diary:

'For a few moments, I lost sight of Yamamoto's plane and finally located the Betty far to the right. I was horrified to see the plane flying slowly just above the jungle, headed to the south with bright orange flames rapidly enveloping its wings and fuselage. About four miles away from us, the bomber trailed thick black smoke, dropping lower and lower. Sudden fear for the Admiral's life gripped me.'

Ugaki then lost sight of the plane as his own aircraft took evasive action to avoid attack. When he looked for the Admiral again, his plane was gone:

'Yamamoto's aircraft was no longer in sight. Black smoke boiled from dense jungle into the air. Alas! It was hopeless now!'

Ugaki's plane, which went down at sea, had only three survivors including himself. In Yamamoto's plane there were no survivors. The cockpit had exploded upon impact and the Admiral himself had been killed prior to the crash by a fusilade of .50 caliber bullets through his head. The fact that his unburned body still clutched a ceremonial sword led to an apocryphal postwar legend that Yamamoto committed *hari-kiri* when the Americans were first encountered.

The score for the day was a single American lost versus three Japanese fighters, two Japanese bombers and the mastermind of the Pearl Harbor atrocity. Captain Lanphier was officially given credit for shooting down Yamamoto, but evidence showed that

Above left: Developed in England during World War II by Lockheed engineers, the P-38 'Droopsnoot' Lightning had a glass bubble in its nose, outfitted for a bombardier. Acting as a sort of self-propelled squadron bombsight, the Droopsnoot flew as the lead plane for special formations of Lightnings, each plane of which carried 4000 pounds of bombs.

Dick Bong—America's top World War II ace, with 40 Japanese aircraft downed—was photographed in 1945, at Lockheed's Burbank facility with the two 'Marges' in his life: his wife (*at right*) and his P-38 (*above*). Bong died in an accident in August 1945 while test flying the Lockheed P-80 jet aircraft. *Below right:* Somewhere in the South Pacific in 1942, Lt M M Sealy sat for this photo in his P-38, which he had named *Haleakala* for the volcano on the Hawaiian island of Maui.

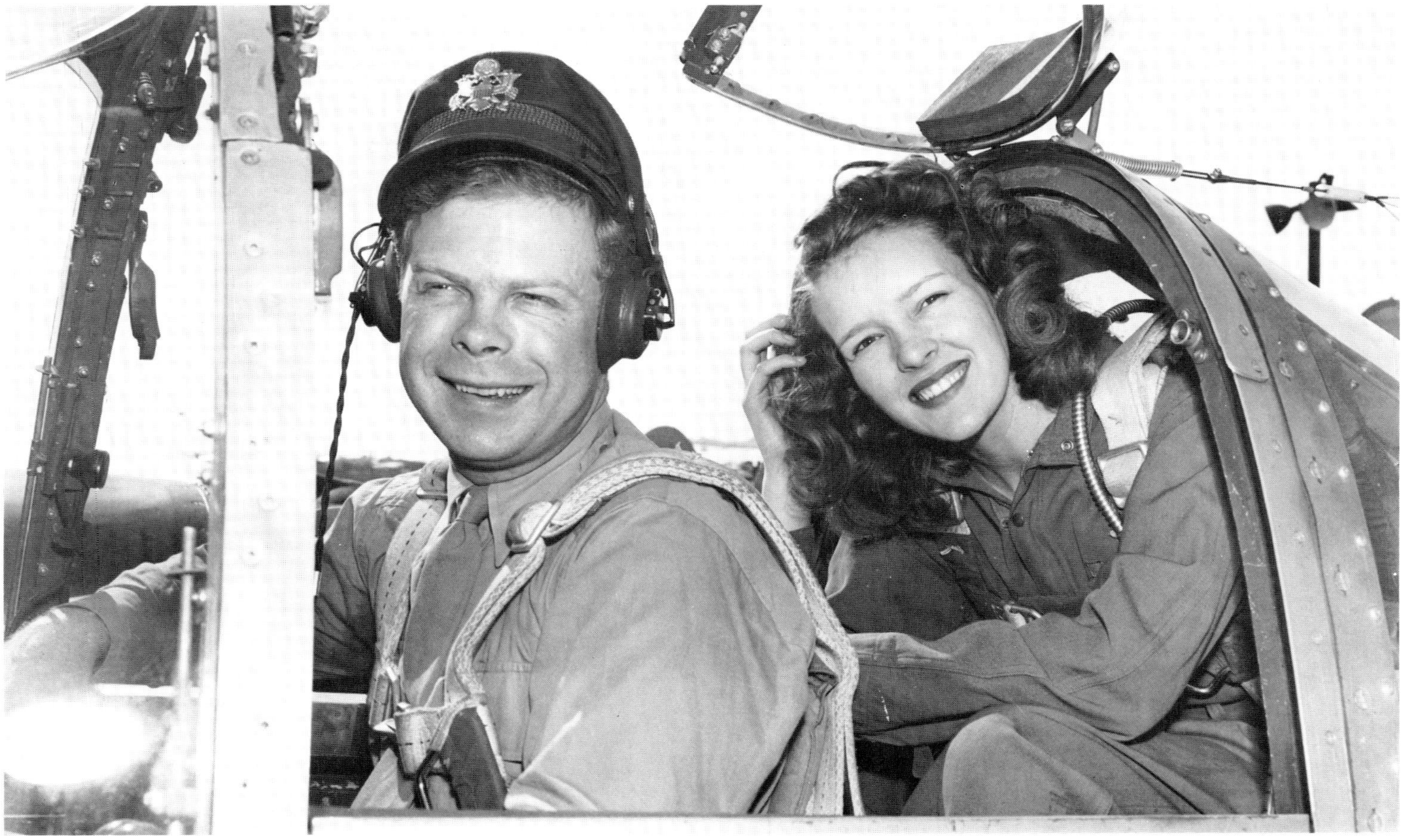

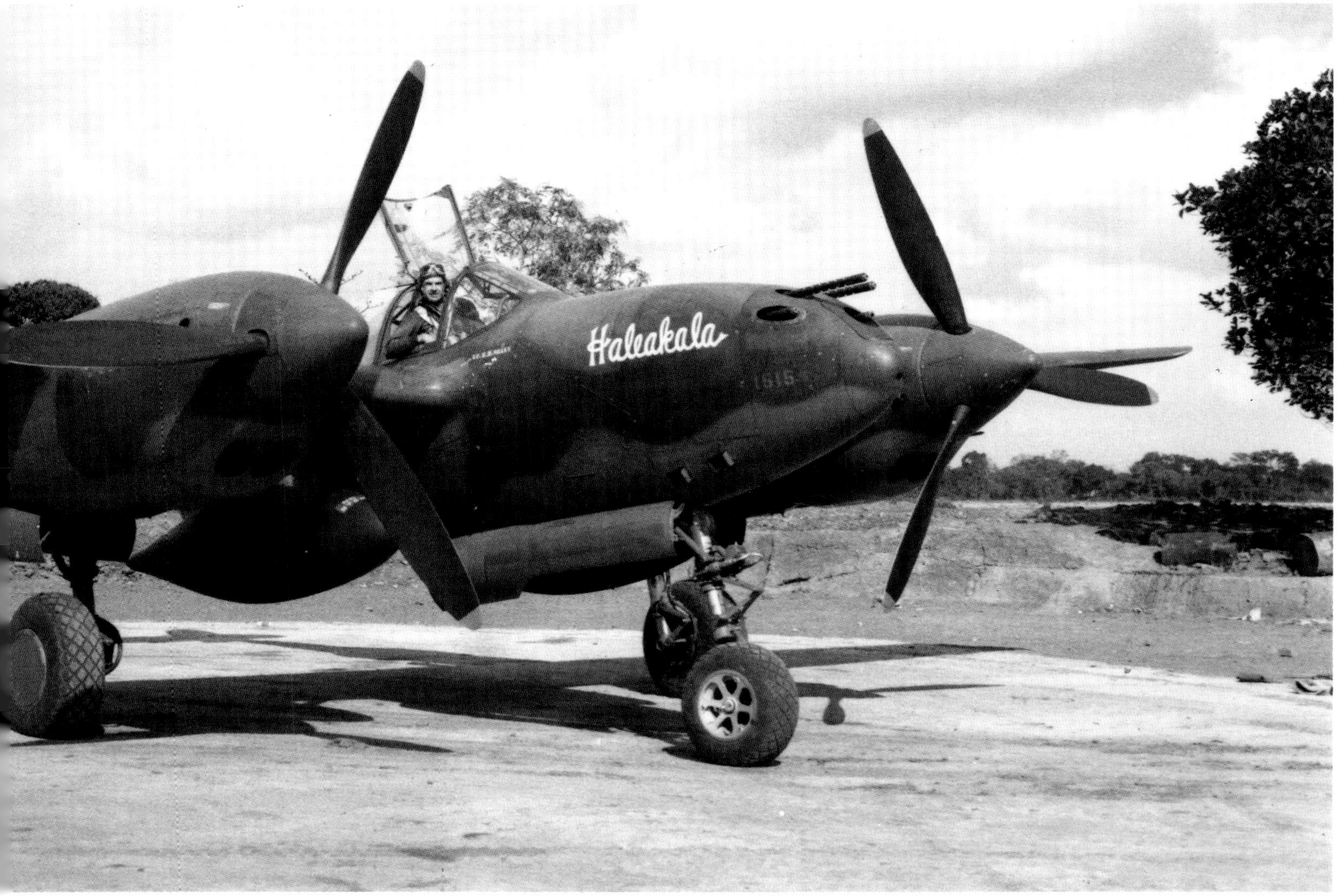
Haleakala

HIDDEN LIGHTNINGS

Prior to the end of 1944, when camouflage paint was generally abandoned by the USAAF in favor of a natural metal finish, P-38 Lightnings were delivered from the factory in olive drab coloring with neutral gray undersurfaces. More than eighty percent of the F-4s and F-5s, however, were painted in what was called 'Haze Paint'. As aviation historian Dana Bell points out in his book *Air Force Colors:*

> 'Haze Paint has been an unguarded secret for some 40 years, not that there has been any effort to keep the facts hidden from the public. Rather, it is a camouflage story that "slipped through the cracks." It was never listed in any Technical Order, being withdrawn from use before the appropriate revisions could be printed. Color chips were never circulated since the peculiar properties of the paint made samples impractical. Though it was the standard high altitude photo reconnaissance camouflage from March to October 1942, and was applied to almost 130 photographic P-38s (F-4s and F-5s), most will not even be aware of its existence. If (it is possible for) a camouflage (to) be invisible, Haze Paint achieved that goal.'

In 1940 Boston paint manufacturer Samuel Cabot approached the Air Corps with his L31340 zinc oxide white paint which he described as having grains with a diameter less than the wavelength of blue or violet light. His theory was that L31340 could be sprayed over a dark blue base and the resulting color would allow only blue and violet to be reflected, with all other colors being absorbed. What this meant was that under some conditions at high altitudes an airplane could be rendered virtually invisible. Early tests with the paint, now called Haze Paint, under the auspices of the Massachusetts Institute of Technology and the USAAF Material Division were promising. In March 1942 Lockheed was directed to paint all of the F-4s with Haze Paint.

In practice, however, there were a number of problems with Haze Paint: variations in thickness seriously altered the effectiveness of the camouflage, and the blue Haze Paint darkened as it weathered. In October 1942 the USAAF told Lockheed that it could stop the time-consuming process of applying Haze Paint and begin painting the F-4s in conventional olive drab.

In January 1943 Lockheed and the Sherwin-Williams Paint Company began development of what would be known as Synthetic Haze Paint, a suitable substitute for the cumbersome original. Finally, a new color scheme was created. First, the F-4s and F-5s would be painted sky blue, then the shadow areas would be tinted with a lighter color until the Lightning appeared to be the same color overall. In a test at 30,000 feet, an F-5 painted with Synthetic Haze Paint remained invisible to six observers in a B-17, until the Lightning closed to within 300 yards. By March 1943 the new color was adopted for use on all photo reconnaissance Lightnings.

Since World War II very little has been written about Haze Paint, but it is interesting—in light of the current interest in radar-invisible 'Stealth' technology—that Lockheed was creating *'invisible'* aircraft as early as 1942.

Above: A Haze-Painted F-4 in formation with a P-38 in conventional olive drab.

At left: This photograph is dated by the US national insignia displayed on these USAAF Lightnings—a star with sidebars and a red surround, which was a design that was displayed on US military aircraft for the brief period between 29 June and 14 August, 1943. This was replaced in August 1943 by the same design with a blue surround. The F-4 *in the foreground* is a reconnaissance plane (*see text*).

Right: Britain's Royal Air Force also put Lightnings to good use. *Below:* This photo brings us 'nose to nose' with the radar pod of the P-38 'Night Lightning'—a fast night fighter with extra crew space for a radar operator—which sought out and destroyed Japanese aircraft. An aerial battleship loaded with rockets, guns and bombs, it served as a nocturnal prowler late in World War II.

the bomber may have been fatally crippled by Barber's attack. In current US Air Force publications both men are now credited with the kill. In either case, credit for the mission that severely crippled subsequent Japanese strategic planning must certainly be shared by the airplane that made it all possible—the Lockheed P-38 Lightning.

On 18 April 1943, the same day that the Thirteenth Air Force P-38s were shooting down Yamamoto, other P-38s were escorting B-17 and B-25 bombers in raids against Algharo-Fertilia and Porto Torres, Sicily; while 22 Eleventh Air Force P-38s in the Aleutians were raiding Japanese positions on occupied Kiska.

Not only were the Lockheed Lightnings virtually ubiquitous, they were highly effective warplanes. Three out of the ten top-scoring aces of World War II flew P-38s, as did Dick Bong, the top-scoring USAAF ace.

In Europe alone USAAF Lightnings flew 129,849 sorties, shot down 1771 enemy aircraft, and dropped 20,139 tons of bombs. The number of Lightnings in service with the USAAF grew from 96 in December 1941 to 1123 in December 1942, to 1805 in December 1943 and to 2759 in December 1944. The peak

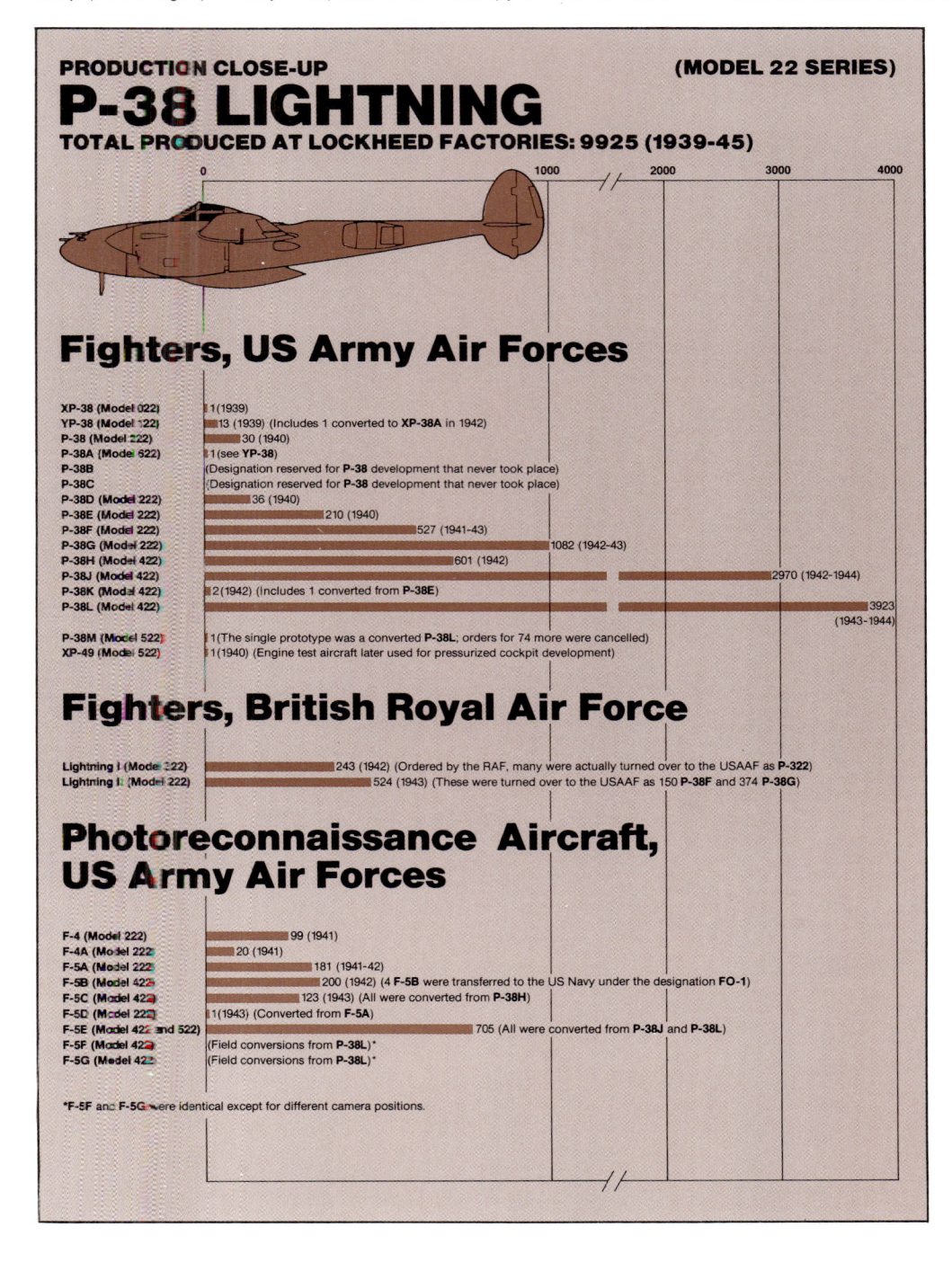

Above: A P-38 warms up in Gibraltar, prior to the 1942 Allied invasion of North Africa. Note the Constellation *at the rear* of this P-38 assembly shop (*below right*). Nearly completed P-38s occupy the middle aisle.

PRODUCTION CLOSE-UP (MODEL 22 SERIES)
P-38 LIGHTNING
TOTAL PRODUCED AT LOCKHEED FACTORIES: 9925 (1939-45)

Fighters, US Army Air Forces

Model	Production
XP-38 (Model 022)	1 (1939)
YP-38 (Model 122)	13 (1939) (Includes 1 converted to XP-38A in 1942)
P-38 (Model 222)	30 (1940)
P-38A (Model 622)	1 (see YP-38)
P-38B	(Designation reserved for P-38 development that never took place)
P-38C	(Designation reserved for P-38 development that never took place)
P-38D (Model 222)	36 (1940)
P-38E (Model 222)	210 (1940)
P-38F (Model 222)	527 (1941-43)
P-38G (Model 222)	1082 (1942-43)
P-38H (Model 422)	601 (1942)
P-38J (Model 422)	2970 (1942-1944)
P-38K (Model 422)	2 (1942) (Includes 1 converted from P-38E)
P-38L (Model 422)	3923 (1943-1944)
P-38M (Model 522)	1 (The single prototype was a converted P-38L; orders for 74 more were cancelled)
XP-49 (Model 522)	1 (1940) (Engine test aircraft later used for pressurized cockpit development)

Fighters, British Royal Air Force

Model	Production
Lightning I (Model 222)	243 (1942) (Ordered by the RAF, many were actually turned over to the USAAF as P-322)
Lightning II (Model 222)	524 (1943) (These were turned over to the USAAF as 150 P-38F and 374 P-38G)

Photoreconnaissance Aircraft, US Army Air Forces

Model	Production
F-4 (Model 222)	99 (1941)
F-4A (Model 222)	20 (1941)
F-5A (Model 222)	181 (1941-42)
F-5B (Model 422)	200 (1942) (4 F-5B were transferred to the US Navy under the designation FO-1)
F-5C (Model 422)	123 (1943) (All were converted from P-38H)
F-5D (Model 222)	1 (1943) (Converted from F-5A)
F-5E (Model 422 and 522)	705 (All were converted from P-38J and P-38L)
F-5F (Model 422)	(Field conversions from P-38J)*
F-5G (Model 422)	(Field conversions from P-38L)*

*F-5F and F-5G were identical except for different camera positions.

number in service in any given month was 2863 in March 1945. In September 1945, as the last Lightning rolled off the Lockheed assembly line, 2222 aircraft of the Lockheed Model 22 series were in service.

AFTER THE WAR

Between December 1945 and December 1946, as the USAAF scrapped its vast inventory, the number of Lightnings decreased from 1370 to just 113. Redesignated as F-38 when the US Army Air Forces became the US Air Force in 1947, a handful of Lightnings remained in service with the US Air Force until 1949.

Most of the surplus Lightnings were sold for scrap but many were simply abandoned in the jungles of the Pacific islands. Of those which remained in flying condition, some served with the Chinese Nationalist air forces in the 1946-1949 civil war, while others served in air forces from Italy to Central America. In the 1980s, a handful of Lightnings are still on the air race circuit in the United States

THE CHAIN LIGHTNING

In February 1940, with the Model 22 Lightning project already well on track, the US Army Air Corps approached Lockheed with an ambitious idea for a scaled-up, two-seat, long-range interceptor version of the Model 22. Developed as the Lockheed Model 20 and given the Air Corps designation XP-58, the plane was known as the Chain Lightning.

In July 1940, after preliminary design work had been done, the Air Corps changed the specifications and instructed Lockheed that the Chain Lightning would be powered by the Pratt & Whitney X-1800 engine, which did not yet exist. In October the engine specification changed again and Lockheed engineers were literally back to the drawing board adapting the XP-58 to use the Wright 42-cylinder R-2160 'Corncob.' Over the next three years the specifications were changed repeatedly. The armament was changed from two .50 caliber machine guns and a 75mm cannon to four high velocity 37mm cannons. The mission of the Chain Lightning changed from high-altitude interceptor to low-altitude tank destroyer, and back again.

In 1943, after 90 percent of the subassemblies were complete, the idea of a Wright 'Corncob' engine was replaced by the notion of combining four P-39-type Allison V-1710 engines into a pair of Xs to drive the two propellers.

The XP-58 Chain Lightning finally made its first flight on 6 June 1944, the day of the Normandy Invasion. When it should have been in service battling the Luftwaffe, it was making its maiden voyage over the California desert.

The Chain Lightning was a marvelous airplane. Though it was larger and heavier than the Lightning, it cruised faster than the P-38 could fly at its emergency top speed. For its rear-firing turret, the XP-58 had one of the most modern fire control systems yet designed. It was designed with interchangeable parts for easy field maintenance, but it never got into the field. It was one of the first planes designed to be built with small, easily-assembled subsections for fast, smooth mass production but only two examples were ever built. By the time the XP-58 was ready for flight testing, Lockheed was already building jets and the Chain Lightning was obsolete.

LOCKHEED PATROL PLANES

THE NEPTUNE

In a business sense there was no airplane more important to Lockheed in the immediate postwar years than the P2V Neptune series. In 1946 Lockheed had suffered an operating loss of $21,860,000. That was just the beginning; the slump continued through 1947 and 1948. It was the consistent and continuing series of orders for Neptunes that provided Lockheed with its bread and butter during those lean years.

During World War II Lockheed had built nearly 20,000 airplanes, from Hudsons and Flying Fortresses to Lightnings and Lodestars. More than half the planes built in Lockheed's entire history from 1913 into the 1980s were built during the space of a half dozen years. When the war ended in September 1945, there were suddenly no more orders for the planes that had been in production by the dozens just a few months before. In the meantime, a great deal of development money had been spent on projects like the Model 75 Saturn and Model 89 Constitution that had become dead ends. This overall situation must have been an incredible shock to Lockheed, and the orders for Neptunes must have indeed been welcome.

Ironically, the first work order on the Neptune was issued on 6 December 1941, the day before the attack on Pearl Harbor. The idea behind the Neptune had originated with Mac Short, the president of Lockheed's Vega subsidiary. At a time when the US Navy was concentrating on the Ventura and Harpoon as near-term successors to the Hudson, Short was promoting the Neptune as a long-term successor. Convincing the Navy to consider its distant future requirements when it had serious and overpowering immediate needs was an uphill battle, but Short succeeded. During the early years of World War II, however, there was little time to devote to the new project and it was not until April 1944 that Lockheed got the go-ahead to build a prototype of its Model 26 under the Navy designation XP2V-1

The first XP2V-1 Neptune flew on 17 May 1945 and proved to be a happy blend of aeronautical ingredients. The 17-foot tail provided outstanding stability and improved single-engine controllability. The wing surfaces, exactly 1000 square feet in area, provided outstanding lift. The Neptune was everything that the engineers had hoped for and proved to be the ideal patrol bomber for the postwar Navy.

The single characteristic most important in a patrol bomber is of course range. Lockheed engineers had designed the Neptune for extremely long range and were confident of success. On 29 September 1946 the US Navy decided to make a demonstration of the aircraft's capability. The third production P2V-1, nicknamed *The Turtle*, took off from Perth, Australia and subsequently captured the world's distance record. Aboard were Cdr Thomas Davies, Cdr E P Rankin, Cdr W S Reid, Lt Cdr R A Tabeling, 8467 gallons of aviation fuel, and a nine months old joey kangaroo named Joey. *The Turtle* flew 9000 miles to California, where an air traffic controller didn't believe them when they said they'd flown from Australia nonstop. Having convinced the controller that they had really done it, *The Turtle* and crew continued without stopping to Columbus, Ohio, having flown 11,236 miles in 55 hours and 17 minutes, a new distance record that was over 3000 miles farther than the existing

The P2V-1 'Truculent Turtle,' is shown *at left,* at the time of its famous flight in 1946. Between it and the P2V-7 (*above*), the Neptune patrol plane's entire history is spanned. The original P2V looked and acted like an Air Force bomber, but the Neptune gradually took on such distinctive features as (visible in the photo *above*) its long tail boom, wingtip tanks and jet engines.

record. The record set by the plane that the press renamed *The Truculent Turtle* stood as an absolute record for 16 years until a Boeing B-52H Jet bomber covered 12,532 miles nonstop.

Eleven P2V-3s were specially modified for use as carrier-launched strategic nuclear bombers. Stripped down to conserve weight, these Neptunes were designed to carry a five ton nuclear bomb. When they were first test flown from the deck of the USS *Coral Sea* in 1948, they were the largest airplanes ever to be launched from an aircraft carrier. In February 1950, using Rocket-Assisted Takeoff (RATO), a P2V-3 took off from the USS *Franklin D Roosevelt* and flew 5156 miles from the Atlantic Ocean near Jacksonville, Florida to the Panama Canal, then on to Moffett Naval Air Station near San Francisco, California. The demonstration was inspired by an interservice rivalry due to the fact that US Air Force strategic bombers were being favored in the Defense Budget over new US Navy aircraft carriers. The Navy wished to show that it was feasible to base strategic bombers on aircraft carriers, but Neptunes never became operational in this role.

Hall Hibbard and Kelly Johnson designed a series of Neptune upgrades that averaged roughly one new type per year from the P2V-2 series in 1947 to the P2V-7 series in 1954. The P2V-4,

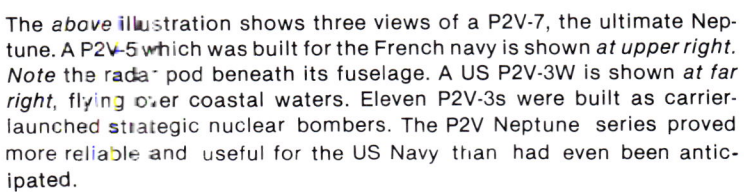

The *above* illustration shows three views of a P2V-7, the ultimate Neptune. A P2V-5 which was built for the French navy is shown *at upper right*. Note the radar pod beneath its fuselage. A US P2V-3W is shown *at far right*, flying over coastal waters. Eleven P2V-3s were built as carrier-launched strategic nuclear bombers. The P2V Neptune series proved more reliable and useful for the US Navy than had even been anticipated.

	P2V-1 (Model 26)	P2V-2 (Model 126)	P2V-3 (Model 326)	P2V-4 (Model 426)
First Flight:	1946	1947	1948	
Wing Area:	1000 ft	1000 ft	1000 ft	1000 ft
Wingspan:	100	100	100	100
Length:	75 ft, 6 in	75 ft, 6 in	75 ft, 6 in	75 ft, 6 in
Height:	28 ft, 1 in	28 ft, 1 in	28 ft 1 in	28 ft, 1 in
Engines:	two Wright R-3350-779C18BB-1	two Wright R-3350-24W	two Wright R-3350-26W	two Wright R-3350-30W Turbo-Compound Cyclones
Engine hp:	2300	2100	3200	2650
Gross Weight (lb):	54,000	54,000	54,000	54,000
Empty Weight (lb):	32,936	34,100	34,100	45,495
Operating Altitude (ft):	27,200	26,000	27,100	31,000
Cruising Speed (mph):	176	178	180	312
Top Speed (mph):	296	320	338	352
Max Range (miles):	4130	3985	3935	4200

PRODUCTION CLOSE-UP
NEPTUNE
(MODEL 26 SERIES)

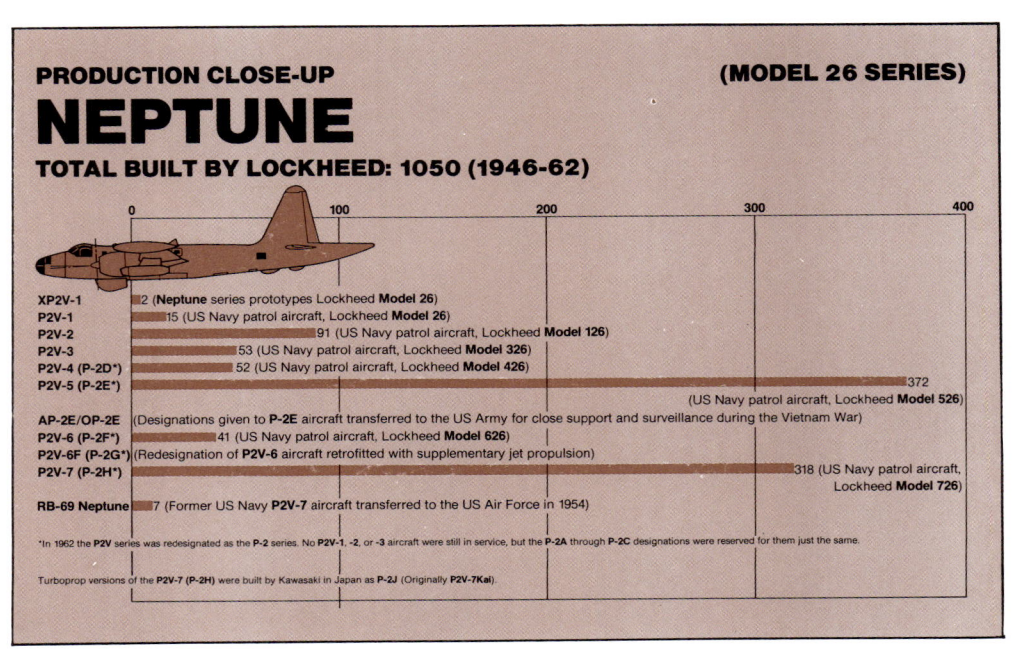

TOTAL BUILT BY LOCKHEED: 1050 (1946-62)

XP2V-1	2 (**Neptune** series prototypes Lockheed **Model 26**)
P2V-1	15 (US Navy patrol aircraft, Lockheed **Model 26**)
P2V-2	91 (US Navy patrol aircraft, Lockheed **Model 126**)
P2V-3	53 (US Navy patrol aircraft, Lockheed **Model 326**)
P2V-4 (P-2D*)	52 (US Navy patrol aircraft, Lockheed **Model 426**)
P2V-5 (P-2E*)	372 (US Navy patrol aircraft, Lockheed **Model 526**)
AP-2E/OP-2E	(Designations given to **P-2E** aircraft transferred to the US Army for close support and surveillance during the Vietnam War)
P2V-6 (P-2F*)	41 (US Navy patrol aircraft, Lockheed **Model 626**)
P2V-6F (P-2G*)	(Redesignation of **P2V-6** aircraft retrofitted with supplementary jet propulsion)
P2V-7 (P-2H*)	318 (US Navy patrol aircraft, Lockheed **Model 726**)
RB-69 Neptune	7 (Former US Navy **P2V-7** aircraft transferred to the US Air Force in 1954)

*In 1962 the **P2V** series was redesignated as the **P-2** series. No **P2V-1**, **-2**, or **-3** aircraft were still in service, but the **P-2A** through **P-2C** designations were reserved for them just the same.

Turboprop versions of the **P2V-7** (**P-2H**) were built by Kawasaki in Japan as **P-2J** (Originally **P2V-7Kai**).

	P2V-5 (Model 526)	P2V-6 (Model 626)	P2V-7 (Model 726)
First Flight:	April 1951		April 26, 1954
Wing Area:	1000 ft	1000 ft	1000 ft
Wingspan:	100	100	101 ft, 4 in
Length:	75 ft, 6 in	75 ft, 6 in	91 ft, 8 in
Height:	28 ft, 1 in	28 ft, 1 in	29 ft, 4 in
Engines:	Wright R-3350-30WA	Wright R-3350-32W	two WrightR-3350-32W Cylones and two J34-WE-36 jets
Engine hp:	2550-3250	3250-3500	2400-3400
Gross Weight (lb):	71,400	67,500	67,500
Empty Weight (lb):	43,000	46,022	44,460
Operating Altitude (ft):	23,200	20,200	22,400
Cruising Speed (mph):	207	201	188
Top Speed (mph):	323	303	312
Max Range (miles):	3194	4126	4293

which first flew in 1949, was the first Neptune to incorporate fixed wingtip fuel tanks into its design. Between 1946 and 1962, Lockheed built a total of 1051 Neptunes of all types and they continued in production in Japan, under a license granted to Kawasaki, until 1979.

In 1962, when the separate US Air Force/US Army and US Navy/US Marine Corps nomenclature systems were merged, the P2V series was redesignated from P2V (Second Lockheed Patrol type) to simply P-2 (Patrol, second). The P-2A, B and C designations were reserved for the P2V-1, 2 and 3 which had been retired from service but the P2V-4 became P-2D, the P2V-5 became P-2E and the P2V-6 became P-2F. The P2V-5F, with its 3400 hp, 16 thrust J34 turbojets, became P-2G, and the P2V-7 became P-2H. The Kawasaki version was redesignated P-2J for P-2, Japan.

During the Vietnam War an unspecified number of US Navy P-2Es were transferred to the US Army for use as ground support gunships under the designation AP-2E.

By Lockheed's reckoning, perhaps the Neptune's biggest contribution—beyond helping to keep the company afloat during the late 1940s—was in its pioneering Antisubmarine Warfare (ASW) systems integration. Literally filled to the brim with electronics gear for search and detection, it used sonobuoys dropped from its own bays to locate submerged submarines. It boasted a long-range navigation system and powerful radar. Later the APR-4 'black box' Electronic-Countermeasures (ECM) system was installed, not only to detect enemy radar but to provide a directional fix. In the APR-4 the radar bombsight computer and autopilot were integrated so that the navigator/bombardier could talk the pilot into position for the bomb run. The Neptune's APR-4 system is primitive by today's standards, but it was the system from which all succeeding ASW systems have evolved.

THE ELECTRA AND THE ORION

The successor to the Neptune and the longest produced Lockheed patrol plane was originally conceived as a turboprop airliner. The Lockheed Model 188 Electra was ill-timed for the airline market of the late 1950s but it begat the Model 186 Orion which is still in use and still in production thirty years later.

In the summer of 1955 Lockheed began work on a short-range turboprop airliner designed around the specification set down by Eastern Airlines and American Airlines, which had ordered 40 and 35 aircraft respectively. Though the new design contradicted the trend toward jets, it was hoped that the efficiency of Electra turboprop would allow it to compete successfully with the new turbojet-powered aircraft that were being introduced by Boeing and Douglas.

The Model 188 Electra, named for the successful Model 10 Electra of a quarter century before, was smaller and less graceful in appearance than the sleek Constellation, and had more in common with the Model 100 Hercules freighter.

By the time the Model 188 first flew on 6 December 1957, a total of 144 had been ordered. They soon were in service with KLM in the Netherlands and Garuda in Indonesia, as well as with three Australian airlines (Ansett, Qantas and TAA), and seven American carriers (American, Braniff, Eastern, National, Northwest, PSA and Western).

Very quickly, however, the Electra encountered unexpected and severe structural problems in its engine mountings, which in turn led to wing damage. Two fatal accidents in the first year of service, combined with competition from pure jet aircraft, spelled an early end to the Model 188 production run. Lockheed successfully corrected the problem by strengthening the wings beyond what would normally have been required. From a tech-

Facing page: The P2V-7 as a US Navy submarine patrol plane. This Lockheed Model 188 Electra (*above*) is shown as a Northwest Airlines passenger ship in 1958. Northwest Airlines was one of the original Model 188 customers. By 1986, the Electras that were still in service (*below*) were serving their second or third owners, but by golly, they were still at work.

nical point of view the modification of the wings and of the engine nacelles completely corrected the problems that had been encountered by the Electra. However when the last Electra was completed in 1962, only 26 had been ordered beyond the initial block of 144 aircraft.

By the late 1960s the Electra had generally been withdrawn from first-line service, but in 1967 Lockheed undertook contract modification of some 41 of the used aircraft. In service primarily as cargo planes with secondary carriers in remote corners of the world, some of these Electras are still in use in the mid-1980s.

The Electra was born at an inopportune time, had a difficult early life, and disappeared from view at a young age. However, for the military derivative of the Electra—named Orion for another early Lockheed airplane—the story was quite the opposite.

In August 1957, even before the Model 188 made her first flight, the US Navy had expressed an interest in a new antisubmarine patrol plane to succeed Lockheed's own P2V Neptune. The Navy wanted the new plane but they wanted it *fast*. To meet the latter specification, Lockheed suggested a modified Model 188, and the Navy nodded its approval, choosing Lockheed's proposal over the others submitted. The contract was signed on 8 May 1958 and the prototype first flew three months later on 19 August 1958. Designated Model 186, the new aircraft was actually the third prototype Model 188 that was snatched from the assembly line and heavily modified. The most noticeable modification was a mock-up of the 14-foot Magnetic Anomaly Detection (MAD) boom extending from the rear fuselage.

On 25 November 1959 the Model 186, now given the Navy service test designation YP3V-1, made its first flight with most of its planned avionics and submarine detection equipment. By the time that the production prototype P3V-1 took to the air on 15 April 1961, the name Orion had been made official. The unified Department of Defense nomenclature system was implemented before the first Orions entered squadron service on 13 August 1962, so they joined the Navy as P-3A rather than P3V-1. The P-3B made its appearance in 1965 with more advanced detection equipment. The P-3B was followed by the P-3C in 1970, which has in turn been through a series of 'updates,' which included P-3C Update I in January 1975, P-3C

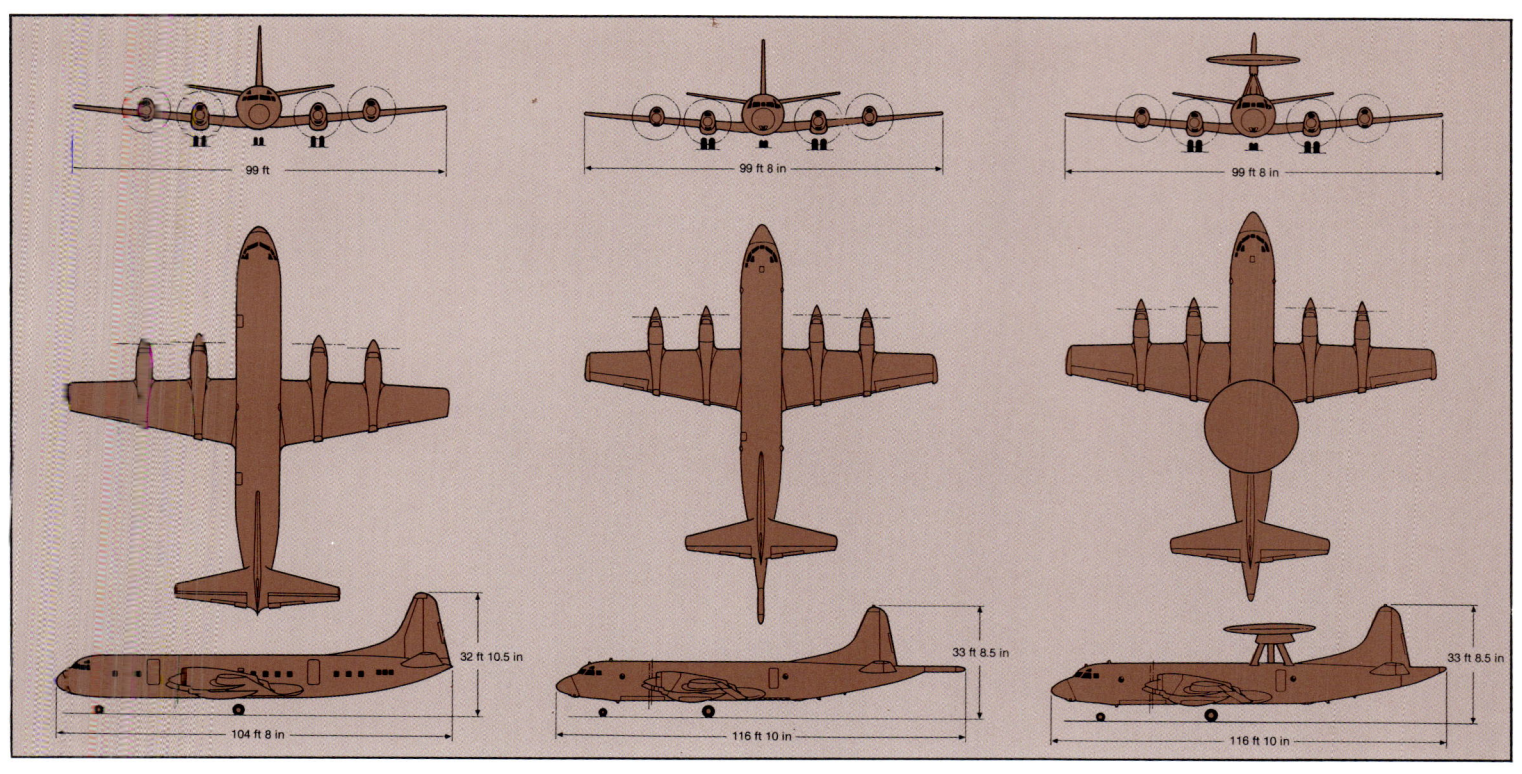

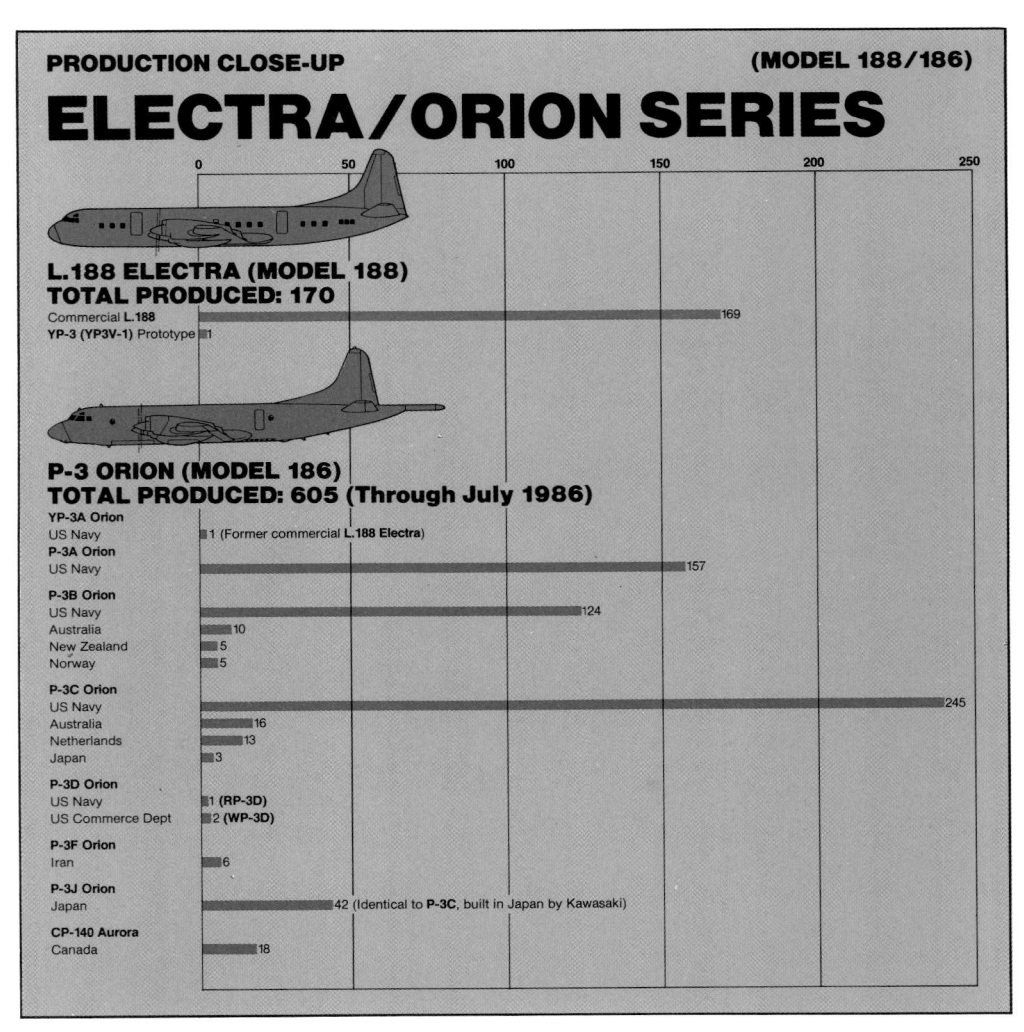

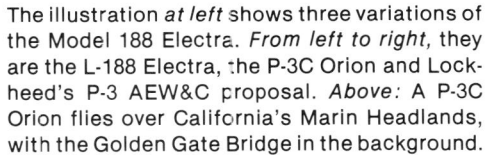

PRODUCTION CLOSE-UP
ELECTRA/ORION SERIES
(MODEL 188/186)

L.188 ELECTRA (MODEL 188)
TOTAL PRODUCED: 170

Commercial L.188	169
YP-3 (YP3V-1) Prototype	1

P-3 ORION (MODEL 186)
TOTAL PRODUCED: 605 (Through July 1986)

YP-3A Orion — US Navy	1 (Former commercial L.188 Electra)
P-3A Orion — US Navy	157
P-3B Orion — US Navy	124
P-3B Orion — Australia	10
P-3B Orion — New Zealand	5
P-3B Orion — Norway	5
P-3C Orion — US Navy	245
P-3C Orion — Australia	16
P-3C Orion — Netherlands	13
P-3C Orion — Japan	3
P-3D Orion — US Navy	1 (RP-3D)
P-3D Orion — US Commerce Dept	2 (WP-3D)
P-3F Orion — Iran	6
P-3J Orion — Japan	42 (Identical to P-3C, built in Japan by Kawasaki)
CP-140 Aurora — Canada	18

The illustration *at left* shows three variations of the Model 188 Electra. *From left to right,* they are the L-188 Electra, the P-3C Orion and Lockheed's P-3 AEW&C proposal. *Above:* A P-3C Orion flies over California's Marin Headlands, with the Golden Gate Bridge in the background.

L-188 Electra

First Flight:	1957	Empty Weight (lb):	61,500
Wingspan:	99 ft	Passengers:	77
Length:	104 ft, 6 in	Operating Altitude (ft):	27,000
Height:	32 ft, 10 in	Cruising Speed (mph):	374
Engines:	four Allison 501-D13A turboprops	Top Cruising Speed (mph):	405
Engine hp:	3750	Max Range (miles):	2500
Max Takeoff Weight (lb):	116,000		

	P-3A Orion	P-3B Orion	P-3C Orion
First Flight:	1959		1969
Wingspan:	99 ft, 8 in	99 ft, 8 in	99 ft, 8 in
Length:	116 ft, 10 in	116 ft, 10 in	116 ft, 10 in
Height:	33 ft, 8 in	33 ft, 8 in	33 ft, 8 in
Engines:	four Allison T56-A-10W turboprop	four Allison T56-A-14 turboprop	four Allison T56-A-14 turboprop
Engine hp:	4500 at takeoff	4910 at takeoff	
Gross Weight (lb):	127,500	132,990	135,000
Operating Altitude (ft):	24,000	24,000	24,000
Cruising Speed (mph):	357	331	325
Top Speed (mph):	460	460	460
Max Range (miles):	5570	5620	5200

Below right: This US Navy P-3C Orion is banking over American Pacific coastal waters, the plane's turboprops pulling its 135,000 pounds through the air with the greatest of ease.

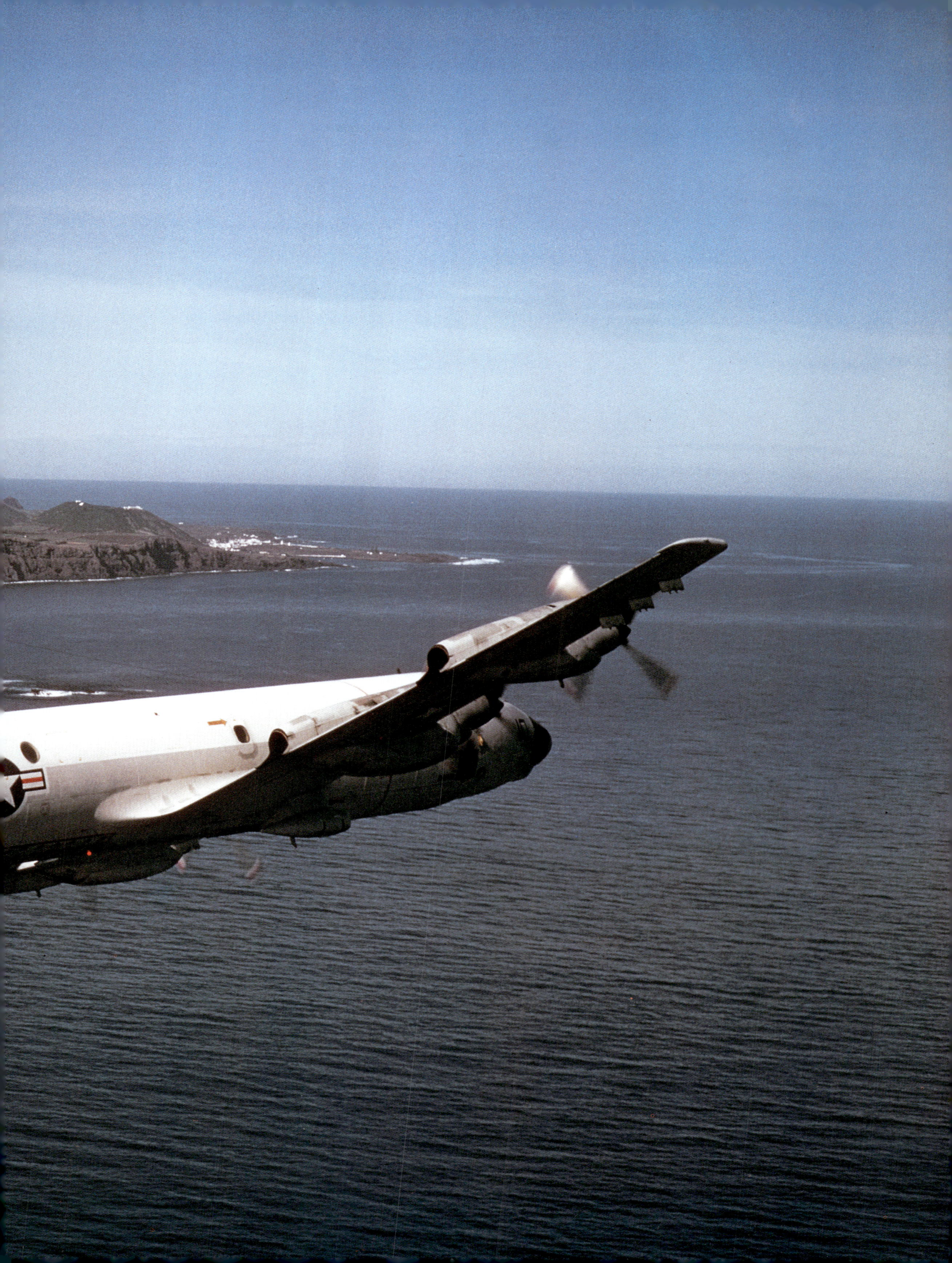

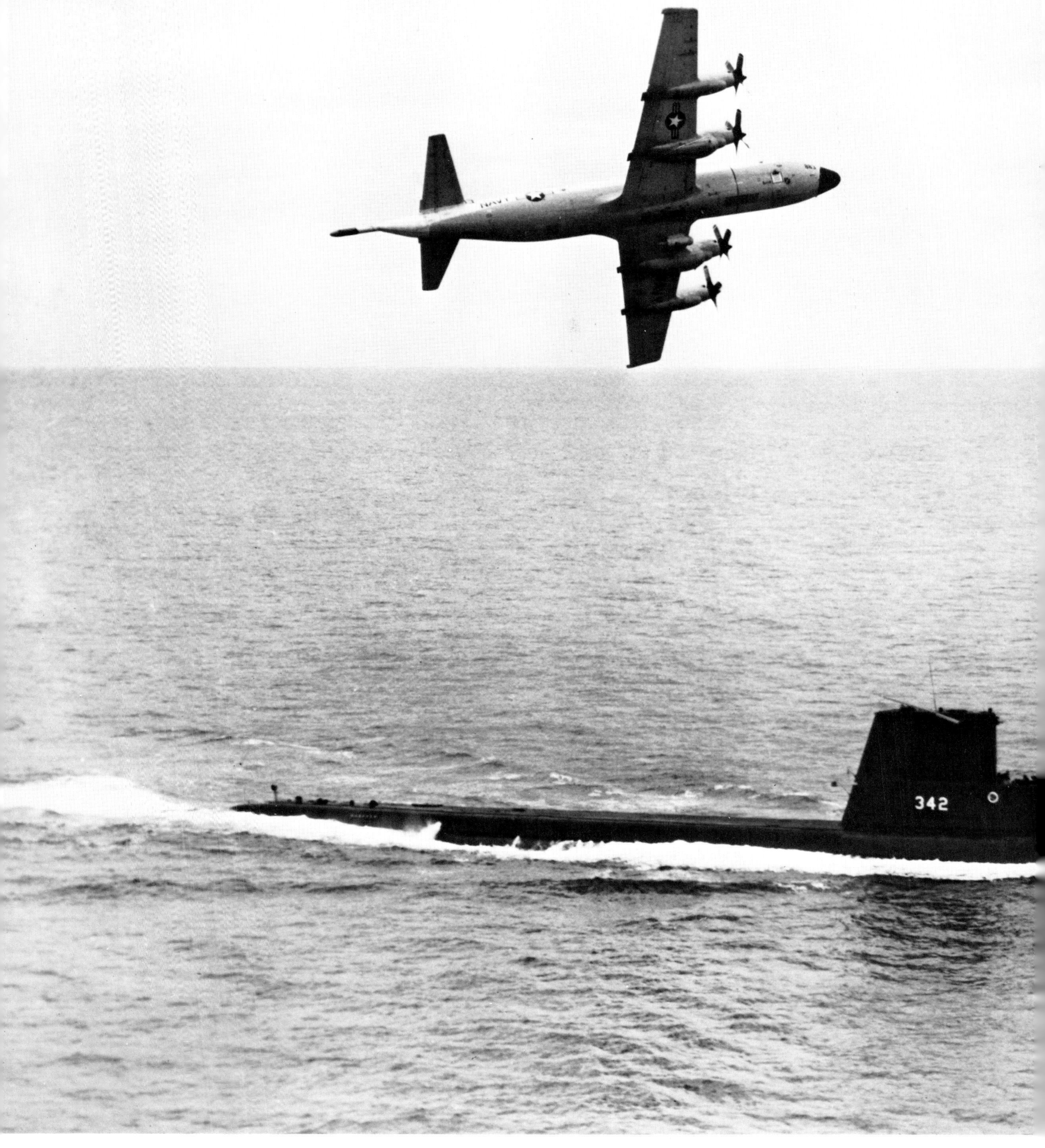
342

A United States Navy P-3 Orion (*at left*), loaded with electronic gear, overflies the US conventional submarine SS 342 *Chopper* (*below*) in the open sea. P-3s like this one are typical of the US Navy's peace-keeping reconnaissance force and a less-pleasant sight for Soviet subs. In addition to having excellent electronic 'eyes and ears,' US Navy P-3s pack a powerful anti-submarine punch, with torpedoes, depth bombs, mines, rockets and air-to-surface Bullpup missiles. The P-3 Lockheed Orion is the Navy's most advanced long range, land-based anti-submarine patrol craft.

Update II in August 1977 and P-3C Update III in May 1984.

Though the P-3C will remain in production until the 1990s and in service until the twenty-first century, the original decision to develop it began in 1960, even before the P-3A went into service. The impetus was the development of the A-NEW advanced ASW avionic system, which eventually was first flown with the YP-3C designation on 18 September 1968.

The P-3C Update I came at a time when new avionics were ready for incorporation into the P-3C, but the computer memory and access channels were saturated. Update I removed these limitations and introduced the highest priority improvements in avionics. These included: a 393,000 word drum memory and 4th logic unit; OMEGA worldwide navigation system; significant improvements in DIFAR; an added tactical display at sensor stations 1 and 2 for improved crew effectiveness; a new operational program providing computer-aided acoustic analysis, ESM signal sorting and refinement of OMEGA navigational signals; and a lighter-weight, more reliable digital magnetic tape transport.

P-3C Update II improvements included: an Infrared Detection System (IRDS); accommodation for the Harpoon all-weather, anti-ship missile; a new acoustic tape record with 28 track capability; and the Sonobuoy Reference System (SRS) for continuous monitoring of sonobuoy positions. Additional improvements added in subsequent years included: a new inertial navigation system; a new doppler system; new radio navigation aids; Tactical Coordinator IRDS display; increased acoustic processing; integrated Acoustic Communication System (IACS) for underwater communication; and the Digital Magnetic Tape Set (DMTS) for computer program loading and data extraction.

P-3C Update III featured an entirely new underwater acoustic monitoring system based on the PROTEUS analyzer unit. Accompanying the entirely new acoustic signal receiving, processing, display and control system were improvements in the air conditioning system to ensure that the densely packed avionics were adequately cooled. A redesigned Transparent Logic Unit was also incorporated, which will form the basis for future modernization of the the data processing system.

In addition to supplying the various P-3 subtypes to the US Navy, Lockheed has sold P-3Bs to Norway, New Zealand and Portugal, and P-3Cs to Australia, Japan and the Netherlands. Prior to the collapse of the Iranian monarchy in 1979, a handful of modified P-3Cs were sold to the Imperial Iranian Air Force under the designation P-3F. The US Navy in turn sold P-3As to Spain.

The Orions in service with the Canadian Armed Forces are similar in outward appearance to the P-3C but carry specialized avionics and bear the CAF designation CP-140 and the name Aurora. Having first flown on 22 March 1979, the CP-140 Aurora has the same airframe and aircraft systems as the P-3C but the cabin interior was substantially altered to suit CAF specifications, which grouped the tactical crew in a tactical crew compartment. The CP-140 is also configured for a variety of missions other than ASW. These include maritime surveillance, arctic surveillance, aerial survey, mapping, resource location, pollution control and search and rescue.

Among the features of the CP-140 that differ from the P-3C are: the pilot's and copilot's instrument panel layouts are revised to provide a basic 'T' arrangement, and blue filtered white lighting is provided in the flight station; a total of 36 underfloor 'A' size sonobuoy launch tubes are installed in lieu of 48; a new magnetic anomaly detector with a fully automatic compensator is incorporated; a 'C' size free-fall chute is installed in lieu of a 'B' size chute; a photo illuminator for night photography and a day/night reconnaissance camera are added; new long-range/

polar and airways navigation systems are included, as well as new communications equipment including VHF, IFF, Data Link, SIMOP and HF. Provisions have been made for a detachable weapons bay canister that is designed to carry additional civil and military sensor equipment, as well as provisions for a mapping camera and an airborne radiation thermometer. Space and power provisions have also been made for Side-Looking Airborne Radar (SLAR).

Also incorporated into the CP-140 is such improved S-3A equipment as: an advanced acoustic data processing system modified to further improve effectiveness and performance; dual processor Navigation/Tactical (NT) central digital computer; expanded tactical displays and controls; multi-mode radar with capability to detect small targets; Electronic Support Measures (ESM); an operational system test, and diagnostic software programs modified for increased weapon system performance; a sonobuoy locating system; and a Forward Looking Infrared (FLIR) system.

As a further development of the Orion, Lockheed in 1984 began test flying a company-funded Airborne Early Warning and Control demonstrator aircraft. Designated P-3 AEW&C, the new plane had the familiar Orion airframe with the addition of a large saucer-shaped rotodome on its back. This is similar in form and function to the rotodome on the US Air Force's Boeing E-3A Sentry Airborne Warning and Control System (AWACS) aircraft and the US Navy's carrier-based Grumman E-2C Hawkeye AWACS aircraft. The P-3 AEW&C, however, is available at roughly half the cost of the E-3A while providing three times the range of the E-2C and slightly greater range than the E-3A.

The function of the P-3 AEW&C, like that of the other AWACS aircraft is to provide an airborne radar platform for monitoring air space for potential intruders. In this sense, the P-3 AEW&C is designed to do in the air what the P-3 ASW aircraft do with potential submarine intruders under water. Like the other AWACS aircraft, the P-3 AEW&C can also control and direct fighters to intercept intruders and provide aerial battlefield management.

The heart of the P-3 AEW&C is the General Electric AN/APS-138 radar antenna contained within the slowly rotating 24-foot rotodome. With the AN/APS-138 radar, the P-3 AEW&C can patrol 1.5 million square miles while flying 3400 nautical miles. The radar can detect and monitor large aircraft and surface ships to the radar horizon and smaller planes and boats at distances in excess of 200 miles. The inherent long-range capability of the Orion allows the P-3 AEW&C, like the other P-3s before it, to remain for eight hours at a station 800 nautical miles from its base.

One of the major reasons for the continued success of the Orion series has been its durability and long range.

At left, left to right: P-3C Orions, belonging to the Netherlands Navy (*Konincklijk Marine*); the Japanese Marine Self Defense Force; and the US Navy, rest on the asphalt. Joint ASW patrols between nations employing P-3s are common. P-3s destined for the Australian Navy (*immediately below*) and the US Navy (*at right*) are shown *here* on Lockheed's Burbank production line.

THE VIKING

In 1969 the US Navy awarded Lockheed the primary contract to build its S-3 carrier-based Antisubmarine Warfare (ASW) aircraft. Small by comparison to the P-2 and P-3, the S-3 would be the only Lockheed airplane developed for use from aircraft carriers. As prime contractor for the S-3, Lockheed would build the fuselage and conduct final assembly—while the secondary contractor, LTV(Ling/Temco/Vought), would produce the wings, tail engine pods and landing gear. The two other major contractors were General Electric, which built the two TF34 turbofan engines and Univac, which provided the Univac 1832 general purpose digital computer. The S-3 would also be equipped with a Forward Looking Infrared (FLIR) scanner and a Magnetic Anomaly Detection (MAD) sensor in a retractable tail boom. Sounding buoys could be carried in the S-3's bomb bay, as could armament consisting of torpedoes, mines or bombs. Additional bombs or rockets could be carried on wing racks.

The first of eight service test prototypes was flown on 21 January 1972 under the designation YS-3A. Given the name Viking, the first production aircraft entered squadron service with training squadron VS-41 at NAS North Island in 1974 and with ASW squadron VS-21 aboard the USS *John F Kennedy* in 1975. The Viking continued in production until 1978, by which time 179 production S-3As were built.

In 1976 the Navy began the modification of six S-3As for use as utility transports for carrier on-board delivery operations. Modified and redesignated as US-3A, these Vikings seated six passengers and carried 202 cubic feet of cargo. During the Iranian crisis in 1980-81, the first US-3A carried 2700 passengers and a million pounds of mail between the naval base at Diego Garcia and the US Navy carrier battle groups operating in the Indian Ocean. Another Viking was later modified as an aerial refueling tanker under the designation KS-3A, and is the single such aircraft in service.

In service in their primary role as ASW aircraft, the US Navy's Vikings are based at two home bases: NAS North Island on the west coast and NAS Cecil Field, Florida on the east coast. From these bases they are operationally deployed in ten-plane squadrons to carriers with the Atlantic and Pacific Fleets.

In 1981 the Naval Air Systems Command awarded a full-scale engineering development contract to Lockheed for an improved S-3 avionics system. The company modified two aircraft to the new configuration, designated S-3B. Advancements incorporated included: a stand-off classification radar system that can classify enemy targets at extended ranges; an improved acoustic processing system; an updated electronic support measures system; a new sonobuoy receiver with expanded capabilities; an electronic countermeasure capability; and a new analog tape recorder. Also, the Harpoon air-to-surface missile has been added to the aircraft's armament.

Above left: The S-3A Viking is Lockheed's contribution to Antisubmarine Warfare (ASW). Each US aircraft carrier, excepting USS *Midway* and USS *Coral Sea,* carries a 10-plane squadron of S-3As. The subhunters *shown in this photo* are part of Squadron 29, deployed to the USS *Enterprise.* S-3As are deployed to US Atlantic and US Pacific fleet vessels from home bases NAS Cecil Field, in Florida, and NAS North Island, on the West Coast, respectively. *Above:* The experimental KS-3A refuels its design counterpart, an S-3A sub hunter from Squadron 41. These sub chasers have stood guard over US carriers for more than 15 years.

	S-3A Vikiing
First Flight:	1971
Wingspan:	68 ft, 8 in (29 ft, 6 in, folded)
Length:	53 ft, 4 in (49 ft, 5 in, tail folded)
Height:	22 ft, 9 in (15 ft, 3 in, tail folded)
Engines:	two General Electric TF-34-2 high-bypass turbofans
Engine thrust (lb):	9,000
Gross Takeoff Weight (lb):	42,500
Crew:	4
Operating Altitude (ft):	40,000
Cruising Speed (knots):	160
Top Speed (knots):	450

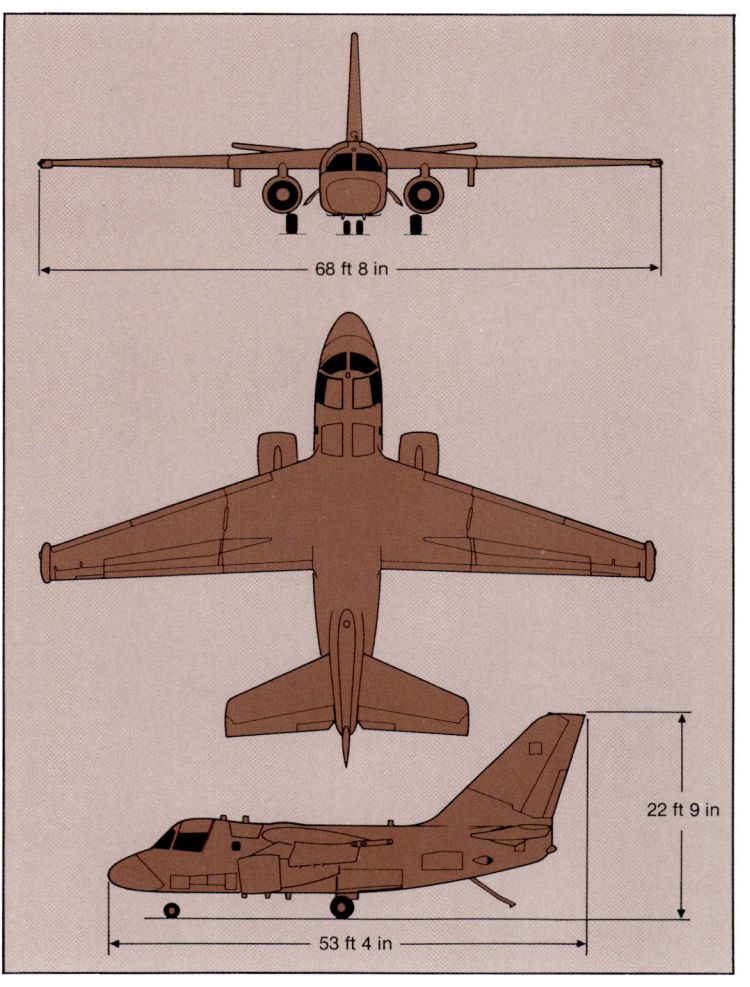

LOCKHEED'S POSTWAR LIGHT PLANES

The Vega Aircraft Company (later Vega Aircraft Corporation) had been organized as a wholly-owned Lockheed subsidiary in 1937 for the purpose of developing a line of light planes for the general aviation market. Shortly thereafter, World War II intervened and Vega became little more than an overflow warplane production facility for the parent company, and in 1943 it was merged into Lockheed. In early 1944 Lockheed president Robert Gross looked into the company's postwar future and once again saw a favorable general aviation market.

The idea of a small, general aviation aircraft evolved from the Lockheed Model 33 Airtrooper—a tiny one-place 'flying motorcycle' that had been developed by Mac Short, the former Vega president who now was heading Lockheed's special projects division. The 425-pound Airtrooper originally had been designed for use by the Army as a possible substitute for paratrooper assaults. Instead of giving each soldier a parachute, the Army might issue each man an *airplane*! However, with an eye towards a postwar civilian market, the Airtrooper was described as the 'plane for everybody.'

The one and only Airtrooper prototype made its first flight in 1944, taking off easily in 100 feet and landing in 75 feet. Rechristened 'Little Dipper,' the Model 33 failed to impress the Army and did not attract any civilian contracts.

Undaunted by the failure of the Little Dipper, Gross moved ahead with a new concept for a 'plane for everybody,' which he called (what else?) the *'Big Dipper'*! The Model 34 Big Dipper was a two-place aircraft, with a single pusher-type propeller and a gross weight roughly three times that of its predecessor. Whereas the Little Dipper was conceived as a 'flying motorcycle' the Big Dipper was more like a 'flying automobile.' With a projected retail price of $2500, Gross saw it as 'safe, cheap flight for the average man.'

The first Big Dipper emerged from the Lockheed factory for its first flight on 10 December 1945 after 14 months in secret development. Said test pilot Prentice Cleaves:

'The Big Dipper was an aerodynamic dream. I've been flying since 1928 and I've never before or since been in such a good plane. Its handling characteristics were amazing.

You could trim out for an indicated speed, chop the throttle and the plane would "hunt" through two slight oscillations, then establish itself in a glide at the set airspeed. Then you could pour on the coal and where an ordinary plane would come up in a whipstall, this plane would just oscillate slightly, seek out the trimmed airspeed and resume level flight. It approached a one-control airplane.'

The Big Dipper's career however was short-lived. On 6 February 1946 during a routine takeoff, the plane stalled twice. At the controls, Prentice Cleaves realized that to abort the takeoff meant that the Model 34 would be damaged, so he applied maximum power and hoped he could get it airborne. He missed by just a few inches; the Dipper clipped an embankment and crashed just a few hundred feet from where it had been built. Although Cleaves and project engineer Frank Johnson survived the crash, both were badly injured.

At the same time that the Big and Little Dipper were under development, Lockheed was working on a third small airplane, the Model 75 Saturn. The idea behind the Saturn was just the opposite of that behind the huge Constellation. Whereas the latter was conceived as a long-range intercontinental transport that would serve major international airlines on globe-spanning postwar routes, the Saturn was conceived as a short-range aircraft for the small feeder airlines that would funnel passengers into big regional 'hub' airports.

The Saturn was one of the most carefully conceived and designed airliners of its era. No expense was spared in its development and no detail, however minute, was overlooked. When plans for the Model 75 were presented at the International Air Conference in Chicago in the fall of 1944, potential buyers flocked to Lockheed's booth. The company came away with 'conditional sales contracts' for almost 500 Saturns.

The problem was that Lockheed had projected an $85,000 unit cost, but by the time the Saturn was ready in mid-1945, a price of $100,000 would have been optimistic. In the meanwhile, the US government had disposed of over 30,000 war-surplus transports. There were thousands of two-engined C-47s (the military version of the legendary Douglas DC-3) for sale at $25,000. This virtually destroyed the postwar market for newly designed twin-engined aircraft.

The first of two Saturns finally flew on 17 June 1946. The plane that had been so carefully designed was found to have serious stability problems and engines that overheated. A second Saturn with improved engines flew on 8 August 1947, but by then Robert Gross had already made the decision to abandon the Model 75 project, which to date had cost Lockheed six million dollars.

In 1946 Lockheed suffered a $21,860,000 operating loss, due in part to the time and energy that had been invested in small commercial projects that faced stiff competition from war surplus aircraft.

Facing page: The Little Dipper (*top*) was originally a 'flying motorcycle' to be used by American combat troops in World War II; while the Big Dipper (*bottom*) was a four-seater meant to be produced as a 'personal airplane' for the masses. *This page, above:* The Saturn was intended as a short-range transport for 'feeder' airlines.

LOCKHEED JET FIGHTERS

THE SHOOTING STAR

On 18 June 1943 ace aircraft designer Kelly Johnson was called into the office of Lockheed president Robert Gross for a chat. The subject was jet aircraft, specifically the subject of how soon Johnson could design and build a high-performance jet fighter and deliver the prototype to the US Army Air Corps. Johnson thought it could be done in 180 days.

At that time however, the Germans were way ahead in the jet airplane race. It had been just under four years since the world's first jet airplane—Dr Ernst Heinkel's He-178—had made its maiden flight in Germany. In the ensuing years, designers in Germany, Britain and the United States had been hard at work on the development of jet aircraft. In Germany, several different prototypes were under development, and Dr Willy Messerschmitt's Me-262, destined to be the world's first operational jet fighter, was well into its flight test program. Lockheed itself developed a design for a sleek jet fighter. The Lockheed Model 133 fighter was intended to be powered by a Model L-1000 jet engine designed by Lockheed engineer Nathan Price, but the plane was never built.

Chief of Staff General Henry 'Hap' Arnold and the US Army Air Forces knew what was going on and they were eager to catch up. The experimental Bell P-59 Airacomet was already in development, but had proven to be disappointingly slow. The USAAF wanted to see the team that had produced the P-38 put to work on an operational jet fighter that could go into action against the Me-262 as early as possible.

The clock began ticking on 23 June 1943 when the USAAF delivered the contract to Burbank. The new design, Lockheed Model 140, was sleek, yet it was much simpler and more straightforward than the Model 133 would have been. The USAAF also abandoned the idea of the Lockheed Model L-1000 engine in favor of the more well developed DeHavilland Goblin engine from Britain.

Johnson and Lockheed chief engineer Hall Hibbard were assigned a staff of 23 engineers and 1205 shop men, but there was not even a cubbyhole in the sprawling Lockheed complex in which to house the men and secret activity, so a crude wood and canvas building was slapped together near the wind tunnel and work began. The drafty shack was a most unlikely site for the home of the nation's most advanced aircraft project. Because of the secrecy surrounding the place, people began to wonder what was going on inside. Kelly Johnson recalls in his autobiography how, when one of his designers was asked what he was doing, he replied that Johnson was 'stirring up some kind of brew.' As Johnson explains it, this brought to mind the character in Al Capp's *Lil' Abner* comic strip who was regularly seen stirring a big, foul-smelling brew called *Kickapoo Joy Juice*—to which he added such ingredients as live skunks. It was from this analogy that Lockheed's most high technology development center came to be known as the *Skunk Works*.

Working 60 hour weeks, the *Skunk Works* crew proceeded quickly on the airframe. Even though Johnson had forbidden work on Sunday to make sure that the men would get some rest, gremlins somehow managed to get a lot of work done between Saturday night and Monday morning. A major problem was encountered when the engine finally arrived seven days before the airframe was completed and was found to be the wrong size! The necessary changes were made and the XP-80 prototype was finished and trucked to Muroc Army Air Field (now Edwards Air Force Base) in the dead of night.

Engine tests were begun on the 139th day and the prototype was accepted by the USAAF six days later on 15 November 1943. The new type was given the experimental pursuit designation XP-80. Lockheed meanwhile designated it as Model 80 for manufacturing purposes. The Model 140 designation had been a design designation. The Model 80/P-80 series aircraft would be known generically by the name Shooting Star, but the first prototype—Lockheed's first jet—was nicknamed *Lulu Belle*.

On the cold, wet morning of 8 January 1944, with Lockheed chief engineering test pilot Milo Burcham at the controls, *Lulu Belle* made her first flight. As the *Skunk Works* engineers that were huddled around bonfires applauded, Burcham eased the screaming XP-80 off the lake bed runway. The XP-80 began to shimmy and shake and the test pilot quickly came around and touched down. Burcham told Johnson that perhaps he was being overly cautious, but that *Lulu Belle* 'felt funny on the ailerons. Pretty touchy.'

'You've got a 15 to 1 boost and a hot ship that's naturally sensitive—maybe you were overcontrolling,' Johnson told him.

'Could be,' Burcham replied as he returned to the jet fighter for another try. The second flight went like clockwork. Kelly Johnson and the *Skunk Works* crew were elated, as were the USAAF officers who were observing the flight.

The USAAF quickly ordered a second prototype under the designation XP-80A. This aircraft, nicknamed *Gray Ghost* because of its gloss gray finish, made its first flight on 10 June 1944 with Lockheed test pilot Tony LeVier at the controls. The XP-80A differed from the XP-80 in that it was a bit larger and

Facing page: Lockheed's prototype of the Model 80/P-80 series, *Lulu Belle*, looks skittish in this 1944 photo, taken at Muroc. The second Model 80/P-80 prototype, the *Gray Ghost,* is shown *below* while under the tender ministrations of Kelly Johnson (in suit) and others of the *Skunk Works* crew. *Above:* F-80s in production.

incorporated the powerful General Electric J33 turbojet engine (originally I-40) in place of the DeHavilland Goblin. The USAAF ordered 13 YP-80A service test Shooting Stars on the spot.

By midsummer 1944, however, the Messerschmitt Me-262 had reached operational service with the Luftwaffe. Soon after the YP-80A first flew on 13 September 1944, the USAAF placed orders for 5000 P-80A Shooting Stars. The production scheme called for Lockheed to build 3063 of the planes in Burbank, while North American Aviation would set up a second assembly line in Kansas City to build the rest under license. However, the war ended before the USAAF could be flooded with sleek jet fighters. The Kansas City line never opened, and only 563 P-80As were built in Burbank.

In early 1945 two Shooting Stars were sent to England and another pair to Italy. They actually went on patrol searching for Me-262 and Heinkel He-162 jet fighters, but there was to be no air-to-air combat between jets during World War II.

There were several postwar triumphs for the Shooting Star. Colonel William Council established a new transcontinental speed record in January 1946, and Colonel Albert Boyd captured the world's absolute speed record of 623.7 mph the following year.

But the Shooting Star had its postwar tragedies as well. Milo Burcham died in a P-80 crash when his fuel system failed on takeoff. An emergency backup was designed but failure to turn it on cost the life of America's ace of aces, Major Richard Bong. Having shot down 40 Japanese aircraft during World War II with a Lockheed P-38, Bong was the top USAAF ace and a natural candidate to take a turn at the controls of the hot new fighter. On 6 August 1945, the day that the atomic bomb fell on Hiroshima, Bong lifted off Lockheed's Burbank runway for a

Right: The P-80s of the 94th 'Hat in the Ring' Fighter Squadron, which was ace Eddie Rickenbacher's in World War I. Photographed in mid-1948 after the red bar had been added to the US insignia, they retain the 'P' for Pursuit designation rather than 'F' for Fighter adopted later in the year.
Above: F-80s awaiting delivery on the eve of the Korean War.

short flight. Seconds later his life was claimed by the same sort of unforgiving fuel system that had killed Milo Burcham.

At the end of World War II in September 1945, there were just 44 Shooting Stars, but by the close of that year there were 215. Over the next six years Lockheed produced an average of 287 Shooting Stars annually, with the last four aircraft being produced in 1951. During these years, against the backdrop of the growing cold war, the Shooting Star was the top fighter in the USAAF. In September 1947 the USAAF became the US Air Force. In June 1948 a new nomenclature was adopted in which the P for 'pursuit' designation was replaced by the F for 'fighter' designation, and the P-80 series became the F-80 series.

Meanwhile, the P-80B series was introduced. Designated F-80B in June 1948, the new Shooting Star incorporated an ejection seat for pilot escape, M-3 machine guns (firing 1200 rpm versus 800 rpm) and a water-alcohol injector to provide extra power to the engine. Lockheed produced 240 F-80Bs and undertook to upgrade existing F-80As.

In March 1948 the P-80C was introduced. Quickly going into production as the F-80C, this aircraft featured a more powerful Allison J33 turbojet than that of the A and B series Shooting Stars, and had provisions for carrying greater ordnance.

By the time the Korean War began in June 1950, there were over 900 Shooting Stars in service—roughly half the US Air Force's jet fighter inventory. F-80Cs entered combat on 27 June 1950—two days after the Korean War began—shooting down

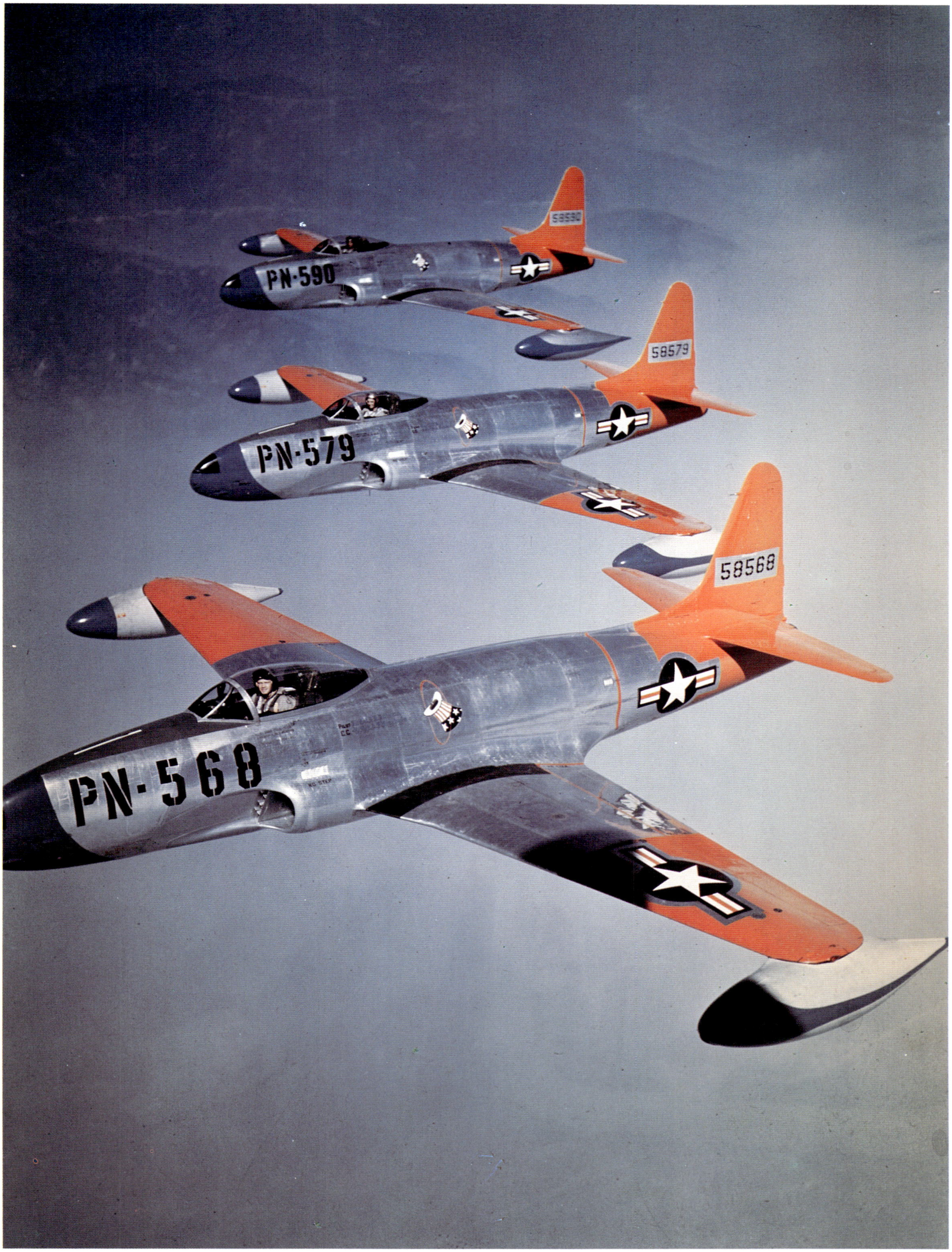
58590
PN-590
58579
PN-579
58568
PN-568

Stealth before 'Stealth': Lockheed's Hall Hibbard (*at right*) holds a model of the Lockheed Model 133, the 1943 precursor to the P-80 that was designed around Lockheed's L-1000 jet engine. The P-80 wing is evident in the Model 133, but the 'canard' (tail-forward) design and rounded corners are characteristic of the F-19 'Stealth' aircraft that caused so much interest in the mid-1980s.

The Model 133's family tree is shown *below right, bottom and center*. The Model 30 *directly below* was a twin-engined, three-seat warplane that combined the canard idea with the stabilizers used on the P-38. *Bottom right:* The Model 30 evolved into a one-seat jet fighter that looks somewhat like the hood ornament of a 1950s automobile. This idea gradually evolved into the Model 133 (*below, center*) which was still a single-seat fighter.

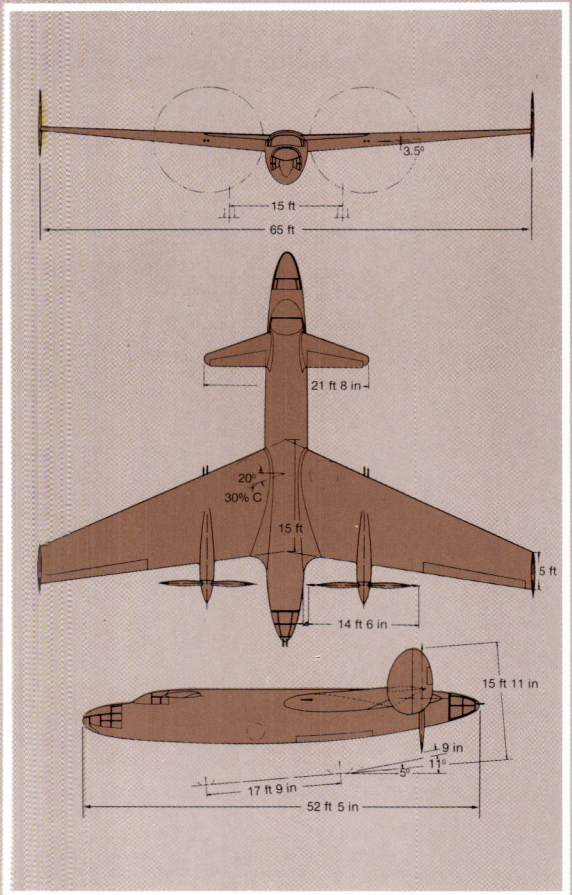

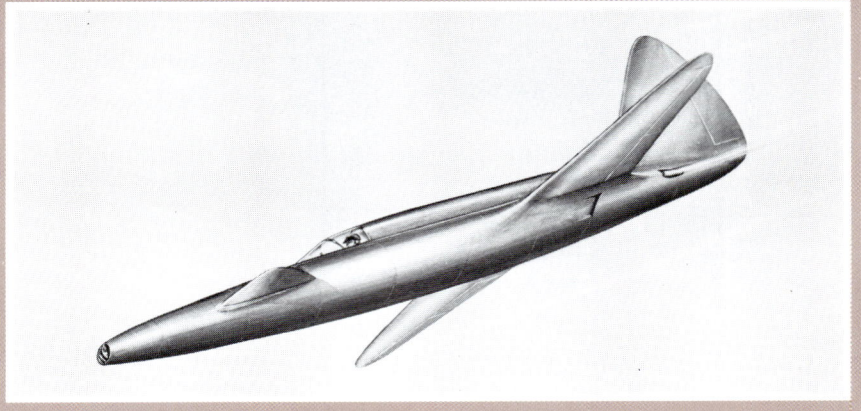

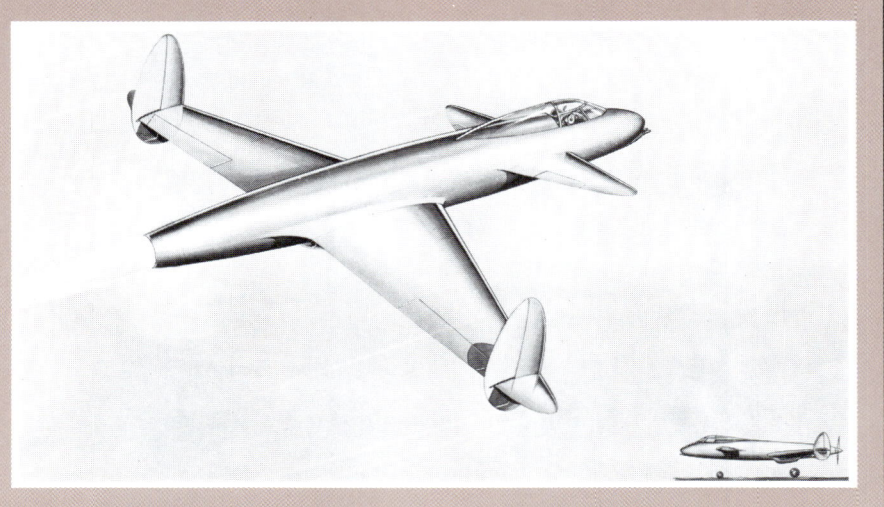

four Ilyushin Il-10 bombers. In November 1950 the Chinese entered the war, and Shooting Stars tangled with Soviet-built MiG-15 jet fighters for the first time. On 8 November, in the world's first jet-vs-jet dogfight Lt Russell Brown of the US Air Force 51st Fighter Interceptor Wing, flying an F-80C, shot down a Chinese MiG-15.

By the early fifties, however, the Shooting Star's 1944 technology had relegated it to second line status among the squadrons in Korea and it served primarily in Fighter Bomber Squadrons. Most of the US Air Force jet jockeys, who became aces in Korea, flew the North American F-86 Sabre Jet, the world's state-of-the-art in fast jet fighters. However, Captain Ralph Parr of the 7th Fighter Bomber Squadron became a 'double ace' (ten aerial victories) while flying 165 missions in a F-80C.

Altogether, Shooting Stars flew 98,515 sorties in the Korean War and performed well. In aerial combat they shot down 37 enemy aircraft against a loss of 14 F-80s.

Captain Ralph Parr became a 'double ace' with 10 aerial victories while flying an F-80C during the Korean War; Lockheed's Model F-80C Shooting Star (*above*) claimed its first MiG-15 on 8 November 1950.

After Korea, the Shooting Star remained in service with the US Air Force until 1957. Many of the surplus F-80s were scrapped but others were exported to the air forces of Brazil, Chile, Ecuador, Peru, Uruguay and Venezuela. The last F-80s in service were the 14 aircraft that were retired by Uruguay in 1975.

In its fighter configuration, the Shooting Star is just a memory, but along with that is a memory of the verse composed by Korean War veterans:

Bless 'em all, bless 'em all;
Bless tailpipe, tiptanks, and all.
Bless Old Man Lockheed for building this jet,
No finer airplane we're willing to bet.
Bless 'em all, bless 'em all.

Model 80 Shooting Star Series

	XP-80 *Lulu Belle*	**P-80A**	**F-80B**	**F-80C**
First Flight:	1943	1944	1947	1948
Wingspan:	37 ft	39 ft, 11 in	39 ft, 11 in	39 ft, 11 in
Length:	32 ft, 10 in	34 ft, 6 in	34 ft, 6 in	34 ft, 6 in
Height:	10 ft	11 ft, 4 in	11 ft, 4 in	11 ft, 4 in
Engines:	De Havilland Halford H-13 'Goblin'	Allison J33-A-11	Allison J33-A-21	Allison J33-A-23
Engine thrust:	2460	4000	4500	5400
Gross Weight (lb):	8620	11,700	11,975	15,336
Empty Weight (lb):	6287	7920	8176	8240
Crew:	1	1	1	1
Operating Altitude (ft):	41,000	45,000	36,800	42,750
Cruising Speed (mph):	400	410	386	349
Top Speed (mph):	502	558	577	580
Max Range (miles):	1200	1440	1210	1380

The Lockheed Model 580/T-33 'T-Bird' is shown *below* in a cutaway view. *Note* (*left to right*) the electronics in the plane's nose; the two-seater cockpit; the engine's air intake ducts; wingtip fuel tanks; and the Allison J33-A-35 turbojet engine.

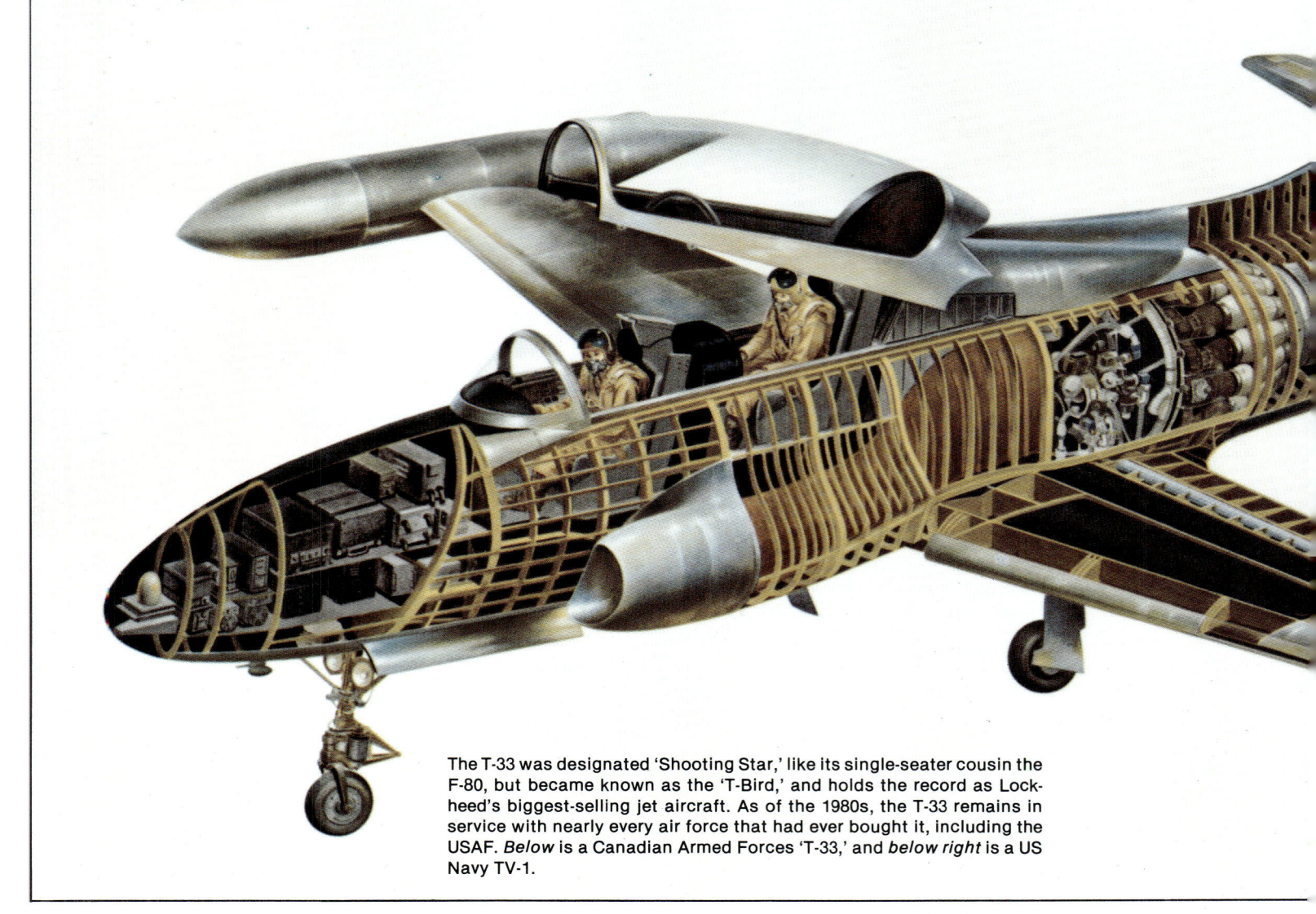

The T-33 was designated 'Shooting Star,' like its single-seater cousin the F-80, but became known as the 'T-Bird,' and holds the record as Lockheed's biggest-selling jet aircraft. As of the 1980s, the T-33 remains in service with nearly every air force that had ever bought it, including the USAF. *Below* is a Canadian Armed Forces 'T-33,' and *below right* is a US Navy TV-1.

THE T-BIRD AND SEASTAR

The Shooting Star first flew as a fighter, but it survived far longer as a trainer. When the P-80 was first introduced as a fighter, its pilots were people who learned to fly in piston-engined airplanes and then made the transition to the jets. But, 1947 there was a clear need for a jet-powered trainer. The Air Force made what was in retrospect, a wise and obvious choice in picking Lockheed to simply build a two-seat version of the Shooting Star. Based on the F-80C and originally designated TF-80C, the trainer, Lockheed Model 580, went into service under the designation T-33A. The T-33A was, like its predecessor, named Shooting Star, but that name has been universally supplanted by the unofficial nickname 'T-Bird.' Anyone who refers to a T-33 as Shooting Star around an Air Force pilot will be promptly corrected.

While Lockheed built 1732 P-80/F-80 Shooting Stars of all types, the company built 5871 T-33As alone, and these were followed by a number of other variants. The T-33 was to become Lockheed's biggest selling jet ever, second only to the P-38 Lightning in terms of the number of aircraft produced in the history of the company. The basic T-33A trainer was followed by the RT-33A, a reconnaissance aircraft with a camera in the nose and electronic equipment in the rear cockpit.

The T-33A made its first flight in March 1948 and quickly became the centerpiece of US Air Force flight training. Fifty of the new aircraft were transferred to the US Navy under the designation TO-1 (later changed to TV-1). The Navy subsequently received an additional 699 T-33As from the Air Force, which were designated TV-2. When the multi-service nomenclature system was adopted in 1962 the Navy TV-2s still in service were redesignated as T-33B.

In the meantime, the US Navy ordered a follow-on to the TV-1/TV-2. Built as Lockheed Model 245, the new plane was similar to the Model 80 trainer, but it had a redesigned tail and dorsal fin, and was equipped with an arrestor hook for aircraft carrier operations. The Model 245 entered service under the Navy designation T2V-1 and was named SeaStar. It was the first American production aircraft with a boundary layer control system and it first joined the Fleet in January 1956. There were 150 T2V-1

T-33 T-Bird (Model 580)

First Flight: 1949
Wingspan: 38 ft, 10½ in
Length: 37 ft, 8½ in
Height: 11 ft, 8 in
Engines: Allison J33-A-35 turbojet

Engine thrust (lb): 4600
Gross Weight (lb): 15,100
Empty Weight (lb): 8084
Armament: two .50 cal machine guns on some early aircraft only
Crew: 2 (trainer)
Operating Altitude (ft): 47,500
Top Speed (mph): 543
Max Range (miles): 1200

T2V-1 SeaStar (Model 245)

First Flight: 1956
Wingspan: 42 ft
Length: 38 ft
Height: 13 ft
Engines: Allison J33-A-24 or 24A turbojet

Engine thrust (lb): 6100
Gross Weight (lb): 15,500
Empty Weight (lb): 11,965
Crew: 2 (trainer)
Operating Altitude (ft): 40,000
Cruising Speed (mph): 580
Top Speed (mph): 600
Range (miles): 970

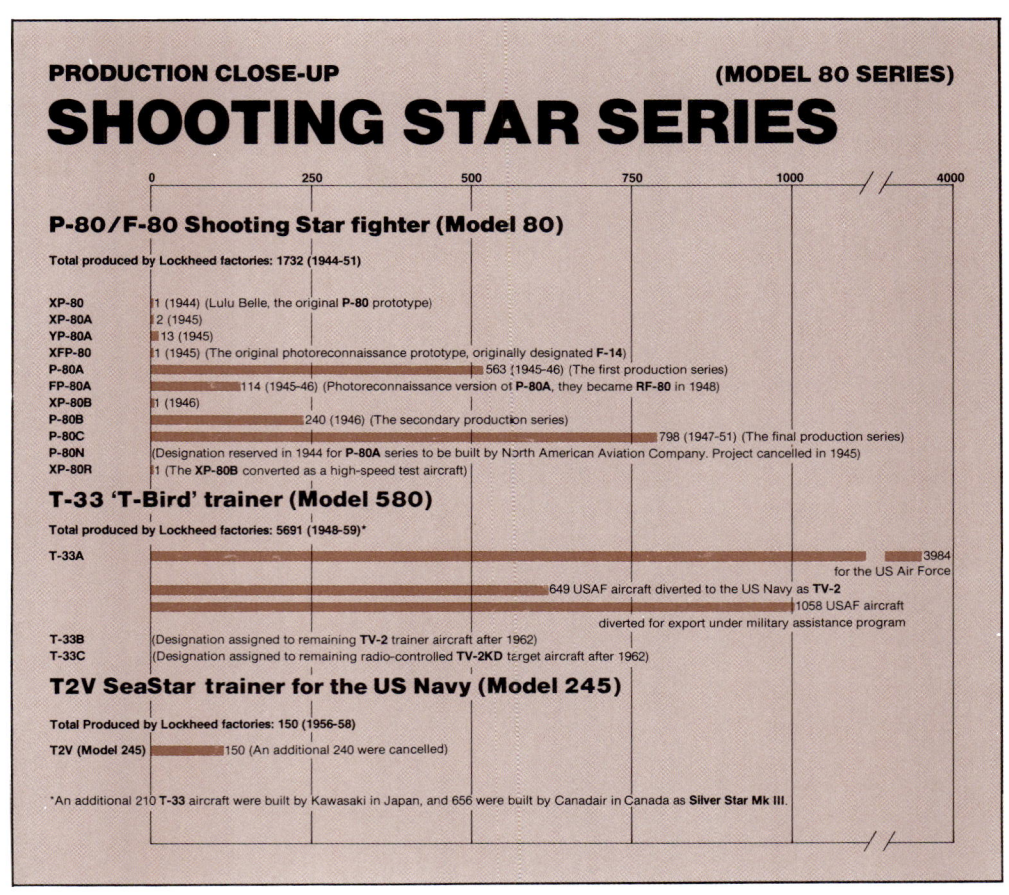

PRODUCTION CLOSE-UP
SHOOTING STAR SERIES
(MODEL 80 SERIES)

P-80/F-80 Shooting Star fighter (Model 80)
Total produced by Lockheed factories: 1732 (1944-51)

XP-80	1 (1944) (Lulu Belle, the original P-80 prototype)
XP-80A	2 (1945)
YP-80A	13 (1945)
XFP-80	1 (1945) (The original photoreconnaissance prototype, originally designated F-14)
P-80A	563 (1945-46) (The first production series)
FP-80A	114 (1945-46) (Photoreconnaissance version of P-80A, they became RF-80 in 1948)
XP-80B	1 (1946)
P-80B	240 (1946) (The secondary production series)
P-80C	798 (1947-51) (The final production series)
P-80N	(Designation reserved in 1944 for P-80A series to be built by North American Aviation Company. Project cancelled in 1945)
XP-80R	1 (The XP-80B converted as a high-speed test aircraft)

T-33 'T-Bird' trainer (Model 580)
Total produced by Lockheed factories: 5691 (1948-59)*

T-33A	3984 for the US Air Force
	649 USAF aircraft diverted to the US Navy as TV-2
	1058 USAF aircraft diverted for export under military assistance program
T-33B	(Designation assigned to remaining TV-2 trainer aircraft after 1962)
T-33C	(Designation assigned to remaining radio-controlled TV-2KD target aircraft after 1962)

T2V SeaStar trainer for the US Navy (Model 245)
Total Produced by Lockheed factories: 150 (1956-58)

T2V (Model 245)	150 (An additional 240 were cancelled)

*An additional 210 T-33 aircraft were built by Kawasaki in Japan, and 656 were built by Canadair in Canada as Silver Star Mk III.

Above left: A US Navy T2V-1 Seastar trainer cruises above the clouds; *note* the redesigned tail and rear stabilizers—a bit more 'sprightly' than the old T-33. This plane is equipped for carrier landings, touching down at 97mph.

Below: Canadian Forces pilot Captain William M Tarling (*on the left*) was given a Lockheed special recognition award—for his 6000 hours of flying time in the T-33—by Tony Levier (*on right*), the first pilot ever to fly the T-33, in 1978.

SeaStars built, although a follow-on order for 240 was canceled. In 1962 they were redesignated as T-1A.

The T-33, however, continued in production at Lockheed until 1959. In the meantime, licenses were granted to Kawasaki in Japan and Canadair in Canada for further production. Kawasaki built 210 and Canadair built 656 under the designation Silver Star Mk III (the Mk I designation had gone to 20 Lockheed-built T-33As delivered to the Canadian Air Force and the Mk II designation was the single airplane that Canadair received as a 'pattern' when it was given the production license.)

Many of the T-33As delivered to the US Air Force were later transferred to other air forces under the Military Assistance Program, or as Foreign Military Sales. The countries who received T-33As included Belgium, Bolivia, Brazil, Canada, Chile, Colombia, Cuba (pre-Castro), Denmark, Ecuador, Ethiopia, France, Greece, Guatemala, Honduras, Indonesia, Iran, Italy, Japan, Laos, Libya, Netherlands, Nicaragua, Norway, Pakistan, Philippines, Peru, Portugal, Saudi Arabia, South Korea, Spain, Taiwan, Thailand, Turkey and even Yugoslavia. The West German Luftwaffe was the biggest foreign customer for Lockheed T-33As, and also took delivery of Canadair Silver Stars.

An attack aircraft conversion of the T-33A was delivered to Brazil, Burma, Colombia, Indonesia, Mexico, Peru, South Korea, Venezuela and Uruguay. Designated AT-33A, this aircraft was seen as a low-cost alternative to more expensive attack planes based on high-priced fighters.

In 1987, as the T-33A marked its 40th birthday, it was still in service with nearly every air force that had ever used it including the original customer—the US Air Force.

THE STARFIRE

In 1948, with the F-80 and T-33 already in service, the US Air Force suddenly realized a need for an all-weather interceptor. The need was immediate. The Soviet Union had developed long-range bombers, and for the first time in history, the United States was vulnerable to air strikes from land-based heavy bombers.

The Air Force had already commissioned Northrop to begin work on the F-89 Scorpion all-weather interceptor, but it was also an *all new* aircraft and as such, it would take a long time to get it into squadron service. Lockheed, on the other hand, could bring an interim all-weather interceptor into service by basing it on the F-80 design, which was already in service and in production. On 12 October 1948 Lockheed was given the go-ahead to develop its Model 780 design under the designation F-94.

An all-weather interceptor, the F-94 Starfire would have 75 percent of its parts in common with the F-80 or the T-33. The basic shape would be the same, and the F-94 would have a two-place cockpit like the T-33 to accommodate the pilot and radar/weapons system operator. The YF-94 prototype, which made its first flight on 1 July 1949, was actually the rebuilt prototype TF-80C!

The F-94A went into production on 26 August 1949 after less than two months of YF-94 tests, and 1100 were delivered. The early F-94A, like the F-80, had a 165 gallon drop tank attached below each wingtip and, as such, it is distinguished from the later F-94As and the subsequent F-94B, which had 230 gallon fuel tanks permanently mounted on the center of the wingtips like the T-33A. The F-94B was ordered on 3 March 1950, and 356 production aircraft were delivered by January 1952.

The first Starfire entered service with the US Air Force in May 1950 with Fighter Interceptor Squadrons at McChord AFB, Washington and McGuire AFB, New Jersey. Starfires were also deployed to Fighter Interceptor Squadrons overseas. Those of the 58th FIS at Itazuke AB in Japan were the first to go into combat when they were deployed in December 1951 to provide air defense for American bases in Korea. In March 1952 the 319th FIS from McChord AFB also arrived in Korea. Because these F-94Bs were equipped with the most sophisticated radar

Opposite, below: Mechanics set the E-5 fire control system into the nose of an F-94C. This particular plane had been an F-94B which was modified with streamlined wings and heavier armament to become the prototype F-94C; *note* the 'barber-pole' nose probe. *Below left:* A row of new F-94Bs are shown being given a going over before they take to the skies, in the early 1950s.

At right: An F-94C fires high-velocity 'Mighty Mouse' rockets from its missile pods. *Opposite:* A needle-nosed F-90 with wingtip tanks. *Below right:* Lockheed's F-80, F-94 and F-90.

and fire-control systems yet used by the US Air Force, they were restricted to offensive operations over friendly territory lest their avionics fall into enemy hands. In November 1952, however, the F-94Bs were permitted to escort B-29 bombers on raids against North Korea.

On 30 January 1953 the 319th FIS, whose motto was 'We Get Ours at Night,' got its first. Captain Ben Fithian and Lt Sam Lyons shot down a Soviet-built La-9 fighter. By the the end of the Korean War in July 1953, the Starfires of the 319th FIS had shot down three enemy aircraft and damaged several more. A fourth enemy plane was destroyed in a mid-air collision that also destroyed the Starfire. The 319th FIS F-94Bs remained on alert in Korea until April 1954.

As early as 1950 Lockheed had begun to develop its Model 88C, a more sophisticated Starfire. Originally designated YF-97 in January, the aircraft was given the more appropriate F-94C designation in September. The F-94C's most important new design feature was a redesigned nose which could accommodate 24 Mighty Mouse air-to-air rockets. It also had a more powerful Pratt & Whitney J48 turbojet engine and was capable of supersonic speeds in a dive.

There were 387 F-94Cs delivered from May 1952 to May 1954, and the first ones went into service with the US Air Force Air Defense Command in March 1953. In the meantime, Lockheed had interested the US Air Force in a ground-attack Starfire to supercede the F-80 in its ground-attack role. There were 112 of these single-seat Starfires ordered in May 1951 under the designation F-94D, but they were canceled.

Built as an interim answer to the Air Force need for an all-weather interceptor, the F-94 remained in service even after the more sophisticated F-89, F-102 and F-106 came into service. By 1955, however, only three F-94 wings remained, and between 1956 and 1959 there was only one.

THE XF-90 PROJECT

Lockheed gave the US Air Force its first jet fighter in 1944 when it was still the USAAF. The company then turned the basic Model 80 concept into the F-94 interceptor that served until 1959, and developed the T-33 trainer that will probably still be in service after the year 2000.

Among its other requirements, the postwar US Air Force had identified the need for a long-range fighter capable of escorting its Strategic Air Command B-36 bombers on intercontinental missions. Eventually, aerial refueling would give nearly any fighter intercontinental range, but in the late 1940s, the call was out for long-range fighters. North American Aviation offered its F-93, which was based on its F-86 Sabre Jet, while McDonnell proposed its F-88, which later evolved into the successful F-101 Voodoo. Lockheed, meanwhile, proposed its F-90 concept. The Strategic Air Command ordered two each of the F-88, F-90 and F-93 for flight testing before contracting with McDonnell to build the F-101 series based on the F-88.

Lockheed's F-90, which first flew on 6 June 1949, could be described as being like an enlarged F-80 with a pointed needle nose, and with the wings and tail surfaces swept back. The F-90 had the same rounded tailtop as the F-80, similar engine intakes, and wingtip fuel tanks. Flight testing of the XF-90 prototypes continued until July 1950, but the Westinghouse XJ34 engines failed to develop the desired thrust, so the program was canceled.

	F-94A Starfire (Model 780)	F-94C Starfire (Model 880)
First Flight:	1949	1950
Wingspan:	38 ft, 11 in	37 ft, 4 in
Length:	40 ft, 1 in	44 ft, 6 in
Height:	12 ft, 8 in	14 ft, 11 in
Engine:	Allison J33-A-33	Pratt & Whitney J48-P-5
Engine thrust (lb):	6000	8750
Gross Weight (lb):	12,219	20,824
Crew:	2	2
Operating Altitude (ft):	49,750	51,400
Cruising Speed (mph):	443	493
Top Speed (mph):	602	
Max Range (miles):	1097	1275

XF-90

First Flight:	1949
Wingspan:	40 ft
Length:	56 ft, 2 in
Height:	15 ft, 9 in
Engines:	two Westinghouse XJ34-WE-11
Engine thrust (lb):	4000 (each)
Gross Weight (lb):	27,200
Empty Weight (lb):	18,050
Armament:	Six 20 mm guns under air intakes, external store provisions, plus 220 gallon drop tank on each wing tip
Crew or passengers:	1
Operating Altitude:	39,000
Cruising Speed (mph):	437
Top Speed (mph):	667
Max Range (miles):	2000

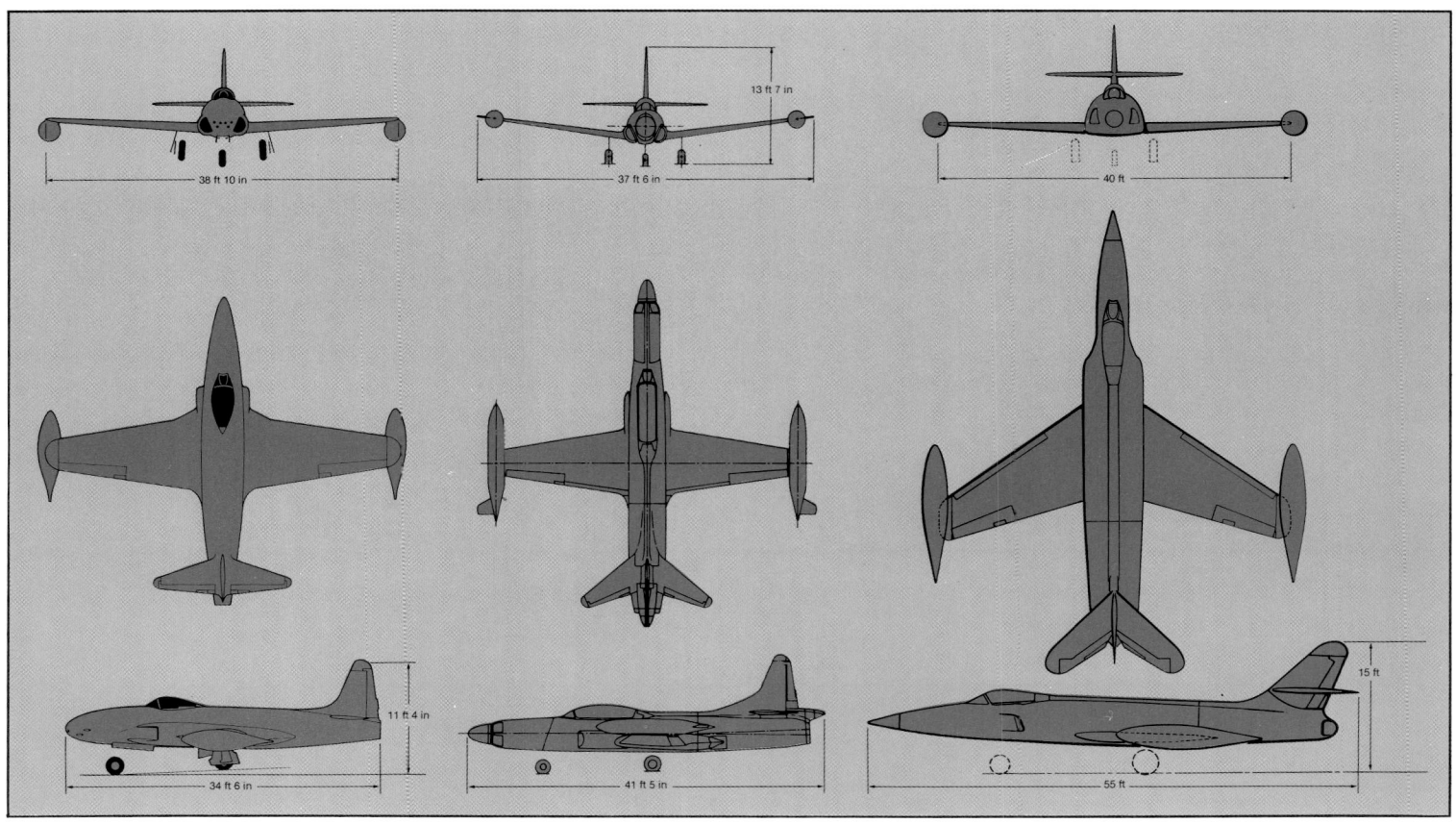

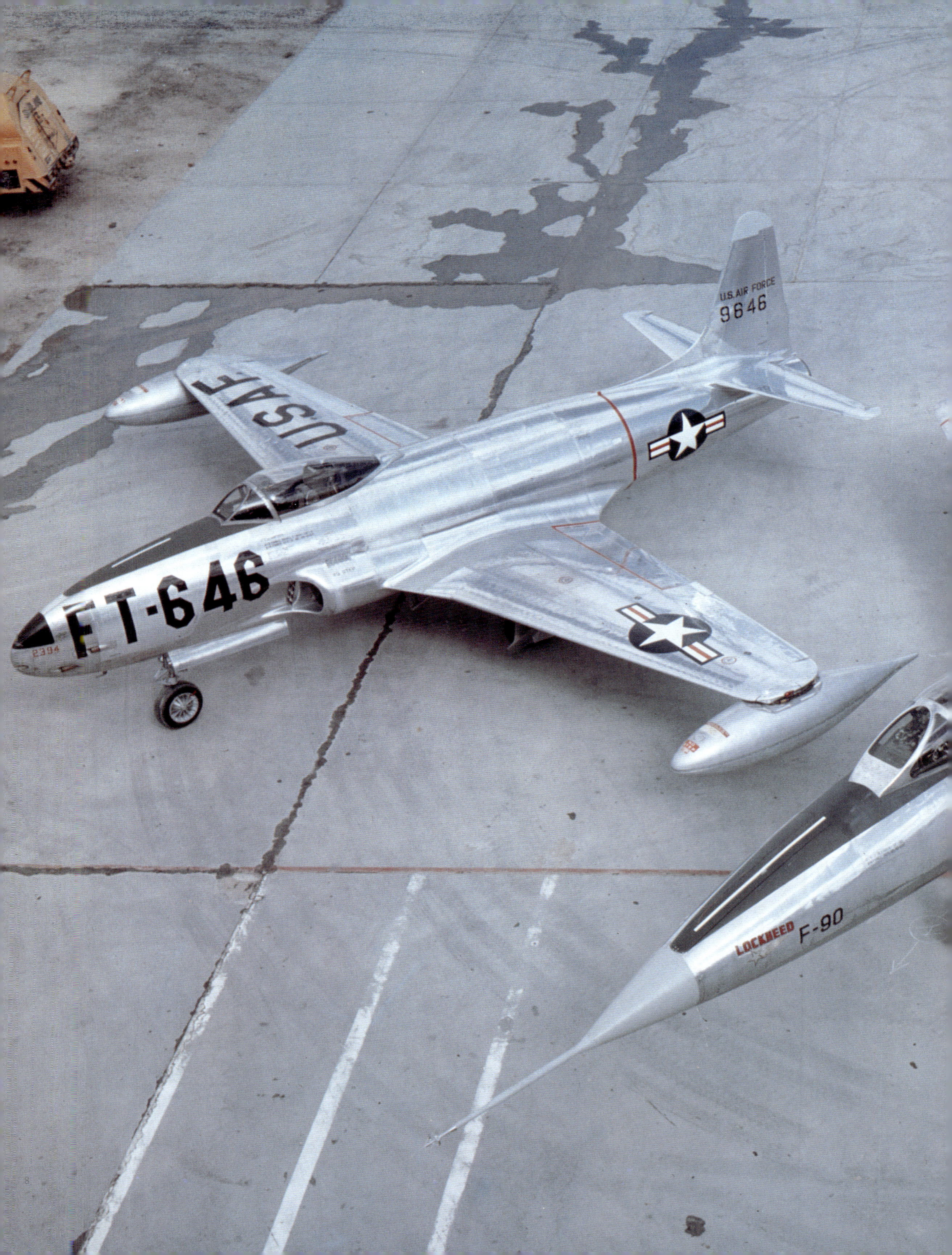
U.S. AIR FORCE
9646
USAF
FT-646
LOCKHEED
F-90

Above left to right, respectively: An F-80 and F-90 are shown *here* together in this rare vintage photo. *Note* that *this* F-90 has no wingtip fuel tanks. *Note also* the 'north' directional chalk mark *just left of* the F-90's forward wheel.

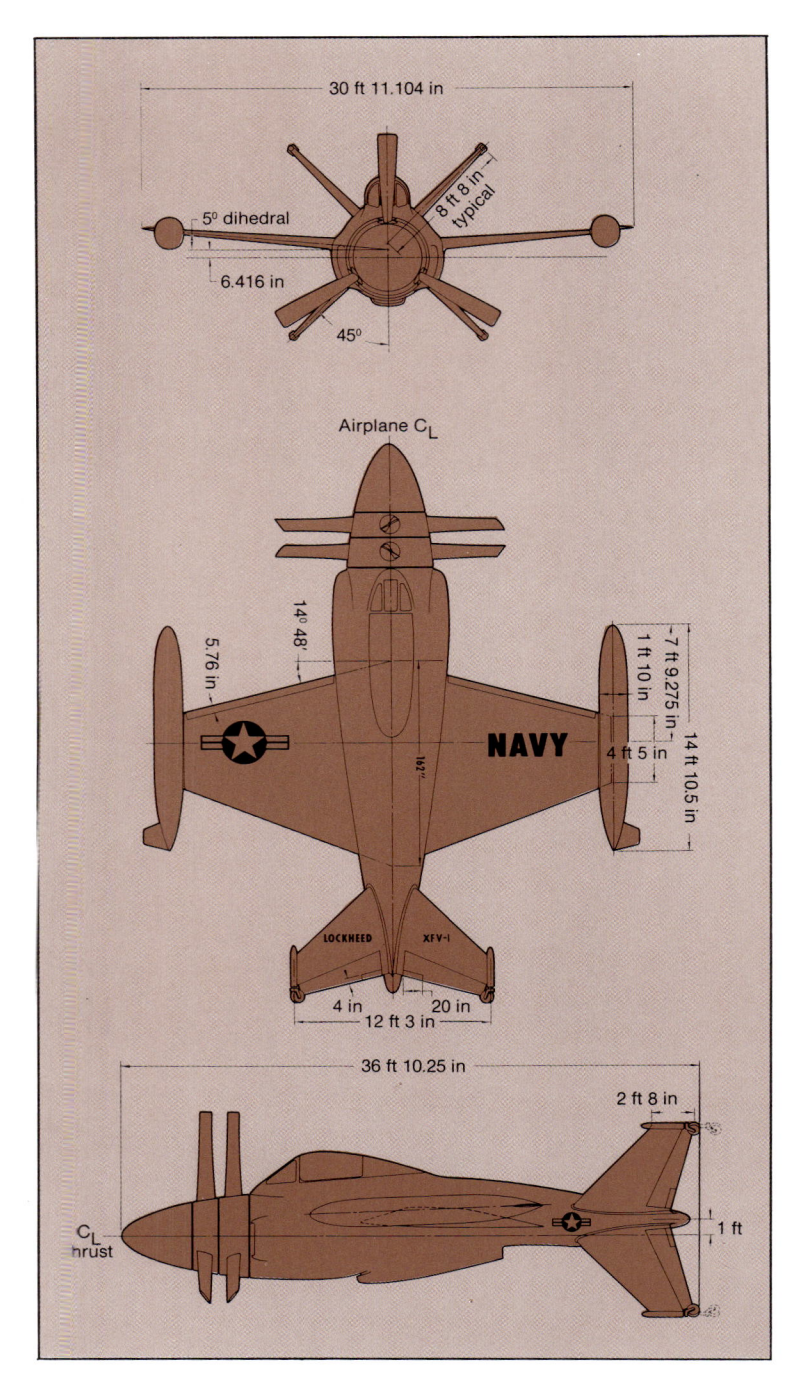

THE POGO

In the aerospace technology boom of the late 1940s and early 1950s, a proliferation of new ideas were tried and many were put into production. First there was jet propulsion itself, then swept wings and delta wings. The first jets set speed records immediately, but within a decade the notion of supersonic flight had gone from an unprovable theory to a commonplace activity.

In the same time period, and within the same feeling of technological euphoria, a number of new ideas failed. Rocket-powered aircraft were successfully tested but never proven economical enough to go into production. The same was true of ramjet engines. There was just too much fuel consumption to deliver acceptable range.

Another idea that was tried, and which failed in the original form, was vertical takeoff and landing (VTOL) aircraft. The idea of an aircraft that could take off straight up like a helicopter, then perform like a high-performance airplane, was not fully realized until the British Aerospace Harrier went into service in the 1970s, but it was not for want of trying.

The original concept (which was eventually discarded in the case of the Harrier) was fairly simple: (a) stand the airplane on its tail; (b) give it a powerful engine and large propeller; and (c) crank it up and take off *straight up*.

The idea probably originated with Heinz von Halem, an engineer with the Focke-Wulf Aircraft Company in Germany. In September 1944 von Halem proposed his Triebfluegel, a wing-

	XFV-1 Pogo
First Flight:	1954
Wingspan:	30 ft, 11 in
Length:	36 ft, 10¼ in
Height:	12 ft, 3 in (span of tail)
Engine:	Double Allison XT40-A-14 turboprop
Gross Weight (lb):	16,221
Empty Weight (lb):	11,599
Crew or passengers:	1
Operating Altitude (ft):	43,300
Cruising Speed (mph):	410
Top Speed (mph):	580

less VTOL airplane with a huge three-bladed propeller around its waist. This propeller, which had a diameter greater than the length of the airplane itself, was powered by a vectorable ramjet on the end of each blade. The Focke-Wulf Triebfluegel would need no runway and could take off from any patch of level ground. If it had been built, and had it worked, it would have been a perfect air/defense fighter because the Luftwaffe could have based it almost *anywhere*.

After World War II, the US Navy was interested in the same idea. It would be to their advantage to have a fighter aircraft that could provide fleet air defense even if no aircraft carrier were available. In March 1951 the Navy ordered prototypes from Convair and Lockheed under the designations XFY-1 and XFV-1 (originally XFO-1).

The first Lockheed XFV-1 Pogo was completed in 1953, but the huge Allison XT40-A-16 engine was not available, so the plane had to be fitted with the less powerful XT40-A-14 engine instead. Because of this, it was decided not to attempt a vertical takeoff with the Pogo, and it was fitted with a crude auxiliary landing gear for horizontal takeoffs. Taxi tests began in December 1953 and Herman 'Fish' Salmon made the first horizontal takeoff on 16 June 1954. In the course of 32 test flights, Salmon never took off vertically but he did make the transition from horizontal to vertical flight many times.

Because of the necessity to back the XFV-1 down to a vertical landing, the plane was considered impractical and even dangerous.

'We practiced landing on clouds, and we practiced looking over our shoulders,' said Kelly Johnson. 'We couldn't tell how fast we were coming down or when we would hit. We wrote the Navy: "We think it is inadvisable to *land* the airplane." They came back with one paragraph that said "we agree".'

In 1955, the XFV-1 program was canceled without the second prototype having been completed, or the XT40-A-16 having been installed on the first prototype. The Pogo's intended armament—four wingtip pods with 20mm cannons—was also never installed. The Pogo was Lockheed's only fighter project initiated by the US Navy and it was probably Lockheed's most unsuccessful postwar military airplane.

The XFV-1 Pogo (*above*) was designed to take off vertically, but was fitted with crude auxiliary landing gear (*below and below, facing page*) to accommodate a weaker-than-planned power plant. Herman 'Fish' Salmon piloted the Pogo's 32 test flights.

THE STARFIGHTER

The Korean War was raging at full tilt when the US Air Force asked Lockheed designer Kelly Johnson to tour the forward air bases in 1952. The Air Force wanted the *Skunk Works* boss to meet and talk to fighter pilots as they returned from their missions so he could find out what characteristics they wanted to see in their airplanes. The answer was simple: speed and altitude.

Upon his return to Burbank, Johnson wrote the specifications for a fighter that would fly higher and faster than anything else in service anywhere. Design work on the Lockheed Model 246 Starfighter began in November 1952, and in March 1953 the Air Force ordered two under the experimental designation XF-104. The resulting airplane, which was manufactured as Lockheed Model 83, was known informally as Kelly Johnson's 'missile with a man in it' because of its missilelike shape and short, stubby wings. In fact, the wings were so short that when Lockheed test pilot Tony LeVier first saw the Starfighter he asked, 'Where are the wings?'

Tony LeVier made the first flight in the XF-104 on 7 February 1954 at Edwards AFB. The initial XF-104 prototypes were built around the Wright XF65 engine which delivered 10,000 pounds of thrust. However, the 17 YF-104 flight test aircraft (Lockheed Model 183) had the General Electric J79 engine which delivered 17,000 pounds of thrust. On 25 March 1955 a Starfighter reached a speed of Mach 1.79, and on 27 April 1955 an XF-104 flew at twice the speed of sound for the first time.

The YF-104A service test version was first flown on 17 February 1956, and it was first flown at Mach 2 on 27 April of the same year. The F-104B—the unarmed, two-seat trainer version of the F-104A—flew for the first time on 7 February 1957.

Because of problems with the then-experimental J79 engine and structural defects in the tail, the early flight test program was marred by the loss of several planes and their pilots. After the initial problems were corrected, the Starfighter entered service with the 83d Fighter Intercept Squadron of the US Air Force Air Defense Command (ADC) at Hamilton AFB, California, on 16 January 1958. In May 1958 an F-104A flew to a record altitude of 91,249 feet and four days later another

Left: Kelly Johnson stands next to his baby—the 'manned missile' F-104, which was a Mach 2-plus jet and won the 1962 Fighter Weapons Meet as the only F-104 against 13 competitors.

Above right: The F-104s in this photo give sleek evidence of their short 7½ foot wings—only four inches thick at their deepest point. These F-104s were armed with the 20mm Vulcan electric cannon, Sidewinder heat-seeking missiles and provisions for additional armament. The F-104 set speed and altitude records in the late 1950s.

U.S. AIR FORCE
70923
FG-923
U.S. AIR FORCE
FG-927
U.S. AIR FORCE
FG-915
U.S. AIR FORCE

Above: This 1954 photo catches a Lockheed test pilot as he climbs into the XF-104. *Right:* Air Defense Command F-104 Starfighters from Hamilton Air Force Base fly over San Francisco, with the smoke from the Hills Brothers Coffee roasting plant wafting up from *below*.

F-104A flew at a record speed of 1404.9 mph. Thus, the Starfighter became the first airplane to set both records, winning the 1958 Collier Trophy for the Year's Greatest Achievement in Aviation. The *same day* that the trophy was being awarded, the Starfighter set another altitude record of 103,395.5 feet.

In 1960 ADC began to phase out its interceptor F-104As and F-104Bs, while the US Air Force Tactical Air Command (TAC) was beginning to take delivery of the F-104C fighter bomber and the complementary F-104D trainer version. In service with TAC, the F-104C made a brief appearance in Thailand in 1966 and 1967 during the Vietnam War, but its limited range and bomb load made it of little use in a war unlike the one for which it had been developed. In July 1967 F-105Cs and F-104Fs followed their predecessors—into retirement from the US Air Force, and into service with the US Air National Guard, from which they were finally retired in July 1975.

In October 1963 the US Air Force took delivery of three Starfighters equipped with tail-mounted, Rocketdyne AR-2 rocket motors which delivered 6000 pounds of thrust. Designated NF-104A (later known as F-104N), these Starfighters were to be used by the US Air Force Aerospace Research Pilots School at Edwards AFB. Until 1969 the US Air Force had its own astronaut program parallel to that of NASA, and the Aerospace Research Pilots School with its NF-104As would provide flight training. Pilots could take the Starfighters up to 100,000 feet and maneuver them into a trajectory that provided 90 seconds of weightlessness that simulated being in a space capsule. The commandant of the school was Colonel Chuck Yeager, the first man to fly faster than the speed of sound, and the students included men like Frank Borman, James McDivitt and Tom Stafford, who all went on to serve as astronauts with NASA's Apollo Lunar program.

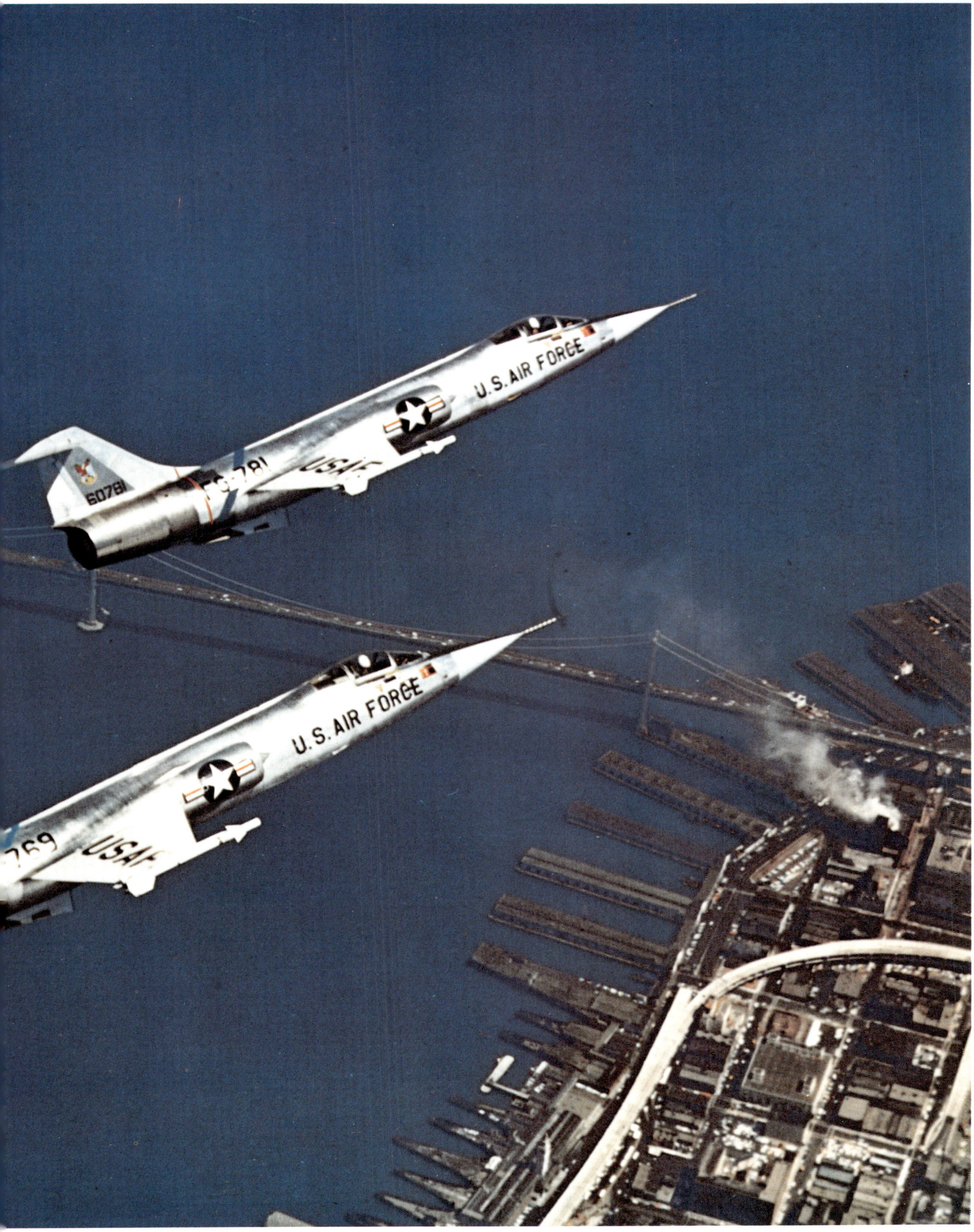
U.S. AIR FORCE
USAF
FG-781
60781
U.S. AIR FORCE
USAF
769

118

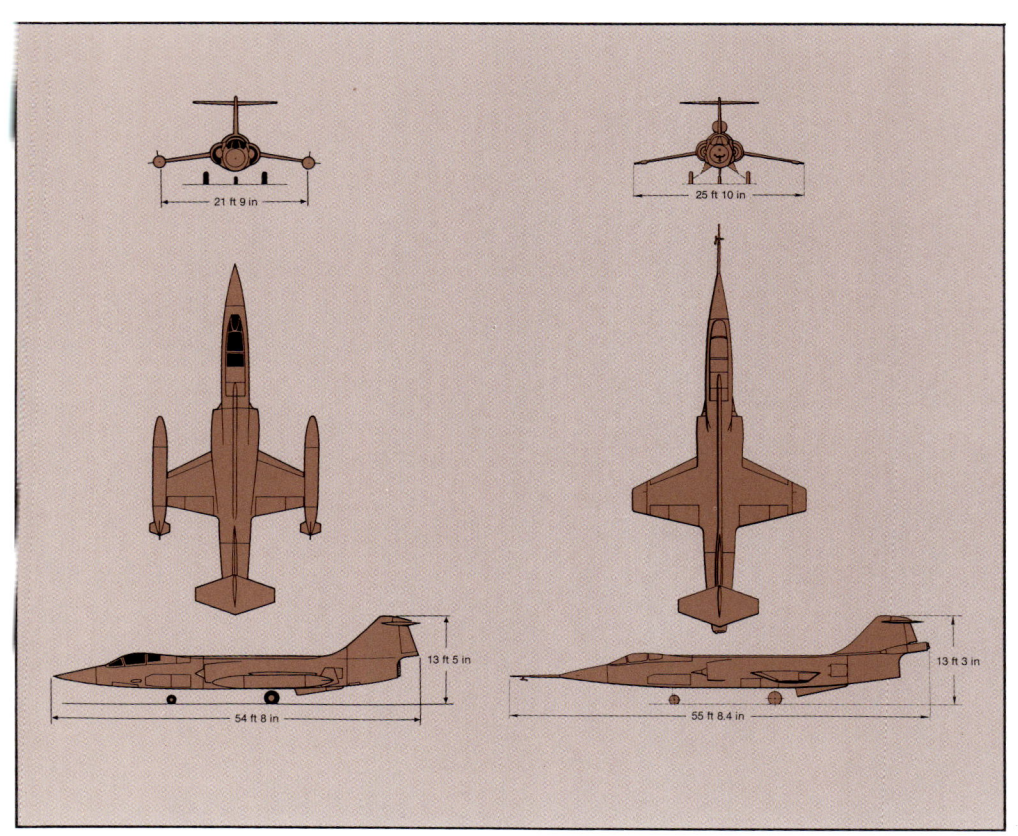

Below left: This NF-104A shows its Rocketdyne AR-2 rocket (*at base of vertical stabilizer*), which helped boost NASA trainees—to 10,000 feet and simulated weightlessness. The particular NASA training program which used this aircraft was headed by test pilot and combat ace Colonel Chuck Yeager, the first man to fly faster than the speed of sound.

Bottom left: Comparative three-dimensional views of the F-104A and the NF-104A, respectively. *Directly below:* The 'arm' projecting from the second to bottom F-104C fuselage is the aircraft's refueling arm, a feature which gave F-104s extended range as tactical aircraft.

The US Air Force manned space program had envisioned a Manned Orbital Laboratory (MOL) served by NASA-type, two-man Gemini space capsules. The program was however canceled, and the astronauts and the NF-104As were transferred to NASA.

In terms of sales, the most successful Starfighter was the F-104G, which was developed not for the US Air Force but for the export market. In the beginning, Lockheed financed the F-104G program itself with the idea that it could produce the aircraft abroad under license and, if a sufficient number were built, this could provide participating nations with a low-cost, multi-role combat aircraft. The German Defense Ministry was at the same time searching for just such an aircraft and, in October 1958, they picked the F-104G. In contracts signed in February and March 1959, West Germany ordered 66 F-104G fighters, 30 F-104F trainers (based on the F-104D), 84 TF-104G trainers (a two-seat F-104G) and arranged for 210 F-104Gs to be produced in West Germany by a consortium of German aircraft manufacturers headed by Messerschmitt—including Heinkel, Siebel, Focke-Wulf, Hamburger Flugeuglban and Westerflug. The Starfighter trainers ordered by West Germany were assigned to the Luftwaffe Combat Crew Training Wing established at Luke AFB, Arizona.

In September 1959 Canadair agreed to establish a Starfighter assembly line in Montreal and the Canadian government ordered 84 F-104Gs and 29 TF-104Gs from Lockheed. In January 1960 the Japanese government ordered 3 F-104Js and 20 two-seat F-104DJs (F-104Ds built to Japanese specifications) from Lockheed, and Mitsubishi was granted a license to build another 177 F-104Js in Japan.

In January 1960 Lockheed visited the Netherlands, which decided to join the F-104G program, and in March the Belgians also came on board. Italy joined its northern neighbors in November 1960, and in June 1961 the multination production program officially became a NATO project, with a NATO Starfighter Management Organization established at Koblenz, West Germany.

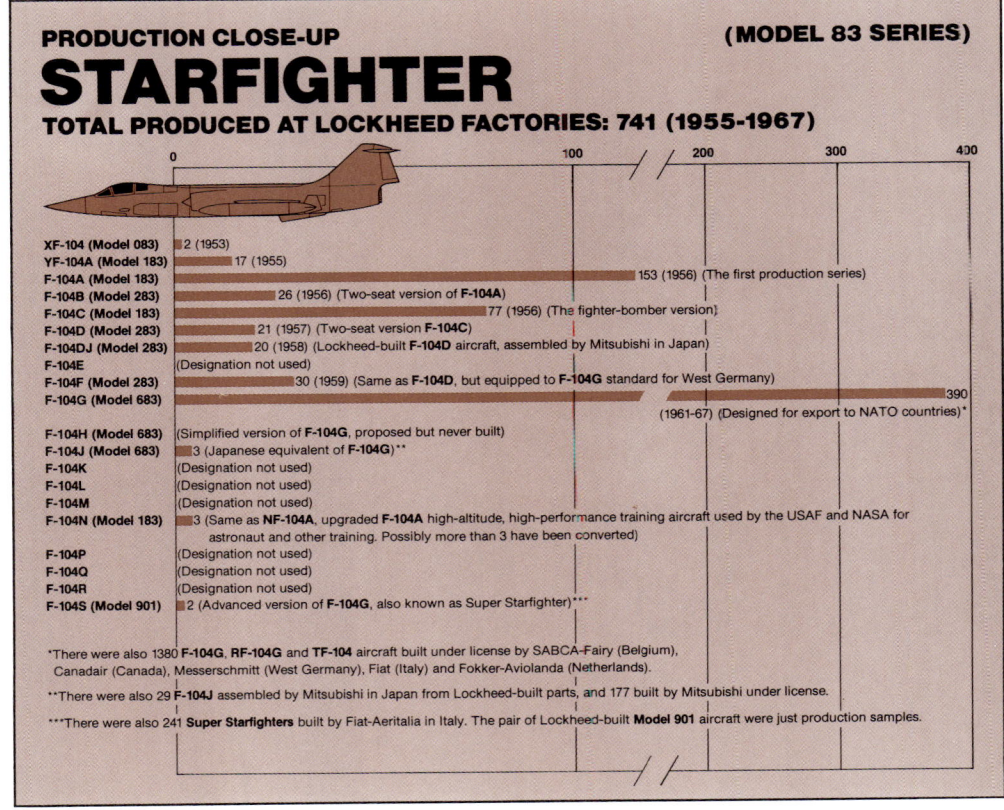

PRODUCTION CLOSE-UP (MODEL 83 SERIES)
STARFIGHTER
TOTAL PRODUCED AT LOCKHEED FACTORIES: 741 (1955-1967)

Model	Production
XF-104 (Model 083)	2 (1953)
YF-104A (Model 183)	17 (1955)
F-104A (Model 183)	153 (1956) (The first production series)
F-104B (Model 283)	26 (1956) (Two-seat version of F-104A)
F-104C (Model 183)	77 (1956) (The fighter-bomber version)
F-104D (Model 283)	21 (1957) (Two-seat version of F-104C)
F-104DJ (Model 283)	20 (1958) (Lockheed-built F-104D aircraft, assembled by Mitsubishi in Japan)
F-104E	(Designation not used)
F-104F (Model 283)	30 (1959) (Same as F-104D, but equipped to F-104G standard for West Germany)
F-104G (Model 683)	390 (1961-67) (Designed for export to NATO countries)*
F-104H (Model 683)	(Simplified version of F-104G, proposed but never built)
F-104J (Model 683)	3 (Japanese equivalent of F-104G)**
F-104K	(Designation not used)
F-104L	(Designation not used)
F-104M	(Designation not used)
F-104N (Model 183)	3 (Same as NF-104A, upgraded F-104A high-altitude, high-performance training aircraft used by the USAF and NASA for astronaut and other training. Possibly more than 3 have been converted)
F-104P	(Designation not used)
F-104Q	(Designation not used)
F-104R	(Designation not used)
F-104S (Model 901)	2 (Advanced version of F-104G, also known as Super Starfighter)***

*There were also 1380 F-104G, RF-104G and TF-104 aircraft built under license by SABCA-Fairy (Belgium), Canadair (Canada), Messerschmitt (West Germany), Fiat (Italy) and Fokker-Aviolanda (Netherlands).

**There were also 29 F-104J assembled by Mitsubishi in Japan from Lockheed-built parts, and 177 built by Mitsubishi under license.

***There were also 241 Super Starfighters built by Fiat-Aeritalia in Italy. The pair of Lockheed-built Model 901 aircraft were just production samples.

Above: A US Air Force F-104A cruises over Arizona's Painted Desert. The cutaway view *at right* shows the F-104A's elegant internal structure, featuring the pilot's compartment, and *just aft of that,* the Vulcan electric cannon, and *behind that,* the air intake duct leading to one of the aircraft's two General Electric J79-GE-3A jet engines. *At the bottom of this page,* another cutaway view explicates some of the F-104A's finer points. Now phased out of the US Armed Forces, the F-104 is still used by NASA, and by several European nations. Italy and Turkey now use the F-104S Starfighter, which is armed with the Sparrow air-to-air missile.

RADAR
FORWARD ELECTRONICS COMPARTMENT
AFT ELECTRONICS COMPARTMENT
AIR CONDITIONING PACKAGE
STABILIZER POWER CONTROL ASSEMBLY
RUDDER POWER CONTROL ASSEMBLY
AILERON POWER CONTROL ASSEMBLY
AERIAL REFUELING PROBE
PYLON TANK
TIP TANK

	F-104A Starfighter (Model 183)	**F-104C Starfighter** (Model 283)	**F-104G Starfighter** (Model 683)
First Flight:	1956	1957	1961
Wingspan:	21 ft, 11 in	21 ft, 11 in	21 ft, 11 in
Length:	54 ft, 9 in	54 ft, 9 in	54 ft, 9 in
Height:	13 ft, 6 in	13 ft, 6 in	13 ft, 6 in
Engines:	two General Electric J79-GE-3A	two General Electric J-79-GE7	two General Electric J-79-GE-11A
Engine thrust (lb):	12,782	15,800	15,800
Gross Weight (lb):	22,614	22410	29,038
Crew:	1*	1*	1
Operating Altitude (ft):	35,000	36,900	35,000
Cruising Speed (mph):	599	584	586
Max Range (miles):	1585	1727	1875

*The F-104B and F-104D were 2-place trainer versions of the F-104A and F-104C

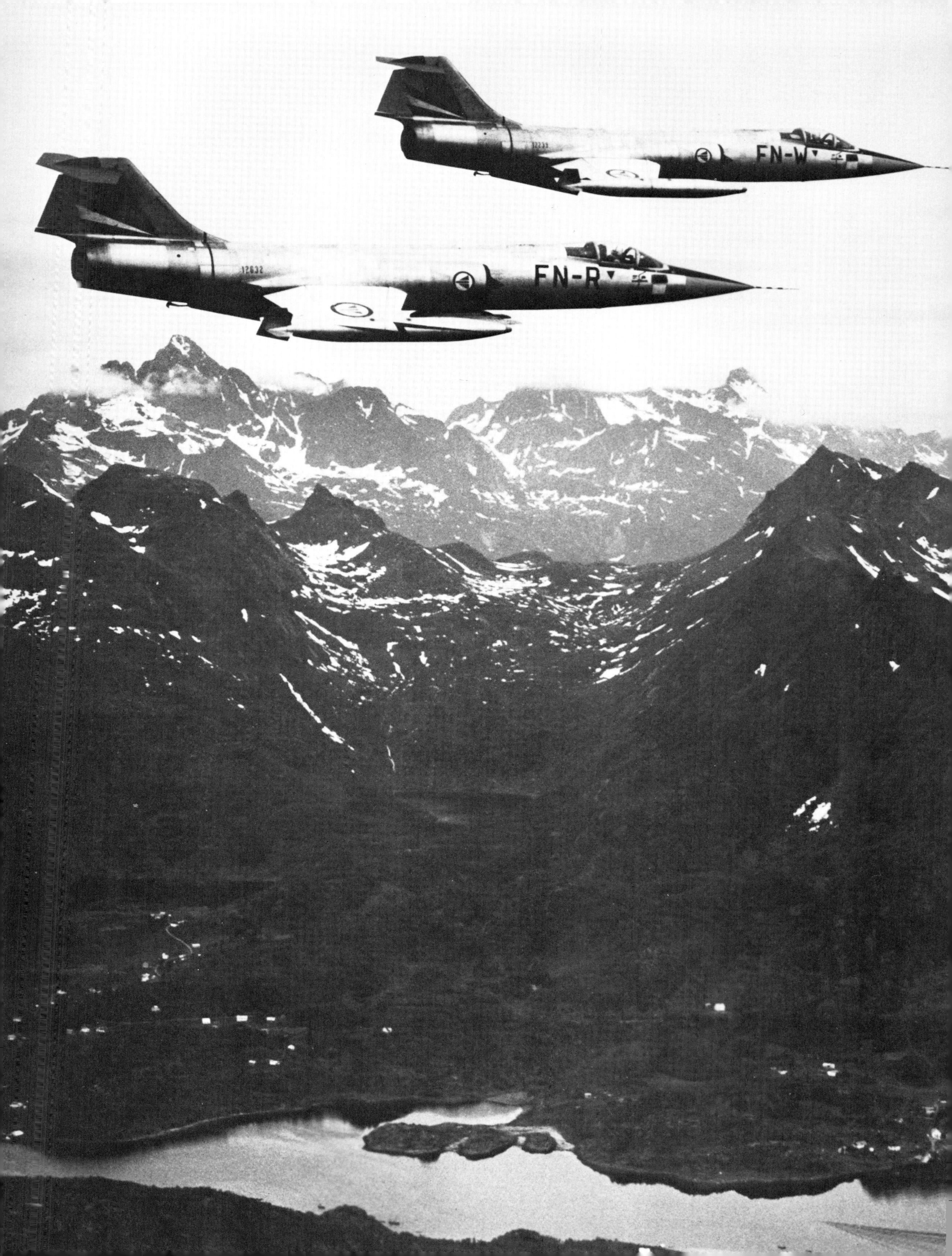
FN-W
12632
FN-R

F-104Gs have been built and distributed internationally, by agreement with Lockheed and the US government. Left: Royal Norwegian Air Force F-104Gs; and a West German Luftwaffe F-104G (above).

The first Lockheed Burbank-built F-104s were delivered in July 1962 and entered service with the Tactical Air Command in October at George AFB, California and Luke AFB, Arizona, where they were utilized in the Military Assistance Program pilot training. MAP F-104 pilot training was later consolidated at Luke AFB, where Luftwaffe pilots had been the first trainees.

On 20 February 1962 Jagd bombergeschwader (Fighter Bomber Wing) 31 was the first Luftwaffe combat unit in Germany to become operational with the F-104G. During their first year in service seven of the Starfighters crashed, and although none were lost in 1963, a further eleven crashed in 1964. This began to earn a negative reputation for the F-104G. When *thirty* were lost in 1965, the F-104G came to be perceived by the West German public as a pariah and a widowmaker. The Bundestag debated and the press investigated. The root of the problem seemed to lie in the fact that many ground crews lacked experience and pilots often had relatively few flying hours. Both of these circumstances could be traced to the fact that the entire postwar Luftwaffe was only *six years old* when the Starfighter entered service. However it should be pointed out that after six years of service with the Luftwaffe, only 8.4 percent of its F-104 fleet had crashed, compared to 14.6 percent of the Canadian and 15.3 percent of the Italian Starfighter fleets during the same time period. By the mid-1970s the Starfighter losses finally began to diminish as air and ground crew proficiency increased.

At the start of 1985 there were five fighter-bomber squadrons in the Luftwaffe, and a year later there were three. By the start of 1985 Belgium had retired its F-104 fleet in favor of the F-16, while the Netherlands had two squadrons which had been phased out by the beginning of 1986 in favor of the F-16. Canada had three fighter squadrons equipped with CF-104s at the beginning of 1985 which were scheduled for conversion to the CF-18 by 1988. Italy had two RF-104G reconnaissance squadrons at the beginning of 1985 which remained in place a year later. Japan had two interceptor squadrons at the start of 1985, which had been reduced to one a year later.

Lockheed data shows that ultimately there were 160 F-104Gs built in Germany by the consortium headed by Messerschmitt; 340 Canadair (including 140 underwritten by the United States for delivery to third countries under the Military Assistance Program); 207 F-104Js built by Mitsubishi in Japan; 350 F-104Gs built by Fokker and Aviolanda in the Netherlands; 188 F-104Gs built by SABCA and Avions Fairey in Belgium; and 199 F-104Gs built in Italy by a consortium of Fiat Aerfer, Alfa Romeo and Macchi. Deliveries of this series took place between 1960 and 1972, and were *in addition to* total deliveries of 741 *Lockheed-built* F-104s of *all* types.

Some Lockheed-built F-104As and F-104Bs were transferred abroad by the US Air Force in 1967 under the Military Assistance Program. These included 47 to Taiwan, 20 to Jordan and 14 to Pakistan. In December 1971 F-104s of the Pakistani air force became the only Starfighters ever to be used in actual combat.

Lockheed-built and Canadair-built Starfighters were also delivered to other countries under the US Military Assistance Program. These included 95 to Taiwan, 55 to Turkey, 54 to Norway, 36 to Greece, 29 to Denmark and 21 to Spain.

The final Starfighter type was the F-104S. The original F-104S prototype was built by Lockheed and first flown in December 1966. Subsequently there were 245 built by Fiat in Italy between 1968 and 1980 for use by the Italian and Turkish air forces. The F-104S was an advanced variation of the F-104G that incorporated many avionics systems that didn't exist in the early days of the Starfighter program. Most important, however, was the ability of the F-104S to carry the advanced Sparrow air-to-air missile. In fact, it is from the Sparrow's initial that the suffix in F-104S is derived. At the beginning of 1986 the Italian Air Force had seven fighter squadrons and one fighter-bomber squadron equipped with the F-104S, while the Turkish air force had two squadrons with the F-104S.

SKUNK WORKS PROJECTS

A PLACE SO SECRET

Named for the foul-smelling factory in Al Capp's *Lil' Abner* comic strip, the *Skunk Works* was born in 1943 along with the P-80 Shooting Star project. Under the direction of Kelly Johnson, Lockheed's California Advanced Development Projects (ADP) office, as the *Skunk Works* is officially known, grew into one of the most advanced aircraft design centers in the world. Since 1954 the *Skunk Works* has also been one of the most *secret* aircraft design centers in the United States, if not the world. It has operated almost autonomously, with a high level of security and with its own manufacturing facilities. From the start the *Skunk Works* has been given the maximum freedom to explore design concepts. The end result of a particular design would be given to the engineers there in the form of a goal to be attained, but they were then free to reach the finished product by any route they chose.

THE U-2 PROJECT

In the early days of the Cold War, the United States conducted surveillance flights over Soviet territory with a variety of aircraft, such as RB-36s and RB-47s. By 1953, advances in Soviet air defenses precluded such flights, causing the Air Force and the CIA to ask Lockheed to develop a new type of aircraft that would be capable of flying above the operational altitude of Soviet interceptors.

Secretly funded by the CIA with the approval of President Dwight Eisenhower, the new aircraft would be operated by the Air Force, which camouflaged the project by designating the secret new aircraft as an innocuous utility airplane. While most of the other military aircraft designated as utility types were simply government-owned light planes from Piper, Cessna and Beechcraft, the U-2 was even more exotic than the most advanced fighter project.

The specifications for the U-2 called for an aircraft with a service ceiling in excess of 70,000 feet and a range of 4000 miles. Lockheed went into the project in 1954 thinking that the F-104 might provide the basis for the new aircraft because of its high altitude capability, and the Model 282, a high altitude version of the XF-104 with a 70 foot wing span was advanced. However a very different design soon evolved. Where the F-104 was designed to fly high and *fast,* the U-2 would have to be designed to fly high and *long*. For the U-2, speed was not as important as the ability to cover great distances in stable, level flight. The U-2 was a camera platform, not a pursuit plane. Also, the U-2 could not be farther from the F-104 in appearance. While the F-104 was a sleek bird with tiny wings, the U-2 was based on a glider design and had a very large wing area: this greatly enhanced the U-2's range.

Because the U-2 project was so secret, its development took place not in Burbank, but at the Lockheed facility in the Mojave Desert at Palmdale. When the time came for flight testing, the U-2 was transported not to the Air Force test flight center at Edwards AFB, but to a secret airfield constructed on a dry lake bed at Groom Lake in the Nevada desert, cynically named 'Paradise Ranch.' Kelly Johnson was later to recall that the name Paradise Ranch was used 'because we thought it would attract people' to come to work there on the U-2 project. Johnson was to add that the misleading name was 'kind of a dirty trick since Paradise Ranch was a dry lake where quarter-inch rocks blew around every afternoon.'

Left: Kelly Johnson, the *Skunk Works'* director and aircraft designer *par excellence.* Responsible for many of Lockheed's most successful designs, Johnson is shown *here* smiling affably. The *Skunk Works* —aka the Advanced Development projects office—was born in 1943 with the P-80 project, and has produced such 'sensitive' progeny as the U-2 high altitude surveillance aircraft (*above*).

The gliderlike wing design of the U-2 proved so successful that the first flight of the new aircraft happened accidentally! On 4 August 1955 Lockheed test pilot Tony LeVier was taking the plane through routine taxi tests, but the wings provided so much lift that he was 35 feet off the ground almost before he realized what was happening. The U-2 proved so airworthy that LeVier actually had trouble getting it back on the ground from its accidental first flight.

By mid-1956 the first operational U-2s had been deployed to Europe and had made reconnaissance flights over Moscow and Leningrad. Meanwhile, the National Advisory Committee on Aeronautics (NACA, predecessor of NASA) had released preliminary data about the U-2 in a statement that further obscured the airplane's true purpose. The statement read in part that the specific research goals of the aircraft included the gathering of more precise information about air turbulence, convection clouds, wind shear and jet streams.

The U-2 successfully continued its covert activities for four years without any but the vaguest of details about it becoming public. This routine, however, came to a sudden and disastrous end on 1 May 1960. Francis Gary Powers took off at dawn from a base near Peshawar, Pakistan to conduct the second U-2 surveillance of what appeared to be the first Soviet ICBM site. The 2900 mile flight was to have taken Powers to a landing at Bodo, Norway, but west of the Russian city of Sverdlovsk a Soviet SA-2 surface-to-air missile blew off the U-2's right stabilizer, knocking it into a spin which in turn ripped the plane's wing off. Powers managed to bail out of the aircraft but was captured and put on trial as a spy. The spectacular spy trial made banner headline news throughout the world and catapulted the U-2 from obscurity to dubious notoriety as the press dubbed it 'the U-2 Spy Plane.'

Even as the term 'spy plane' became synonymous with the U-2, the routine overflights of the Soviet Union were terminated.

In May of 1960, a U-2 (*above*) piloted by Francis Gary Powers (*below*) was shot down over the USSR, an event which mightily upset both Soviet Premier Nikita Khruschev and US President Dwight D Eisenhower, shown *at left* together, during a happier time at Camp David. President Eisenhower had hoped for a summit meeting with the Soviets—a feat which would have crowned his presidential career, but Powers' capture dashed that hope. Powers himself was freed by the Soviets, and went on to become a traffic reporter, and died some years later in a helicopter crash on a Los Angeles freeway.

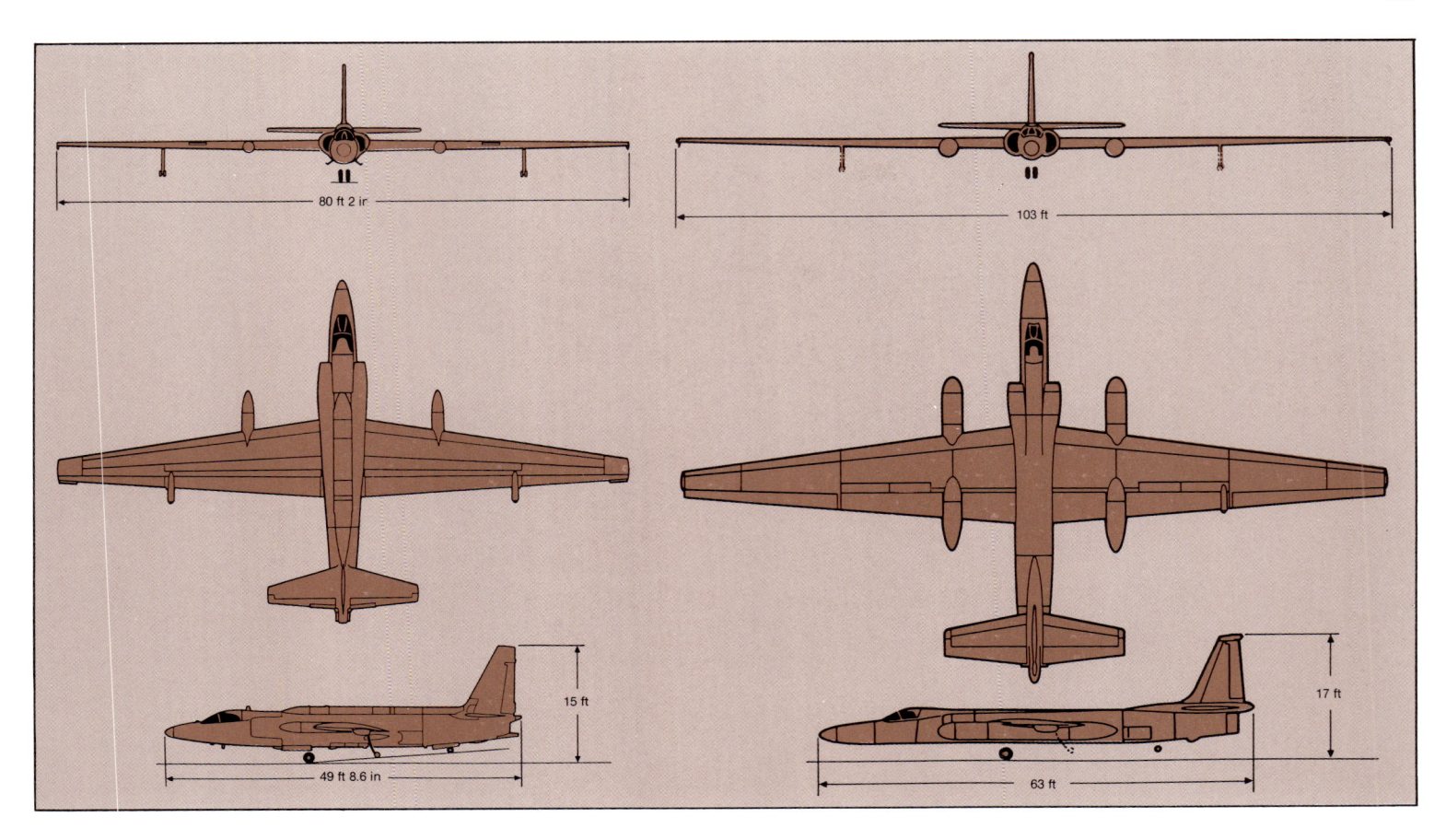

However, the planes continued to be used for high altitude reconnaissance in other parts of the world, and in October 1962 photographs taken by U-2s revealed that the Soviets were secretly putting offensive missiles in Cuba. President Kennedy demanded that the missiles be removed, and when Soviet Premier Krushchev grudgingly conceded, U-2s helped monitor the dismantling of the missile sites.

During the 1960s and 1970s, the U-2 continued in service not only with the US Air Force but with NASA as well. The NASA U-2s were used for high altitude photographic studies of earth resources and for weather research.

	U-2	TR-1
First Flight:	1954	1981
Wingspan:	80 ft	103 ft
Length:	49 ft, 7 in	63 ft
Height:		
Engine:	Pratt & Whitney J75-P-13 turbojet	Pratt & Whitney J75-P-13B turbojet
Engine thrust (lb):	17,000	17,000
Gross Weight (lb):	17,270	40,000
Crew:	1	1
Operating Altitude (ft):	80,000	90,000
Cruising Speed (mph):	528	430
Max Range (miles):	4000	4000

The aircraft *at above left* is a U-2B, which has wing pods (noticeably missing in the photo of the earlier U-2 *at far left*). The plane *at above right* is the U-2R configuration, which went into production as the comparatively slower but higher-flying TR-1. Also, *note* the TR-1's longer wings and fuselage.

The Air Force U-2s have been used not only for military reconnaissance missions but for a variety of other uses as well. These have included search flights for missing boats and downed aircraft, data gathering for geothermal energy projects, and flood and hurricane damage assessment, as well as land management and crop estimate projects for the US Department of Agriculture.

The details of the U-2 production run still remain largely secret, but the run is known to have included the original U-2A with the 11,200 pound thrust Pratt & Whitney J57 turbojet engine, and the U-2B with a 17,000 pound thrust version of the J57. In turn, some of these aircraft were rebuilt with multiple seating for training purposes under the designations U-2C, U-2D and U-2CT (tandem-cockpit) trainer. Those aircraft used for weather reconnaissance were redesignated as WU-2. Other redesignations have included U-2EPX (Electronics Patrol, Experimental), and HASPU-2 (High Altitude Sampling Program).

By 1968 there were 25 early U-2s which had been rebuilt with much larger wings, better avionics and more internal fuel capacity. These aircraft were redesignated U-2R and one of them served as the prototype for the successor to the U-2 project in 1980.

THE TR-1 PROJECT

In 1980 the US Air Force decided to reopen the U-2 production line with an all-new variant based on the U-2R, but redesignated TR-1 for 'Tactical Reconnaissance, First.' According to Kelly Johnson, Air Force General David Jones, Chairman of the Joint Chiefs of Staff, concocted the new

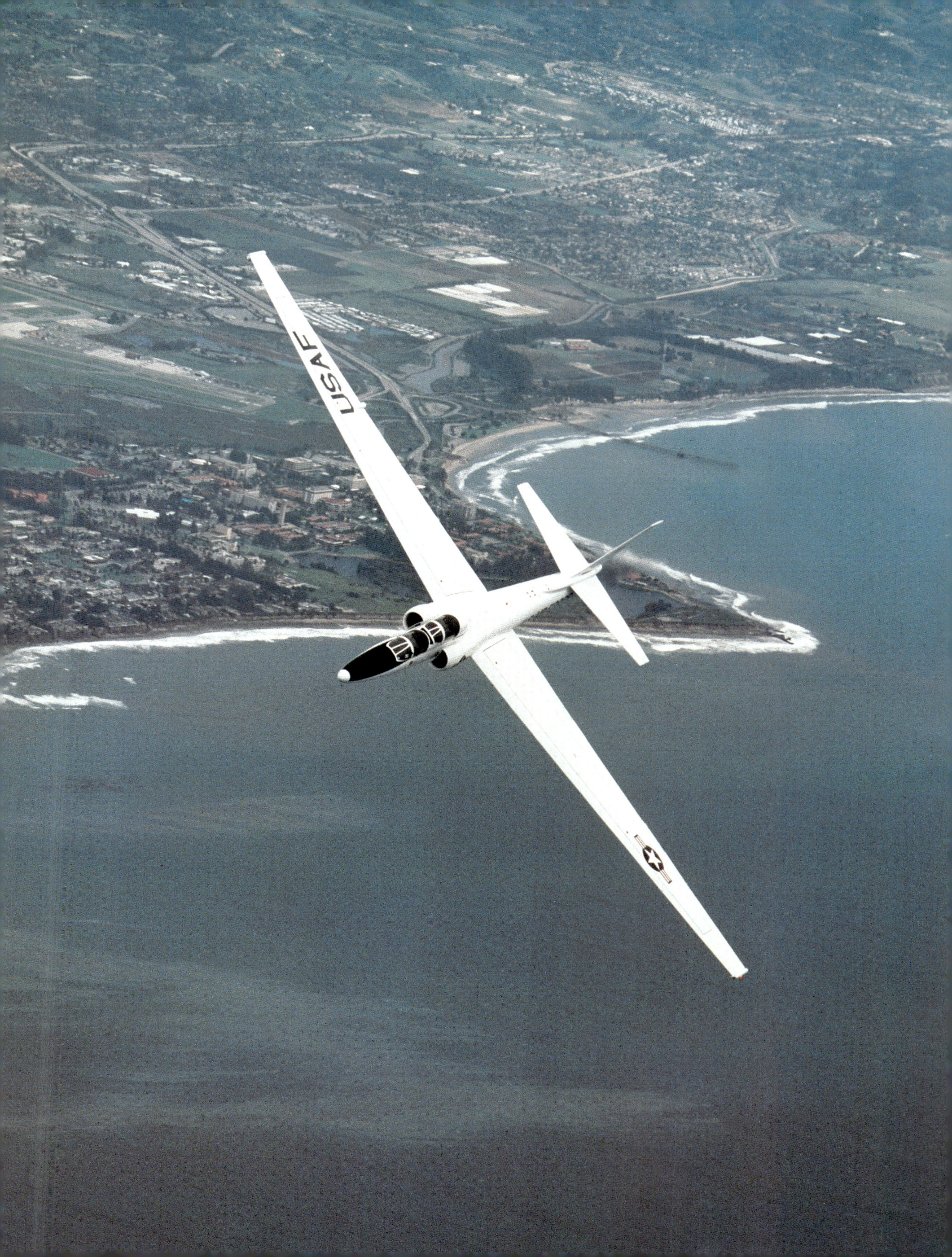
USAF

designation off the top of his head just to relieve the plane from the old 'U-2 spy plane' stigma.

The first TR-1, with its thousand square foot wing area, flew on 1 August 1981. Since then, deliveries have included not only the basic TR-1A single-seat reconnaissance version, but a pair of two-seat TR-1B trainers for the Air Force and an earth resources survey version delivered to NASA under the designation ER-2.

The NASA ER-2 is based at NASA's Ames Research Center at Moffet Field NAS, California, while the Air Force TR-1s are divided between the Strategic Air Command's Beale AFB, California and the Royal Air Force base at Alconbury, England, where they are managed by the Strategic Air Command for the US Air Forces in Europe.

The TR-1 is designed to accommodate interchangeable components for various reconnaissance missions. Not only are the 'black boxes' located in the bays within the fuselage interchangeable, but so is the TR-1's *entire nose*. In addition to the reconnaissance equipment that can be carried internally, the aircraft can carry wing pods packed with two tons of instruments and sensors. Current surveillance hardware technology gives the TR-1 the 'stand-off' capability to identify targets and threats 300 miles behind enemy lines without actually having to penetrate hostile airspace.

LIQUID HYDROGEN-POWERED AIRCRAFT

In the 1950s, as jet propulsion rapidly replaced piston engine propulsion in high-performance aircraft, engineers began to study various power systems that might theoretically replace hydrocarbon fuels for jet aircraft.

The US Navy was in the process of developing nuclear reactors which could give their submarines and surface ships virtually unlimited range. At the same time, the US Air Force and various aircraft manufacturers including Lockheed, undertook studies aimed at the development of nuclear-powered aircraft. In September 1955 a converted Convair B-36 bomber was flown with a nuclear reactor aboard, although the reactor did not power the aircraft. Beyond these tests, the course of the Air Force nuclear-powered aircraft project still remains classified.

Lockheed, among others, produced design studies for such aircraft, but solving the problem of how to shield the crew from reactor radiation would have produced an airplane too heavy to be practical.

Another potential replacement for jet propulsion that was seriously studied in the 1950s, and which remains of interest in the 1980s, is the concept of liquid hydrogen fuel. Between 1955 and 1957 the Air Force commissioned the study that led to the design of Lockheed's Model 325, a Mach 2.25 aircraft that would have been powered by a pair of Rex III liquid hydrogen engines, each delivering 4500 pounds of thrust.

The Model 325 design was later superseded by that of the Lockheed Model 400, a sleek aircraft with the overall general appearance of the F-104 Starfighter—although it was more than three times the size of the Starfighter. The Model 400 was designed to be powered by a pair of wingtip-mounted Pratt & Whitney 304 liquid hydrogen engines. In April 1956, under its

Facing page: The TR-1B is a two-seat training version of the TR-1A reconnaissance plane (*overleaf*), and both are related to the ER-2 NASA Earth resources survey plane (*top of page*). *Below:* The 1950s period of Lockheed experimentation gave birth to this design for a nuclear-powered aircraft.

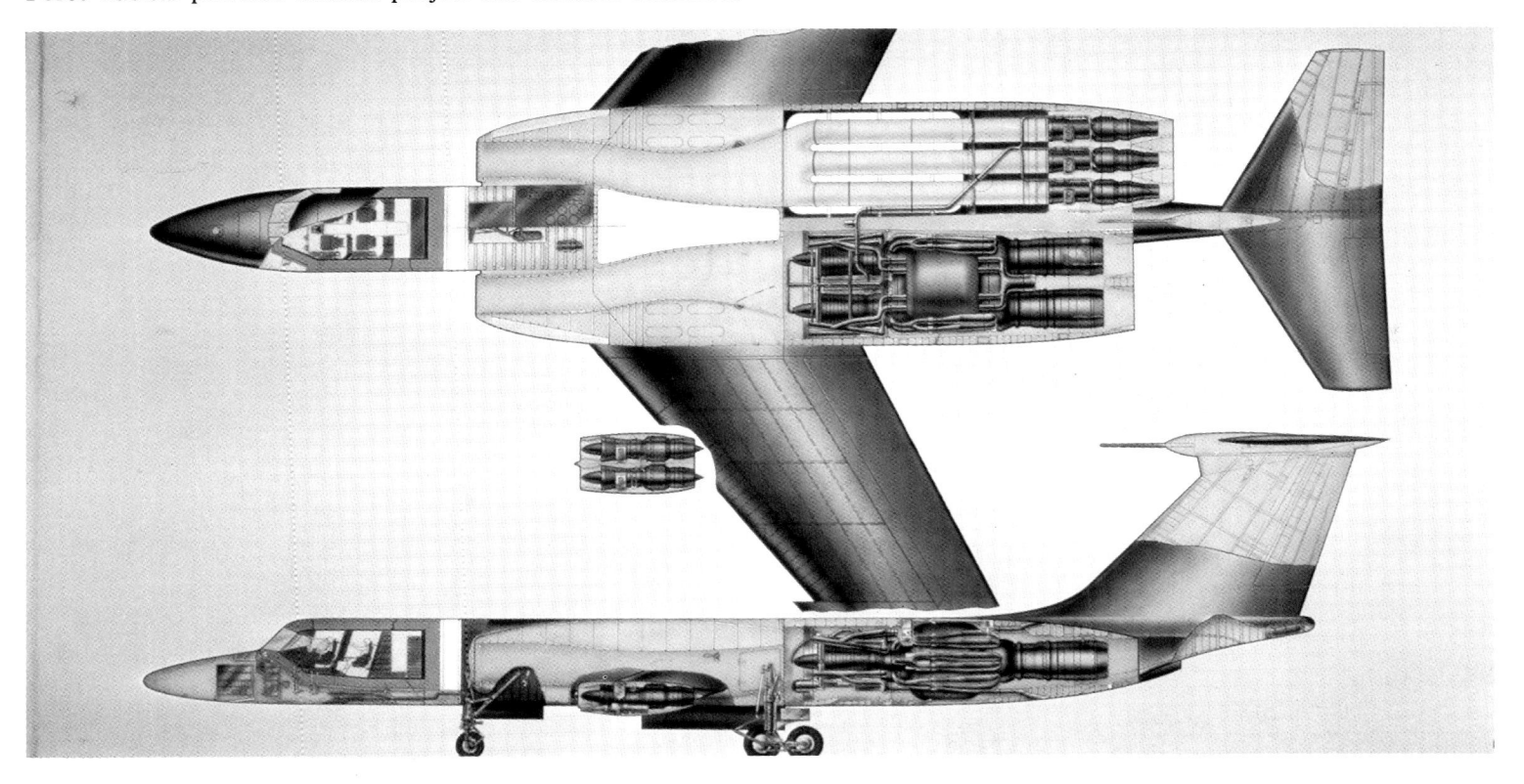

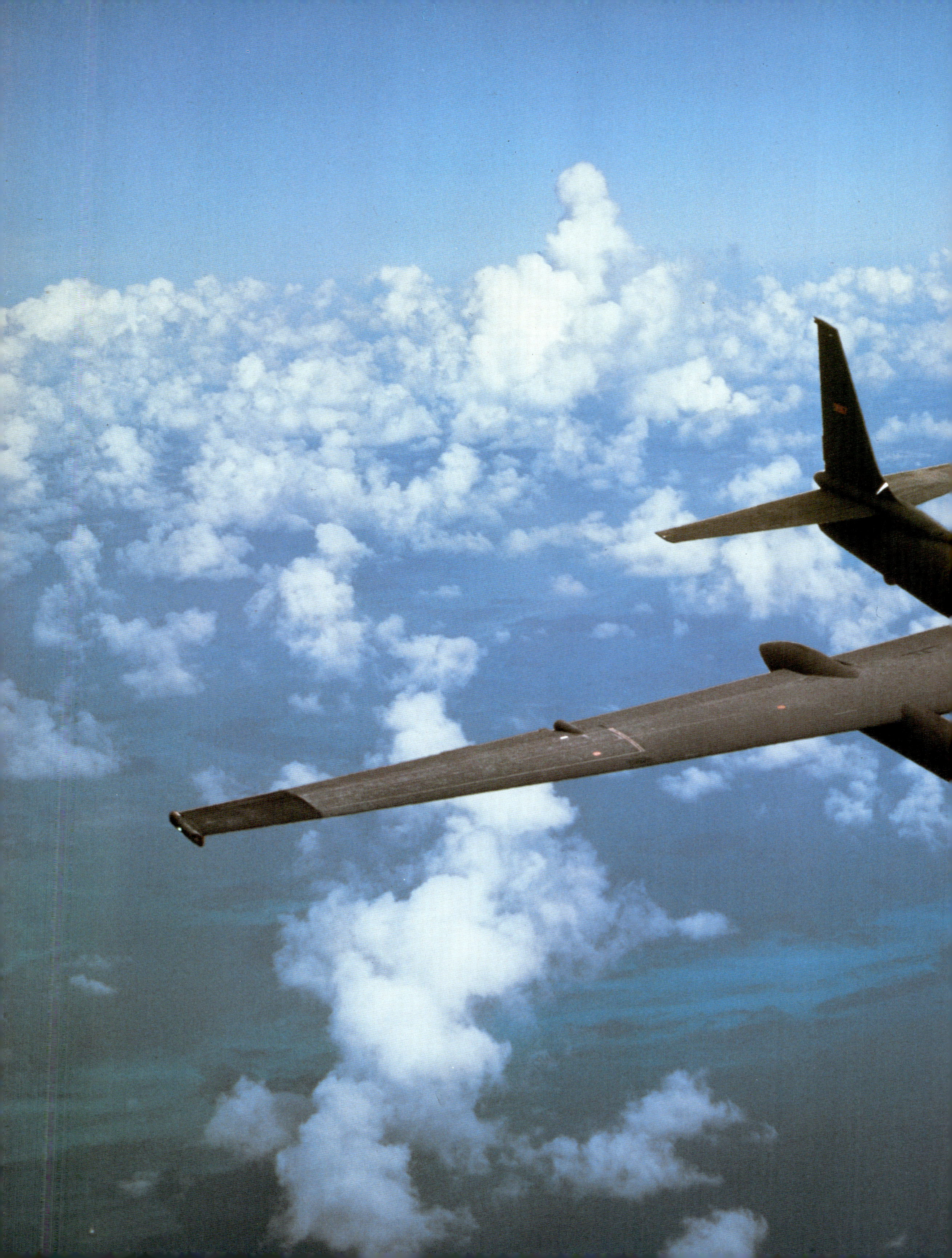

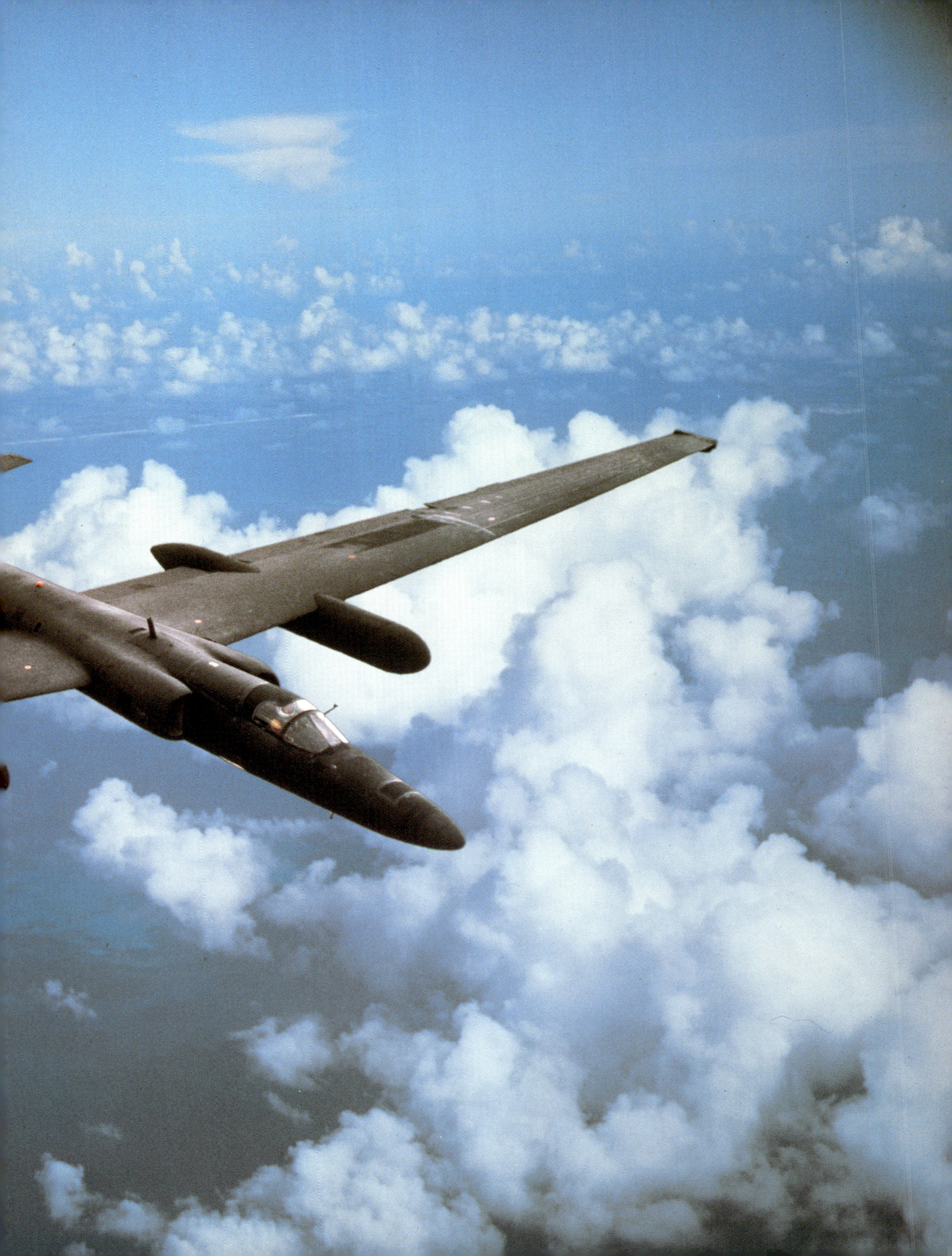

secret *Suntan* liquid hydrogen aircraft program, the US Air Force gave Lockheed an order for two prototype Model 400s, to be followed by six service test aircraft. In 1957, with prototypes already under construction at the *Skunk Works*, Kelly Johnson recommended that the program be terminated. While the Model 400 would have delivered spectacular performance in terms of speed and altitude, its range would have been severely lacking. Beyond this was the problem of the extreme volatility of the liquid hydrogen, as well as the problem of how to safely store and transport the fuel. It was estimated that the hydrogen liquefication plant that Lockheed would have built near its Palmdale factory would have consumed 10 percent as much natural gas as the city of Los Angeles by the year 1972. Also, the Air Force would have had to build an entire network of such plants and storage facilities and/or tanker aircraft just to serve the voracious appetites of the Lockheed 400s!

As liquid hydrogen continues to be discussed as a possible fuel for future aircraft, the preceeding are some of the issues which still need to be addressed.

THE A-12/YF-12 PROJECT

In 1958, in the wake of the cancellation of the *Suntan* project, the US Air Force and the CIA teamed up to solicit proposals for an ultra high-performance Mach 3+ jet-propelled aircraft. The contenders that were evaluated a year later included General Dynamics' delta-winged Kingfisher (aka as Kingfish), and a US Navy in-house design—a fantastic ramjet-powered inflatable rubber Machine that would have required a 5000 foot balloon to carry it aloft. Lockheed, for its part, submitted a series of twelve designs under the general code name *Oxcart*. Originating at the *Skunk Works*, these designs began with the Model A-1 which was submitted on 21 April 1958 and culminated with the Model A-12, which was selected on 29 August 1959 as the winning proposal. On 30 January 1960 Lockheed was given the go-ahead by Richard Bissell of the CIA to build twelve A-12s.

Even before the first A-12 flew on 26 April 1962 at Paradise Ranch, Kelly Johnson had proposed that the Air Force should also consider the A-12 as the basis for a new interceptor to replace the Mach 3-capable North American F-108 Rapier which had been canceled in September 1959 because of budget restraints. The F-108's advanced ASG-18 radar and AIM-47A missile system had already been developed and could be adapted for an interceptor version of the A-12, so the idea made sense to the Air Force. The first service test interceptor variant made its first flight on 7 August 1963 under the designation YF-12.

Powered by the all new Pratt & Whitney J58 turbo-ramjet engine, the YF-12 was the first aircraft ever built that could cruise in level flight at speeds in excess of Mach 3. Because the J58 engine was designed for *continuous* afterburner operation it provided a very high cruising speed, but it also created some intensive design problems. As a result, the J58 and even its J-7 fuel are unlike anything that has ever been developed before or since.

The A-12/YF-12 program remained a carefully guarded secret until 29 February 1964 when it was revealed by President Lyndon B Johnson, who erroneously referred to it in a press conference as the A-11. Johnson announced that 'the United States has developed an advanced experimental jet aircraft, the A-11, which has been tested in sustained flight at more than 2000 mph and at altitudes in excess of 70,000 feet. The performance of the A-11 far exceeds that of any aircraft in the world today.'

After the president made the YF-12 public, the US Air Force went on to use the aircraft to set a series of official speed and altitude records on 1 May 1965. These included an Absolute Sustained Altitude of 80,258 feet, an Absolute Closed Circuit Speed of 2070 mph and a 1000km/1000kg payload Absolute

	Model 325	Model 400
Wingspan:	79 ft, 10½ in	83 ft, 9 in
Length:	153 ft, 4 in	164 ft, 10 in
Engines:	two Rex III (liquid hydrogen)	two Rex III (liquid hydrogen)
Gross Weight (lb):	45,705	69,955
Operating Altitude (ft):	100,000	100,000
Cruising Speed (mph):	Mach 2.25	Mach 2.5

	A-12	YF-12A	SR-71 Blackbird
First Flight:	1962	1963	1965
Wingspan:	55 ft, 7 in	55 ft, 7 in	55 ft, 7 in
Length:	102 ft	101 ft, 8 in	107 ft, 5 in
Height:	18 ft, 3 in	18 ft, 3 in	18 ft, 6 in
Engines:	two Pratt & Whitney J58 turbo ramjets	two Pratt & Whitney J58 turbo ramjets	two Pratt & Whitney J58 turbo ramjets
Engine thrust (lb):	32,500	32,500	32,500
Gross Weight (lb):	140,000	136,000	172,000
Empty Weight (lb):	38,000	60,000	60,000
Armament:	none	AIM 47A (formerly GAR-9)	none
Crew:	2	2	2
Operating Altitude (ft):	95,000+	85,000+	100,000+
Cruising Speed (mph):	Mach 2.5+	Mach 2.5+	Mach 2.5+
Top Speed (mph):	Mach 3.5+	Mach 3.5+	Mach 3.5+
Max Range (miles):	2500	2500	3250

Speed of 1688.9 mph. The CIA-owned A-12s, which were lighter and hence capable of higher performance than the YF-12, were never entered for any *official* speed records out of security considerations.

In conjunction with the A-12, the *Skunk Works* developed an equally top-secret remotely piloted D-21 reconnaissance drone, which could be launched from the back of an A-12. These drones, of which 38 were built, were 43 feet 2 inches long with a wingspan of 10 feet. They were powered by single Marquardt RJ43 ramjet engines capable of speeds above Mach 4. The expendable D-21s were designed to eject their film cartridges after a mission, whereupon they would be destroyed by an internal explosive charge. The details and operational record of the D-21 program still remain a secret, even though it was apparently terminated in the mid-sixties without having been particularly successful. While most of the D-21s were test flown from B-52s, some were actually flown from A-12s. One of two A-12s converted as a D-21 carrier was lost on 30 July 1966 as a result of a D-21 malfunction.

The YF-12 never made it beyond the service test stage of its career. Its performance was exceptional—it was the world's first and only Mach 3+ interceptor—but it was deemed to be an expensive luxury when no threat of Mach 3 bombers evolved in the Soviet Union or elsewhere. On 27 November 1967 the YF-12 program was terminated.

Ironically, even as the US Air Force canceled the YF-12 interceptor because there was no bomber threat fast enough to make it necessary, the Soviet Union was moving forward with the technology that resulted in the Tupolev Tu-22M (Tu-26) bomber. This bomber, which is NATO codenamed Backfire, became operational in the 1980s—long after the YF-12 had been aban-

NASA's Dryden Research Center YF-12s (*above*) in flight. The tube suspended under the *upper* craft tests the effects of rapid heat buildup at speeds in excess of 2000 mph. *Below:* A USAF Air Defense Command YF-12A. *Overleaf:* YF-12s and SR-71s under construction in the supersecret *Skunk Works* Palmdale facility.

IT'S SERIOUS
WATCH OUT FOR
F.O.D.

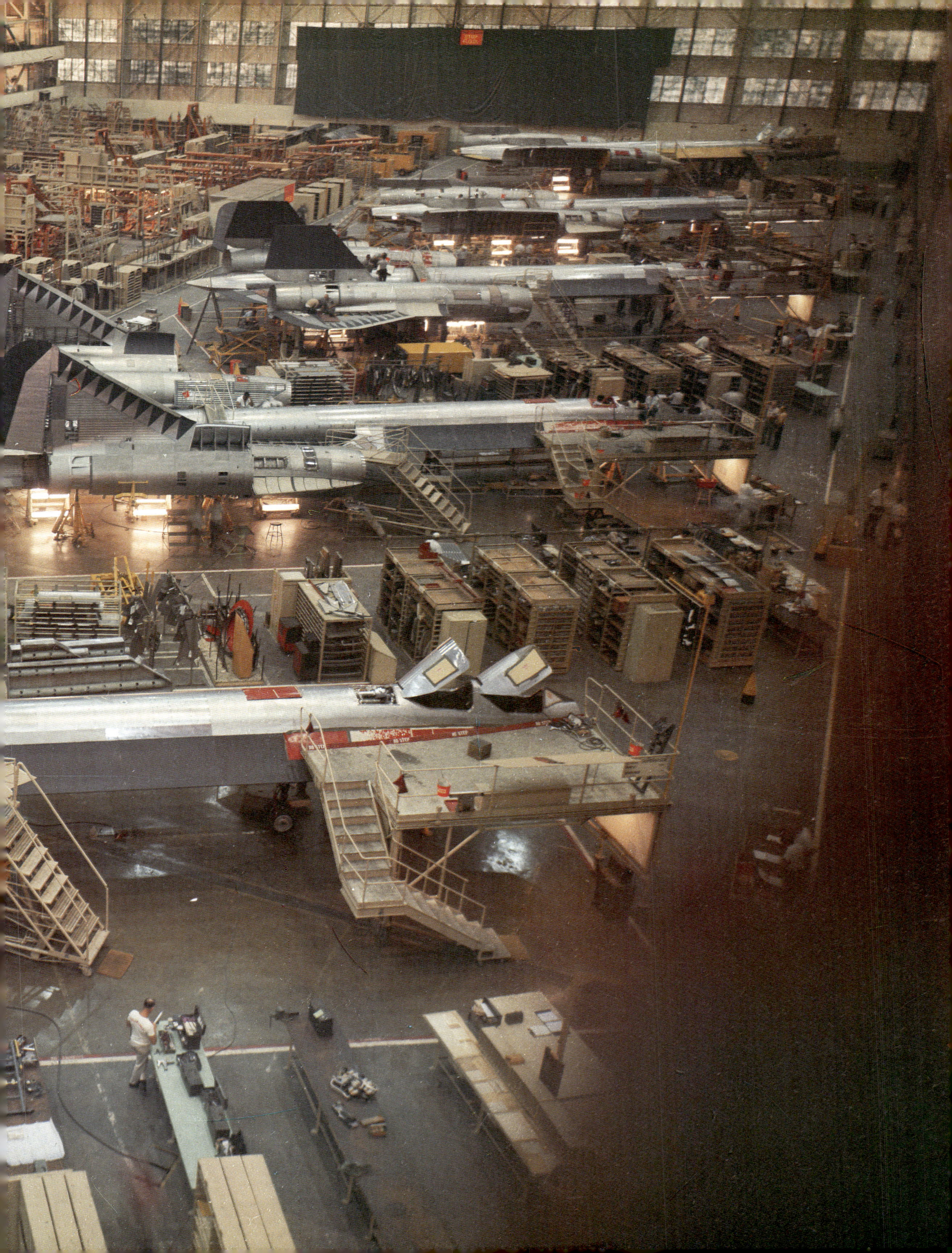

dored in favor of the slower but newer F-14, F-15 and F-16. Capable of cruising speeds greater than Mach 2, the Backfire can cruise faster than any interceptor in the world except the YF-12.

The last A-12 flight took place six months later in June 1968. Nine of the known surviving A-12/YF-12 aircraft were placed in storage at Lockheed's Palmdale facility, and one YF-12a was flown to the US Air Force Museum at Wright Patterson AFB, Ohio.

THE BLACKBIRD

At the same time that the *Skunk Works* were developing the Mach 3 technology that would lead to the A-12 and YF-12, North American Aviation (now Rockwell International) was developing its own Mach 3 stable, which included the F-108 Rapier interceptor and the B-70 Valkyrie strategic bomber. However, both of these planes fell victim to the congressional budget-cutting axe. The F-108 project, canceled in 1959 before a prototype could be built, created the void that led to the adaptation of the A-12 as the YF-12 interceptor. The huge stainless steel B-70, originally intended as a replacement for the Strategic Air Command's B-52s, was built but it was clear long before the completion of the prototypes in 1964 and 1965 that it, too, would never see service as a bomber.

Even as the B-70 was downgraded to the role of a Mach 3 research vehicle, the US Air Force Strategic Air Command considered the development of a long range 'Reconnaissance Strike' version under the designation RS-70. This idea was also rejected by Congress, but in January 1961 Kelly Johnson had already suggested that the Air Force consider a 'reconnaissance strike' version of the A-12. The Strategic Air Command carefully considered the Lockheed proposal, and in December 1962 the US Air Force gave the company a contract for six reconnaissance strike aircraft which would be delivered under the designation RS-71.

On 24 July 1964, even before the new plane made its first flight, President Lyndon Johnson announced that it was under development. However, he referred to it as the SR-71 rather than as the RS-71, catching both SAC and the *Skunk Works* off guard. The designation was revised to accommodate the SR christening, and RS for 'Reconnaissance Strike' officially became SR for 'Strategic Reconnaissance.'

On 23 December 1964 the SR-71 prototype made its first flight. On 7 January 1966 the first SR-71A went into service with SAC's 4200th Strategic Reconnaissance Wing (Ninth SRW after June 1966) at Beale AFB, California. Like some of the A-12/YF-12 series, the SR-71 prototype and all the succeeding SR-71s were painted entirely in a specially developed heat-and radar-reflective indigo blue paint. This paint, which appears flat black when the aircraft is not exposed to the heat and friction of the Mach 3 environment, quickly earned it the now-official nickname 'Blackbird.'

During the next six years, SR-71s were deployed to Kadena AB on Okinawa, where they were used for numerous reconnaissance missions over North Vietnam. Because of their Mach 3+ capability, the Blackbirds were able to avoid interception by North Vietnamese fighters or surface-to-air missiles.

After the Vietnam War, SR-71s became somewhat more public as they demonstrated their incredible speed and range. On 26 April 1971 an SR-71 flew 15,000 miles in 10½ hours, earning Major Thomas Estes and Major Dewain Vick the 1971 McKay and 1972 Harmon International Trophies. In September 1974 a Blackbird flown by Major James Sullivan and Major Noel Widdlefield made an appearance at the Farnborough International Air Show, having flown from New York to London in just *one* hour and 56 minutes.

In October 1967, a Soviet Mikoyan E-266—the prototype of the MiG-25 fighter—had beaten the World Absolute Speed and Altitude records established in 1965 by the YF-12, so in July 1976 SAC set out to recapture the records with their SR-71s. Major Larry Elliot and Captain Robert Heit flew at 85,069 feet in horizontal level flight; Major John Fuller and Major Adolphus Bledsoe flew 2092.3 mph over a 1000 km closed circuit; while Major George Morgan and Captain Eldon Joerz attained a straight line speed of 2193.2 mph, while operating at less than full power.

While the actual top speed of the SR-71 is classified, it is sufficiently higher than 2193.2 mph to keep it the fastest airplane in the world for the foreseeable future. As this writer was told in a briefing at SAC's Ninth SRW—operator of the Air Force Blackbird fleet—should any of the Absolute Records ever be lost, 'We'd just take up one of our birds and step down a little harder on the accelerator.'

An outgrowth of the A-12 and YF-12 programs, the SR-71 is clearly the most advanced of the three. This is partly due to its being the third stage in the series and partly to the fact that SAC is an extremely demanding customer.

At right: An airborne stiletto, SR-71 Blackbird is so fast that *many of those who fly it* have not experienced its top speed. *Overleaf:* Washed in an otherworldly suffusion of light, a black birdlike, yet otherworldly creature approaches the camera—is this thing in the hangar at Beale AFB really a plane, or... something else?

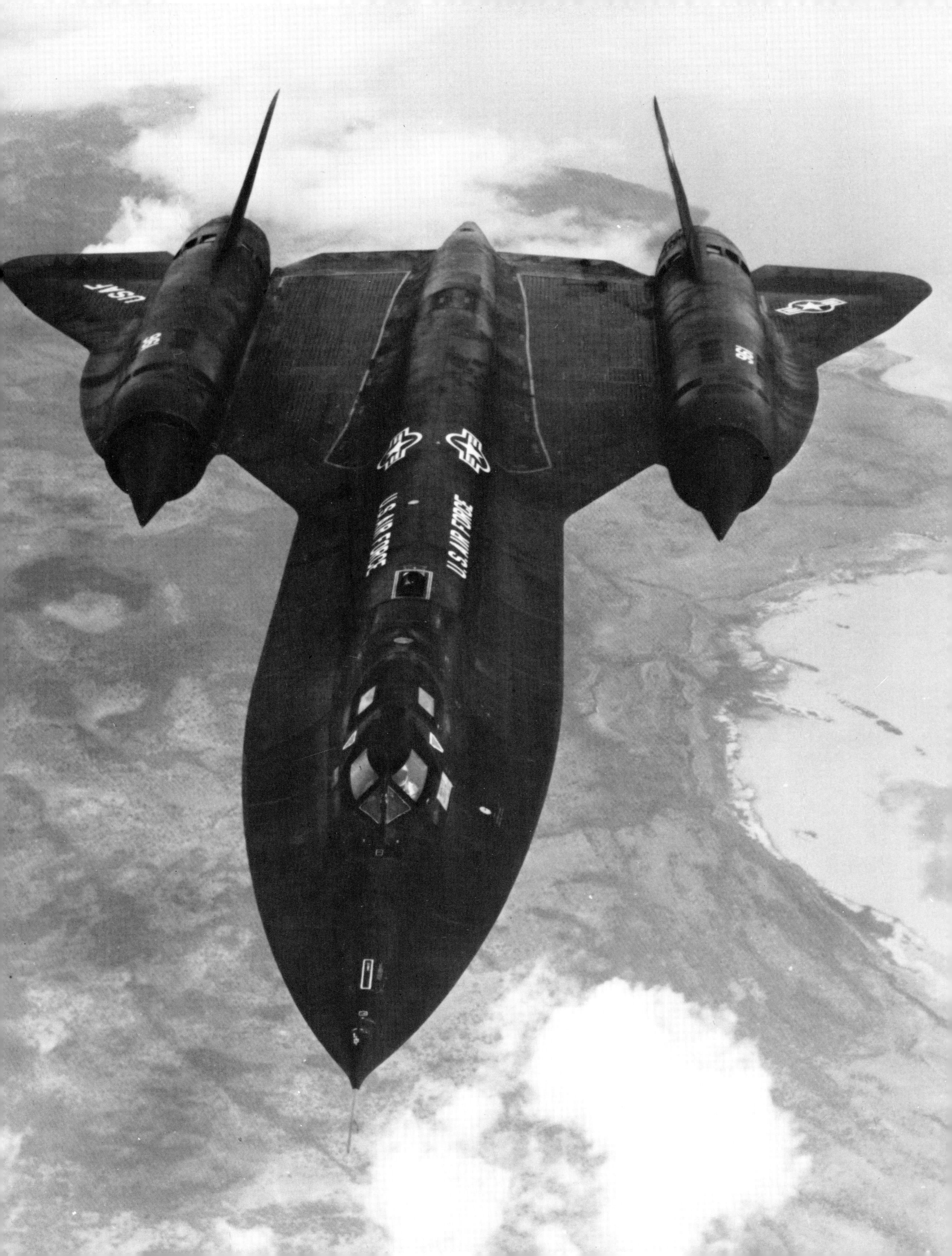
USAF
U.S. AIR FORCE
U.S. AIR FORCE

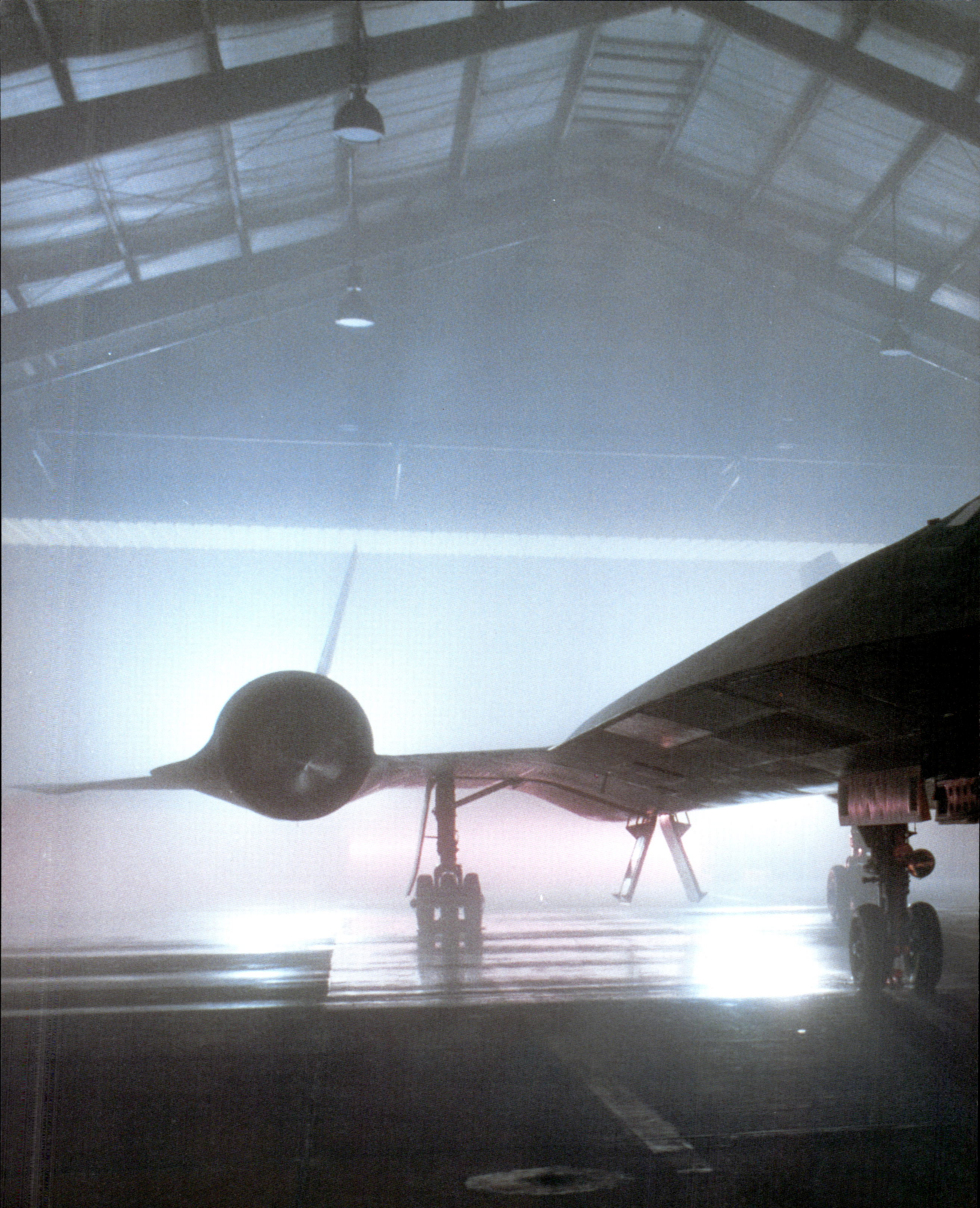

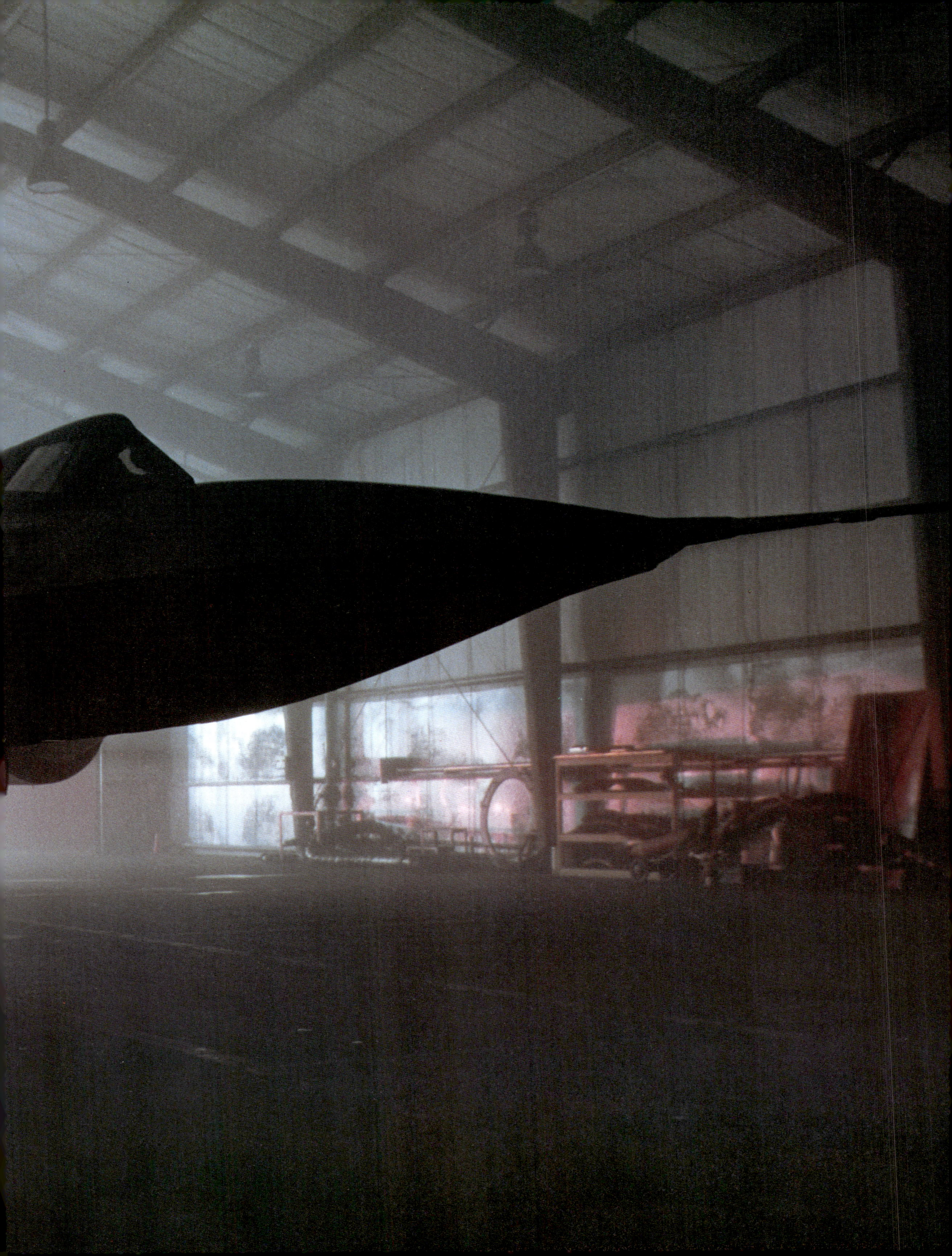

Like the early planes in its lineage, the SR-71 is constructed almost entirely of Beta B-120, a specially developed titanium alloy which is as strong as stainless steel at half the weight. Like its predecessors, the SR-71 is powered by a pair of Pratt & Whitney J58 turbo-ramjet engines capable of continuous operation at speeds above Mach 3.

Because of the high temperatures in the Mach 3 environment, special lubricants had to be developed. Rubber gaskets (O-rings) could not be used, so steel gaskets were developed for the fuel system. When the Blackbird is in flight at high speed, the heat causes the steel gaskets to expand and seal perfectly—but when the plane is on the ground the fuel tanks are perceived to leak. There is little cause for alarm, however, because the JP-7 fuel (ordinary jet engines are powered by JP-4 fuel) has an extremely high ignition temperature. The JP-7, in fact, has such low volatility that the engines have to be started with a chemical ignition system using tetraethyl borane.

The SR-71's surveillance systems include a wide variety of optical cameras, as well as infrared and laser sensors. These are contained in bays located on the underside of the fuselage and are among the most secret aspects of one of the most secret aircraft in the US Air Force arsenal.

The SR-71 production run consisted entirely of the basic SR-71A reconnaissance version, but two of these were retrofitted as trainers—with a tandem two-seat cockpit and a raised second cockpit. These two aircraft were then redesignated SR-71B. A third pilot trainer designated SR-71C, was created from an existing YF-12, with its forward section reportedly taken from an A-11 or A-12 engineering mock-up.

All of the SR-71s in the US Air Force are still assigned only to SAC's Ninth SRW at Beale AFB, which evolved out of the 4200th SRW in June 1966. The Ninth SRW contains two Strategic Reconnaissance Squadrons, the First and 99th, but since 1976 the 99th SRS has operated only U-2s and TR-1s, leaving the First SRS as the only Blackbird Squadron in the US Air Force. Supported by KG135Q refueling aircraft carrying JP-7 fuel, the Ninth SRW/First SRS Blackbirds are continuously on deploy-

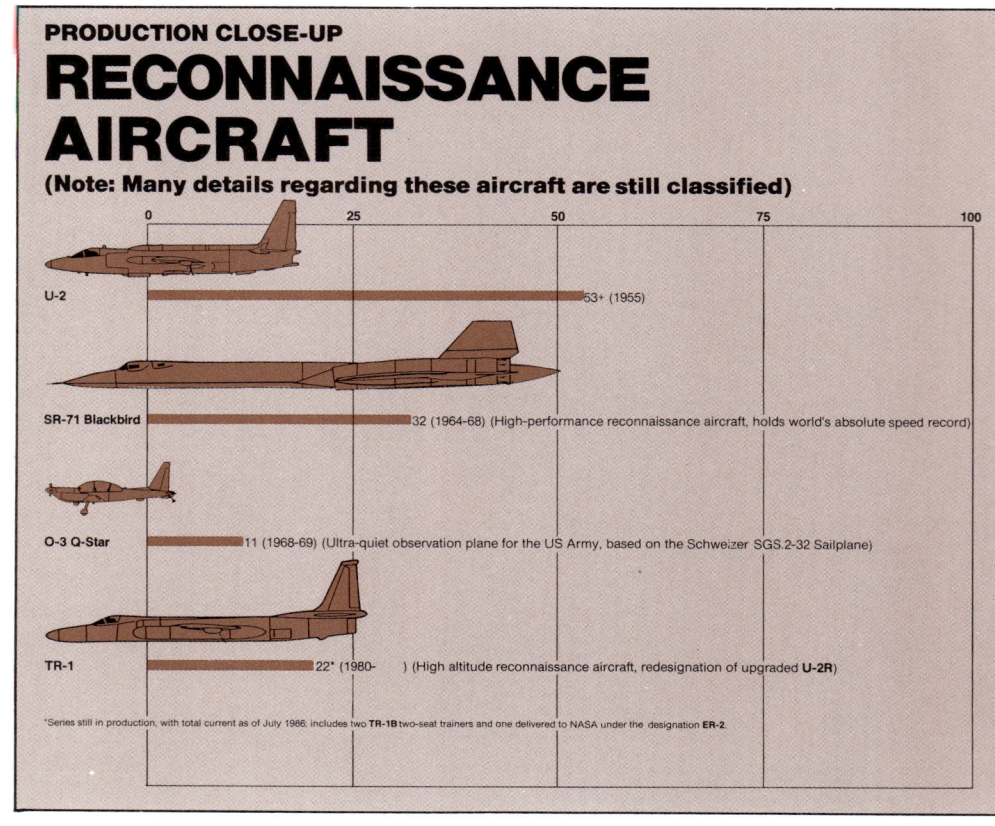

PRODUCTION CLOSE-UP

RECONNAISSANCE AIRCRAFT

(Note: Many details regarding these aircraft are still classified)

Aircraft	Production	Notes
U-2	53+ (1955)	
SR-71 Blackbird	32 (1964-68)	High-performance reconnaissance aircraft, holds world's absolute speed record
O-3 Q-Star	11 (1968-69)	Ultra-quiet observation plane for the US Army, based on the Schweizer SGS.2-32 Sailplane
TR-1	22* (1980-)	High altitude reconnaissance aircraft, redesignation of upgraded U-2R

*Series still in production, with total current as of July 1986, includes two TR-1B two-seat trainers and one delivered to NASA under the designation ER-2.

141

Left: A pilot straps in, and the 'bird' will shortly 'come alive.' *Above, and lower left:* Though these two SAC Ninth Strategic Reconnaissance Wing SR-71s are elegant and fragile-looking sculptures in Beta-B 120 titanium, they and other SAC Blackbirds do grueling continuous military reconnaissance duty throughout the world. *Overleaf:* A ground crew prepares the Blackbird to fly, at Beale AFB in northern California.

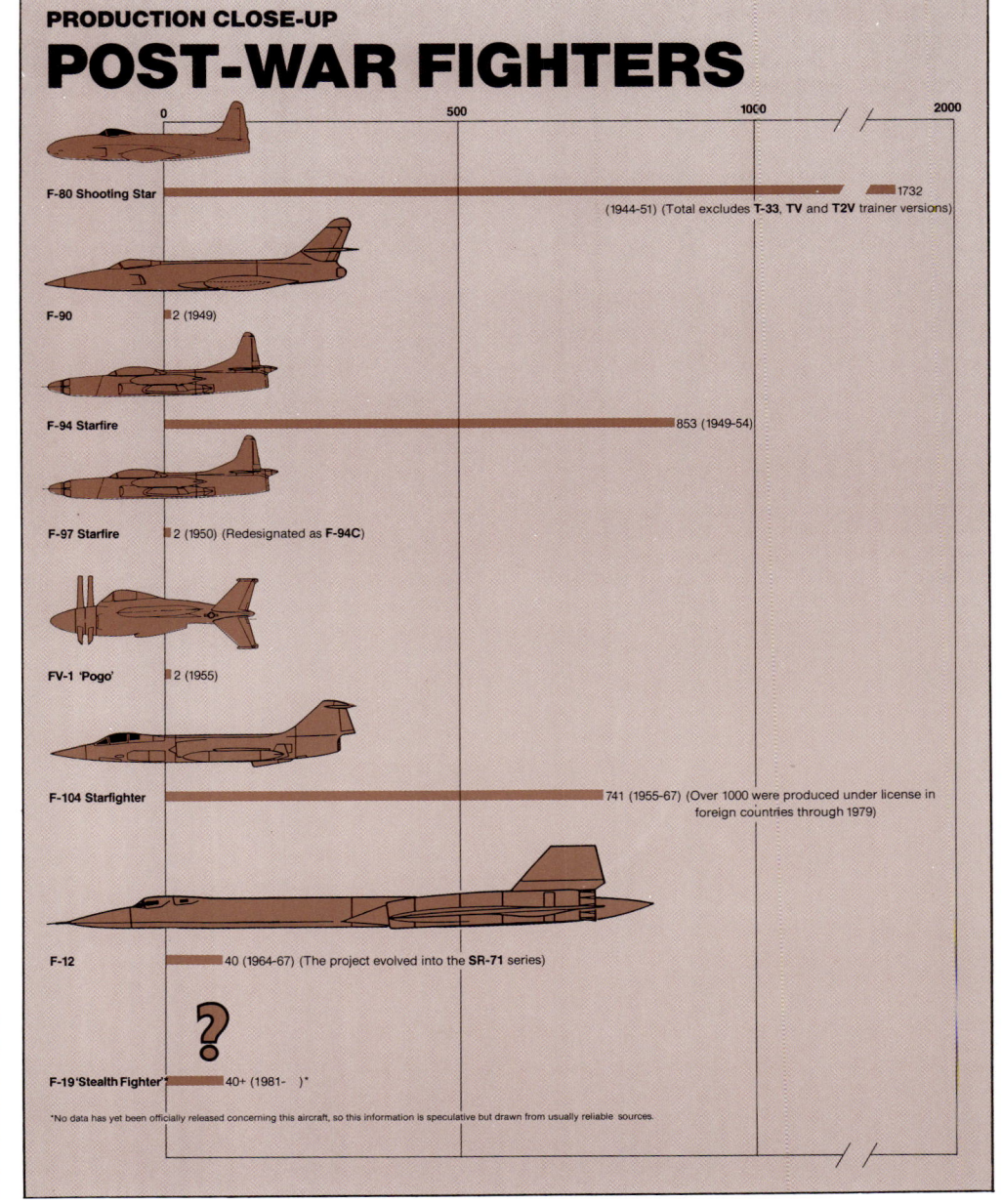

PRODUCTION CLOSE-UP
POST-WAR FIGHTERS

F-80 Shooting Star — 1732 (1944-51) (Total excludes **T-33**, **TV** and **T2V** trainer versions)

F-90 — 2 (1949)

F-94 Starfire — 853 (1949-54)

F-97 Starfire — 2 (1950) (Redesignated as **F-94C**)

FV-1 'Pogo' — 2 (1955)

F-104 Starfighter — 741 (1955-67) (Over 1000 were produced under license in foreign countries through 1979)

F-12 — 40 (1964-67) (The project evolved into the **SR-71** series)

F-19 'Stealth Fighter' — 40+ (1981-)*

*No data has yet been officially released concerning this aircraft, so this information is speculative but drawn from usually reliable sources.

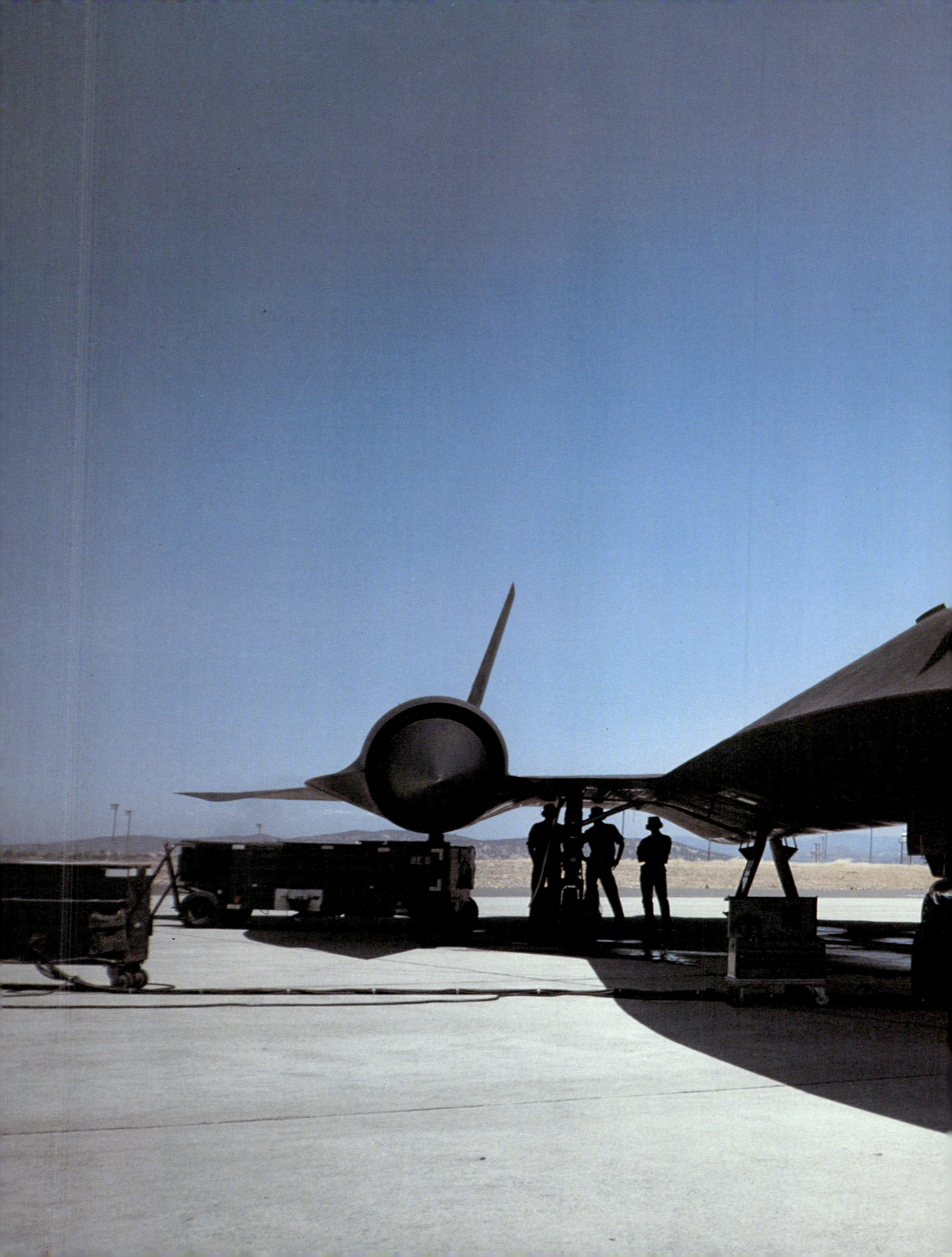

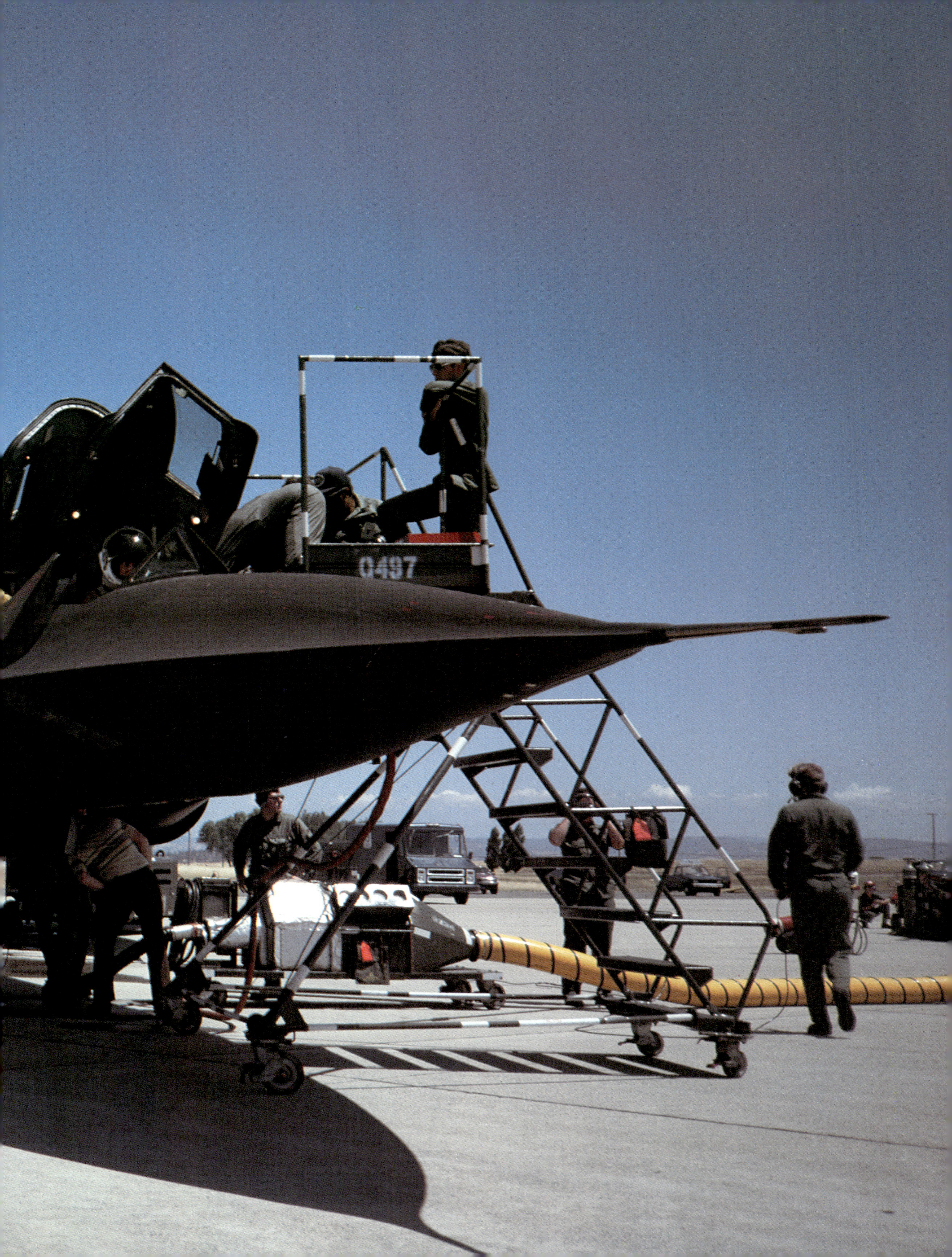
0497

Lockheed's first designs (from 1985) for the US Air Force Advanced Tactical Fighter (*above*) incorporate configurations that have evolved out of the SR-71 experience. Such designs, and such actual successes as the SR-71 (*right*), keep the *Skunk Works* 'jumping.'

ment throughout the world. Both Kadena AB in Okinawa and RAF Mildenhall in England have facilities for regular SR-71 operations.

The notion that SR-71 was ahead of its time is an understatement, and to describe this statement as an 'understatement' is in itself an understatement. The Blackbird and its predecessors are a profound tribute to the foresight of Kelly Johnson and Ben Rich (who has since succeeded Kelly as head of the *Skunk Works*), as well as to the brilliant engineers and staff of the *Skunk Works* who *invented* nearly every aspect of this unique aircraft from *scratch*. As one Blackbird pilot described it, the SR-71 is 'high-nineties technology that we were lucky to have in the sixties.'

THE SKUNK WORKS AFTER KELLY JOHNSON

Kelly Johnson retired as Lockheed senior vice president in 1975 and was succeeded as head of the Advanced Development Projects office by Ben Rich, a veteran of the SR-71 program and other projects. Because of the nature of its work, much of what the *Skunk Works* have done since Johnson's departure will not be known until the 1990s, and some of its work will *never* be known beyond the walls of the Palmdale plant or the ARP Headquarters in Burbank.

In recent years no secret military aircraft program has attracted more interest without any hard facts being known than that which the media refers to as 'stealth'. By definition, stealth is a system of various technologies employed in the design of an airplane to keep it from being detected by radar. The various stealth technologies cover a wide range of developments, from radar-absorbing paint and structural materials, to simply rounding the airplane's sharp corners because such angles are more 'visible' to radar. Another design feature that has been shown to help is shielding an airplane's jet intakes. The more of these features that are incorporated, the smaller an aircraft's 'radar signature' or 'radar cross section' becomes. An airplane incorporating stealth technology might appear on radar to be one-tenth the size of a nonstealth airplane that has the same actual dimensions. By refining it further, the stealth airplane could be made to appear even smaller until it became virtually invisible on a radar scope.

For example, the B-1A of the 1970s has just ten percent the cross section of the B-52 of the 1950s, even though it is 85 percent the actual size of the B-52. Meanwhile, the B-1B of the 1980s is almost exactly the same size as the B-1A, but subtle design treatments have given it a radar cross section that is *one percent* the size of the B-52!

While stealth technology is known to have been applied successfully to conventional aircraft designs, it is also reported that certain advanced aircraft have been built using stealth technology as the starting point. In 1980 the Carter administration revealed the existence of a stealth bomber program and gradually it became known that Northrop was developing a bomber that was a 'flying wing' type aircraft for use by US Air Force Squadrons in the 1990s. Simultaneous unconfirmed rumors have indicated that Lockheed is the primary contractor for a stealth fighter identified as the F-19A Specter.

Reportedly, the Air Force invited proposals for a stealth fighter in 1973 under a program known as *Have Blue*. Several major aerospace firms with experience in the fighter field submitted designs. The contract reportedly was awarded to Lockheed in 1976. A year later, the *Skunk Works* allegedly produced a stealth demonstration aircraft which was first flown from the secret Paradise Ranch airfield near Groom Lake, Nevada. In 1981, reportedly on the basis of the performance of this demonstrator, Lockheed was given the go-ahead to build a production series of Covert Survivable In-weather Reconnaissance Strike (CSIRS) aircraft under the oft-reported but unconfirmed designation F-19A. The aircraft was said to be powered by a pair of General Electric F404 turbofan engines.

On 11 July 1986 the crash of a secret airplane in the desert near Bakersfield, California again fueled conjecture about the CSIRS program. Though the Air Force did not identify the type of airplane involved, extraordinary security measures were taken and the crash site was declared a national security area. Firefighters, called in to fight a brush fire started by the crash, were ordered by Air Force officials not to discuss what they had seen or heard. In its coverage of the crash, the respected aerospace journal *Aviation Week* suggested that the aircraft *had* been a Lockheed F-19 and reported that 'sources familiar with the Lockheed stealth fighter program . . . believe 40-50 of the twin-engine attack aircraft have been produced.'

Whatever the reality of the Lockheed stealth fighter program, it takes little stretching of the imagination to picture Lockheed's *Skunk Works* at the forefront of advanced aircraft design as the twenty-first century approaches.

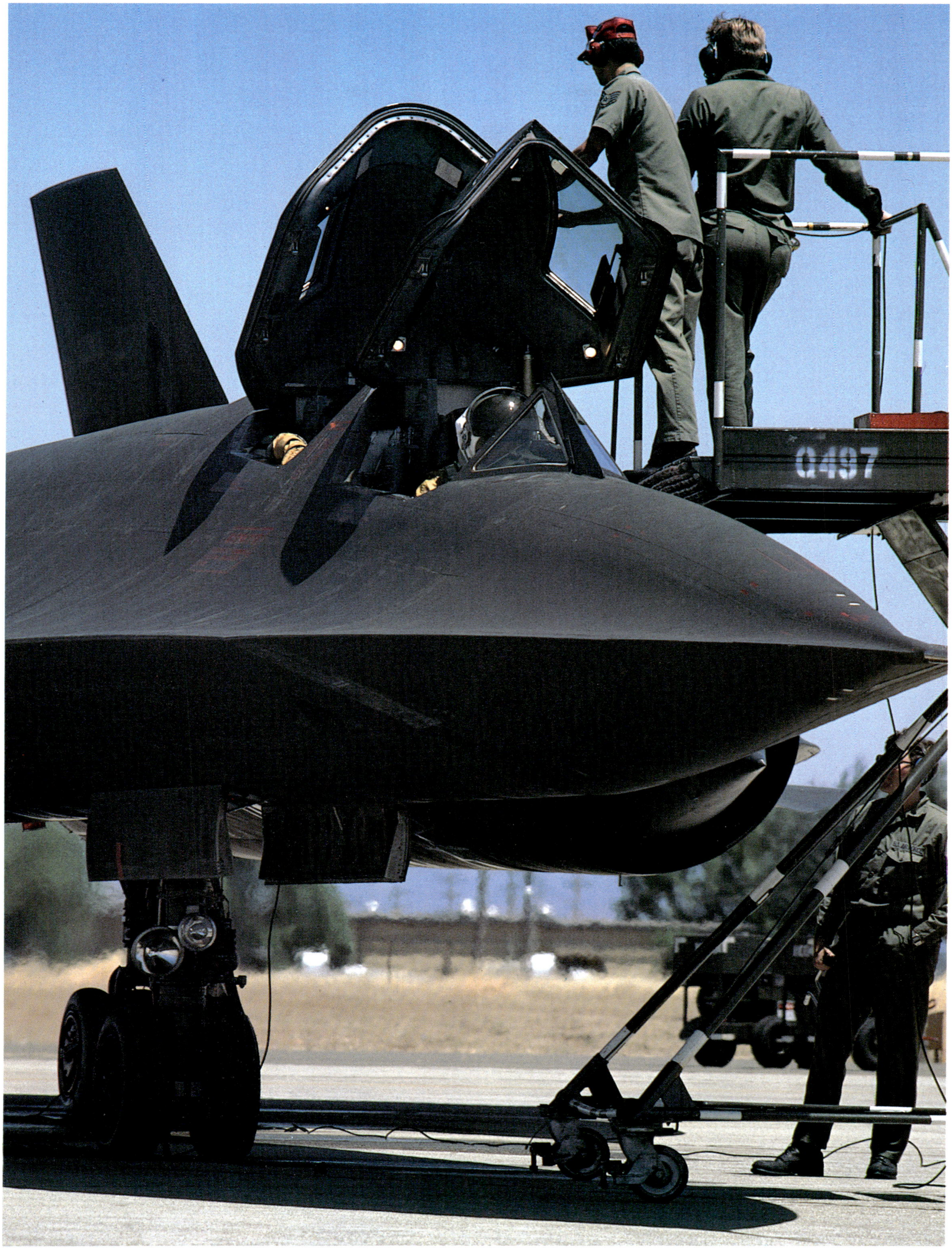
0497

LOCKHEED HELICOPTERS

THE MODEL 475

In the decade beginning in 1957, Lockheed undertook a series of three helicopter projects before finally abandoning the helicopter field as commercially nonviable.

The original 1957 studies were directed toward a low-cost, mass market commercial helicopter. A design was developed by Lockheed engineer Irven Culver for a 'rigid-rotor' helicopter whose handling characteristics were like those of a fixed wing aircraft. In the rigid-rotor design, pilot control forces are applied to a gyro which is connected by gimbals to the rotor mast and which rotates *with* the rotor. The gyro then controls the pitch angle of each rotor blade through control rods. When the helicopter is hovering, the blade pitch angle remains unchanged during rotation, but in *forward* flight each rotor blade follows through an identical cycle in which the blade pitch changes during rotation to compensate for any differential lift forces from the rotor.

To demonstrate the rigid rotor concept, Lockheed's California Division (now Lockheed California Company) produced a single Model 475, civil designation CL-475. Initially flight tested in 1959, the CL-475 was Lockheed's first helicopter.

THE MODEL 186/286 SERIES

The CL-475 demonstrator led to development of the Model 186 Aerogyro, of which two were built for joint US Army/Navy studies under the designation XH-51A. The XH-51A had an aerodynamically clean design with retractable landing skis to reduce drag. The original 35-foot, three-bladed rotors were constructed of stainless steel and aluminum honeycomb.

The first hovering flight was made on 29 September 1962 with test pilot Ray Goudey at the controls; Donald Segner took the XH-51A prototype through its first transital flight on 2 November. In 1964 the XH-51A became the first helicopter under 10,000 pounds to fly faster than 200 mph.

The second XH-51A was later modified by the addition of a Pratt & Whitney J60 jet engine installed on its port side. Thus equipped, the Model 186 became the fastest helicopter of the era, capable of speeds in excess of 260 mph at an altitude of 12,000 feet. On 19 June 1967 the second XH-51A was flown at 302.6 mph at an altitude of 5500 feet.

The rigid-rotor Lockheed Model 475 (*at top, above*), aka by civilian designation CL-475, was Lockheed's first helicopter. The 'ring' beneath the rotor on this craft harnessed the rotor's gyroscopic action, and was replaced by three weighted arms on its design successor, the turbine-powered Model 186 Aerogyro (*above*, and *both photos on facing page*), aka the XH-51A, which was successful, but not quite what the Army and Navy—its design sponsors—needed.

In 1964 a third Model 186 was built for NASA under the designation SH-51N. Two Model 286 commercial demonstrators also were built to test the waters for potential civilian sales. There was some interest in the commercial Model 186, but not enough to warrant putting it into production, and the program was canceled.

THE CHEYENNE

In the early days of the Vietnam War, the US Army began to modify some of its utility helicopters into gun platforms. The Bell AH-1 Huey Cobra gunship was factory improvised from the UH-1 Huey along the same lines as the field conversions that had taken place. Soon the AH-1 had revolutionized airmobile battlefield tactics. The helicopter gunship—and an all new mode of modern warfare—had been born.

In 1964 the Army invited proposals for a second generation gunship under its Advanced Aerial Fire Support System (AAFSS) program. The new AAFSS gunship would be the first helicopter designed from the ground up as a gunship. It would be heavily armed, heavily armored and designed expressly for attack purposes. The AAFSS as specified would have to have a speed of 220 mph, which would make it the fastest production helicopter in service.

In November 1965 Lockheed was declared the winner of the AAFSS contract and received an order for ten attack helicopters under the US Army designation AH-56. Following the Army convention under which all helicopter types are named for Indian tribes, the AH-56 was named Cheyenne. The Cheyenne was equipped with a four-blade, rigid main rotor and was armed with a gun turret forward of the cockpit which contained a

	Model 286 (XH-51)	Cheyenne AH-56
First Flight:	1962	1967
Rotor Diameter:	31.8 ft	26.7 ft
Length:	31.8 ft	54.7 ft
Height:	8.2 ft	13.7 ft
Engines:		General Electric T-64-GE-16
Gross Weight (lb):	3700	18,300
Crew or passengers:	5	2
Operating Altitude (ft):	12,000	25,000
Top Speed (mph):	302.6	253
Max Range (miles):		2400

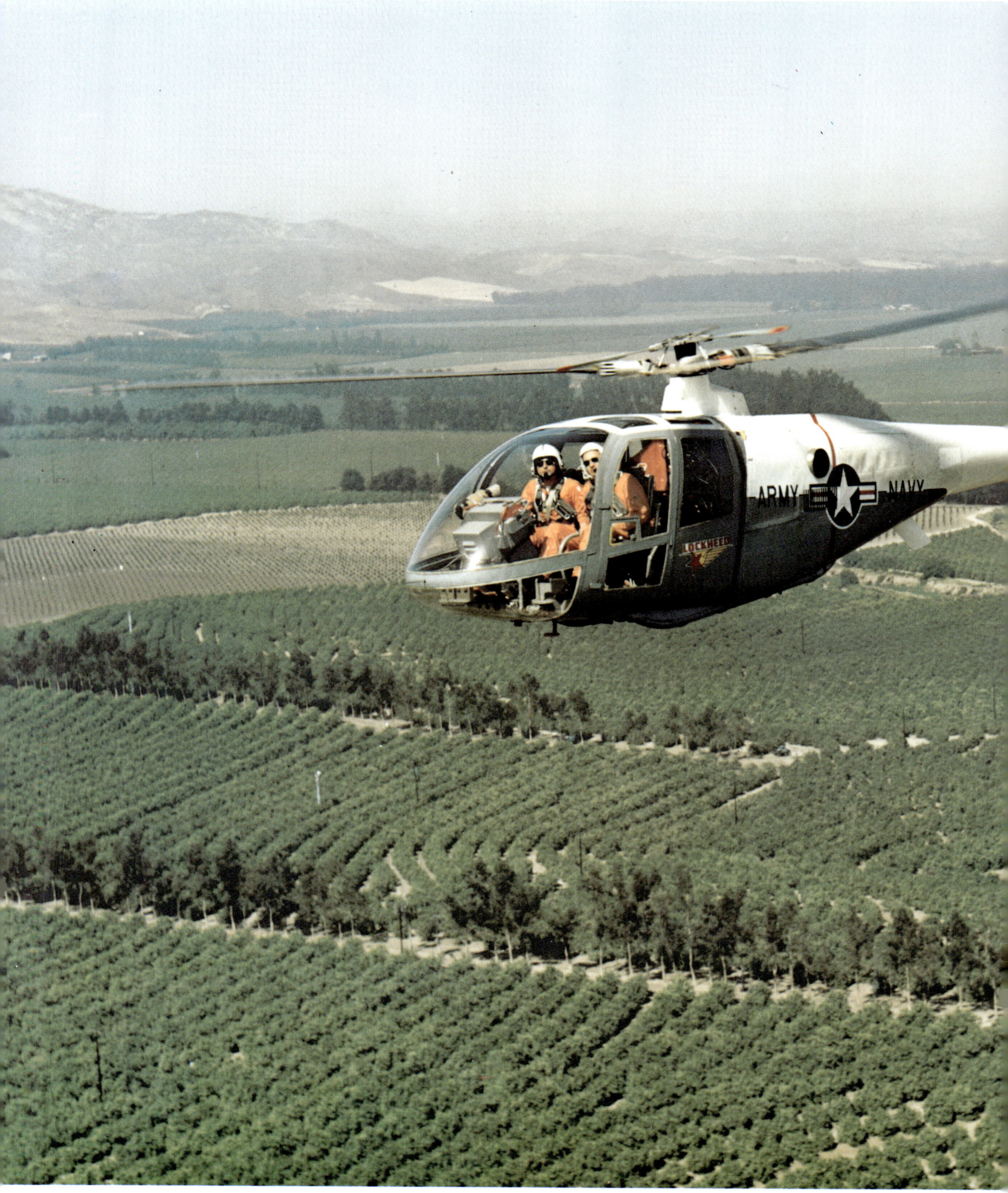
ARMY
NAVY
LOCKHEED

Left: An XH-51A is being flown by orange-clad Lockheed test crewmen over the orange groves of Southern California. *Above:* The YAH-56A Cheyenne takes its first tentative leap into the air in September 1967. 'Cheyenne' accords with the US Army's Indian naming for helicopters.

30mm cannon. Short winglets on the sides of the fuselage contained six attachment points for Hughes TOW antitank missiles.

The first YAH-56A prototype was delivered for ground testing, and the first flight of the Cheyenne involved the second prototype on 21 September 1967. Early flight testing and weapons tests went quite well, but the YAH-51A encountered problems with stability in speeds above 200 mph. Despite its promising performance, the Cheyenne failed to graduate from its trials.

The time and money to invest in correcting the AH-56's problems were simply not forthcoming amid the cuts that befell the defense budget in the late 1960s and early 1970s. Cancellation of the intended 375 helicopter production series was followed by termination of the test program and the end of the Cheyenne. The Army lowered its performance goals and backed away from the idea of a compound helicopter. The concept of an attack helicopter, however, remained alive and the Army entertained proposals for a rigid-rotor helicopter gunship from Lockheed, Bell, Sikorsky and Hughes. The latter, which became part of McDonnell Douglas in 1984, was the winner of this competition which led to the contract for the AH-64 Apache, which entered service in 1984.

In the meantime the attack helicopter idea was also deemed a sound one by the Soviet Union. In 1973 the Mil Mi-24 (NATO code name Hind) helicopter gunship appeared on the scene with an armament scheme that seemed to have been copied from the AH-56. The Mi-24 went on to serve as a potent weapon in the Afghanistan War of the early 1980s. It was due to this development that the US Army continued its own attack helicopter concept and moved into production with the McDonnell Douglas AH-64 Apache.

LOCKHEED OF GEORGIA

GOING SOUTH

During World War II aircraft factories sprang up throughout the United States, but after the war most were converted, abandoned or torn down. One of these factories was US Army Air Force Plant Six at Marietta, Georgia. When the USAAF decided to decentralize production of the Boeing B-29 bomber in order to get the maximum number built as quickly as possible, Plant Six was opened under the management of Bell Aircraft which built 665 B-29s there before the end of World War II.

In January 1951, with the Korean War raging, the US Air Force (the USAAF became the USAF in 1947) had a need to get its B-29 fleet out of mothballs and off to war, so Plant Six was reopened for this purpose—with Lockheed receiving the contract to do the work.

In January 1951 Lockheed's Georgia Division (Lockheed Georgia Company after 1961) was formed with James Carmichael as vice president and general manager and Daniel Haughton (later chairman of Lockheed) as assistant general manager. By the following January the first Lockheed-reconditioned B-29s were ready to fly.

In April 1952 Lockheed's new Georgia Division received an even more ambitious contract. In the face of the Korean War and the expanding offensive, the US Air Force was about to employ a production method that had not been used since World War II: second-source production for combat aircraft. As had been logically demonstrated by Bell Aircraft's having built some of the Boeing B-29s at Marietta, more aircraft of a particular type could be built faster if more factories were building them simultaneously. Reacting to the perceived Cold War threat, the US Air Force asked Douglas Aircraft and Lockheed's Georgia Division to help out with the production of Boeing B-47 Stratojets. For the second time in less than ten years, Boeing strategic bombers were being built at Plant Six in Marietta by a company other than Boeing. Out of a total of 2040 B-47s built for the US Air Force, 394 were built by Lockheed between 1952 and 1957.

THE HERCULES

In July 1951 Lockheed received an auspicious new US Air Force contract for its Model 82 (YC-130) transport. With the Air Force's statutory requirement to provide airlift support to the Army in mind, the new contract called for a faster, longer-ranged new transport that could land large-sized cargo at remote, semiprepared landing strips. The new aircraft, to be built under the Air Force designation C-130, would have to be designed for straight-in rear loading of cargo on pallets and have a ramp that would permit trucks, howitzers, jeeps and even bulldozers or tanks to drive aboard. The two prototypes would be designed and built by Lockheed in Burbank, while the production series would be produced by the Georgia Division.

In 1952 Lockheed's Burbank production facilities became the Lockheed California Division, joining Lockheed Georgia as the two major aircraft production divisions of Lockheed Aircraft Corporation, headquartered in Burbank. The two 'divisions' were redesignated as 'companies' in 1961.

The first service test prototype YC-130 was flown on 23 August 1954 at Burbank with Roy Wimmer and Stanley Beltz at the controls. Less than a year later, on 7 April 1955, the first production C-130A (Lockheed Model 182) made its first flight at Marietta with pilots Bud Martin and Leo Sullivan. The C-130A quickly proved itself to be dependably controllable and stable at low speeds, and it also demonstrated an exceptional performance on takeoff and landing even on short, crude runways.

While the plane was still in early development, Air Force General Joseph Smith, commanding general of the Military Air Transport Service (Military Airlift Command after 1965), said

Above: AC-130 Hercules flies over the Lockheed Georgia Company in Marietta, Georgia—aka the 'Airlift Center of the World'—where Lockheed's Hercules, Starlifters and Galaxies were made. This Lockheed YC-130 (*left*) was one of two service test predecessors of the rugged and versatile C-130 Hercules.

the turboprop-powered transport aircraft 'is the first major step taken in the United States to move into jet transportation aircraft production.' He noted that it had the advantages of the boxcar type cargo compartment configuration; the tail end, straight-in loading characteristics so universally desired for cargo operations; and the safety performance advantages of any four-engine aircraft.

The late Robert Gross (head of the Lockheed Aircraft Corporation at the time) expressed confidence in the Hercules in 1952, stating: 'We believe the C-130 has features which will make it a highly versatile carrier for the Air Force to fill demands of the present, and additional features which will give it other Air Force uses as time goes on.'

After the first flight of the production C-130A in 1955, Air Force Major General Chester E McCarty, commander of the 18th Air Force, Tactical Air Command, told aviation writers: 'The C-130 will make aviation history, giving TAC attack units faster and more effective global mobility—and in dangerous situations could be the difference between success and failure.'

US Army Major General Wayne Smith, commander of the 11th Airborne Division, said the Hercules 'gives us the first chance of global mobility for the airborne effort.' He was impressed with the Hercules' greater range, greater lift and greater safety compared with troop carriers then in service.

The first of 231 C-130A Hercules reached squadron service at Ardmore AFB in Oklahoma on 9 December 1956. The following year Lockheed began producing the first of 230 C-130Bs, with the first flight taking place on 20 November 1958. The C-130B series offered an eight percent increase in gross weight over the C-130A. The new C-130B also was equipped with a quieter and more powerful variant of the Allison T56 turboprop engine.

The C-130C was the unofficial designation of a single C-130B converted as a boundary layer control research aircraft. It was later redesignated NC-130B so that the C-130C designation could be used for the next production series, but it was never used as such.

The C-130D designation went to 13 C-130As which were fitted with skis for arctic/antarctic operations. One of them was later transferred to the US Navy as DC-130A.

Clockwise from below: Versatile variants of the C-130 in US Air Force action: A C-130A wings along the rugged California coast; a California Air National Guard HC-130 tanker prepares to refuel a pair of Air Guard HH-3s near San Francisco; a C-130E Hercules transport of the 36th Tactical Airlift Squadron passes by the pre-eruption Mt Saint Helens; a Special Operations Squadron MC-130E Combat Talon aircraft flies over part of West Germany; and an AC-130H Spectre Gunship readies for a Southeast Asia mission.

The next Hercules production series was the C-130E (Lockheed Model 382), a long-range development of the C-130B. It first flew on 25 August 1961. The C-130E offered a 25 percent increase over the gross weight of the early C-130As and 30 percent more payload capacity. Its longer range was, however, the major improvement offered by the C-130E: it could cross the Atlantic nonstop and the Pacific with one stop. In a typical US Air Force Military Air Transport Command (now Military Airlift Command) mission, a C-130E could leave Travis AFB, California with a 17 ton payload; buck a 58 mph headwind 2467 miles to Hickam AFB, Hawaii; stop for refueling; and then fly 3893 miles to Japan with a 14 ton payload. The C-130E was the largest-selling Hercules type up to that time, with 487 examples having been built. It served and continues to serve in a variety of nonairlift roles such as: the AC-130E gunship first introduced in the Vietnam War; the EC-130E electronic navigation calibration aircraft; the HC-130E search and rescue version; the MC-130E *Combat Talon* aircraft; and the WC-130E weather reconnaissance conversion. The *Combat Talon* aircraft were designed for low-level cover, deep penetration tactical missions by US Air Force Special Operations Squadrons.

The C-130F was the US Navy version of the C-130B which had originally been ordered under the pre-1964 designation UV-1. The series included seven C-130F transports; four LC-130Fs equipped with skis and Jet Assisted Takeoff (JATO) gear for antarctic operations; and 46 KC-130Fs, which would serve as aerial refueling tankers with the US Marine Corps. The latter are equipped with underwing pods.

The C-130G was a series of four C-130E conversions delivered to the US Navy as communications relay aircraft. They were later redesignated EC-130G.

The C-130H series (Lockheed Model 382) constituted the fourth Hercules production series after the A, B and E groups. The C-130H first flew on 30 November 1964 and offered greater range than the preceding types. It also was equipped with an updated avionics system. The initial production series included 142 basic C-130H transports, 43 HC-130H search and rescue variants, and two KC-130H air refueling tankers destined for the Israeli air force. In addition there were four LC-130Hs for US Reserve Forces in the Arctic, 15 WC-130H weather reconnaissance *conversions*, and several advanced AC-130H Spectre gunships armed with two 20mm rotary cannons, two 7.62mm miniguns and a 105mm howitzer, as well as a laser target designater.

The AC-130H Spectre gunship was the first C-130 type in the US Air Force not named 'Hercules.' In 1983 some C-130Hs were converted to MC-130H *Combat Talon II* aircraft for use in covert penetration missions by US Air Force Special Operations Squadrons (SOS). They have been used to supplement MC-130E *Combat Talon I* aircraft already in service with the 1st SOS at Clark AB in the Philippines, the 7th SOS in West Germany and the 8th SOS at Hurlburt Field, Florida. Hurlburt is also home to the AC-130H Spectre gunships.

There was no C-130I because the I and O subdesignations are never used in order to avoid confusion with the numbers one and zero. The C-130J designation was reserved for a development of the C-130E. The C-130K series was the designation originally assigned to 66 C-130H-type aircraft built for the British Royal Air Force, beginning in 1965. In RAF service the C-130K is known as Hercules C MkI. The C-130L designation was not used because of potential confusion with the C-130BL designation, which had once been assigned to the US Navy's four LC-130Fs. The C-130M designation was reserved for future development,

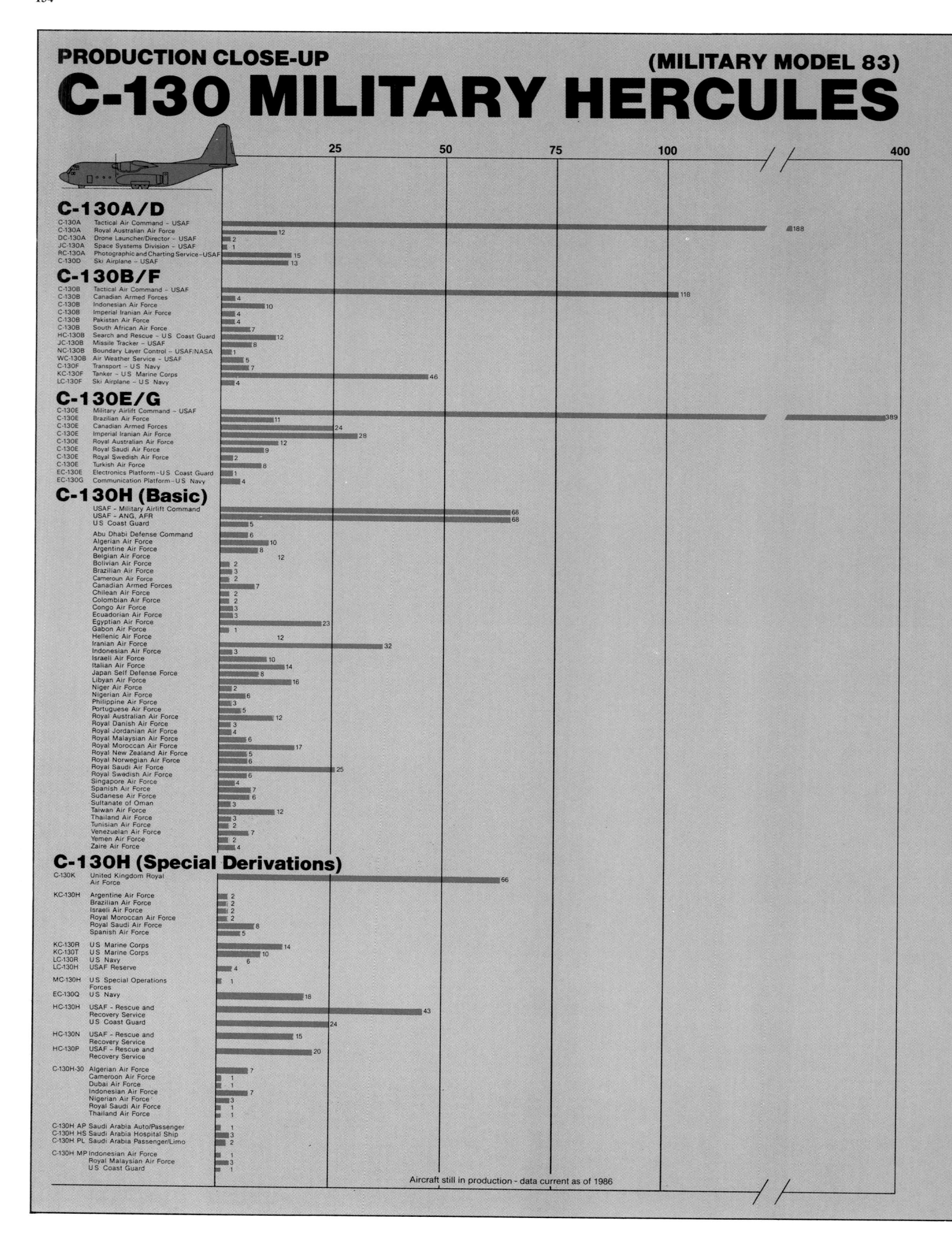

PRODUCTION CLOSE-UP
C-130 MILITARY HERCULES
(MILITARY MODEL 83)

C-130A/D

Variant	Operator	Quantity
C-130A	Tactical Air Command – USAF	188
C-130A	Royal Australian Air Force	12
DC-130A	Drone Launcher/Director – USAF	2
JC-130A	Space Systems Division – USAF	1
RC-130A	Photographic and Charting Service – USAF	15
C-130D	Ski Airplane – USAF	13

C-130B/F

Variant	Operator	Quantity
C-130B	Tactical Air Command – USAF	118
C-130B	Canadian Armed Forces	4
C-130B	Indonesian Air Force	10
C-130B	Imperial Iranian Air Force	4
C-130B	Pakistan Air Force	4
C-130B	South African Air Force	7
HC-130B	Search and Rescue – U.S. Coast Guard	12
JC-130B	Missile Tracker – USAF	8
NC-130B	Boundary Layer Control – USAF/NASA	1
WC-130B	Air Weather Service – USAF	5
C-130F	Transport – U.S. Navy	7
KC-130F	Tanker – U.S. Marine Corps	46
LC-130F	Ski Airplane – U.S. Navy	4

C-130E/G

Variant	Operator	Quantity
C-130E	Military Airlift Command – USAF	389
C-130E	Brazilian Air Force	11
C-130E	Canadian Armed Forces	24
C-130E	Imperial Iranian Air Force	28
C-130E	Royal Australian Air Force	12
C-130E	Royal Saudi Air Force	9
C-130E	Royal Swedish Air Force	2
C-130E	Turkish Air Force	8
EC-130E	Electronics Platform – U.S. Coast Guard	1
EC-130G	Communication Platform – U.S. Navy	4

C-130H (Basic)

Operator	Quantity
USAF – Military Airlift Command	68
USAF – ANG, AFR	68
U.S. Coast Guard	5
Abu Dhabi Defense Command	6
Algerian Air Force	10
Argentine Air Force	8
Belgian Air Force	12
Bolivian Air Force	2
Brazilian Air Force	3
Cameroun Air Force	2
Canadian Armed Forces	7
Chilean Air Force	2
Colombian Air Force	2
Congo Air Force	3
Ecuadorian Air Force	3
Egyptian Air Force	23
Gabon Air Force	1
Hellenic Air Force	12
Iranian Air Force	32
Indonesian Air Force	3
Israeli Air Force	10
Italian Air Force	14
Japan Self Defense Force	8
Libyan Air Force	16
Niger Air Force	2
Nigerian Air Force	6
Philippine Air Force	3
Portuguese Air Force	5
Royal Australian Air Force	12
Royal Danish Air Force	3
Royal Jordanian Air Force	4
Royal Malaysian Air Force	6
Royal Moroccan Air Force	17
Royal New Zealand Air Force	5
Royal Norwegian Air Force	6
Royal Saudi Air Force	25
Royal Swedish Air Force	6
Singapore Air Force	4
Spanish Air Force	7
Sudanese Air Force	6
Sultanate of Oman	3
Taiwan Air Force	12
Thailand Air Force	3
Tunisian Air Force	2
Venezuelan Air Force	7
Yemen Air Force	—
Zaire Air Force	4

C-130H (Special Derivations)

Variant	Operator	Quantity
C-130K	United Kingdom Royal Air Force	66
KC-130H	Argentine Air Force	2
KC-130H	Brazilian Air Force	2
KC-130H	Israeli Air Force	2
KC-130H	Royal Moroccan Air Force	2
KC-130H	Royal Saudi Air Force	8
KC-130H	Spanish Air Force	5
KC-130R	U.S. Marine Corps	14
KC-130T	U.S. Marine Corps	10
LC-130R	U.S. Navy	6
LC-130H	USAF Reserve	4
MC-130H	U.S. Special Operations Forces	1
EC-130Q	U.S. Navy	18
HC-130H	USAF – Rescue and Recovery Service	43
	U.S. Coast Guard	24
HC-130N	USAF – Rescue and Recovery Service	15
HC-130P	USAF – Rescue and Recovery Service	20
C-130H-30	Algerian Air Force	7
	Cameroun Air Force	1
	Dubai Air Force	1
	Indonesian Air Force	7
	Nigerian Air Force	3
	Royal Saudi Air Force	1
	Thailand Air Force	1
C-130H AP	Saudi Arabia Auto/Passenger	1
C-130H HS	Saudi Arabia Hospital Ship	3
C-130H PL	Saudi Arabia Passenger/Limo	2
C-130H MP	Indonesian Air Force	1
	Royal Malaysian Air Force	1
	U.S. Coast Guard	1

Aircraft still in production – data current as of 1986

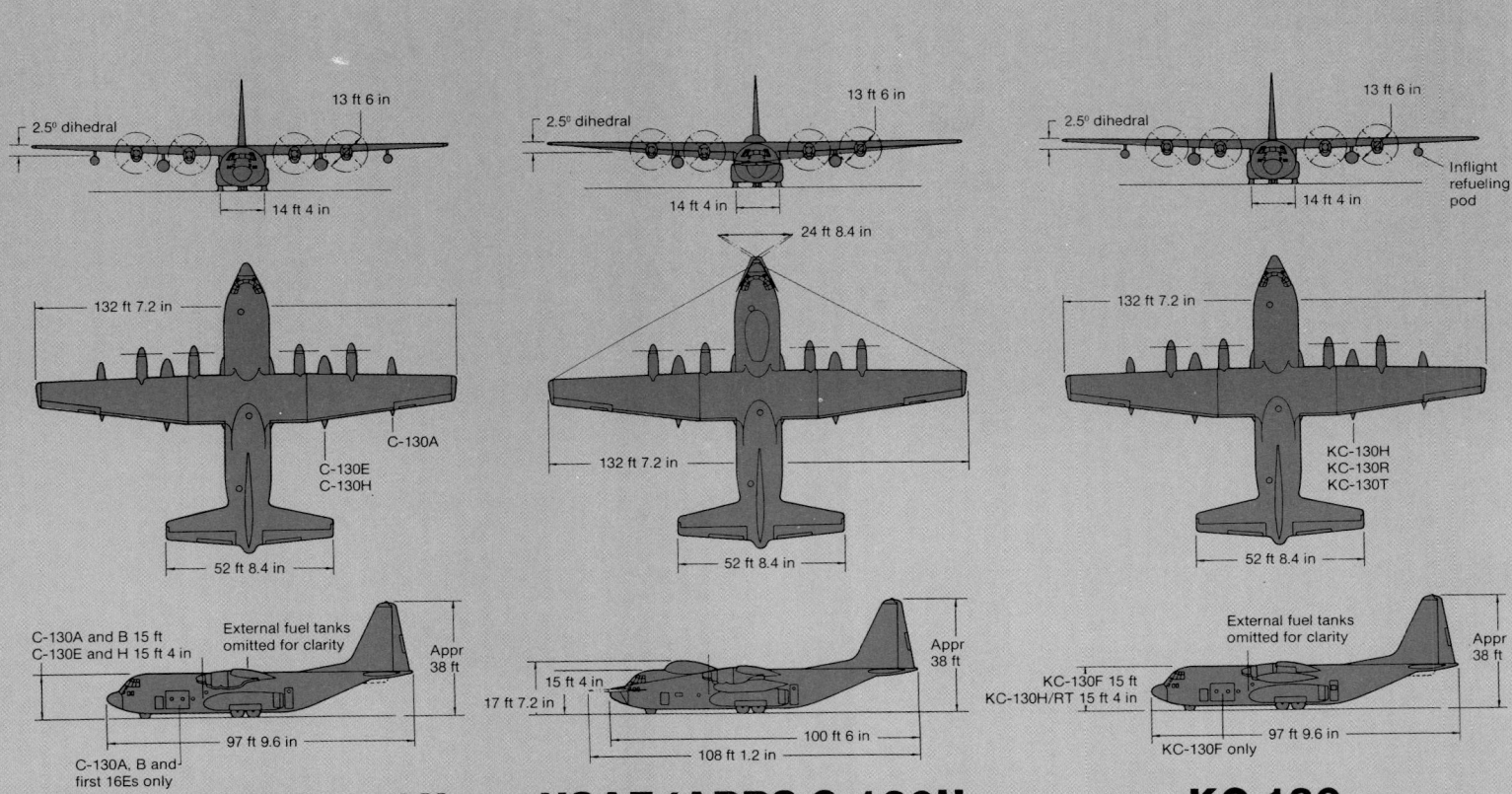

C-130 A, B, E, and H General Arrangement

USAF/ARRS C-130H General Arrangement

KC-130 General Arrangement

		C-130A	C-130B	C-130E	C-130H
Maximum Ramp Weight (2.5g)	lb	124,200	135,000	155,000	155,000
Maximum Landing Weight – 5 fps	lb	124,200	135,000	155,000	155,000
Design Landing Weight – 9 fps	lb	96,000	118,000	130,000	130,000
Operating Weight	lb	61,842	69,376	73,563	80,606*
Maximum Payload (2.5g)	lb	35,000	34,840	45,579	38,536*
Fuel Capacity @ 6.5 lb/gal	lb	39,975	45,240	62,920	60,112*
Internal Tanks	gal	5,250	6,960	6,960	6,652*
External Tanks	gal	900	–	2,720	2,596*
Total Fuel Volume	gal	6,150	6,960	9,680	9,248*
Engine Model		–	T56-A-9	T56-A-7	T56-A-15
Engine Takeoff Power, SL, Std Temp	eshp	3,750	4,050	4,050	4,508
No of Propeller Blades	–	3/4	4	4	4
Propeller Diameter	ft	15/13.5	13.5	13.5	13.5
Outboard Propeller/Ground Clearance	in	68/79	79.0	79.0	79.0
Inboard Propeller/Ground Clearance	in	60.6/69.6	69.6	69.6	69.6
Inboard Propeller/Fuselage Clearance	in	28.8/37.8	37.8	37.8	37.8
Wing Area	sq ft	1,745	1,745	1,745	1,745
Wing Loading	lb/sq ft	71.2	77.4	88.8	88.8
Wing Aspect Ratio	–	10.09	10.09	10.09	10.09
Cargo Compartment Floor Length	ft	41.0	41.0	41.0	41.0
Cargo Compartment Width	in	120.0	120.0	120.0	120.0
Cargo Compartment Height	in	108.0	108.0	108.0	108.0
Cargo Compartment Floor Area	sq ft	533	533	533	533
Cargo Compartment Usable Volume	cu ft	4,500	4,500	4,500	4,500
Wing Tip Turning Radius	ft	85.0	85.0	85.0	85.0
Nose Gear Turning Radius	ft	37.0	37.0	37.0	37.0
Wheel Base	ft	32.1	32.1	32.1	32.1
Main Gear Tire Size	–	20:00-20	20:00-20	20:00-20	20:00-20
Nose Gear Tire Size	–	12:50-16	12:50-16	12:50-16	39 x 13

Notes: Operating weights include external fuel tanks for C-130A, E, and H models.
Cargo compartment floor areas and usable volumes include ramp space.
T56-A-15 engine can produce 4910 eshp but is flat-rated to 4508 eshp for takeoff in order not to exceed nacelle/wing structural capability.

*The FY84 and FY85 Air Reserve Forces versions include blue foam for fire suppression in fuel tanks. International versions do not include blue foam.

Power Plant — Four Allison turboprop, constant-speed engines. Provisions for eight 1000-pound thrust assisted takeoff (ATO) units except on some C-130H airplanes. See Table 5 for engine models and power ratings.

Propeller — Four Hamilton Standard electro-hydromatic, constant-speed, full-feathering, reversible-pitch propellers. Early C-130A models had three-bladed Aeroproducts propellers.

Auxiliary Power — A self-starting auxiliary power unit (APU) supplies air during ground operation for engine starting, air conditioning, and electrical power. Emergency electrical power during flight is also available up to 20,000 feet. C-130A, B, and E models have a gas turbine compressor and an air turbine motor.

Oil — Independent system with twelve-gallon capacity for each engine. (C-130A has eight-gallon capacity).

Fuel — Modified manifold-flow type incorporating fuel crossfeed, single point refueling (SPR) and defueling, and fuel dumping (C-130A is without the fuel dumping provisions). Latest USAF version incorporates blue foam for fire suppression.

Electrical — AC electrical power is provided by five 40 KVA generators, four driven by the engines and one driven by the APU (C-130A, B and E models have a 20 KVA generator driven by an ATM for the fifth generator). DC power is provided from AC sources through four 200 ampere transformer rectifiers and from one 24 volt, 36 ampere-hour battery.

Hydraulic — Four engine-driven pumps supply 3000 psi pressure to the utility and booster systems. An electric motor-driven pump (C-130A uses compressed air) supplies pressure to the auxiliary system and is backed up by a hand pump.

Air Conditioning & Pressurization — Two independent systems for the flight deck and cargo compartment are operated by bleed air from the engine compressors in flight and by the APU on the ground. Maximum pressure differential of 7.5 psi will maintain an 8000-foot cabin at 35,000-foot flight altitude.

Oxygen — C-130A and C-130B have a gaseous-type system which provides 36- and 40-manhours of oxygen, respectively, at 25,000 feet. C-130E and C-130H have a 300 psi liquid-type system which provides 96-manhours of oxygen at 25,000 feet. Both systems use diluter-demand automatic pressure-breathing regulators. Portable units are also provided. International versions may have either gaseous or liquid systems.

Note the JATO exhaust flames just below and behind the wing of this National Science Foundation LC-130R (*at top, above*). *Below:* The US Navy's Blue Angels aerobatic team personnel fly from place to place in this US Marine Corps-provided C-130 transport, which is painted in the Blue Angels colors. *Right:* A Coast Guard HC-130B at rest.

and the HC-130N was a search and rescue variant similar to the HC-130H, of which 15 were produced. The HC-130P was another development of the HC-130H designed for aerial refueling of helicopters from underwing fuel tanks. Twenty HC-130Ps were built.

The EC-130Q was a series of 18 advanced radio relay stations for the US Navy. The C-130R type was a series of fourteen KC-130R and ten KC-130T aerial refueling tankers built for the US Marine Corps and six LC-130Rs built for US Navy use in the Antarctic.

The RC-130S designation was applied to specially classified reconnaissance conversions from existing C-130As.

In service with the US Air Force and more than a dozen other air forces around the world, the 'Herk' has earned a reputation as a 'go anywhere, do anything' workhorse. In Vietnam, US Air Force C-130s were constantly dodging enemy fire as they trucked supplies to the most rugged of frontline airfields. In 1976 Israel Air Force C-130s carried commandos on their daring and successful rescue of civilian hostages at Entebbe airport in Uganda. Royal Air Force Hercules transports were among the first aircraft to land in the Falklands after the 1982 war with Argentina.

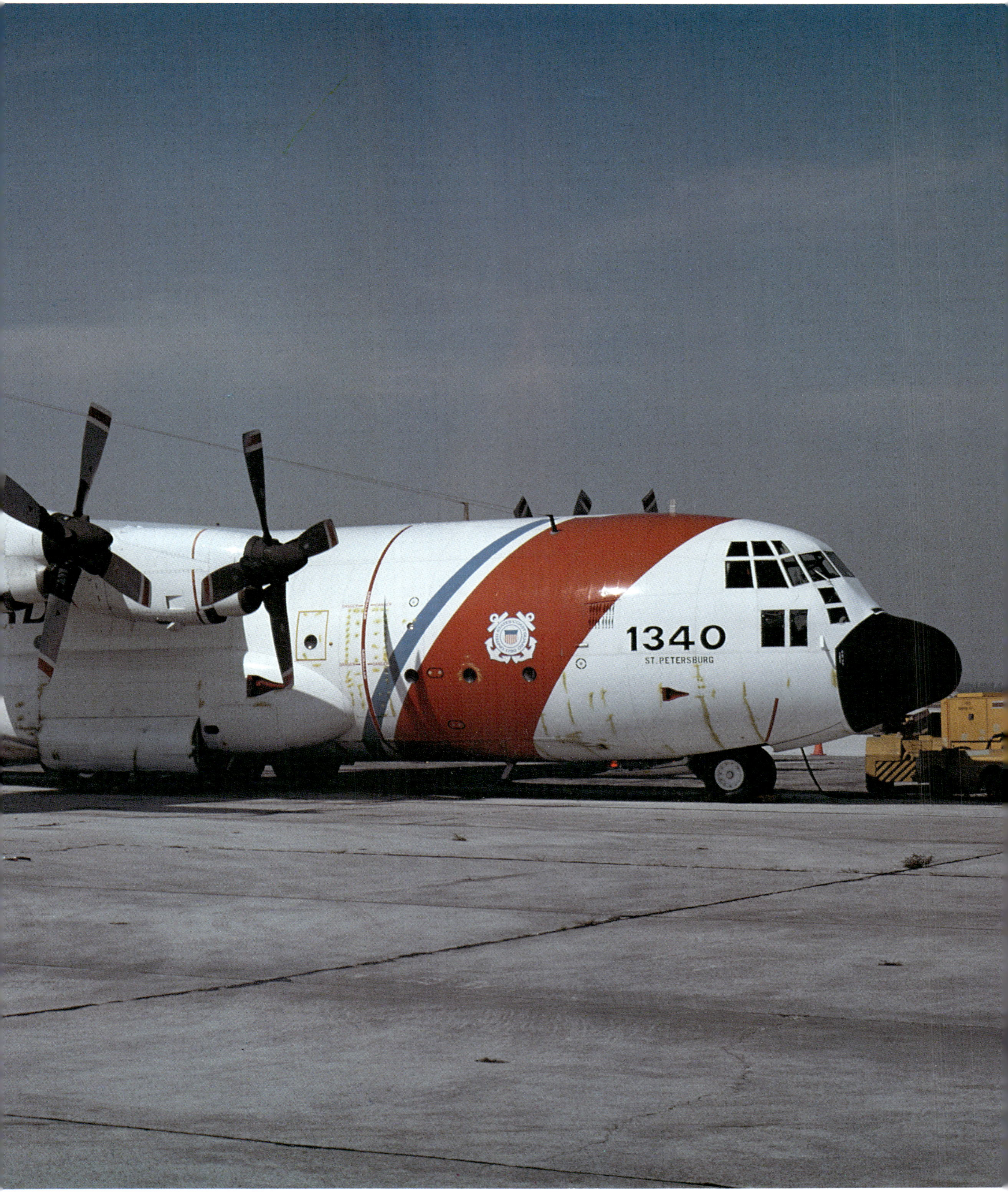
1340
ST. PETERSBURG

158

Low Altitude Parachute Extraction System - (LAPES)

Apply Power and Climb Out | Load Extracted From Aircraft | Parachute Fully Deployed | Release Extraction Parachute | Absolute Altitude 5 to 10 Feet | Final Approach Flaps set to give level pitch attitude Airspeed 120 KIAS

Airspeed 120 KIAS

Approx 600 Ft or 3 Seconds

Parachute Low-Altitude Delivery System - (PLADS)

Load Pulled From Aircraft | Extraction Chute Unfurled | Reefed Extraction Chute Deployed | 120 KIAS

200 Ft Absolute Altitude

Impact Point (Target) | Drop Point (Marked with Panels)

Energy Absorber, Cable Supports, Pendant Cable, Gasoline Engine, Extraction Line, Hook Shank, Hook

A C-130 Hercules transport (*above left*) delivers a jeep via LAPES (*see above right*). *Below left and right:* These historical photos record the landing and takeoff from an aircraft carrier of one of the largest aircraft to do so—a C-130 transport. On 30 October 1963, Pilot Lt James H Flatley II (who received the distinguished flying Cross for this effort and is now an admiral) and crew began a series of 29 touch-and-go landings, 21 un-arrested landings and 21 unassisted takeoffs from the flight deck of the *USS Forrestal*.

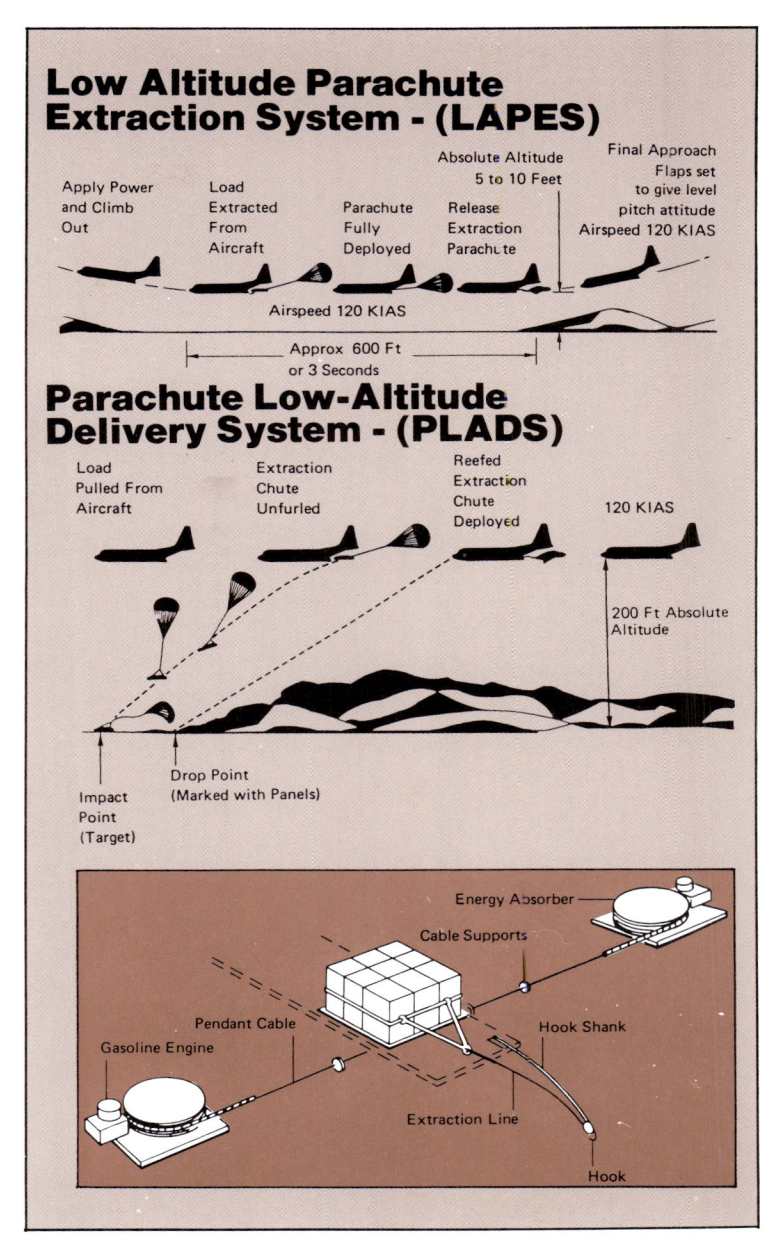

Lockheed Georgia has shipped over 1700 Hercules aircraft to airlines and governments world-wide. *Above* is an Air Botswana L-100-130. Great Britain's Royal Air Force converted many of its C-130K Hercules into the 'stretched' C-130H-30 Super Hercules (shown *below* with a comparatively shorter C-130H *at rear*). *Below right, from left:* Lockheed Georgia VP William Bullock; HTTB Ops Manager Wynne Daughters; Deputy Director for Hercules Projects Terry Graham; Frank Hadden, chief engineering test pilot; and HTTB Hercules.

The Hercules, however, is more than just a military airlifter. Over 100 commercial Hercules transports have been sold to airlines and governments around the world. The airlines have ranged from the well known—like Delta (which no longer uses the Hercules)—to the somewhat more obscure ones—like Air Gabon. Nonairline owners of the commercial Hercules include the likes of Petroleos Mexicanos (PEMEX), the Mexican national oil company. In civilian service the Hercules is Lockheed Model 100 (L-100-20 and L-100-30) while the military Hercules is Lockheed Model 82 (incorporating Models 182, 282 and 382). Technically the L-100-20 is a Model 382E, and the L-100-30 is a Model 382G.

The first Model 100 was based on the C-130E and as such it was built under the Model 382 designation. It was first flown in April 1964, nearly ten years after the first YC-130 flight and almost three years after the first C-130E flight. On 16 February 1965 the Federal Aviation Administration (FAA) certified the aircraft, which Lockheed then began to market as the L-100. There were a total of 22 L-100s, of which 13 were converted to L-100-20 or L-100-30 standard.

In 1968 Lockheed Georgia delivered the first of 27 of the L-100-20 series, which was 100 inches longer than the L-100. The overall wing and tail were the same as the L-100, but the fuselage was stretched 60 inches ahead of the wing and 40 inches aft of the wing. The floor length of the cargo compartment was thus extended from 41 feet to 49.3 feet, allowing the L-100-20 to carry seven rather than six typical cargo pallets. More powerful Allison turboprop engines increased performance by 11 percent.

In August 1970 the L-100-30 'Super Hercules' was introduced. The L-100-30 is 180 inches longer than the L-100 or the C-130, with a 100 inch stretch plug ahead of the wing and 80 inches aft. The cargo space floor length was increased to 65 feet, accommodating eight standard air cargo pallets. As of 1987 the L-100-30 was still in production, with 65 having been built by the factory in Marietta. Including those built from scratch and those L-100s and L-100-20s converted to L-100-30 standard, there were 65 L-100-30s in service in 1986. Southern Air Transport was the largest operator with 15 L-100-30s and two L-100-20s, while Safair Freighters Pty Ltd, was second with eight. Deliveries of L-100-30s have also included those to the air forces of Dubai, Ecuador, Gabon, Indonesia, Kuwait and Saudi Arabia.

The British Royal Air Force converted its G MkI Hercules (C-130K) aircraft to C-130H-30 "Super Hercules" military standard, which is similar in overall appearance to the civil C-100-30.

THE HIGH TECH TEST BED

In 1984 Lockheed Georgia began flying its High Technology Test Bed (HTTB) aircraft, a heavily modified L-100-20 Hercules. Funded through the company's internal research and development budget, the all-black HTTB was described by Lockheed as a 'flying laboratory for testing advanced aviation technologies.'

The HTTB is equipped with the Lockheed Airborne Data System (LADS), a data-gathering, analysis and display system that allows constant monitoring of aircraft systems. LADS includes a 100-channel sensor system that allows structural testing of any part of the HTTB. The HTTB was retrofitted with fins and modifed tail surfaces to enhance its Short Takeoff and Landing (STOL) characteristics. This permitted the aircraft to set several new STOL records, including short takeoff (427 meters); climb to 3000 meters (three minutes, 57.4 seconds); climb to 6000 meters (nine minutes, .4 seconds); and climb to 9000 meters (17 minutes, 41.7 seconds).

In addition to its enhanced STOL capabilities, the HTTB is designed to test a number of new and emerging avionics technologies, including application of a fighter-style Head Up data Display (HUD) in the cockpit. The HUD projects important data such as speed, altitude and flight path on a transparent panel inside the windshield, so that the pilot doesn't have to look down at his instrument panel at such critical moments as during landings or low-level air drops—when his attention should be focused outside.

PRODUCTION CLOSE-UP
COMMERCIAL MODEL 100 HERCULES

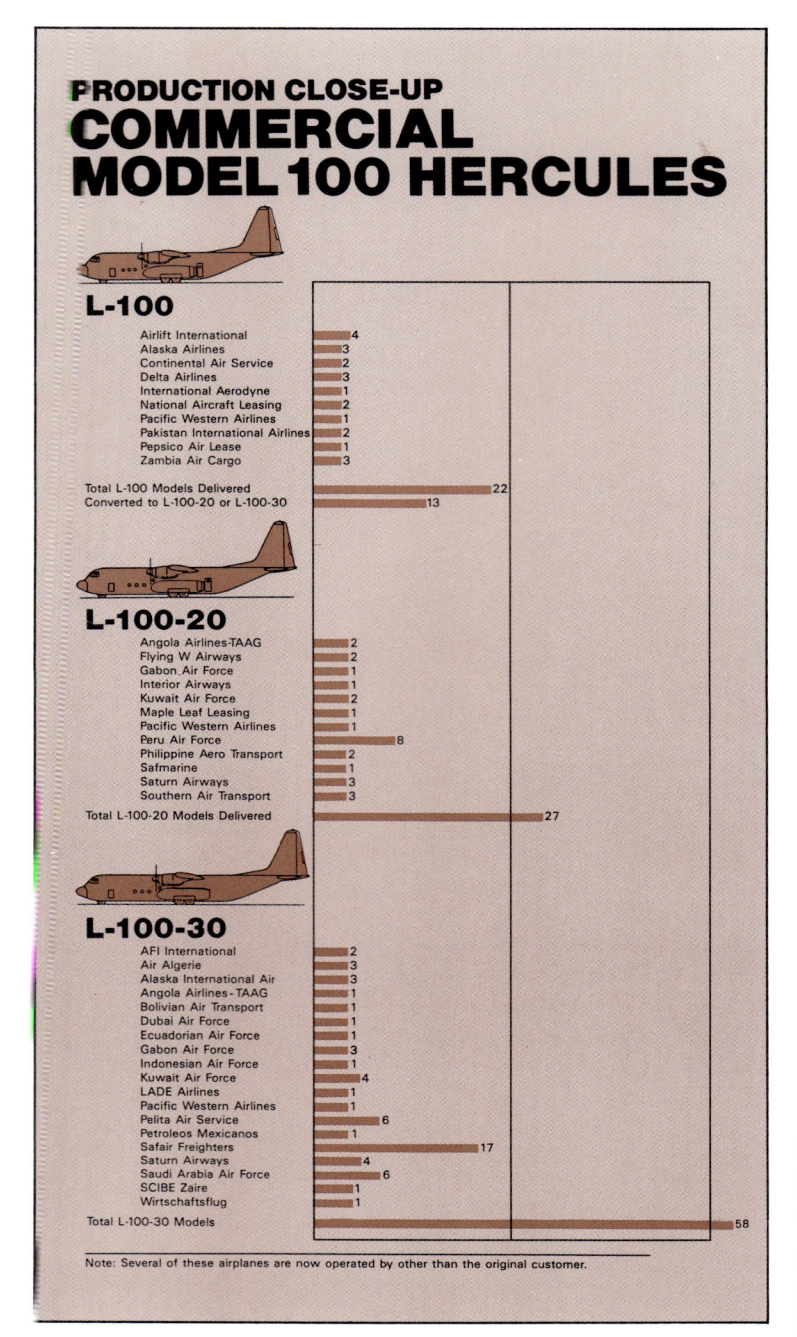

L-100

Operator	Qty
Airlift International	4
Alaska Airlines	3
Continental Air Service	2
Delta Airlines	3
International Aerodyne	1
National Aircraft Leasing	2
Pacific Western Airlines	1
Pakistan International Airlines	2
Pepsico Air Lease	1
Zambia Air Cargo	3

Total L-100 Models Delivered: 22
Converted to L-100-20 or L-100-30: 13

L-100-20

Operator	Qty
Angola Airlines-TAAG	2
Flying W Airways	2
Gabon Air Force	1
Interior Airways	1
Kuwait Air Force	2
Maple Leaf Leasing	1
Pacific Western Airlines	1
Peru Air Force	8
Philippine Aero Transport	2
Safmarine	1
Saturn Airways	3
Southern Air Transport	3

Total L-100-20 Models Delivered: 27

L-100-30

Operator	Qty
AFI International	2
Air Algerie	3
Alaska International Air	3
Angola Airlines-TAAG	1
Bolivian Air Transport	1
Dubai Air Force	1
Ecuadorian Air Force	1
Gabon Air Force	3
Indonesian Air Force	1
Kuwait Air Force	4
LADE Airlines	1
Pacific Western Airlines	1
Pelita Air Service	6
Petroleos Mexicanos	1
Safair Freighters	17
Saturn Airways	4
Saudi Arabia Air Force	6
SCIBE Zaire	1
Wirtschaftsflug	1

Total L-100-30 Models: 58

Note: Several of these airplanes are now operated by other than the original customer.

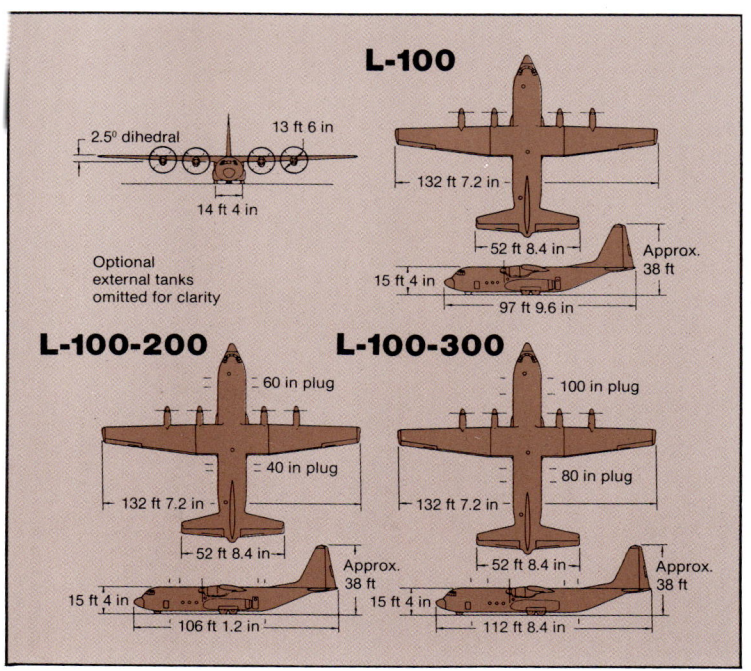

L-100 / L-100-200 / L-100-300 Dimensions

- 2.5° dihedral
- 13 ft 6 in
- 14 ft 4 in
- Optional external tanks omitted for clarity

L-100
- 132 ft 7.2 in
- 52 ft 8.4 in
- 15 ft 4 in
- 97 ft 9.6 in
- Approx. 38 ft

L-100-200
- 60 in plug
- 40 in plug
- 132 ft 7.2 in
- 52 ft 8.4 in
- 15 ft 4 in
- 106 ft 1.2 in
- Approx. 38 ft

L-100-300
- 100 in plug
- 80 in plug
- 132 ft 7.2 in
- 52 ft 8.4 in
- 15 ft 4 in
- 112 ft 8.4 in
- Approx. 38 ft

Specifications

		L-100	L-100-20[1]	L-100-30[1]	L-100-30[2]
Maximum Ramp Weight	lb	155,800	155,800	155,800	155,800
Maximum Landing Weight – 10 fps	lb	130,000	130,000	135,000	135,000
Operating Weight	lb	69,926	75,985	77,113	77,905
Maximum Payload	lb	47,990	52,805	51,677	50,885
Fuel Capacity @ 6.7 lb/gal	lb	64,856	64,856	64,856	64,856
Internal Tanks	gal	6,960	6,960	6,960	6,960
External Tanks[3]	gal	2,720	2,720	2,720	2,720
Total Fuel Volume	gal	9,680	9,680	9,680	9,680
Engine Model	–	501-D22	501-D22A	501-D22A	501-D22A
Engine Takeoff Power, Sea Level, ISA	eshp	4,050	4,508[4]	4,508[4]	4,508[4]
No. of Propeller Blades	–	4	4	4	4
Propeller Diameter	ft	13.5	13.5	13.5	13.5
Outboard Propeller/Ground Clearance	in	79.0	79.0	79.0	79.0
Inboard Propeller/Ground Clearance	in	69.6	69.6	69.6	69.6
Inboard Propeller/Fuselage Clearance	in	37.8	37.8	37.8	37.8
Wing Area	sq ft	1,745	1,745	1,745	1,745
Wing Loading	lb/sq ft	88.8	88.8	88.8	88.8
Wing Aspect Ratio	–	10.09	10.09	10.09	10.09
Cargo Compartment Floor Length	ft	41.0	49.3	56.0	56.0
Cargo Compartment Width	in	120.0	120.0	120.0	120.0
Cargo Compartment Height	in	108.0	108.0	108.0	108.0
Cargo Compartment Floor Area[5]	sq ft	533	602	666	666
Cargo Compartment Usable Volume	cu ft	4,500	5,307	6,057	6,057
Wing Tip Turning Radius	ft	85.0	88.0	90.0	90.0
Nose Gear Turning Radius	ft	37.0	43.0	46.8	46.8
Wheel Base	ft	32.1	37.1	40.4	40.4
Main Gear Tire Size	–	56x20-20	56x20-20	56x20-20	56x20-20
Nose Gear Tire Size	–	12:50-16	39x13	39x13	39x13

Notes:
1. Airplanes up to S/N 4992
2. Airplanes S/N 4992 and subsequent
3. External fuel tanks are optional
4. Engine can produce 4910 eshp but is derated to 4508 eshp to not exceed airplane structure capability.
5. Floor area and volume include space on ramp.

Lockheed's L-100-30 'Super Hercules' commercial transport (in flight, *above*) is flown by airlines and governments world-wide. Its fuselage has a 55-foot cargo bay, and can carry 50,000+ pounds.

The L-100-20 Hercules shown *below,* landing at Port Radium, North West Territories, Canada, demonstrates its 'all-terrain' landing and takeoff capability in the employ of the Echo Bay Mines Company.

Lockheed
USE ONE BOTT_E AT A TIME
NOT TO BE USED
FOR TIRE INFLATION
OR OXYGEN SYSTEM

Photographer George W Hamlin has caught the High Technology Test Bed (HTTB) aircraft at rest (*below left*) on the Lockheed Georgia pavement in Marietta. The HTTB is a much modified L-100-20 Hercules, and therefore has plenty of room for test equipment and devices 'to be tested.' This aircraft, among other special features, is equipped with the Lockheed Airborne Data System (LADS), for swift data processing and storage. The HTTB is modified especially for flight speed versatility, having specialized flaps, spoilers, longer chord rudder, aerlons, and elevators for low speed operation, as well as vertical and horizontal triangular 'fins' (extending *forward* from the tail assembly) for short takeoff and landing 'floatability.'

THE JETSTAR

In 1956, under its UCX (Utility Transport, Experimental) project, the US Air Force expressed an interest in acquiring a small, 10-passenger utility jet. At that time there were few jet transports on the market and those which did exist tended to be designed for a hundred or more passengers. The concept of a small utility jet was as yet unheard of. Lockheed correctly recognized that there would soon be a commercial, as well as military market for this type of aircraft, so they assigned Kelly Johnson's *Skunk Works* the job of coming up with the basic design. Lockheed Georgia would build the production aircraft. Design work began in January 1957 and the prototype made its first flight on 4 September—just 241 days later!

Designated as Lockheed Model 329 (commercial designation CL-329) and named JetStar, the new transport prototype was a sleek little bird powered by a pair of British Bristol Orpheus engines mounted in pods on the side of the fuselage. Lockheed had used the Orpheus in its earlier Model 139 jetliner—which had been designed but never built—in the early 1950s. It was used on the JetStar because of an anticipated deal by which Wright would build the Orpheus under license in the United States. When that deal fell through, Lockheed was forced to redesign the JetStar to be powered by *four* of the smaller Pratt & Whitney JT12 turbojets. The first JT12-powered prototype, Lockheed Model 1329, flew on 2 July 1960.

In 1958 the US Air Force had evaluated the Model 329 prototype and had declared it the winner of the UCX competition, but when the Model 1329 production version was ready, only five were purchased by the Air Force. Designated C-140A, these aircraft were complemented by the sale of 29 JetStars to the Canadian government and the purchase by the US Air Force of five C-140Bs in 1962.

The first commercial Model 1329s were delivered to corporate customers in September 1961, after having been FAA-approved the month before. They were powered by four JT12A-6 engines and marketed under the trade name JetStar 6. When the JT12A-8 came into use in 1967, the new version of the plane was marketed as the JetStar 8. In 1974 a fourth version of the JetStar was prototyped. Powered by four Garret AiResearch TFE 731 turbofan engines, the new version was initially referred to as the JetStar 731, but it was marketed as the JetStar II. The first JetStar II built from the ground up made its first flight in August 1976, and the first commercial delivery was made the following month.

The JetStar I (*above*) was originally designed for two powerful British Bristol Orpheus jet engines, but the deal with the Orpheus manufacturer fell through. The US Air Force C-141A Starlifter (*at right*) introduced in 1965 and 'stretched' to C-141B standard in the 1980s.

	Jetstar I (Model 329)*
First Flight:	1957
Wingspan:	53 ft, 7 in
Length:	58 ft, 9 in
Height:	20 ft, 6 in
Engines:	four Pratt & Whitney turbojet engines
Engine Thrust (lb):	3000
Gross Weight (lb):	40,920
Crew and passengers:	8 passengers, 3 crew
Operating Altitude (ft):	45,000
Cruising Speed (mph):	600
Max Range (miles):	3000

*Military equivalent: C-140 (Model 1329)

In 1978 Lockheed made the decision to stop making the JetStar, and in January 1979 the last six were delivered to Iraqi Airways. When the JetStar production line at Marietta came to a halt, 162 JetStars (some sources say 163) and 40 JetStar IIs had been produced. Of these, only 16 JetStars (no JetStar IIs) were delivered to the US Air Force. Four JetStars were however ordered by the US Navy. Two of these (ordered as UV-1 but redesignated C-140C in 1962) were never delivered. The other pair were transferred to the Saudi Arabian Air Force as C-140A and upgraded to C-140B standard.

THE STARLIFTER

On 13 March 1961, the US Air Force selected Lockheed Georgia to build a large jet transport to complement the fleet of C-130s that were already in production. The new airlifter, Lockheed Model 300, was to be in the same size and performance class as a standard commercial jetliner such as a Boeing 707 or a Douglas DC-8, but it would have a high wing and clamshell loading doors to permit some of the rough terrain versatility of the C-130. In other words, it wouldn't be able to land on as many crude runways and fields of clover as a C-130, but it would be able to fly farther, fly faster and carry a bigger load.

Designated C-141 and named Starlifter, the first new jet rolled out of the Marietta factory door on 22 August 1963. Its first flight occurred on 17 December, the 60th anniversary of the Wright brothers' first powered flight. The first C-141 was delivered to the US Air Force Military Airlift Command at Tinker AFB, Oklahoma for crew training on 19 October 1964. The Starlifter went into squadron service with the 60th Military Airlift Wing at Travis AFB, California on 23 April 1965. Deliveries continued at a rate of roughly eight per month until the 284th and last C-141A delivery was made in February 1968. Lockheed built a 285th Model 300 as a commercial demonstrator but no

	C-141B Starlifter
First Flight:	1979 (**C-141A**, 1965)
Wingspan:	159 ft, 11 in
Length:	168 ft, 3½ in (**C-141A**, 145 ft)
Height:	39 ft, 3½ in
Engines:	four Pratt & Whitney TFF-33-P-7 turbofans
Engine Thrust (lb):	21,000
Gross Weight (lb):	343,000
Max Payload (lb):	90,200
Crew:	5
Operating Altitude (ft):	25,000
Cruising Speed (mph):	566
Top Speed (mph):	570
Range (miles):	4080

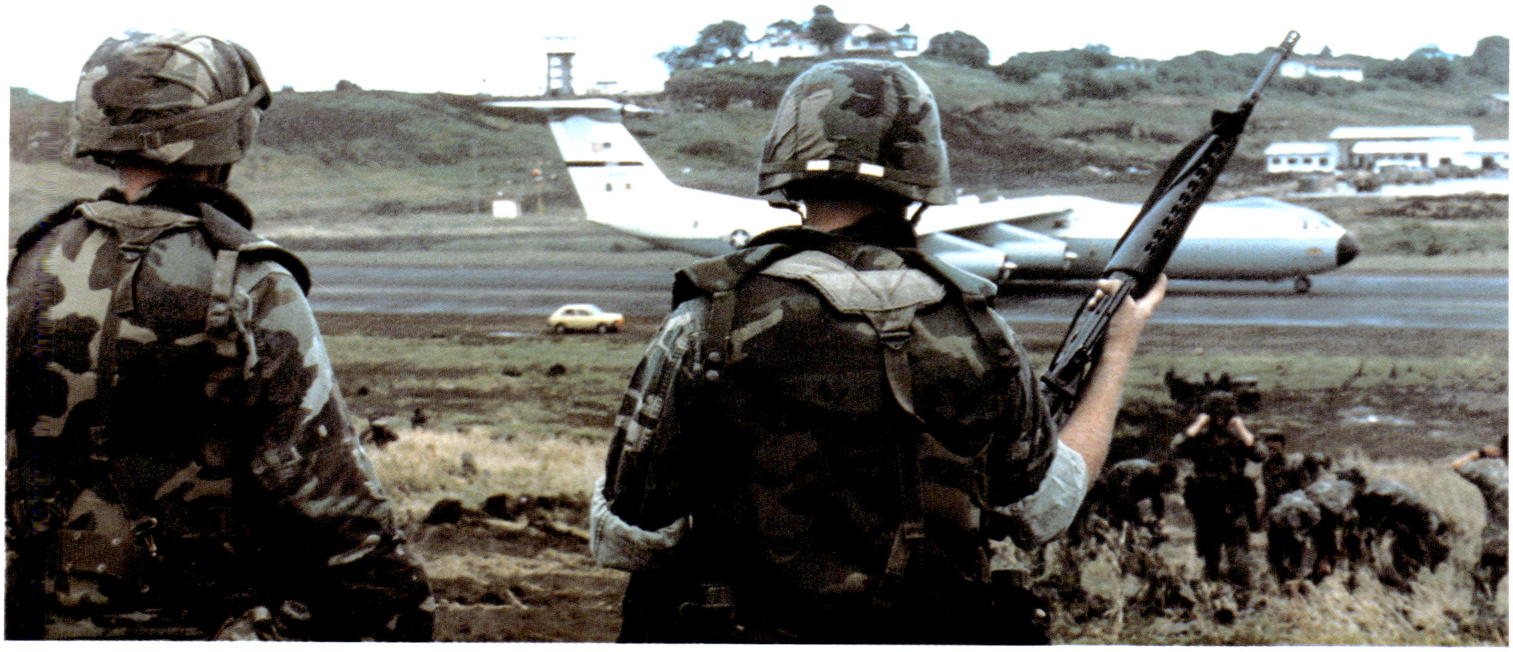

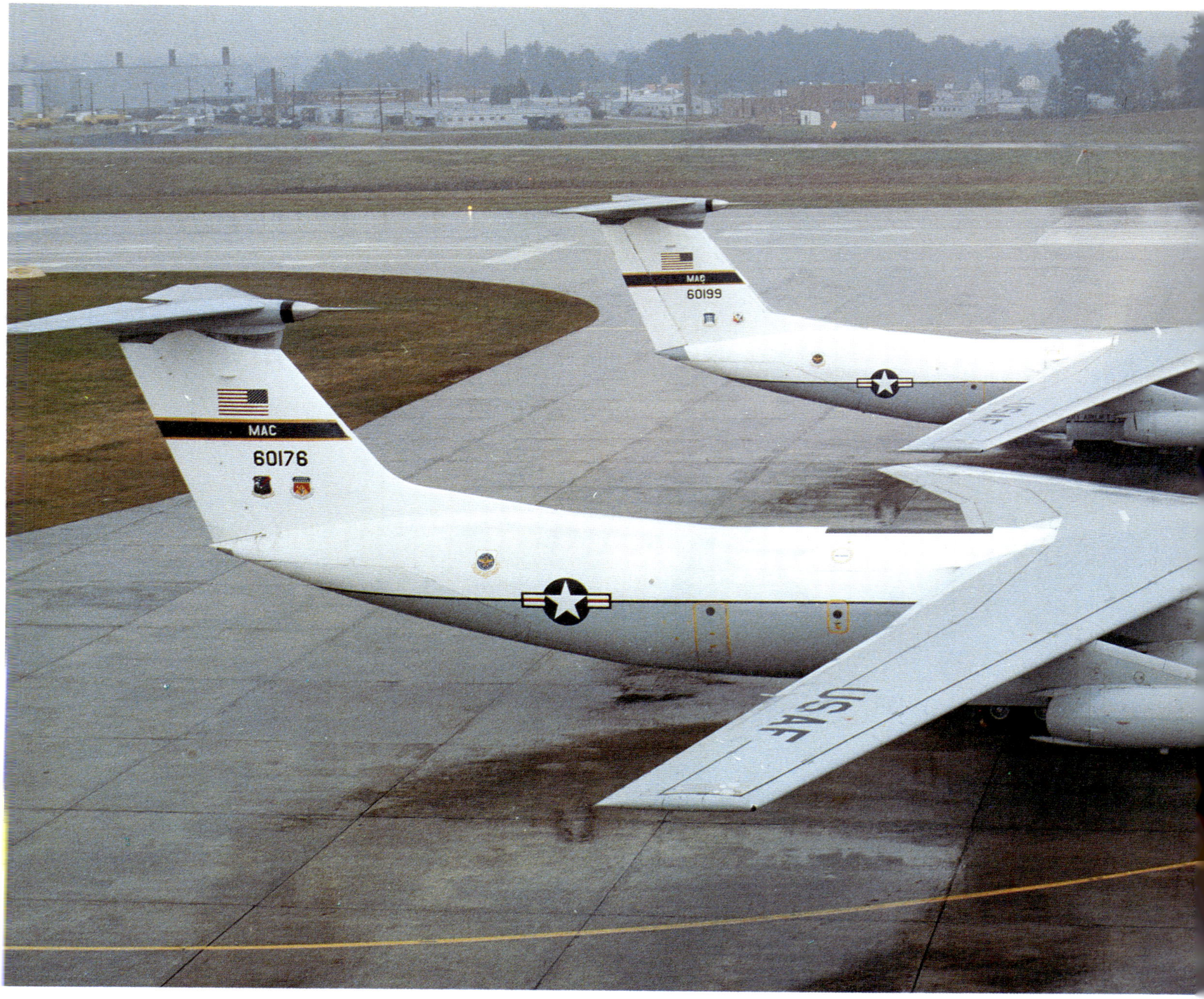
MAC
60176
MAC
60199
USAF
USAF

Facing page, at top: A Military Airlift Command C-141 Starlifter sets down at Grenada's Point Salines Airport during the invasion of Grenada in October 1983. *Above:* US Airborne troops wait to board the C-141s *in the background,* which the troops call 'lizards' because of their European 1 camouflage colors. *Below left:* The C-141A (*background*) and the C-141B (*note* aerial refueling 'cap' above its cockpit), compared for size.

sales were forthcoming, so this aircraft was purchased by NASA and fitted with a high-powered 36-inch astronomical telescope, to become the *Kuiper Airborne Observatory*.

From the moment it went into squadron service and for eight years thereafter, the C-141A Starlifter was an important part of the Military Airlift Command's logistical support for American forces involved in the Vietnam War. Unlike the C-130, the C-141A had the capability of flying nonstop to Saigon from California. Thus, as the Starlifter became available in sufficient numbers, C-130s were freed up for tactical airlift missions involving the disbursal of supplies from places served by Starlifters to frontline field positions.

In 1973, during the Yom Kippur War in the Middle East, the Military Airlift Command set up an aerial pipeline to transport supplies to Israel. It was at this time that the Air Force identified the need to enhance the Starlifter's capability. First of all, the C-141A was not able to be refueled while in the air. Also, since the overall airframe could tolerate a longer fuselage, and a longer fuselage would accommodate a larger load, such a modification would make the Starlifter more valuable.

In 1975 the decision was made to stretch the Starlifter's overall length by 23.3 feet and retrofit it to permit aerial refueling. On 8 December 1975 the first C-141A arrived at Marietta for stretching, and on 8 January 1977 this C-141A had become the stretched YC-141B prototype. On 24 March 1977, more than a month ahead of schedule, the YC-141B made its first flight. On 7 June 1978 the Air Force made the decision to rebuild the *entire* Military Airlift Command (MAC) C-141A fleet to C-141B standard.

In February 1979 MAC began sending its Starlifters down to Marietta for the 23.3-foot stretch, and by 13 July the first production C-141B had rolled out of the factory. By 22 April 1981, 136 C-141Bs had been built and the conversion program had reached the halfway point. Finally, on 29 June 1982, the last of the 270 C-141Bs was completed and the conversion program ended — ahead of schedule and under budget.

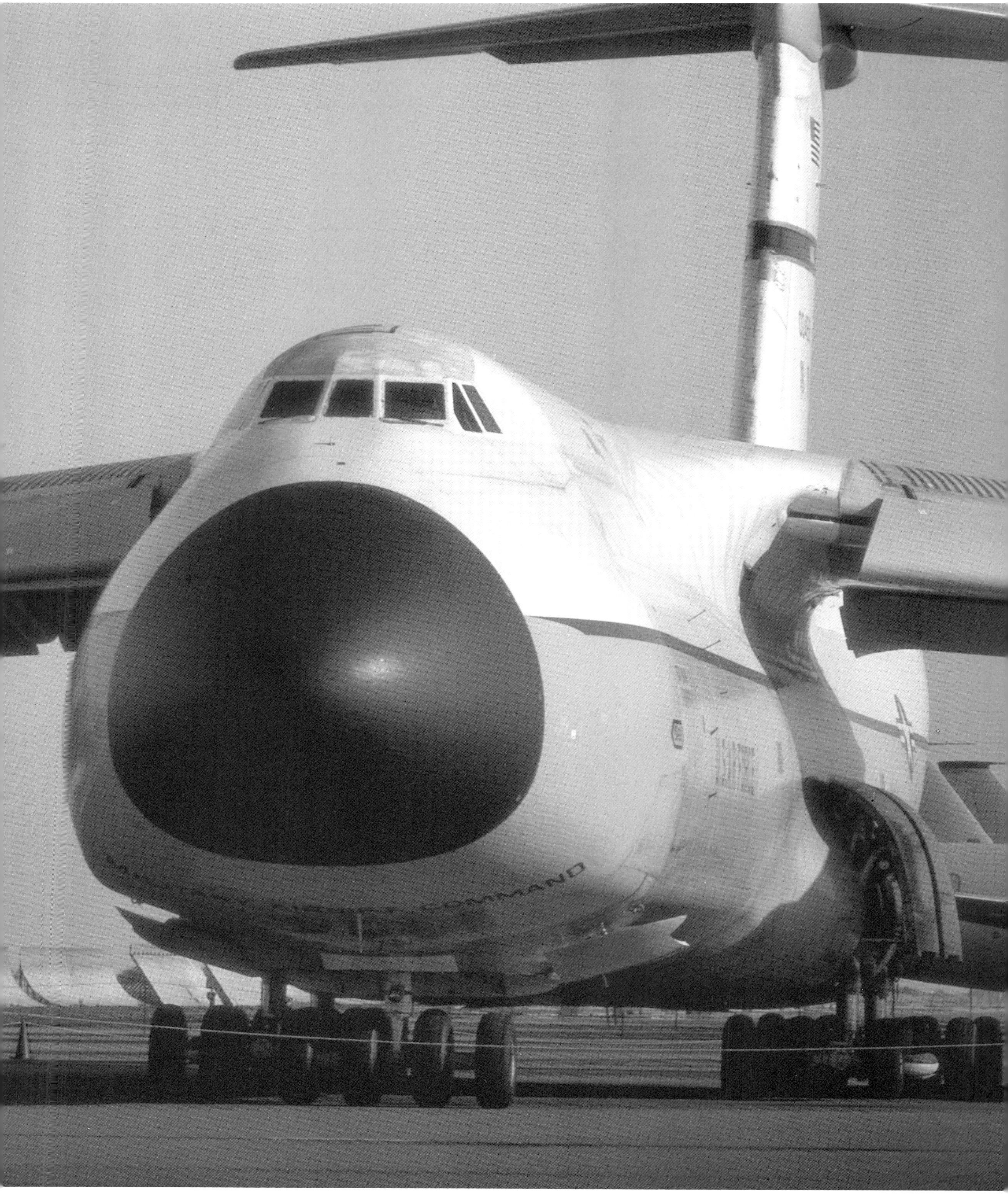
COMMAND

THE GALAXY

By the early to mid-1960s, the US Air Force Military Airlift Command was building a well-planned and standardized core group of transports to serve the many and varied jobs that it was called upon to perform. On the *small* end of the scale were the likes of the Lockheed C-140 JetStar and the Fairchild C-123. In the *medium* category was, of course, the Lockheed C-130 Hercules. At the *large* end of the scale were a few Boeing C-135s, counterparts of the Strategic Air Command KC-135 tankers and, of course, the planned series of Lockheed C-141 Starlifters. This seemed as though it would complete a well-rounded core, but MAC had begun to think about building an *extra-large* airlifter. Thus came the origin of the CX-4 project in 1963.

The CX-4 experimental transport project would call for nothing short of the largest transport the world had ever seen. The nation's three largest builders of large aircraft—Boeing, Douglas and Lockheed—were all given CX-4 study contracts in June 1964, and the process began. Each company knew that the final production contract would be one of the largest the Air Force had ever let, so there was intense competition. What Lockheed and the others didn't realize at the time was that contract would lead the *winner* to the brink of financial disaster.

On 1 October 1965 Lockheed became that winner with the Model 500, which was basically a greatly scaled-up version of its Model 300 (C-141 Starlifter). Lockheed would build 115 Model 500s under the designation C-5A for $1.9 billion, excluding five prototypes and spare parts. The name chosen for the C-5A would be Galaxy, thus keeping with Lockheed's tradition of naming aircraft after stellar bodies and *really large* aircraft (such as the Constellation in its day) after groups of stars.

While a disappointed Boeing turned its C-5 proposal into the hugely successful commercial Model 747, Lockheed Georgia went forward with production of the C-5A prototype on August 1966, hoping for (as reported in *Fortune* magazine in 1969) a $177 million profit. There was also optimism at Lockheed that commercial orders for a civilian L-500 freighter would add to the success of the Galaxy program.

What was not foreseen in the beginning of the Galaxy program, however, was that it would take more than simply scaling-up the Starlifter. The Galaxy would be the world's largest airplane. Nobody had ever built anything so big, and mistaken assumptions proved costly.

On 2 March 1968 the first C-5A Galaxy rolled out of the Marietta factory. She was, as predicted, more costly than at first anticipated, but she also was more than just a scaled-up C-141 would have been. Unlike the C-141—which could be loaded only through its aft doors—the Galaxy's nose opened to permit loading from either end. Vehicles could be driven aboard through one end and *driven* off the other end rather than being backed out. For the first time ever, the US Air Force had a plane that could haul the US Army's largest main battle tanks. In size, the Galaxy was 156 percent larger than the C-130, with five times the gross weight; and 69 percent longer than the C-141A, with more than twice the gross weight. In comparison to other large transports, the Galaxy was 13 percent longer than Howard Hughes' H-4 *'Spruce Goose'*, with more than twice the gross weight; while it was seven percent longer, with about five percent greater gross weight than the Boeing 747, the only other plane in the same class. The huge C-5A was also a good deal more versatile

The C-5A Galaxy (*above left*) is one of the largest aircraft ever built, and that by some whopping dimensions: wingspan of 222 feet, 9 inches; length of 247 feet, 10 inches; and overall height of 65 feet. A Galaxy set a cargo-carrying record of 798,200 pounds in 1968.

Above: In this view of the interior of the Lockheed Georgia manufacturing plant, the details of a C-5 fuselage are very much in evidence.

In the *above* cutaway view of a C-5A, we encounter, *from nose to tail:* the drive on/drive off front loading ramp; the living-room-size flight deck, *behind which* is the forward galley, crew bunks and the crew rest area; *farther back* past the wings is the passenger area and the aft galley. All of this is suspended *above* the enormous cargo bay, which itself terminates in the drive on/drive off aft loading ramp, and *beyond this* is the tail section, with a maintenance ladder built into the interior of the vertical stabilizer.

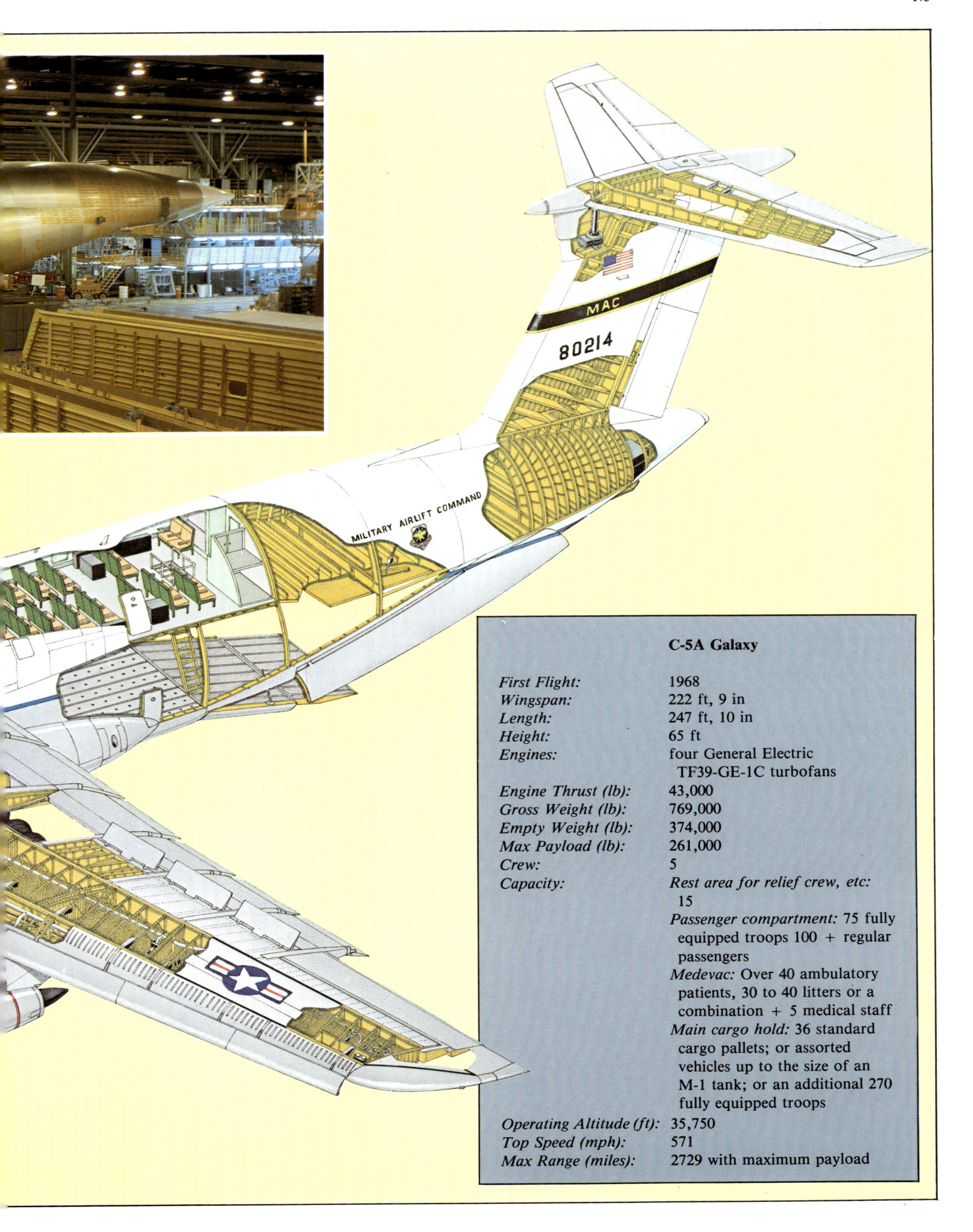

	C-5A Galaxy
First Flight:	1968
Wingspan:	222 ft, 9 in
Length:	247 ft, 10 in
Height:	65 ft
Engines:	four General Electric TF39-GE-1C turbofans
Engine Thrust (lb):	43,000
Gross Weight (lb):	769,000
Empty Weight (lb):	374,000
Max Payload (lb):	261,000
Crew:	5
Capacity:	*Rest area for relief crew, etc:* 15 *Passenger compartment:* 75 fully equipped troops 100 + regular passengers *Medevac:* Over 40 ambulatory patients, 30 to 40 litters or a combination + 5 medical staff *Main cargo hold:* 36 standard cargo pallets; or assorted vehicles up to the size of an M-1 tank; or an additional 270 fully equipped troops
Operating Altitude (ft):	35,750
Top Speed (mph):	571
Max Range (miles):	2729 with maximum payload

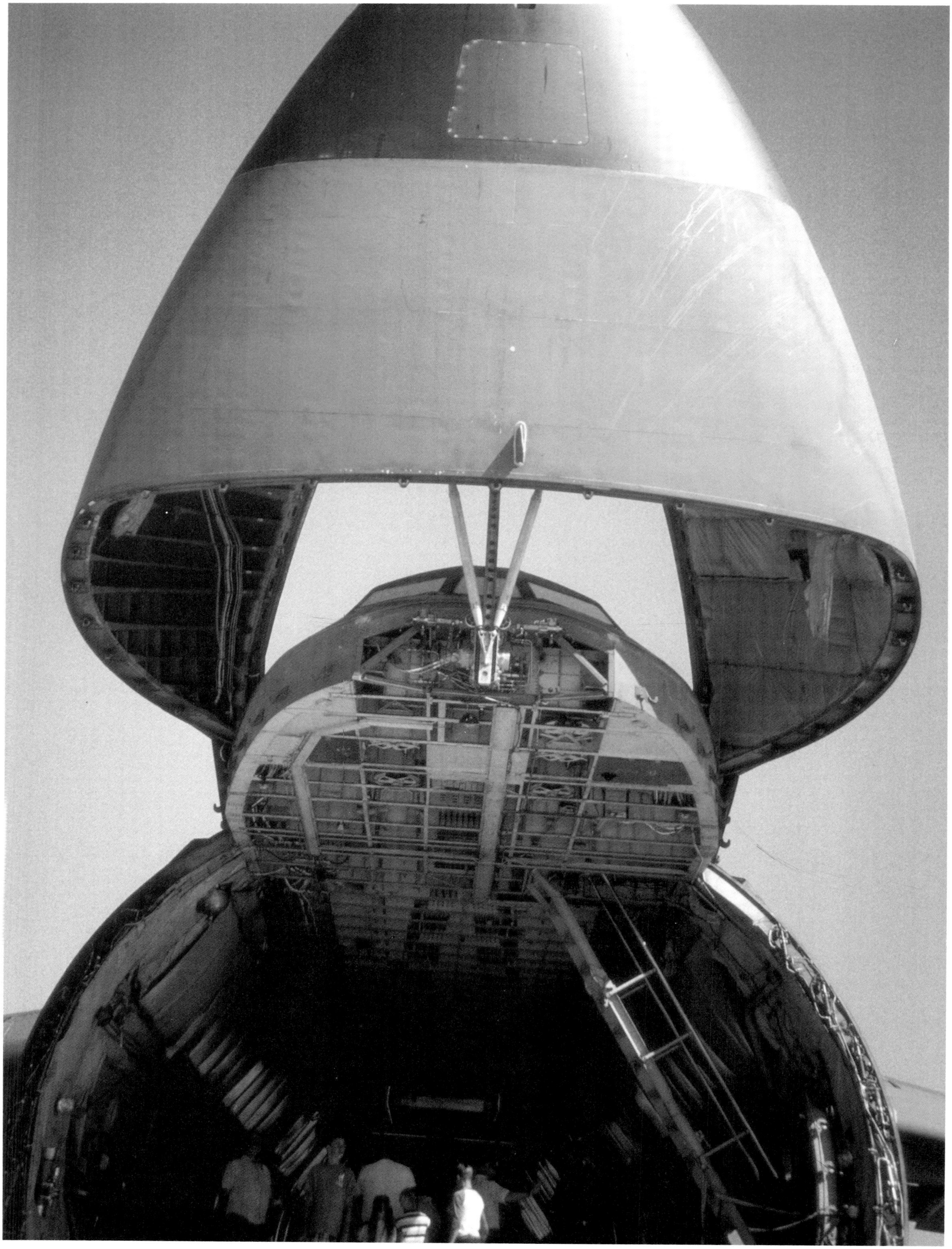

Left: This is a head-on view of the C-5A's 19 foot wide, 13.5 foot high and 144.6 foot deep cargo hold. Despite its size, the Galaxy takes off (*above*) and lands in distances comparable to today's commercial jetliners. *Right:* Three views of the C-5A.

in terms of the types and lengths of runways from which it could operate.

On 30 June 1968, powered by four General Electric TF39s, the world's first high-bypass ratio turbofan engines, the biggest airplane ever constructed made its first flight. On 4 October 1968 a Galaxy took off carrying a record gross weight of 798,200 pounds. On 17 December 1968 the first C-51A was delivered to Altus AFB, Oklahoma for MAC crew training.

In November 1968, however, the C-5A had come under Congressional attack for cost overruns when the Pentagon estimated that the final cost of the program of 115 aircraft could reach $3.5 billion. The overall deal had been structured to call for delivery of the 115 C-5As in two batches of 58 and 57 aircraft. Charges in Congress of waste and cost overruns resulted in a movement toward cancellation of the second batch. In January 1969 a compromise was reached by which the second batch would be chopped to just 23 aircraft. In July 1969 the failure of a C-5A wing during static tests further fueled the controversy, and Lockheed's stock plunged to less than half of its 1968 high. The Air Force predicted that Lockheed could lose as much as $285 million on the project. Even Lockheed chairman Dan Haughton's much more optimistic assessment showed a $13 million loss.

In November 1969, amid charges of design deficiencies, the Air Force confirmed that it would buy no more than a total of 81 C-5As. Lockheed protested the cutoff, noting that there was now no way to avoid a loss. Financially, 1970 was the worst year in Lockheed's history, with corporate losses posted at $187.8 million. Faced with the C-5A troubles on top of the cancellation of the Cheyenne helicopter and the L-1011 jetliner teething troubles, there were many voices in the American business press that predicted Lockheed's imminent demise. In July 1970 Congress authorized a $200 million contingency fund for continued

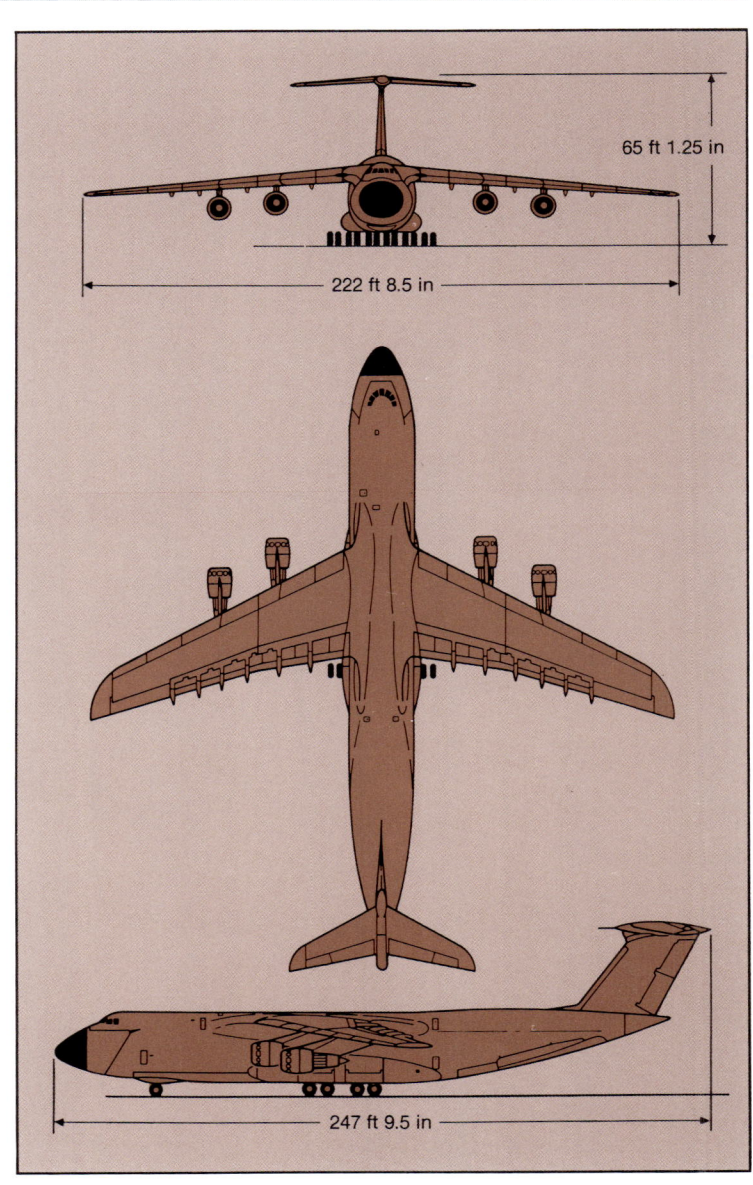

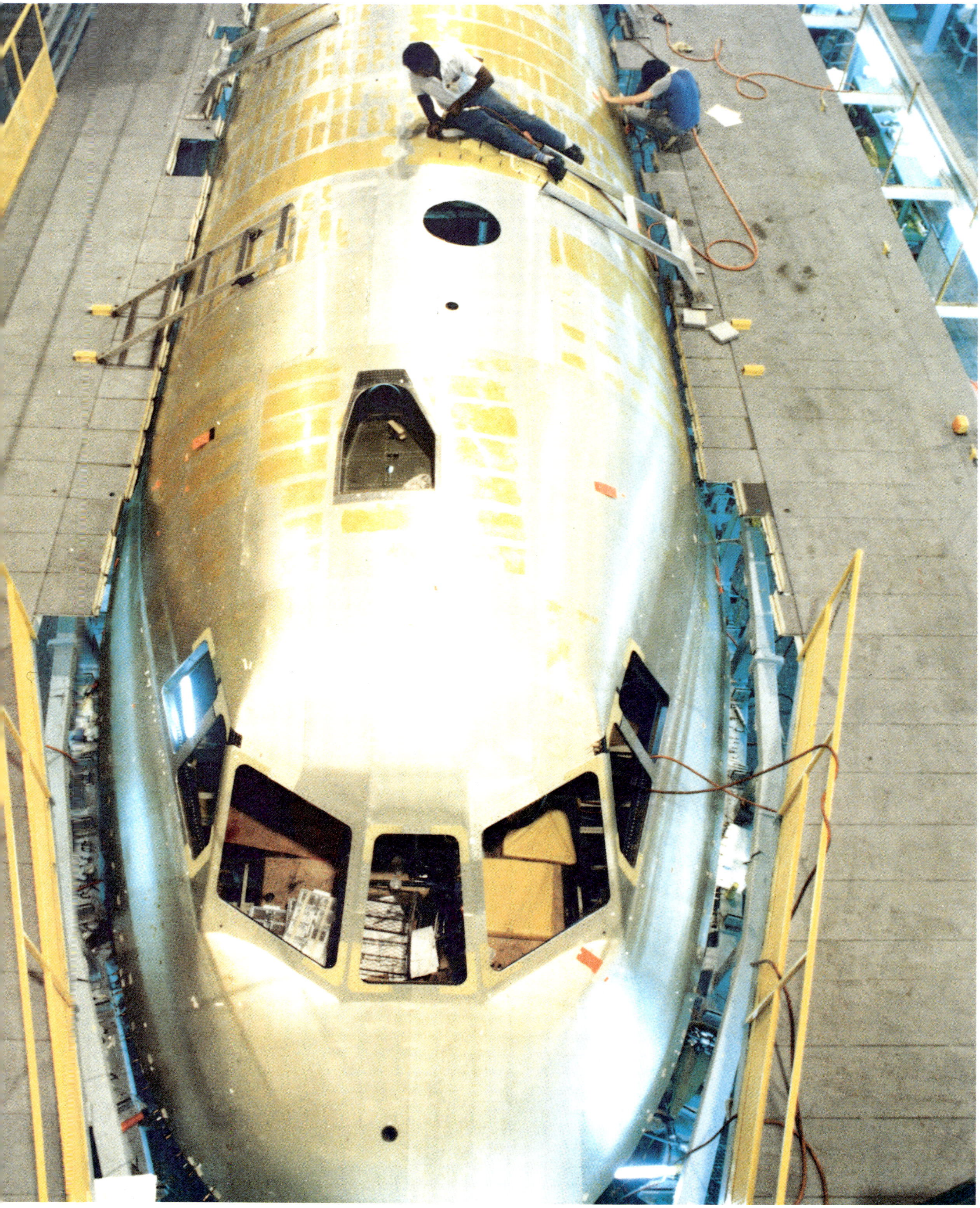

As the result of a contract for 50 updated C-5B military transports, Lockheed geared up again in the early 1980s to begin production on their Galaxy series. The *facing page* is a photograph of Lockheed employees working from a platform built around the huge C-5B's 'second story.'

Among other Galaxy improvements are the C-5B's engines, which are General Electric TF39-1Cs. General Electric's TF39-1C (*immediate left*) high bypass turbofan jet engine replaces the TF39-1, which was designed for the C-5A in the 1960s½ All of the USAF's fleet of 77 C-5As are also being upgraded to the new TF39-1C engine specs. *Note* how this huge engine dwarfs the men who are working on it.

Above: C-5 fuselages are mated together from three initial sections—forward, center and aft. The historic photo *above,* of the interior of Lockheed's Marietta, Georgia C-5B facility, shows a riveting jig (*center, foreground*) which contains a segment of the center section of the first C-5B fuselage to be successfully mated. This blessed event took place 5 December 1984. Also note another segment of the center section—also in its jig—*aloft at right rear.* As the C-5B's fuselage alone is 247.8 feet in length, the successful joining of its three main sections is indeed, as a Lockheed staffmember put it, 'a milestone.'

production of the C-5A, and the company scrambled to fix the problems with the Galaxy's wings. In the end, Lockheed wrote off $250 million on the C-5A project, through it all the company survived, and the US Government made $31 million profit on the loan guarantee. (Please refer to the L-1011 section for a fuller discussion of these trying times.)

The Galaxy itself survived the problems with its wing to become a far better airlifter than had been feared in the early years of the program. On 27 May 1970 a C-5A operated from bare soil for the first time at Harper's Dry Lake in California, and on 6 June the first C-5As entered squadron service at Charleston AFB, South Carolina. Although at that time the American involvement in Vietnam was winding down, the C-5A nevertheless played an important role in the logistical support of American forces between 1971 and 1978. In April 1971 a single C-5A carried three huge twin-rotor CH-47 helicopters to Vietnam, and in August 1971 another C-5A set a world record for a single parachute drop by dropping an incredible *80 tons* of material.

On 18 May 1973, with American involvement in southeast Asia all but concluded, the 81st and last C-5A was delivered to the Military Airlift Command. If the C-5A operations to Southeast Asia demonstrated the Galaxy's capability, the MAC airlift to Israel during and after the Yom Kippur War proved it. After having delivered 21,600,000 pounds of supplies in 145 sorties during October and November 1973, the Galaxy's reputation had turned 180 degrees from white elephant to workhorse.

In the meanwhile, sales for the L-500 commercial Galaxy, an aircraft that could have hauled 87 Volkswagons from Frankfurt to New York in a single hop, failed to materialize. The reason was that $250 million in tooling would be required for the civil L-500, due to the fact it would have only 20 percent of its components in common with the C-5A. The resulting $23.5 million per plane price tag was too steep for any potential customer.

The C-5A, however, continued to establish a solid reputation for itself. In a 1974 demonstration, a live 40-ton Minuteman ICBM was *air-launched* for the first time from a C-5. In both 1978 and 1979 its crews captured the MacKay Trophy for airmanship. By 1979, after ten years in the Air Force and nine years in squadron service, the MAC C-5A fleet had logged 400,000 hours and had airlifted *four billion tons* of cargo.

In 1980 work began on a program to rebuild the wings of the C-5A fleet to extend their service life. The production phase of the program began in July 1981, and in June 1982 the first re-winged C-5A had completed 1400 flight hours. In August 1982 fatigue tests were concluded on the new wing, which the Air Force dubbed a 'super wing.' The tests had included 105,000 cyclic test hours on one set of wings, simulating 3.5 'lifetimes' of flying. The last 15,000 hours included deliberately induced simulated 'battle damage'. On 25 October 1984 one C-5A passed the 10,000 hour mark with its 'super wing'. On 17 December 1984 a 'super wing' C-5A, carrying a 116-ton payload, was flown at a gross weight of 922,000 pounds—the heaviest weight at which an aircraft had ever flown.

In December 1982 Lockheed was awarded a contract for 50 upgraded C-5B transports to join the 77 C-5As that were still in service. Painted in the new European I camouflage scheme, the first C-5B rolled out of the factory on 12 July 1985. This new Galaxy made its first flight on 10 September 1985, and the first C-5B was put into service on 8 January 1986.

The first C-5B (*above right*) to take to the air did so on 10 September 1985 with test pilot Bernie Dvorscak at the controls. Dvorscak said 'It does everything it's supposed to do. The first flight went so well, we extended it by an hour.'

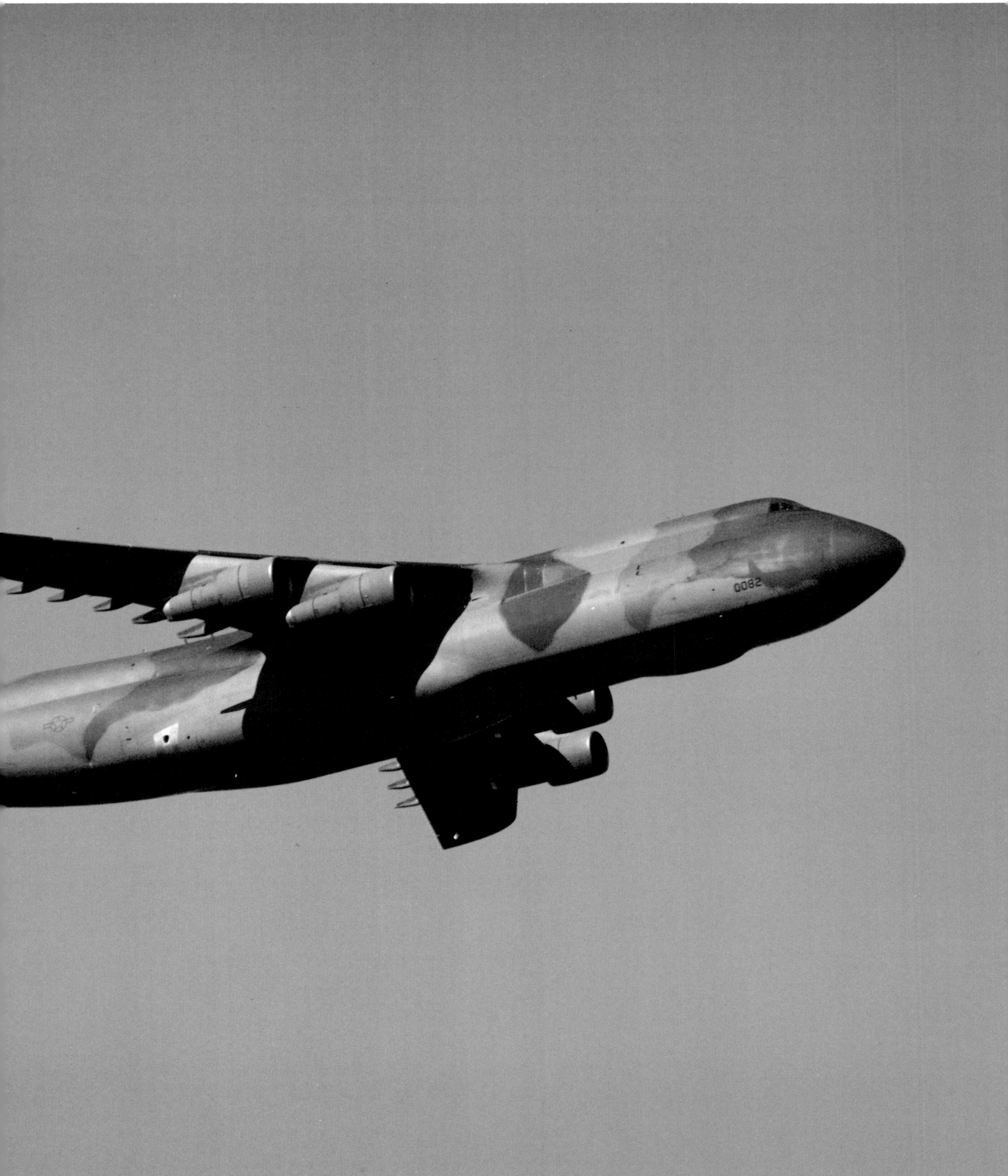
0082

Galaxies on parade: C-5As of the 60th Military Airlift Wing (MAW) are shown *here* on the flight line at Travis Air Force Base. The first C-5A rolled out of Lockheed's Marietta factory on 2 March 1968, and the first aircraft were delivered to the 60th MAW. On 18 May 1973, after five financially unstable and publicly controversial years, the 81st and last C-5A left the factory behind it. The Galaxy program was, despite trouble, hugely successful—the aircraft itself proved reliable and more useful than had even been anticipated. In December 1982, Lockheed was awarded a US Air Force contract to produce 50 improved C-5Bs, the first of which saw the light of day on 12 July 1985.

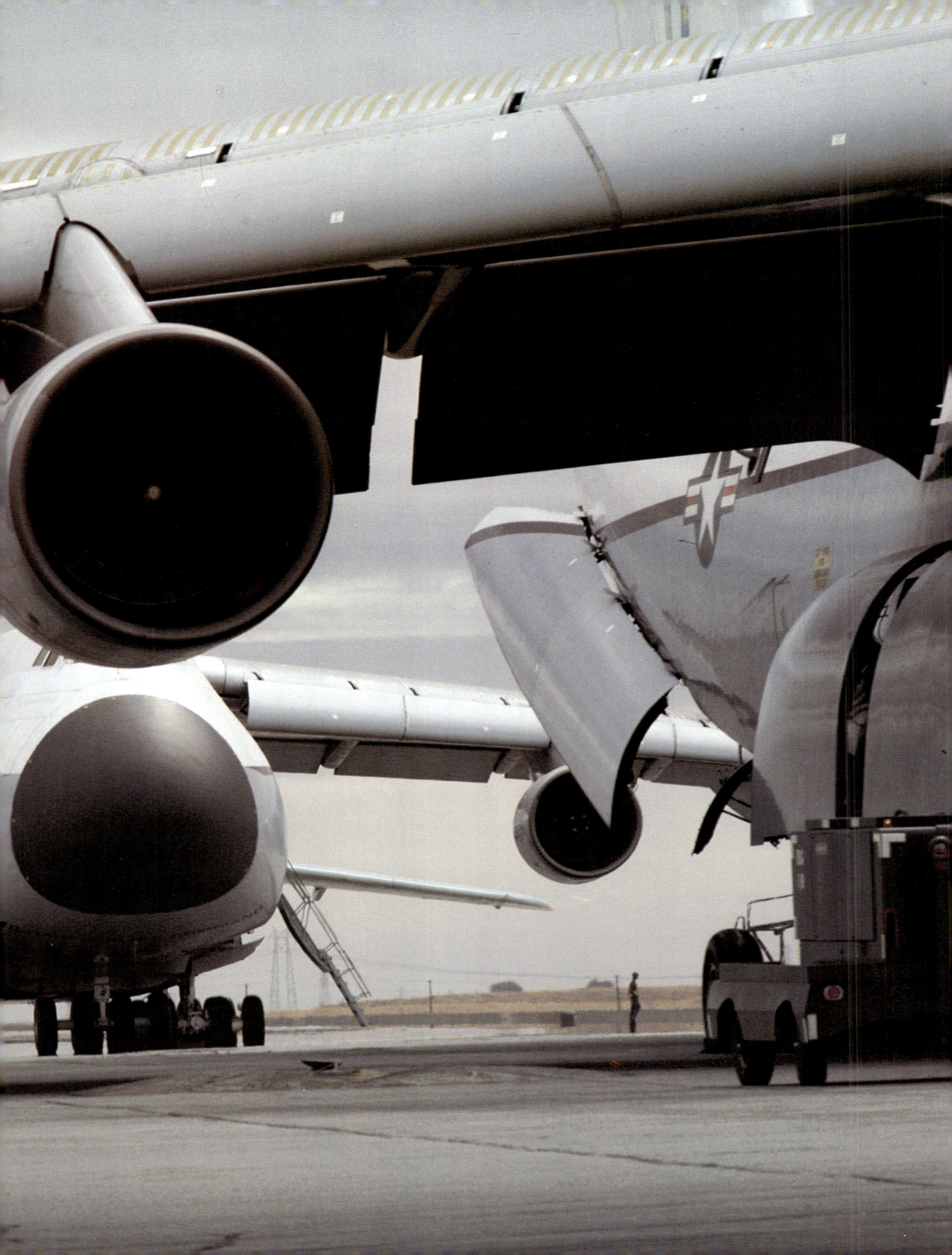

THE L-1011 TRISTAR

PLANNING A JUMBO JET

In 1965 Boeing lost to Lockheed in the competition to build the huge C-5A airlifter for the US Air Force. Undaunted, Boeing turned its engineering studies into its Model 747, the largest commercial jetliner ever built. The Boeing 747, which first flew on 9 January 1969 (seven months after Lockheed's C-5A Galaxy), completely revolutionized commercial air travel.

Meanwhile, Boeing's two principal competitors, McDonnell Douglas (Douglas Aircraft Company prior to the 1967 merger with McDonnell) and Lockheed each had made the decision to build a wide-body, 'jumbo jet' of their own. Both companies had their eye on the portion of the market which could be filled by an airliner in the 250+ passenger range that would be smaller than the Boeing 747 but much larger than any other jetliner that had ever been put into service. What emerged were Lockheed's L-1011 and the McDonnell Douglas DC-10, two planes designed for the same market, nearly identical in appearance and fated to share a market that *would have been* profitable for either, but which was not large enough for both players. Both Lockheed and McDonnell Douglas decided to reach for the same slice of the pie.

McDonnell Douglas had already developed a track record in the jetliner field with its DC-8 and DC-9, while Lockheed had never built a jetliner. Lockheed, in fact, hadn't built a commercially successful airliner since the Constellation, which had been designed in the early 1940s. Lockheed's president (chairman after 1967) Daniel Haughton, however, had watched his company successfully build a family of military airlifters (Hercules and Starlifter) that would soon include the Galaxy, the world's largest airplane. Haughton was determined to balance out Lockheed's product line by returning to commercial aircraft. He also was determined to build a 250+ passenger jetliner that was second to none.

In the meantime, Lockheed had also been developing the design for its Model 2000 Supersonic Transport (SST), again in competition with McDonnell Douglas and Boeing. In December 1966 Boeing was given the SST contract and suddenly, Lockheed California had a large pool of engineers that could go to work on the new 250+ passenger jetliner, Lockheed's Model 1011.

The prototype Lockheed Model 1011 (*above*), known to airline passengers the world over as the L-1011 TriStar, eclipses a seaside sunset. *Upper right:* An Air Canada L-1011 is shown *here* as it tucks its landing gear away, just after takeoff.

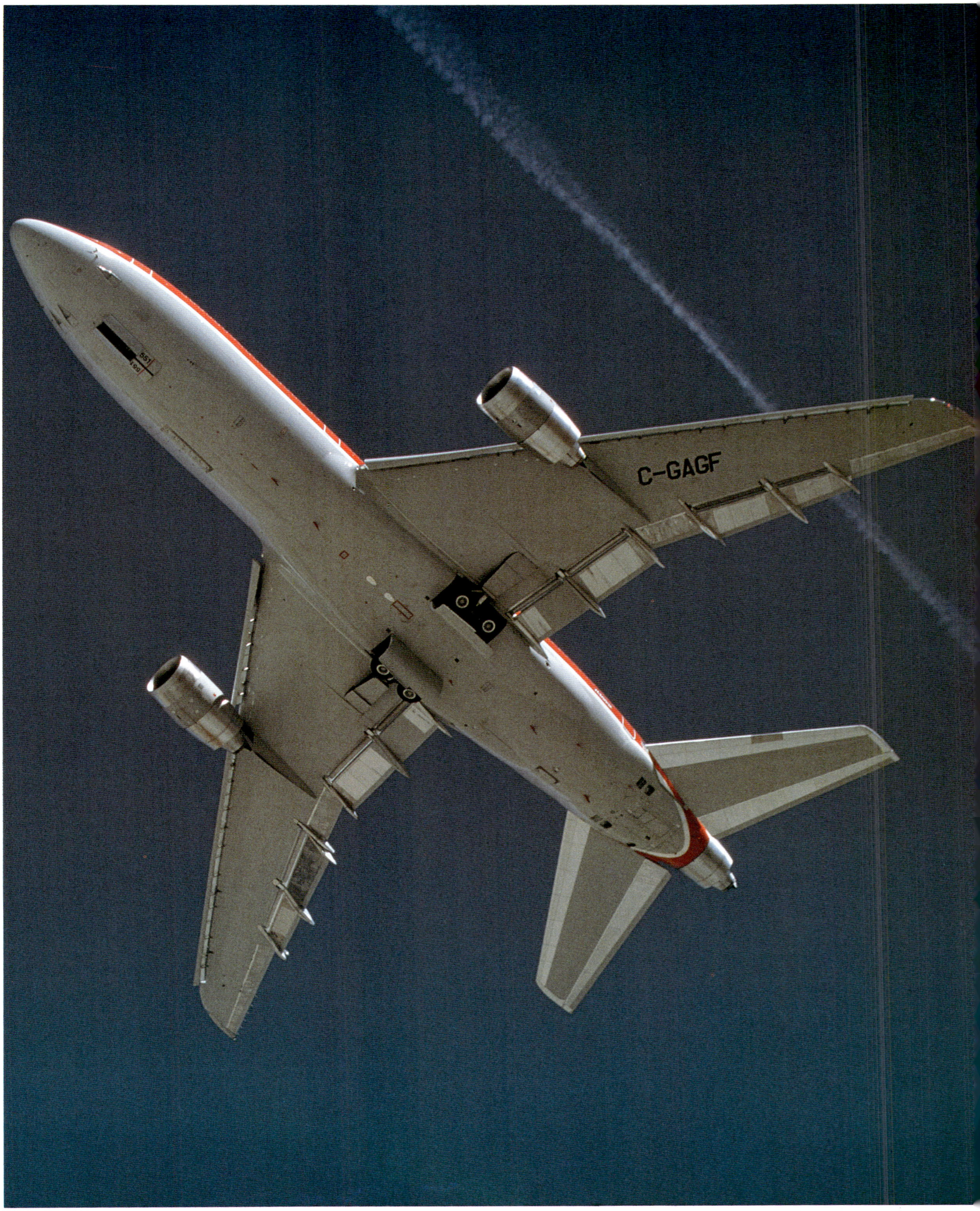
C-GAGF

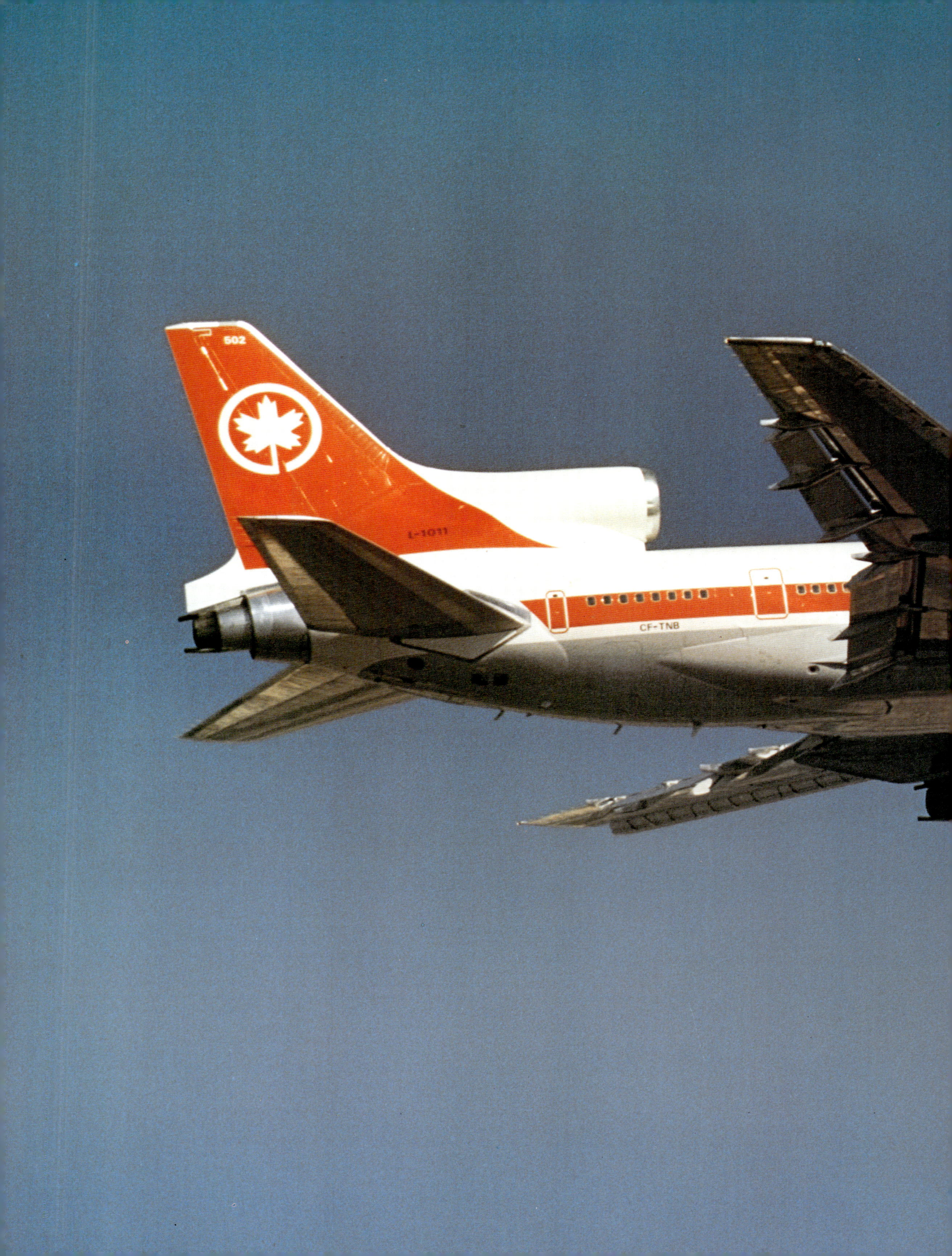
502
L-1011
CF-TNB

Below left: A fitting counterpart to Lockheed's huge cargo craft, the C-5A, the Model L-1011-1 (aka the 'Dash One,' as compared to later versions of the aircraft) is shown *here* in the service of Air Canada, one of the second round of early L-1011 buyers.

EARLY DEVELOPMENT

The L-1011, named TriStar because of its three turbofan engines, and the McDonnell Douglas DC-10 emerged from their respective southern California drawing boards looking almost like twins. Both were wide-bodied, twin-aisled jetliners powered by three high-bypass turbofan engines. They were within seven percent of having exactly the same overall dimensions, and their internal configuration gave them virtually identical passenger capacity. Even side-by-side they were nearly identical. The major distinguishing feature was that the DC-10's tail-mounted engine was of a 'straight-through' design and mounted on the vertical stabilizer, while the TriStar's tail-mounted engine was located in the fuselage, with the intake situated above it and connected to it by an 'S-duct.' *(See photos.)*

Boeing had selected Pratt & Whitney high-bypass turbofan engines for the 747, while McDonnell Douglas had picked General Electric's high-bypass turbofan engines for the DC-10. Lockheed had decided to use General Electric high-bypass turbofans for the C-5A, but when it came time for the TriStar's engines, Daniel Haughton went to Rolls Royce. The British manufacturer, most famous for its luxury automobiles, was also one of the world's three top jet engine builders. The strong US dollar made buying British engines cheaper, and on top of that, Rolls Royce made Lockheed a very good deal on the RB211 (a version of its RB207 engine) which would not only be cheaper, but would offer lower fuel consumption than the General Electric or Pratt & Whitney engines. Lockheed also projected that, by buying a European engine, it would have an inside track on selling the L-1011 to European airline companies. Despite complaints from the US Congress about Lockheed's plan to spend its engine budget overseas, the deal was struck and the RB211 was irrevocably designed into the TriStar.

COMPETITION AND CRISIS

By the beginning of 1968 the designs of both the DC-10 and L-1011 had taken form, and the sales cycle began. American Airlines, the airline which best epitomized the profile of a customer in need of a 250+ passenger airliner, looked closely at both planes. On 19 February 1968 they chose to order 15 DC-10s. On 29 March 1968 Eastern Air Lines and Trans World

At the top of this page: An L-1011-1 lifts off in the service of Eastern Air Lines, which was one of the aircraft's first buyers. *Upper right:* A mechanic services one of the Rolls Royce RB211 Turbofan engines of an Air Canada L-1011-1 TriStar airliner.

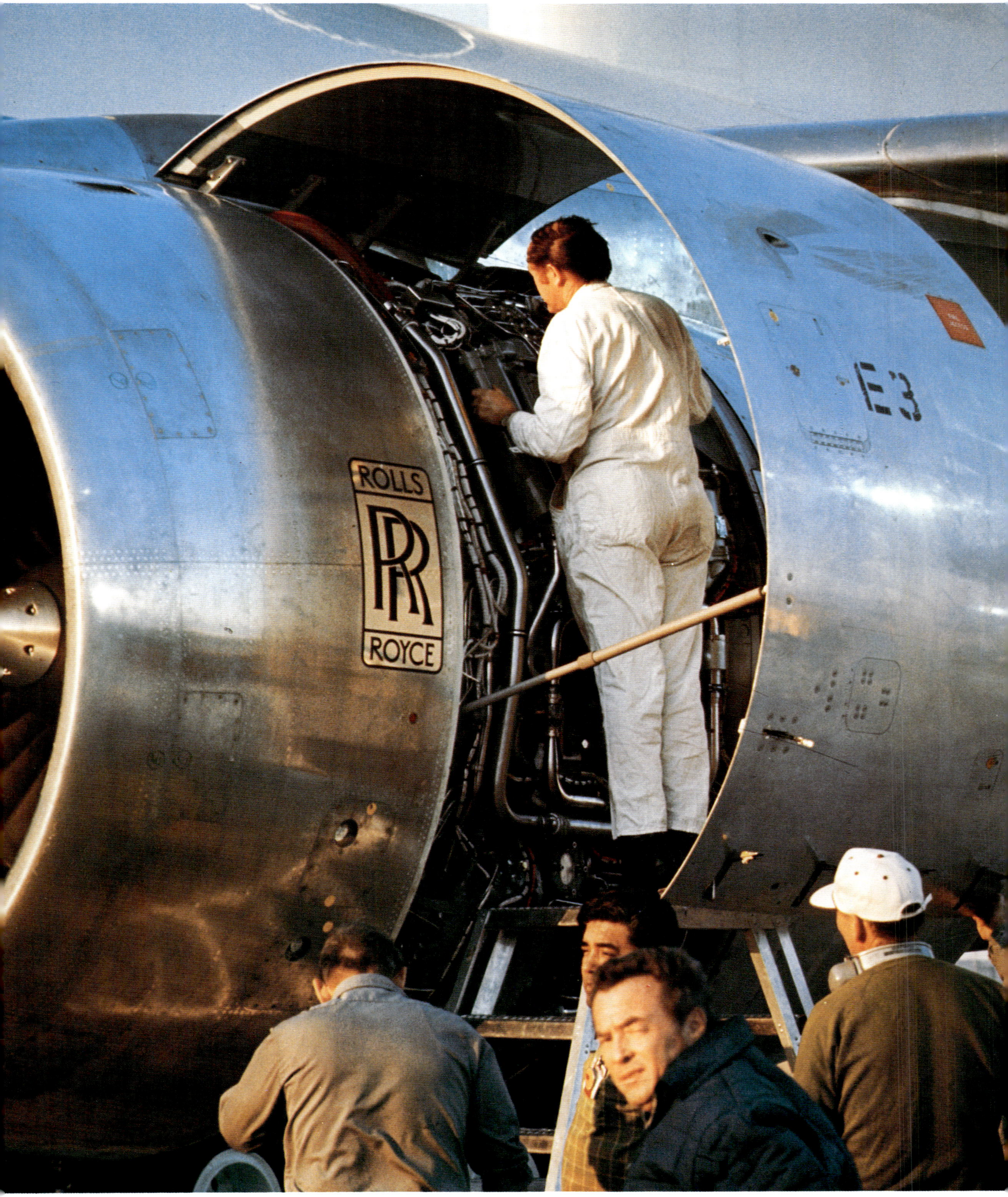
ROLLS
RR
ROYCE
E3

The Lockheed L-1011 TriStar (*below center*) and the McDonnell Douglas DC-10 (*at right*) airliners very strongly resemble one another, but whereas the DC-10 features a straight-through aft engine (integral to its vertical stabilizer), the L-1011 features an 'S-duct' aft engine arrangement, with the engine's intake port mounted in the fore part of the L-1011's vertical stabilizer, and the engine itself mounted in the aft portion of its fuselage. Both are wide-bodied, twin aisled jetliners powered by three turbofan engines (L-1011: Rolls Royce RB211s; and DC-10: General Electric CF6-series or Pratt & Whitney JT9Ds); and have nearly identical (with a mere seven percent overall size difference) overall dimensions.

A close look at the L-1011's horizontal tail fin reveals an arrowhead-shaped seam along its forward junction with the fuselage—this evidences the Lockheed Flying Stabilizer feature; the entire horizontal tailfin is moveable (in addition to the tailfin's own elevator surface), like a giant aerlon, giving the giant jetliner an increased control sensitivity.

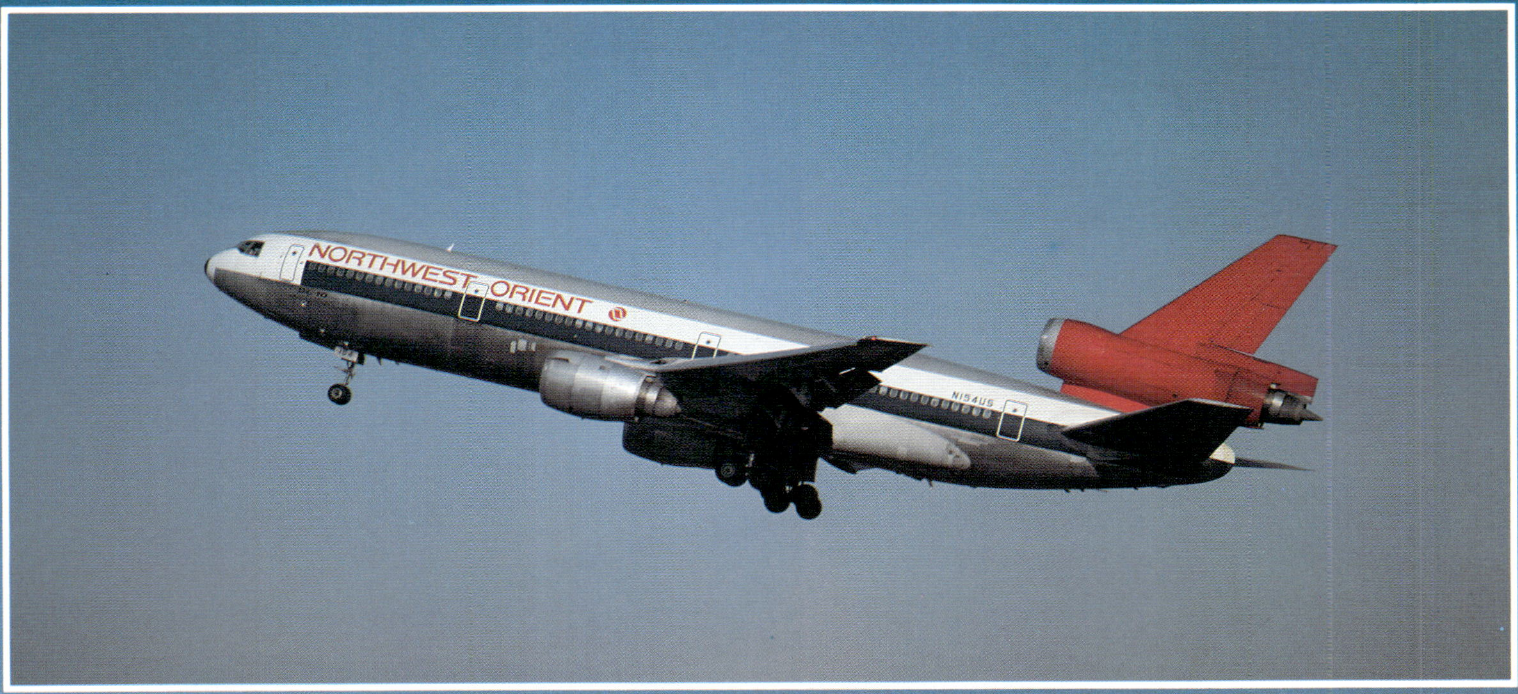
NORTHWEST ORIENT

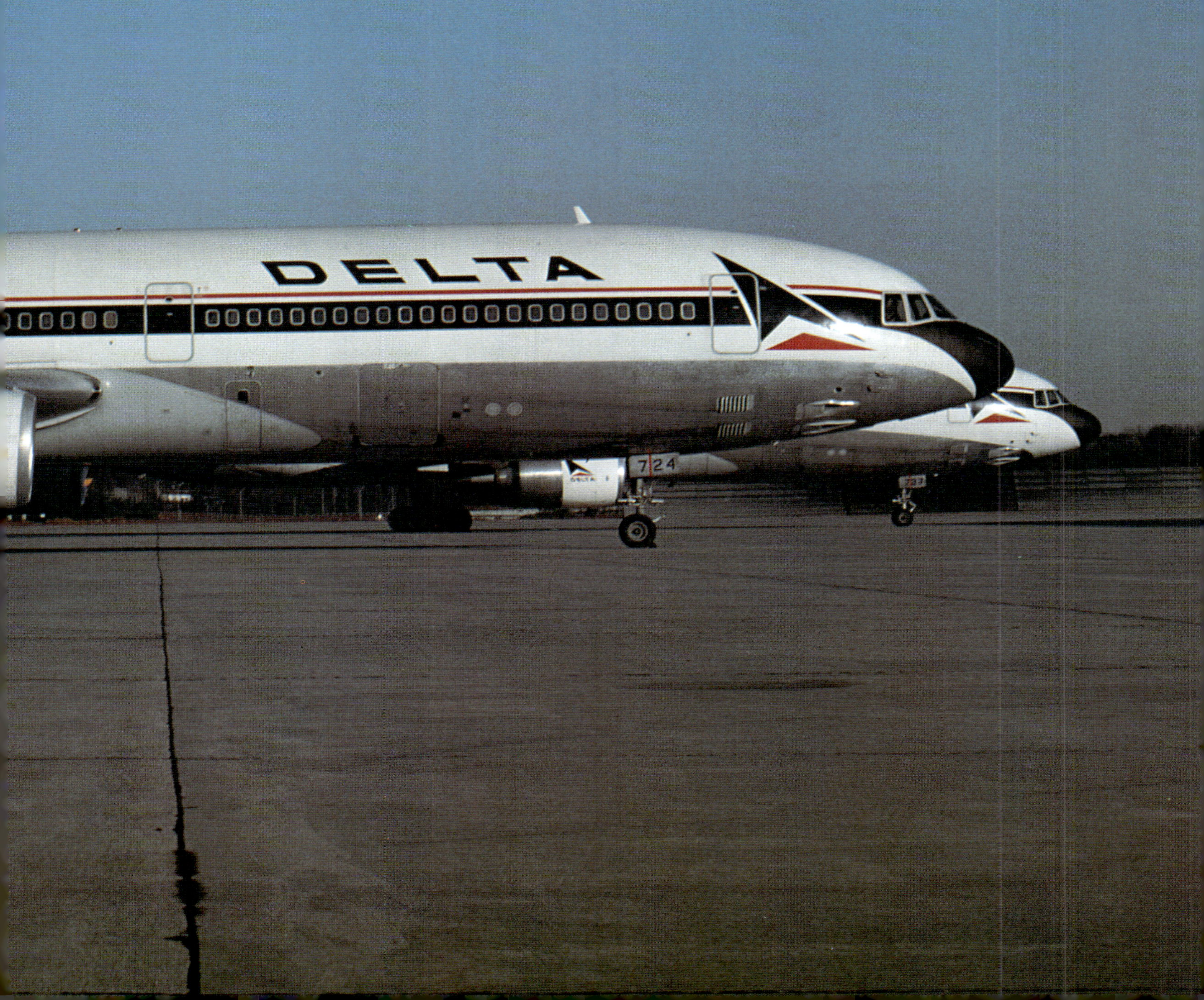
DELTA
724

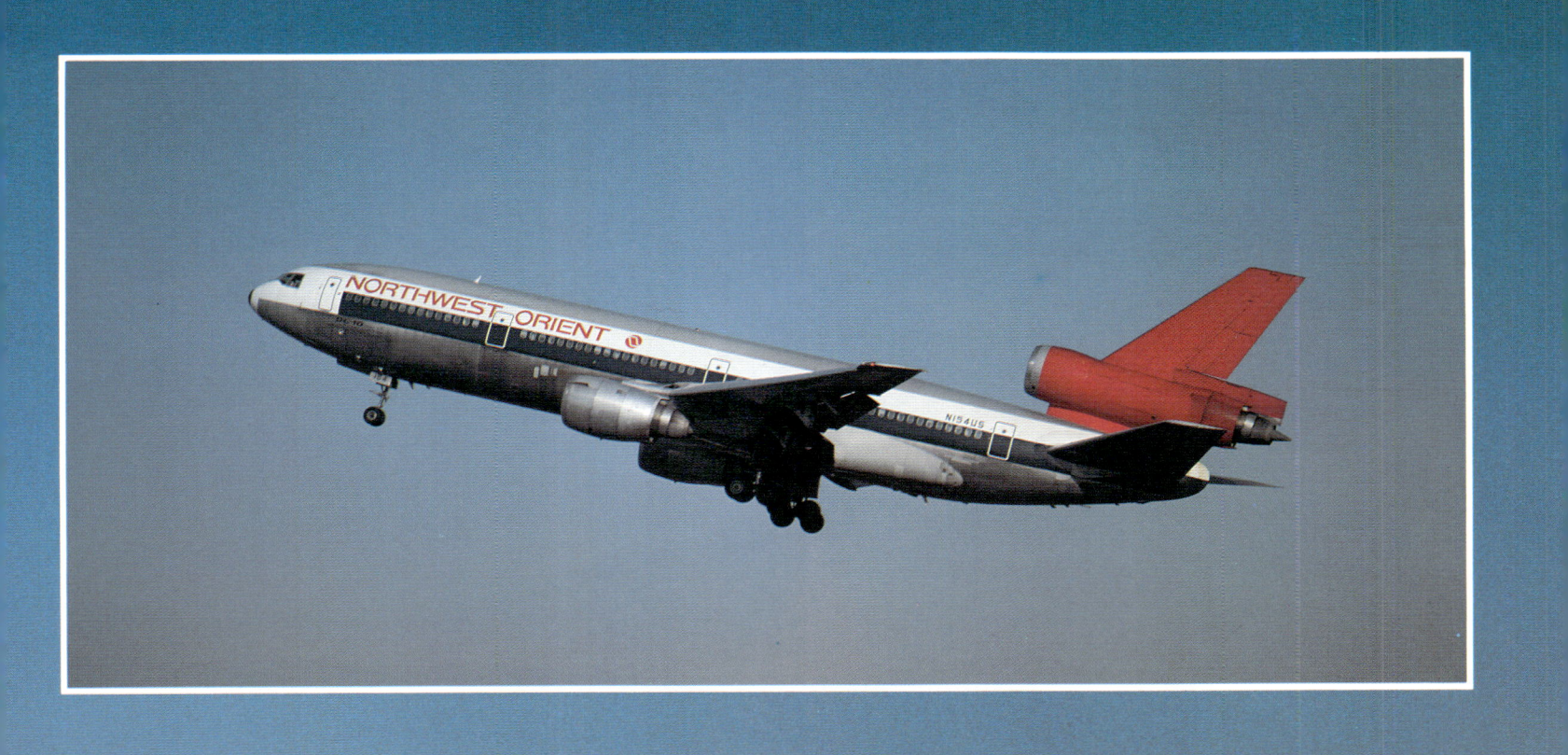

Airlines opted in favor of Lockheed's entry in the race. Delta Airlines followed the lead of Eastern and TWA on 2 April, choosing 24 TriStars for its fleet. The first round of the sales cycle ended on 25 April when United Airlines, the world's second largest airline (after Aeroflot), chose the DC-10. The events of Spring 1968 set the stage for what was to come.

The two largest airlines in the United States—United and American—had bought the DC-10, while the next three largest —TWA, Eastern and Delta—had gone with Lockheed's TriStar. In the first round Lockheed and McDonnell Douglas had split the market. That was the way it would be throughout the production career of the two aircraft. As could have been expected with the Rolls Royce engine, Lockheed won British Airways as a TriStar customer, but the DC-10 sold better in the rest of the European market. Lockheed succeeded in selling a sizable number of L-1011s to Japan's All Nippon Airways, but the sales commission the company paid to middleman Yoshio Kodama added fuel to what the media would call the 'Lockheed bribery scandal'.

The Lockheed L-1011 made its first flight on 16 November 1970, just three months after the DC-10. The TriStar quickly earned a reputation as an outstanding aircraft, but trouble was brewing. Rolls Royce was heavily in debt, the RB211 project was over budget, and Conservative Party Prime Minister James Callaghan was opposed to any notion of government aid to the ailing company.

Lockheed had invested a billion dollars in the L-1011 which was designed around the RB211, so if Rolls Royce went out of business, Lockheed could stand a chance of going down along with it. Chairman Haughton succeeded in working out a deal whereby the L-1011 customers would increase their advance payments. This, along with help from the British government, saved Rolls Royce (which had gone into receivership in February 1971) and the RB211.

Meanwhile, Lockheed itself was in a tailspin. The strain of shelling out development costs for two of the world's four larg-

Above: A stewardess tries on the L-1011's RB211 turbofan engine for size. The L-1011, shown *at upper right* undergoing stress testing, features Relaxed Static Stability for reduced aerodynamic drag, and the 4D Flight Management system, for maximum operational economy.

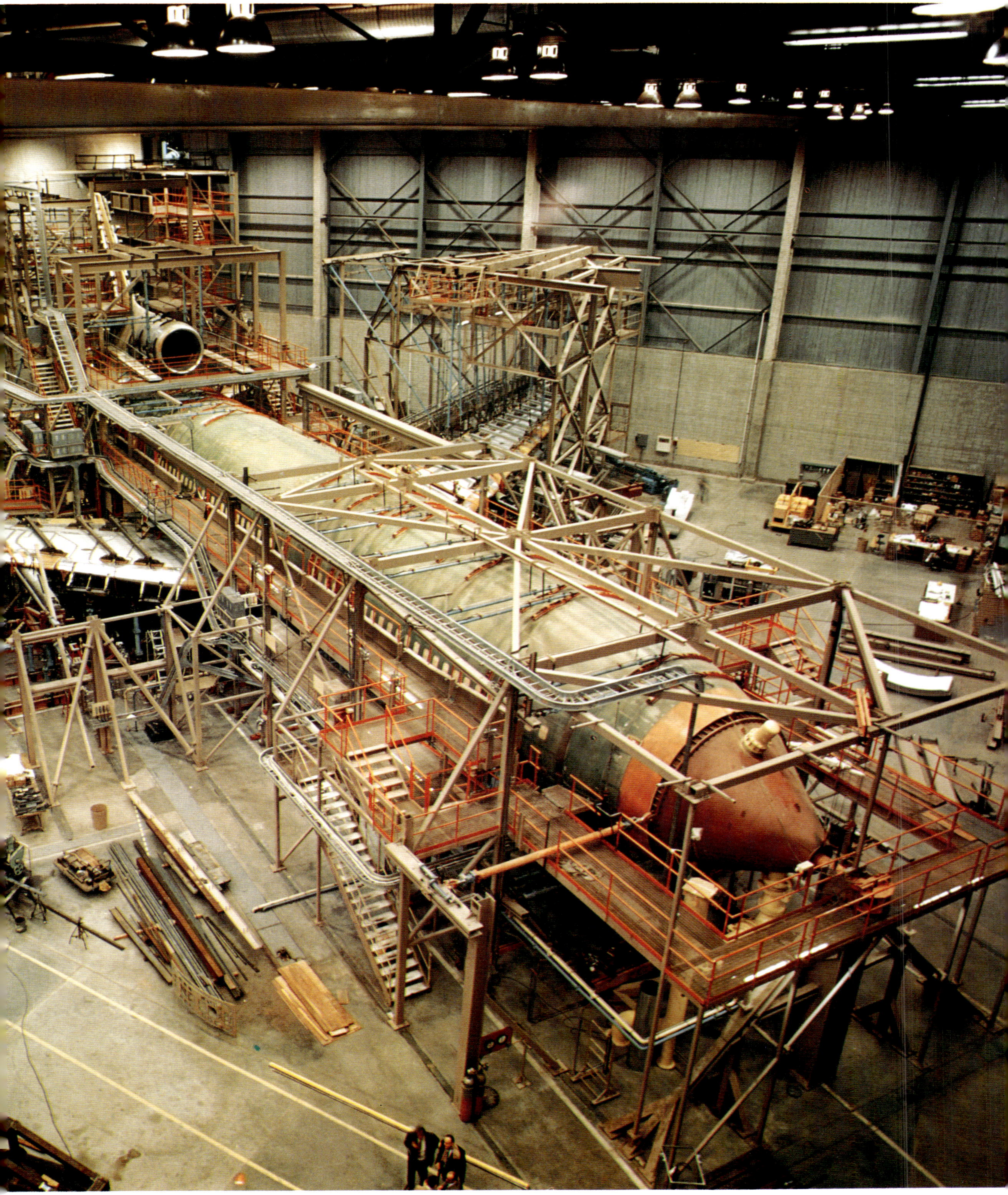

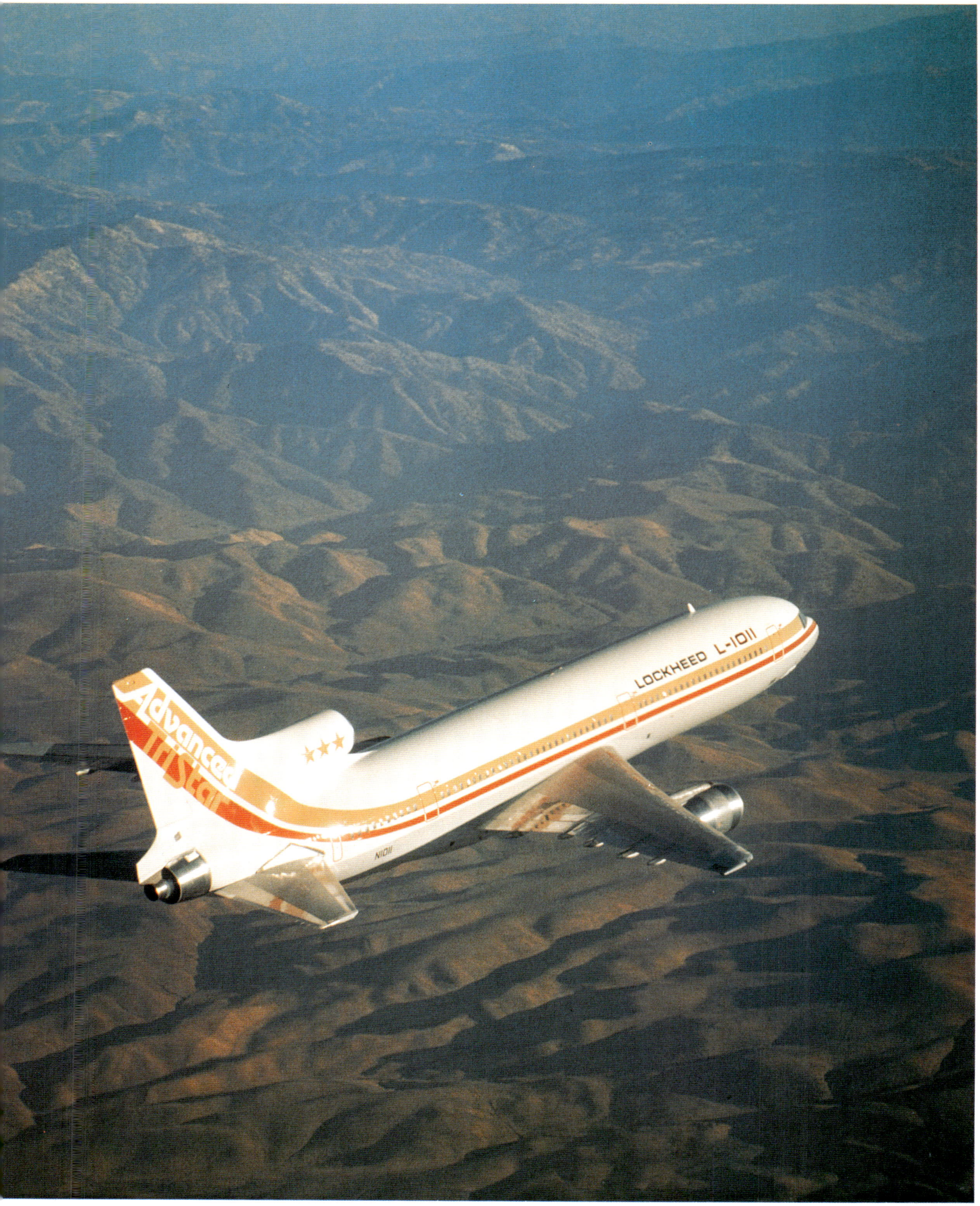
Advanced
TriStar
LOCKHEED L-1011
N1011

est aircraft types (C-5A and L-1011) simultaneously had cost the corporation a record $187.8 million loss in 1970 and 1971. The situation would have been much worse had Congress not guaranteed a $250 million line of credit, which was extended to Lockheed by commercial banks. Contrary to the popular misconception, the US Government neither gave nor loaned any money to Lockheed. In fact, Lockheed paid $30 million to the Federal Government for 'administrative expenses' on top of the interest paid to the banks.

Lockheed survived, repaid the bank loans with interest and over the next eight years the L-1011 TriStar went on to consistently post the best on-time departure record of any widebodied airliner.

THE TRISTAR IN SERVICE

Certified by the Federal Aviation Administration on 15 April 1972, the basic TriStar (L-1011-1 'Dash One') was in service two weeks later. The initial 'launch' customers—Eastern, Delta and TWA—were joined by Air Canada, All Nippon, British Airways, AeroPern, Cathay Pacific and Germany's Lufttransport Unternehmen (LTU). The 'Dash One' was capable of carrying 400 passengers over a distance of 3500 miles.

The next member of the TriStar family was the L-1011-100, which entered service in June 1975. The L-1011-100 was similar to the 'Dash One', but offered a 25 percent increase in range, permitting it to serve on longer transoceanic routes. Customers for the L-1011-100 included Delta, TWA, Air Canada, Cathay Pacific and Gulf Air, the airline of the United Arab Emirates.

Entering service in May 1977, the L-100-200 was similar to 'Dash One,' but combined the increased fuel capacity of the

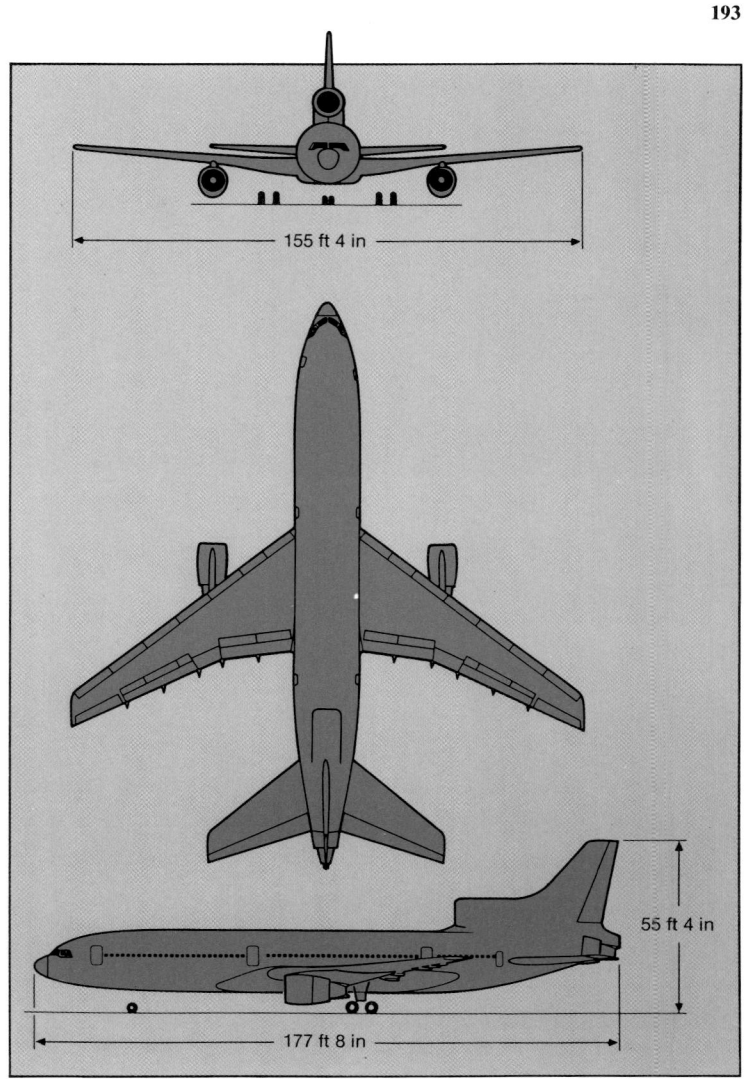

Left: The Tristar prototype cruises over a sparse desert landscape.

	L-1011-1 TriStar	L-1011-200 TriStar	L-1011-500 TriStar
Horizontal Tailspan:	71 ft, 7 in	71 ft, 7 in	71 ft, 7 in
Wingspan:	155 ft, 4 in	155 ft, 4 in	164 ft, 4 in
Wing Area:	3456 sq ft	3456 sq ft	3541 sq ft
Wing Sweep at .25 chordline:	35 deg	35 deg	35 deg
Length:	177 ft, 8 in	177 ft, 8 in	164 ft, 2 in
Height:	55 ft, 4 in	55 ft, 4 in	55 ft, 4 in
Landing Gear, wheel base:	70 ft	70 ft	61 ft, 8 in
Landing Gear, main thread:	36 ft	36 ft	36 ft
External Diameter:	19 ft, 7 in	19 ft, 7 in	19 ft, 7 in
Engines:	three Rolls-Royce RB.211-22 B, 42,000 lb thrust	three Rolls-Royce RB.211-524B, 50,000 lb thrust	three Rolls-Royce 50,000 lb thrust
Takeoff Weight (lb):	430,000	466,000	496,000
Landing Weight (lb):	358,000	368,000	368,000
Manufacturer's Empty Weight (lb):	domestic 224,579; international 225,2371	231,600	232,749
Max Payload (lb):	domestic 84,393; international 82,767	89,400	89,718
Cargo Volume (cubic ft):	2528	3228	3437
Fuel Capacity (lb):	159,560	178,400	213,640
Passengers:	273	304	244
Initial Cruise Altitude (ft):	33,650	34,000	33,000
Operating Altitude (ft):	35,000	36,000	35,000
Cruising Speed (Mach):	0.82 to 0.85	.83	.83
Max Range:	4000 nautical miles	4000 nautical miles	5500 nautical miles

Above: Britain's Princess Margaret christens the first L-1011-500—which was built for British Airways—at Lockheed's Palmdale facility. The L-1011-500 (*at right*) had a shorter fuselage, wider wings and longer range than earlier TriStars.

L-1011-100 with the improved, higher thrust Rolls Royce RB-211-524B turbofan engine. The RB-211-524B was optimized for improved takeoff performance on hot days, a fact that made it attractive to both Gulf Air and Saudia (Saudi Arabian Airlines). In addition to the two Arab carriers, both British Airways and Delta acquired the L-1011-200.

In May 1979 the final TriStar variant, the L-1011-500 Advanced TriStar was delivered into service with British Airways when Britain's Princess Margaret christened the first airplane at Lockheed's Palmdale, California factory. The L-1011-500 Advanced TriStar entered service two years after the L-1011-200 and four years after the L-1011-100. The Advanced TriStar differed from its predecessors by having a shorter fuselage and wider wingspan. Designed to have the longest range of any TriStar, the L-1011-500 had increased fuel capacity and the RB-211-524B engines that had been incorporated in the L-1011-200. Aside from the original 'Dash One' there were more Advanced TriStars produced than any other L-1011 type. After British Airways, L-1011-500s were delivered to Delta and Pan American World Airways in the United States and later to Air Canada, Air Lanka (Sri Lanka), Alia (Jordan), BWIA International (Trinidad and Tobago), LTU (Germany) and TAP (Portugal).

In December 1982 the British Royal Air Force announced that it would be the first military customer for the TriStar. During the war in the Falklands earlier in 1982, the RAF had recognized the need for a long-range aerial refueling tanker and considered both the TriStar and the McDonnell Douglas DC-10. Despite the fact that the US Air Force had selected the McDonnell Douglas airplane as its new generation tanker, the RAF chose the TriStar. The first six were purchased used from British Airways in 1982 and an additional three were acquired from Pan American in 1984. In February 1983 Marshall of Cambridge was given the contract to convert the big jetliners to tanker configuration.

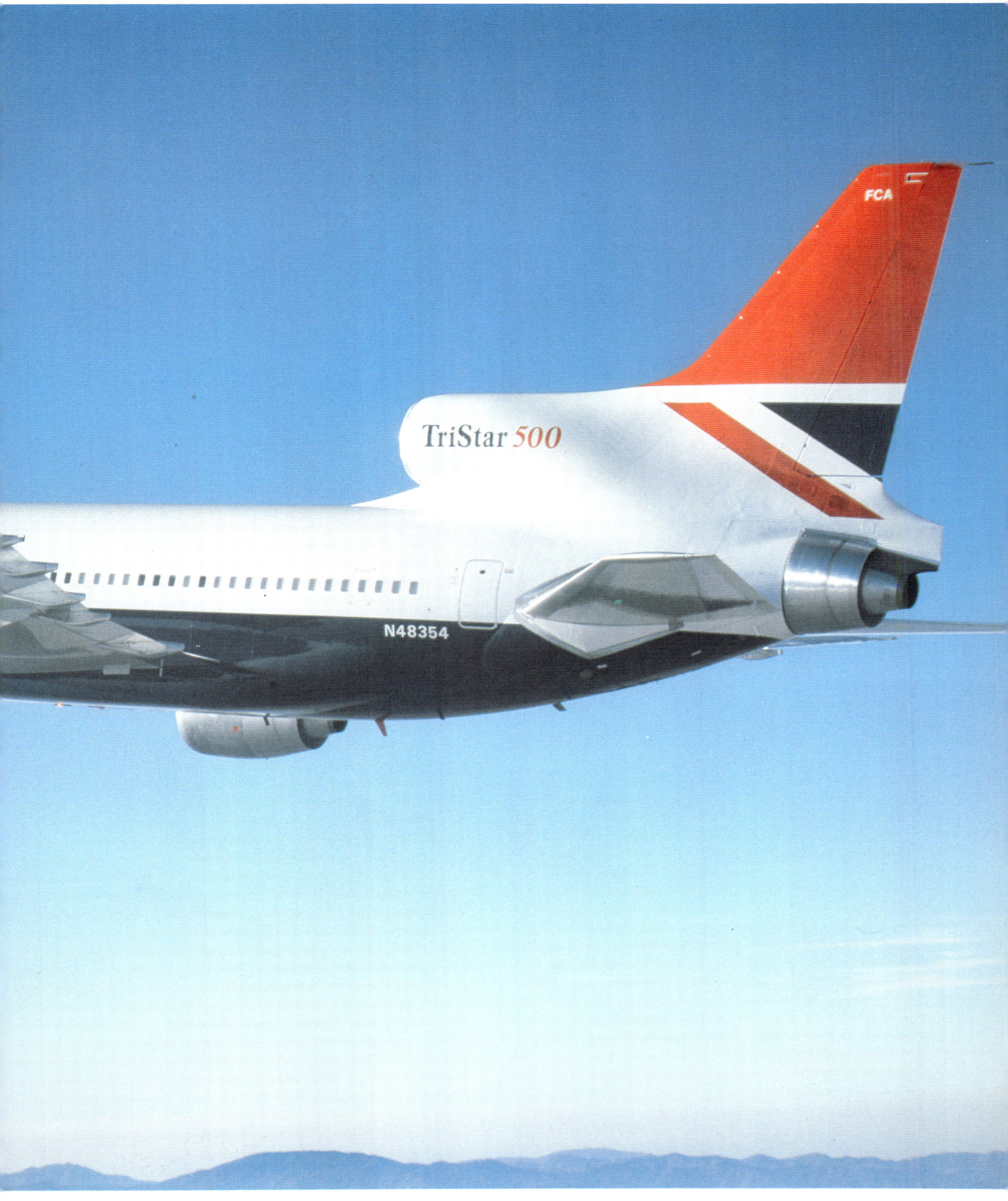
FCA
TriStar 500
N48354

All of the aircraft in question were L-100-500s and serve in the RAF under the service designations TriStar K Mk1 (tanker/passenger configuration), TriStar KC Mk1 (tanker/cargo configuration) and TriStar K Mk2 (the ex-Pan American jets in a tanker/passenger configuration). While the upper deck configurations may vary, the TriStar tankers have a huge lower deck fuel capacity of 100,060 pounds of fuel, and are all equipped with two Mk17 hose drum units (HDUs) located under the aft fuselage. The most noticeable feature on the new TriStar tankers is the aerial refueling probe fitted to the top of the fuselage above and ahead of the flight deck so that the TriStar tankers can themselves be refueled in flight.

L-1011 Service Data

	Apr 1972 - Nov 1980	Nov 1980 - July 1986
Total aircraft ordered:	239	11
Total aircraft delivered:	191	59
Total fleet hours:	2.5 million	3.4 million
Revenue passengers carried:	168.5 million	179.8 million
Revenue passenger miles:	157.4 billion	187.0 billion

The first flight of the TriStar tanker took place in July 1983 with Lockheed test pilot Bill Weaver in the pilot's seat and Marshall test pilot Tim Mason in the copilot's seat. The first flight with an all-RAF flight crew took place in February 1984 and the first flight with an all-RAF cabin crew followed in March 1985. In May 1985 TriStars began making regular cargo flights between Britain and the Falkland Islands in the South Atlantic, setting a new record of 17 hours, 22 minutes for the flight.

On 7 December 1981 Lockheed had made the decision to close the L-1011 production line after building 250 TriStars of all types. The last L-1011 was assembled in August 1983. Of the 250 TriStars constructed, 249 were delivered to airlines, with the original prototype being retained for many years by Lockheed California Company. The biggest number of orders (71) occurred in 1968, the first year that the TriStar was offered for sale. There were 29 TriStars ordered in both 1978 and 1979, and 28 in 1974. The most TriStars built in a single year was 41 in 1974, followed by 39 in 1973.

The biggest TriStar customers were Delta (44), TWA (38), Eastern (37), British Airways (23) and All Nippon Airways (21). In July 1986 there were 239 TriStars in service, with the largest operators being Delta (35), TWA (35), Eastern (24), British Airways (20), Saudia (17) and Air Canada (16).

The last delivery of a factory-new TriStar took place in 1985, but service support of the global L-1011 fleet is still an integral part of Lockheed California's operations. Over 230 L-1011s are in service around the world with 19 airlines and the Royal Air Force, and there is every likelihood that many of them will still be in service in the twenty-first century.

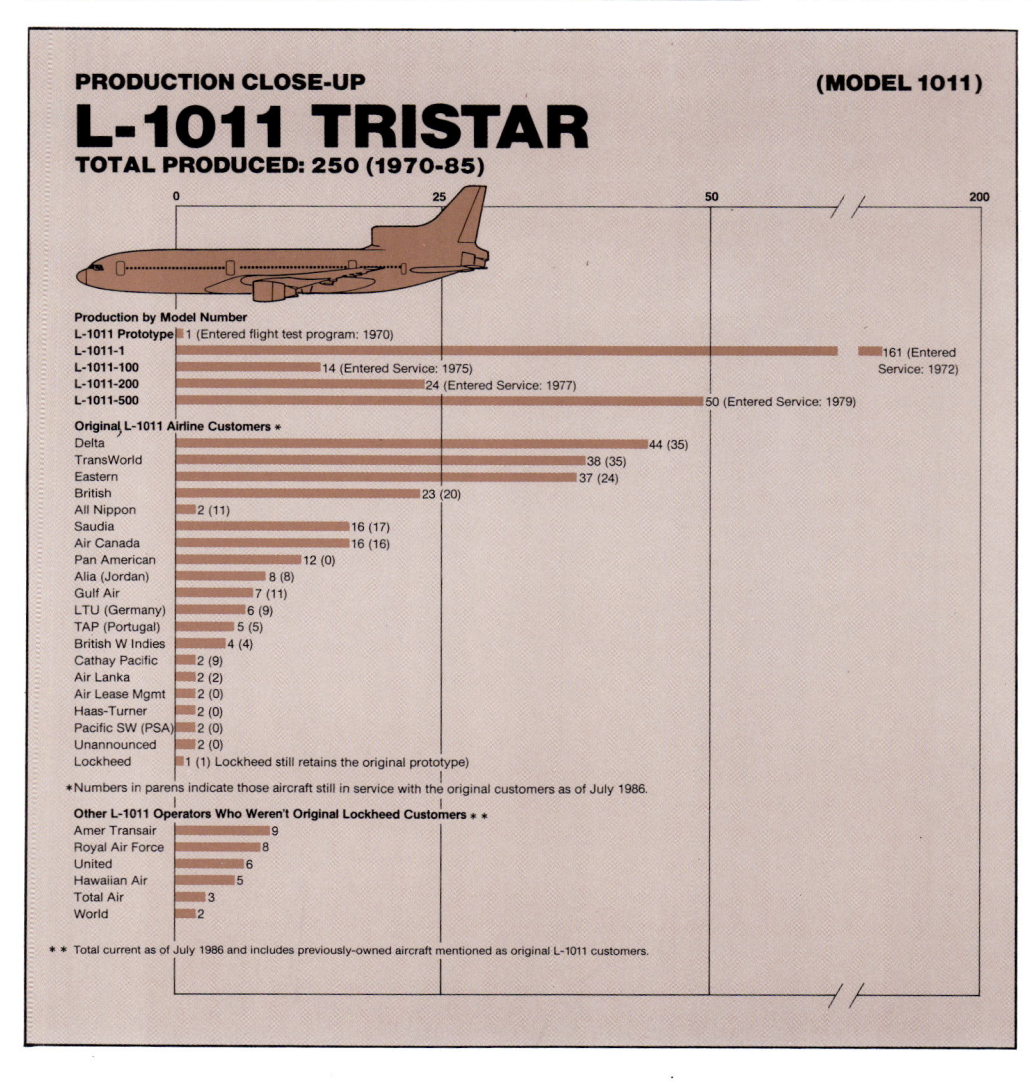

PRODUCTION CLOSE-UP (MODEL 1011)
L-1011 TRISTAR
TOTAL PRODUCED: 250 (1970-85)

Production by Model Number
- L-1011 Prototype: 1 (Entered flight test program: 1970)
- L-1011-1: 161 (Entered Service: 1972)
- L-1011-100: 14 (Entered Service: 1975)
- L-1011-200: 24 (Entered Service: 1977)
- L-1011-500: 50 (Entered Service: 1979)

Original L-1011 Airline Customers *
- Delta: 44 (35)
- TransWorld: 38 (35)
- Eastern: 37 (24)
- British: 23 (20)
- All Nippon: 2 (11)
- Saudia: 16 (17)
- Air Canada: 16 (16)
- Pan American: 12 (0)
- Alia (Jordan): 8 (8)
- Gulf Air: 7 (11)
- LTU (Germany): 6 (9)
- TAP (Portugal): 5 (5)
- British W Indies: 4 (4)
- Cathay Pacific: 2 (9)
- Air Lanka: 2 (2)
- Air Lease Mgmt: 2 (0)
- Haas-Turner: 2 (0)
- Pacific SW (PSA): 2 (0)
- Unannounced: 2 (0)
- Lockheed: 1 (1) Lockheed still retains the original prototype

*Numbers in parens indicate those aircraft still in service with the original customers as of July 1986.

Other L-1011 Operators Who Weren't Original Lockheed Customers **
- Amer Transair: 9
- Royal Air Force: 8
- United: 6
- Hawaiian Air: 5
- Total Air: 3
- World: 2

** Total current as of July 1986 and includes previously-owned aircraft mentioned as original L-1011 customers.

Above: This Delta Airlines L-1011-500 seems to *float* above a river valley. *Below:* An L-1011-500 in the Royal Air Force TriStar KC Mk2 tanker/passenger configuration, with prominent refueling probe on the aircraft's 'forehead.' *Overleaf:* Three nearly finished TriStars enliven Lockheed's Palmdale, California plant with their Air Portugal color scheme. The last brand new TriStar was delivered in 1985.

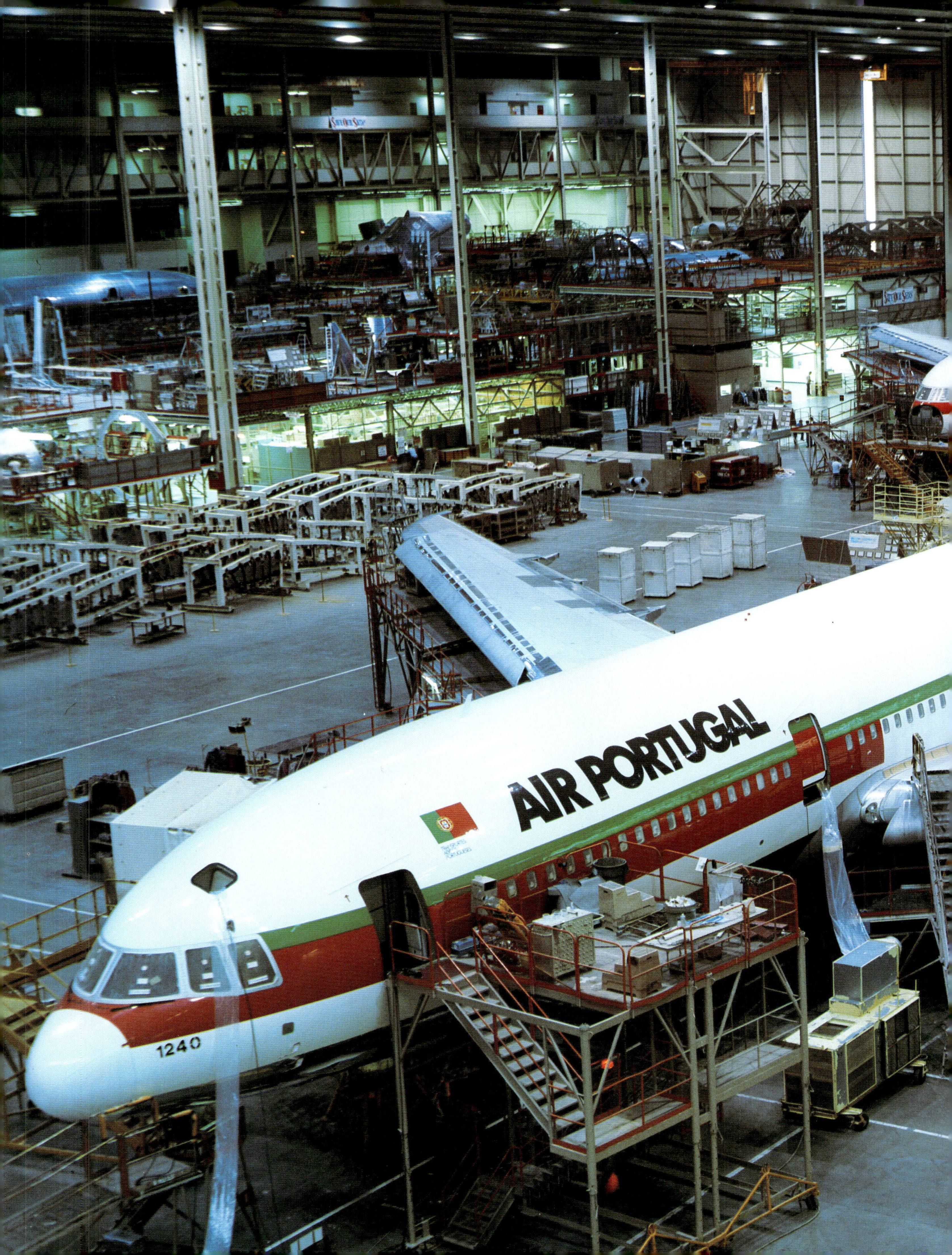
AIR PORTUGAL
1240

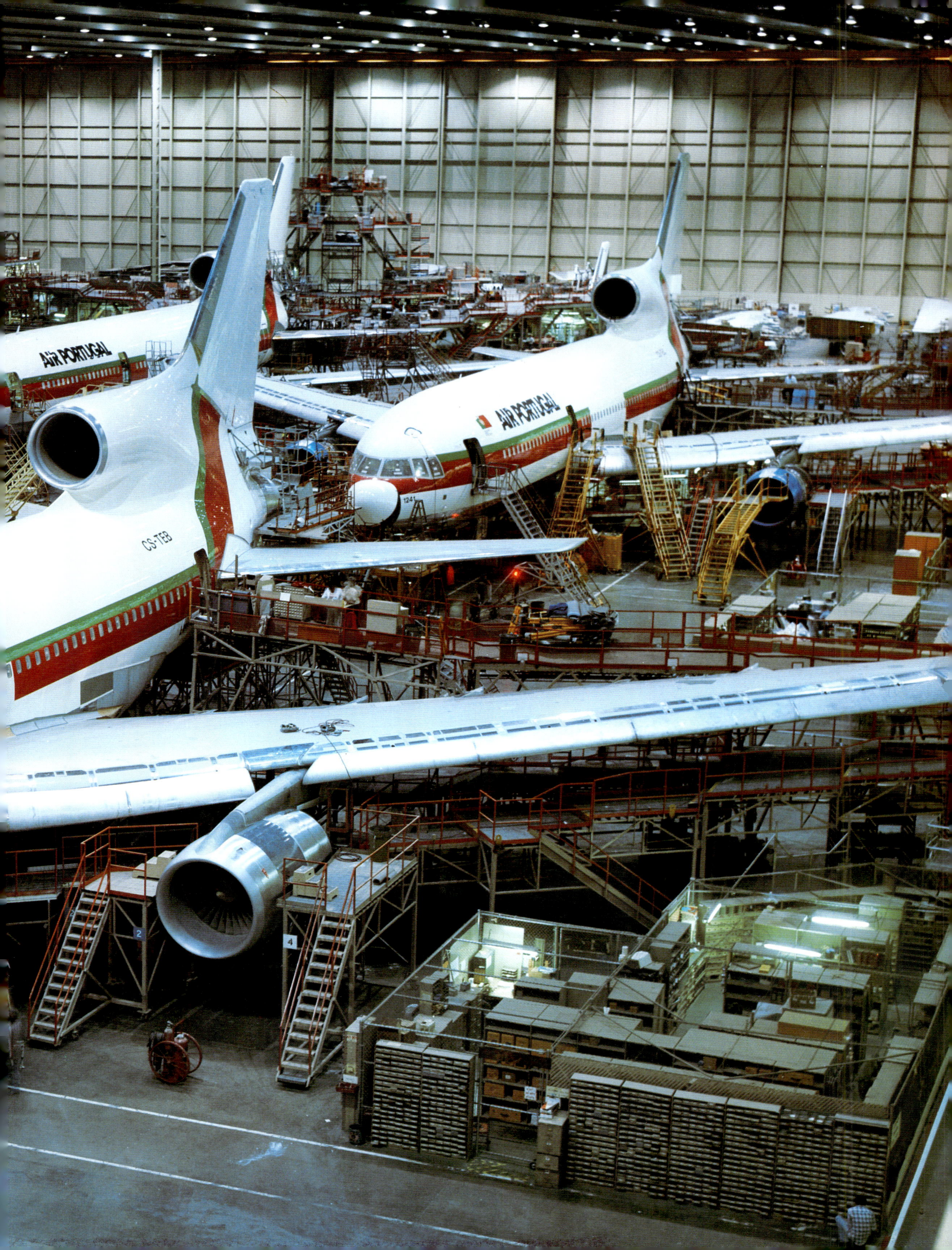
AIR PORTUGAL
AIR PORTUGAL
CS-TEB

LOCKHEED SUPERSONIC TRANSPORT TECHNOLOGY

In 1956, only nine years after a manned aircraft achieved supersonic flight for the first time, Lockheed engineers began work on the concept of a supersonic transport. During the years from 1956 to 1958, Lockheed developed a design for a 68-passenger supersonic military transport. After the cancellation of this project Lockheed continued design studies for future supersonic transports. At the same time in Europe, designers were working on the design for the aircraft which would evolve into the British-French Concorde, the world's first supersonic jetliner.

In June 1963, when Pan American World Airways announced that it was considering the Concorde, President John Kennedy decided that the US government should help to fund an *American* supersonic jetliner. By early 1964 Boeing, North American Aviation and Lockheed had each submitted proposals for Phase 1, which NASA called the Supersonic Commercial Air Transport (SCAT), but which would be known to the public as the Supersonic Transport (SST).

North American Aviation was eliminated from the contest in May 1964 and the remaining companies were asked to refine their proposals into larger and more specific designs. The results were the Lockheed Model 2000 *(above left)* and the Boeing Model 2707, which were submitted in 1966. Boeing won the competition and began work on two prototypes. On 24 March 1971, however, the program was canceled through political pressure in Congress—there was to be no American SST.

Meanwhile, the British-French Concorde had made its maiden flight in March 1969. The Concorde went into service with Air France and British Airways in 1976, but it would be ten years before the venture would begin to make money.

In the meantime, Lockheed continued to refine the SST concept against the day that it might be revived. Major problems that had led to the decision to cancel the American SST included such environmental concerns as noise and air pollution. There was also the problem of fuel effi-

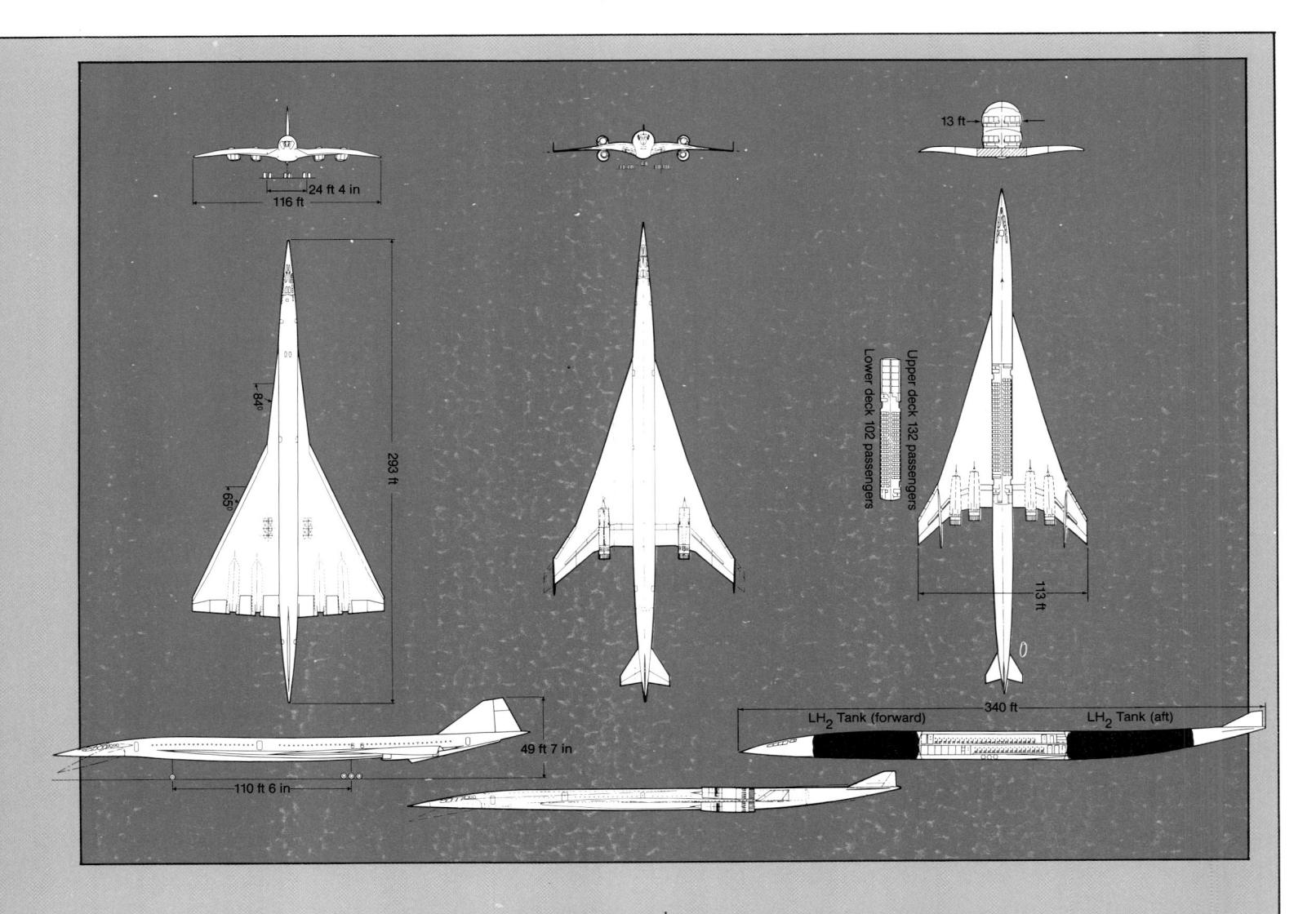

Upper left: Artist Chuck Hodgson's 1977 illustration of a Lockheed California study project depicts an SST which used conventional turbojets for subsonic flight and hydrogen-fuel combustion ram engines for speeds up to Mach 6 + . *Above, from the left:* SST concepts: The Lockheed Model 2000 (circa 1966); the SCV Study Concept (circa 1980); and the Liquid Hydrogen SST (circa 1982).

ciency, which was brought into sharp focus by the energy crisis of 1973-74 (unforeseen during the SST development). These were among the considerations as Lockheed pursued the SST concept in the 1970s and 1980s.

As more scientific evidence came to light, worries about SST damage to the earth's ozone layer were shown to be unfounded. Studies showed tht SST noise levels could be reduced to that of conventional aircraft except for the sonic boom. The Concorde deals with the latter problem by going to supersonic speeds over the ocean, but Lockheed began to design aircraft that could transition to supersonic at high altitudes, thus reducing the impact of the sonic boom.

Lockheed/NASA technology assessment studies culminated in the Supersonic Cruise Vehicle (SCV) design which was unveiled in 1980 *(above center)*. The SCV was designed to carry 290 passengers for 4000 nautical miles at 60,000 feet and at a cruising speed of Mach 2. The SCV was an improvement over the Model 2000 in the refinement of its wing design and in the use of a variety of new materials and materials processing to reduce weight. These materials included advanced nonmetallic composites and advanced aluminum alloys. In fact, well over half the total airframe would be composed of polymide nonmetallic composites.

The over-and-under engine placement served as a passive noise control. It was shown that in vertically superimposed engines, the lower engine shields the ground noise radiated by the top engine, thus reducing the overall effect by up to three decibels.

The final major problem in future SST development rests with the effect of petroleum prices on total operating costs. Two fuels that have been considered as a replacement for JP-4 jet fuel are liquid methane (LCH) and liquid hydrogen (LH_2). Lockheed and other manufacturers have been studying LH_2 for many years because of its efficiency and low weight. The problems with LH_2 rest with the volume of space within an aircraft that would need to be devoted to fuel tanks, the volatility of the LH_2 itself, and finally the high cost of generating LH_2 and of converting airport fueling systems to accommodate an all-new fuel.

Lockheed has been working on concepts for LH_2-powered aircraft since the mid-1950s and has evolved a concept for an LH2-powered SST *(top right)* that might be operational at the turn of the century. By combining the weight-saving characteristics of the materials used in the SCV of 1980 *(above center)* with the inherent light weight of liquid hydrogen, a SST could be produced that would have the same capacity, at little more than half the weight of the Model 2000 of 1966 *(above left)*.

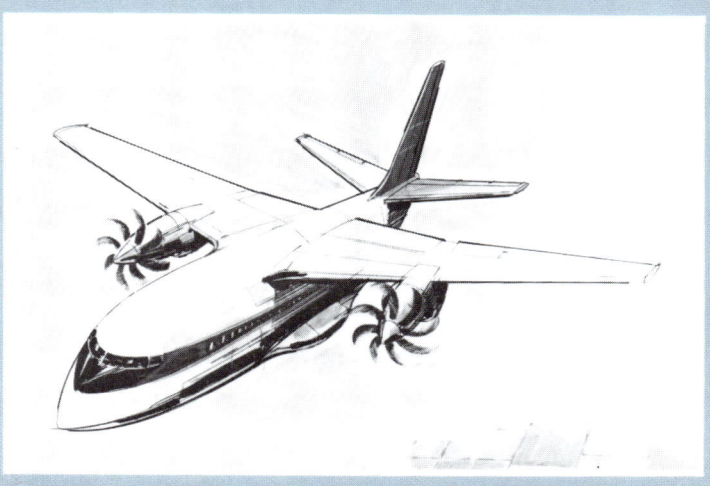

The 'propfan' concept (*above*) was Lockheed's 1981 answer to fuel shortages and short-haul scheduling worries. This plane's eight-to-10-bladed swept propellers would offer high fuel efficiency and speed (up to Mach 0.75) comparable to today's subsonic airliners.

The 1981 Lockheed 'span loader' concept (*above*) combines wide wings for maximum lifting capability and extra wing thickness (for actual cargo storage in the wings themselves) in an aircraft capable of carrying a 600,000 lb payload over distances up to 5,000 miles.

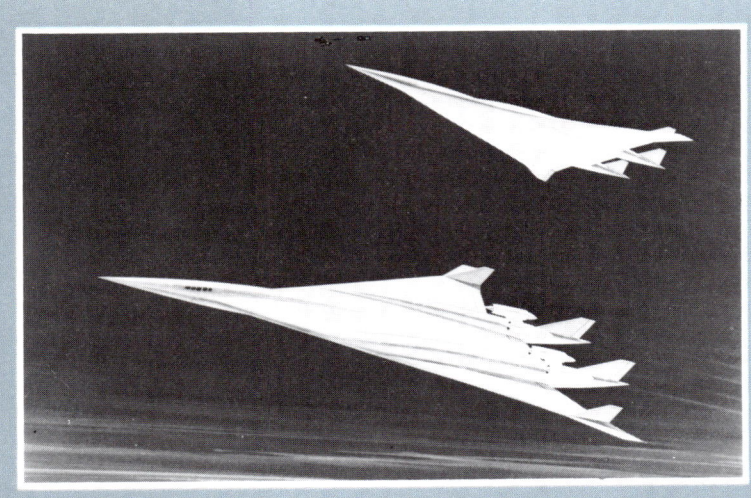

Yet another Lockheed SST concept (*above*) proposed an aircraft large enough to carry 300 to 400 passengers over distances of up to 4000 miles, with cruising speeds between Mach 2 and Mach 2.7. Lightweight alloys and positive controls would aid fuel economy.

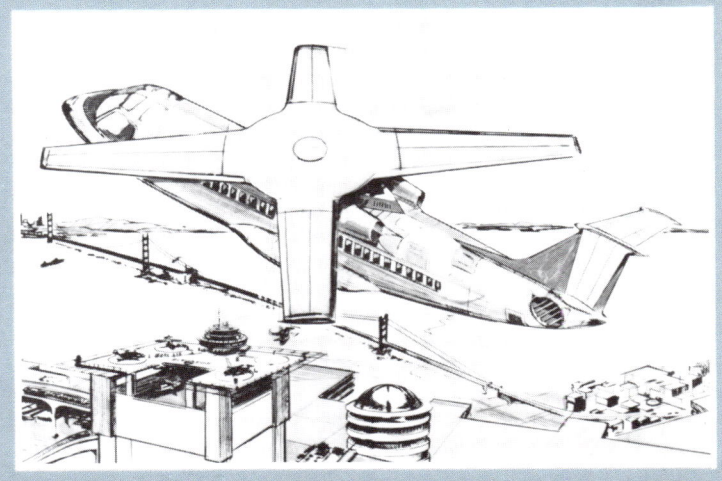

The Lockheed Vertical Takeoff and Landing aircraft concept (*above*) would combine rotor- and fixed-wing capabilities in a traffic congestion-beating aircraft capable of ferrying up to 50 passengers at a cruise speed of Mach 0.6 for up to 1000 miles.

Below left: This recent conceptual design for a liquid hydrogen-fueled subsonic transport aircraft should be capable of carrying 400 passengers for some 5500 nautical miles on 47,670 lbs of fuel—one reason for the plane's proposed fatness; all that LH_2 takes up a lot of space.

LOCKHEED MISSILES & SPACE

NEW FRONTIERS, NEW PROGRAMS

During World War II, the aircraft industry in the United States had evolved faster than it had ever done before. The end of the war sparked an unprecedented cycle of discovery and innovation. New propulsion systems and new airframe designs promised amazing performance and greater speed. The sound barrier was broken and the edge of space beckoned.

All of the major American aircraft builders put their engineers to work on high-speed jets and experimental rockets. For Lockheed the new age took concrete form in March 1947 when the company submitted its proposal for a ramjet test vehicle to the US Army Air Forces (US Air Force after September 1947). Designed by a team of engineers at the *Skunk Works* under the direction of Hall Hibbard and Kelly Johnson, the Lockheed Model 171 was approved by the USAAF and a contract was issued for a series of unmanned ramjet aircraft to be built under the research designation X-7. The vehicle was specified to be capable of speeds between Mach 1.7 and Mach 3.0, at altitudes up to 80,000 feet. The purpose of the X-7 program would be to test a variety of ramjet engines including the USAAF designed XRJ-37-MN-1.

The team developing the X-7 had to develop the technology as they went along because no aircraft had ever reached the kind of speeds that they were trying to achieve with the X-7 designs. They even used a jackhammer to test resistance of the airframe to pressure. The end product was a pencil-thin, ramjet-powered aircraft 33 feet in length, with a 13-foot rocket booster attached.

The first X-7 test flight came on 28 April 1951 when the aircraft was successfully air dropped by a B-29 acting as 'mother

Above: An early model of the USAF/Lockheed X-7 Test Vehicle has just been 'dropped' by its 'mother ship,' a modified B-29. The white, big-finned boost motor (shown *below left*, behind the X-7) pushed it to 1000 mph, then its ramjet test motor (attached to the X-7's belly) took over, and the boost motor was jettisoned.

ship.' The instant the engine was started, however, things came unglued and the bird became a group of separately flying parts! A second test in November also failed, but on 7 May 1952 the third X-7 was successfully flown and recovered.

The X-7 program lasted until 1960 during which time the aircraft made 130 flights, setting new altitude (106,000 feet) and speed (Mach 4.31) records for air-breathing aircraft. During those eight years, Lockheed built a total of 61 of the X-7 series aircraft, which included the X-7, the X-7A, the XQ-5 Kingfisher drone, and a 37-foot X-7B, which was built to test guidance and control systems for high-speed aircraft.

As the test flights of the X-7 series aircraft continued, many Lockheed engineers began pushing for the company to establish a separate missile division. At last, on 1 January 1954, the Lockheed Missile Systems Division (LMSD) was established at Burbank under the direction of Elwood Quesada, a former Air Force General who had served as the first commander of the Tactical Air Command. The LMSD was moved from Burbank to the airport at nearby Van Nuys, but soon that site was also outgrown. On 4 November 1955 Lockheed announced the purchase of a 275 acre tract of land in Sunnyvale on San Francisco Bay. Lockheed thus became one of the original firms in the area which would come to be known as Silicon Valley, the epicenter of American high technology. By September 1956 LMSD was fully established in its new location on San Francisco Bay not far

Above: This X-7 Test Vehicle literally stuck like a dart in the California desert, having buried its nose spike in good old terra firma. The fellow *at rear* pulled it out, cleaned it off, and they sent it up again. The XQ5 (*below*) was a modified X-7A3 which substituted two under-wing boosters for the original X-6 tandem booster.

from where Alan and Malcolm Loughead had once tinkered with automobile engines and dreamed of machines that would fly.

During the mid-fifties LMSD became one of Lockheed's fastest growing components. The first project started by LMSD had been the secret X-17 project. Designed in 1954 the X-17 was slightly longer than the X-7 without its rocket booster. It was a three-stage, spin-stabilized solid fuel rocket designed to research the reentry into the earth's atmosphere of ballistic missile warheads capable of traveling at speeds between Mach 15 and Mach 20.

The first stage was a Thiokol XM-20 Sergeant rocket delivering 50,000 pounds of thrust for 23.8 seconds. This carried the X-17 to an altitude of about 95 miles. The second stage was a trio of Thiokol XM-19 Recruit rockets, delivering a total of 104,580 pounds of thrust for 1.53 seconds. The third stage carried the X-17's telemetry hardware and was powered by a single XM-19. LMSD built a total of 26 X-17s, which performed successfully on 90 percent of their 30 test flights—in which the vehicle flew to 265 miles altitude and reached speeds of 9700 mph.

Between 27 August and 6 September 1958, the X-17 was used in Project Argus: nuclear explosives were detonated at maximum altitude in order to investigate the structure of the earth's Van Allen radiation belt. Some examples of the X-17 were used by the US Navy under the FTV-3 designation during the initial studies for the Polaris Submarine Launched Ballistic Missile (SLBM) program.

THE POLARIS

During the last years of World War II German scientists had developed the A-4, the world's first operational ballistic missile. The unstoppable, supersonic A-4 (which Hitler renamed V-2, for Vengeance weapon, second) opened a whole new chapter in warfare. Combined with nuclear weapons, the ballistic missile had the potential to become the ultimate weapon.

After World War II the United States used captured A-4s for research purposes, but when it was learned that the Soviet Union

Above: The first Polaris undersea launch, as portrayed by artist Chuck Hodgson. *Note* the USS George Washington's mast, *at right.*

was using them as the basis for a new generation of ballistic missiles, the United States reluctantly was dragged into what the press would dub 'the arms race.'

Ballistic missile development in the United States proceeded along three tracks. On the first track was the *Intercontinental* Ballistic Missile (ICBM). The ICBM was the ultimate ballistic missile and the object of Soviet research. Because development of the ICBM would be a long and complex process, the United States decided to proceed with it, and to develop the Thor and Jupiter *Intermediate Range* Ballistic Missiles (IRBM) in the meantime: because they involved a shorter stretch of existing technology, they could be in service sooner than ICBM. In 1955 the Department of Defense decided to begin development of a third type of ballistic missile as well. While the ICBMs and the interim IRBMs would be land-based, this third track led to a sea-based ballistic missile.

On 17 November 1955 the US Navy established its Special Projects Office (SPO) to take charge of the development of the Fleet Ballistic Missile (FBM) program. The SPO, under the direction of Admiral W F 'Red' Raborn, soon realized that the 50-foot, thin-skinned, liquid fuel Jupiter-type IRBM would not be suitable as a shipboard missile, so they set about looking for a contractor to develop an all-new type of missile. It was decided that the FBM would not be based aboard surface ships but aboard a series of huge nuclear submarines. This basing mode, if it could be made practical, seemed ideal. Ballistic missiles aboard submarines would be virtually undetectable, and if they were found, they could easily be moved. In contrast, once the concrete silo of an ICBM was located by the Soviet Union, they would always know where it was. A submarine could be tracked, but it would be a much harder and more uncertain task. Lockheed expressed interest in being the contractor to develop the project. Finally, on 17 December 1956, LMSD was given the go-ahead to produce the FBM, which would be known as Polaris, after the North Star.

Lockheed planned to draw upon its experience with the Air Force X-17 in the development of the Navy Polaris FBM. Therefore, a series of 22 flight test vehicles (FTV) based on the X-17 (including four X-17s redesignated FTV-3) would be employed in early testing. The first FTV test launch took place on 11 January 1957 at Cape Canaveral, Florida.

The Polaris timetable was critical. When the FBM concept had been firmed up at the end of 1955, the thinking had been that a missile based on the Jupiter IRBM could be deployed aboard surface ships by early 1960, but that it would take another five years to make the submarine basing plan workable. This was clearly unacceptable to the Navy, so in May 1957 the Initial Polaris Plan called for submarine deployment of the first Polaris A-series missiles by the end of 1962. In November 1957 the deployment deadline was moved up to mid-1960, and in April 1958, LMSD was given until the end of 1960 to complete its work. The Polaris A was deployed on 15 November 1960, more than two years ahead of the original schedule.

The first prototype Polaris A, AX-1, was ground-launched at Cape Canaveral on 24 September 1958 but had to be destroyed by the range safety officer after 27 seconds. The first successful launch came with AX-6 on 20 April 1959, although a targeting error put it off course. AX-22 was launched from the surface ship, EAG 154 *Observation Island*, and it would have been successful had AX-22 not failed to jettison the second stage, which it carried through to reentry. By 7 January 1960 all the program bugs had been worked out and the first successful Polaris test A1X-7 took place. Finally on 28 July 1960 the nuclear submarine USS *George Washington* (SSBN 598) successfully launched two Polaris A1Xs in the space of three hours from a submerged position. These tests were followed by nine more submerged A1X launches and the launch of the A2X, the prototype for the new Polaris A2 series. On 15 November 1960 the USS *George Washington* became operational with the Polaris A1, and on 31 December it was joined by the USS *Patrick Henry* (SSBN 599).

Even with the Polaris A1 operational, the tests continued. On 6 May 1962 Operation *Frigate Bird* saw the launch of a fully nuclear-armed Polaris A1 from the USS *Ethan Allen*, in the first and only complete test of any American ballistic missile. While Polaris FBM was developed for the US Navy, some were also delivered to Holy Loch in Scotland for use aboard submarines of the British Royal Navy.

The Polaris A1, with its range of 1200 nautical miles, was followed into service on 26 June 1962 by the Polaris A2 (originally designated Polaris B), with a range of 1500 nautical miles. The final development in the Polaris series would be the Polaris A3 (originally designated Polaris C), which became operational on 28 September 1964. The range of the Polaris A3 was 2500 nautical miles, more than double that of the Polaris A1. The Polaris A3, which was 85 percent unlike its predecessors, also was equipped with *three* Multiple Independently Targeted Reentry Vehicles (MIRV), aka multiple warheads. The Polaris A3 would remain in service until 1982, until it was withdrawn in favor of its successor, the Poseidon. Five USS *George Washington* class and five USS *Ethan Allen* class submarines remained as Polaris A3 carriers until their retirement from the fleet, while 31 submarines were converted or built new. This gave the US Navy a total capacity of 496 Fleet Ballistic Missiles, or Submarine Launched Ballistic Missiles (SLBM) as they are often called.

THE POSEIDON

By 1961 the Lockheed Missile Systems Division (LMSD) had grown beyond what had originally been envisioned when it was formed. Thus, along with Lockheed's important Georgia and California aircraft divisions, LMSD was upgraded to the status of 'company' within the Lockheed Aircraft Corporation.

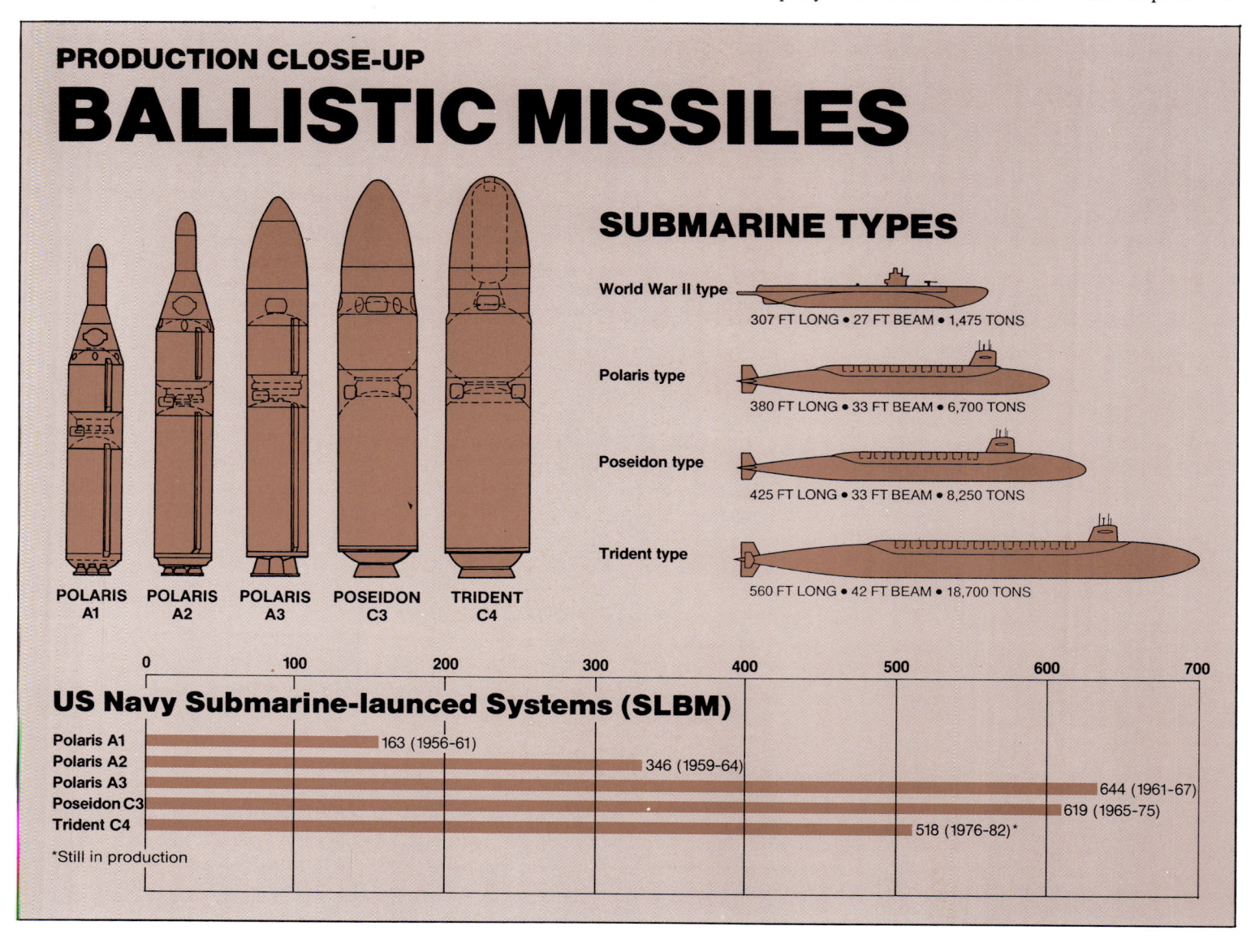

PRODUCTION CLOSE-UP
BALLISTIC MISSILES

POLARIS A1 | POLARIS A2 | POLARIS A3 | POSEIDON C3 | TRIDENT C4

SUBMARINE TYPES

World War II type — 307 FT LONG • 27 FT BEAM • 1,475 TONS

Polaris type — 380 FT LONG • 33 FT BEAM • 6,700 TONS

Poseidon type — 425 FT LONG • 33 FT BEAM • 8,250 TONS

Trident type — 560 FT LONG • 42 FT BEAM • 18,700 TONS

US Navy Submarine-launced Systems (SLBM)

System	Value	Years
Polaris A1	163	(1956-61)
Polaris A2	346	(1959-64)
Polaris A3	644	(1961-67)
Poseidon C3	619	(1965-75)
Trident C4	518	(1976-82)*

*Still in production

LMSD became Lockheed Missiles & Space Company (LMSC).

With the Polaris missiles already being deployed, the first ballistic missile project to be tackled by LMSC was the Poseidon C3. The new Poseidon C3 was similar in appearance to the Polaris A3, but new missile tube technology now permitted an increase in missile diameter from 54 inches to 74 inches in diameter. The first submerged launch of the Poseidon C3 came in August 1970 from the USS *James Madison*, the first of 31 former Polaris submarines to be converted to Poseidon capability.

THE TRIDENT

On 14 September 1971 Deputy Secretary of Defense David Packard approved the US Navy Undersea Long-Range Missile System (ULMS) program. Under ULMS, the Navy would develop larger, quiet, longer range nuclear submarines to be armed with more accurate, longer range ballistic missiles. In December 1971 LMSC began work on the ULMS-1 missile, which was promptly redesignated Trident C4 (or Trident I). The range of the Trident would be 4000 nautical miles, nearly four times the range of the Polaris A-1.

The Trident C4X-1, prototype for the Trident series, was successfully launched on 18 January 1977. A successful test program followed, and on 31 July 1979 the first Trident C4 submerged launch took place from aboard the USS *Francis Scott Key*.

Above: An A-3 Polaris missile breaks the surface, en route to a target which could be up to 2500 nautical miles 'downrange.' *Below:* The USS *Ethan Allan*, part of the US Navy's Atlantic fleet, was the name ship of a class of Polaris A3-type nuclear submarines.

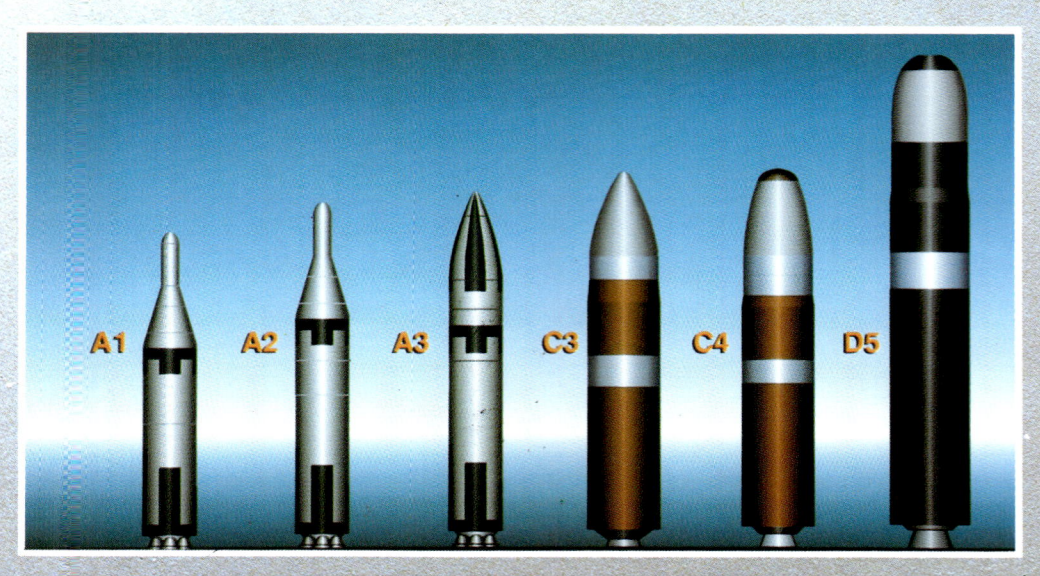

At left, left to right—ballistic missiles of the US Navy: the Polaris A1, A2 and A3 missiles; the Poseidon C3; the Trident I C4 missile and its successor, the awesome Trident II D5, which is 20 percent longer than the C4. *Below:* The first Trident SSBN, the *USS Ohio,* cuts a swath through the cold North Pacific.

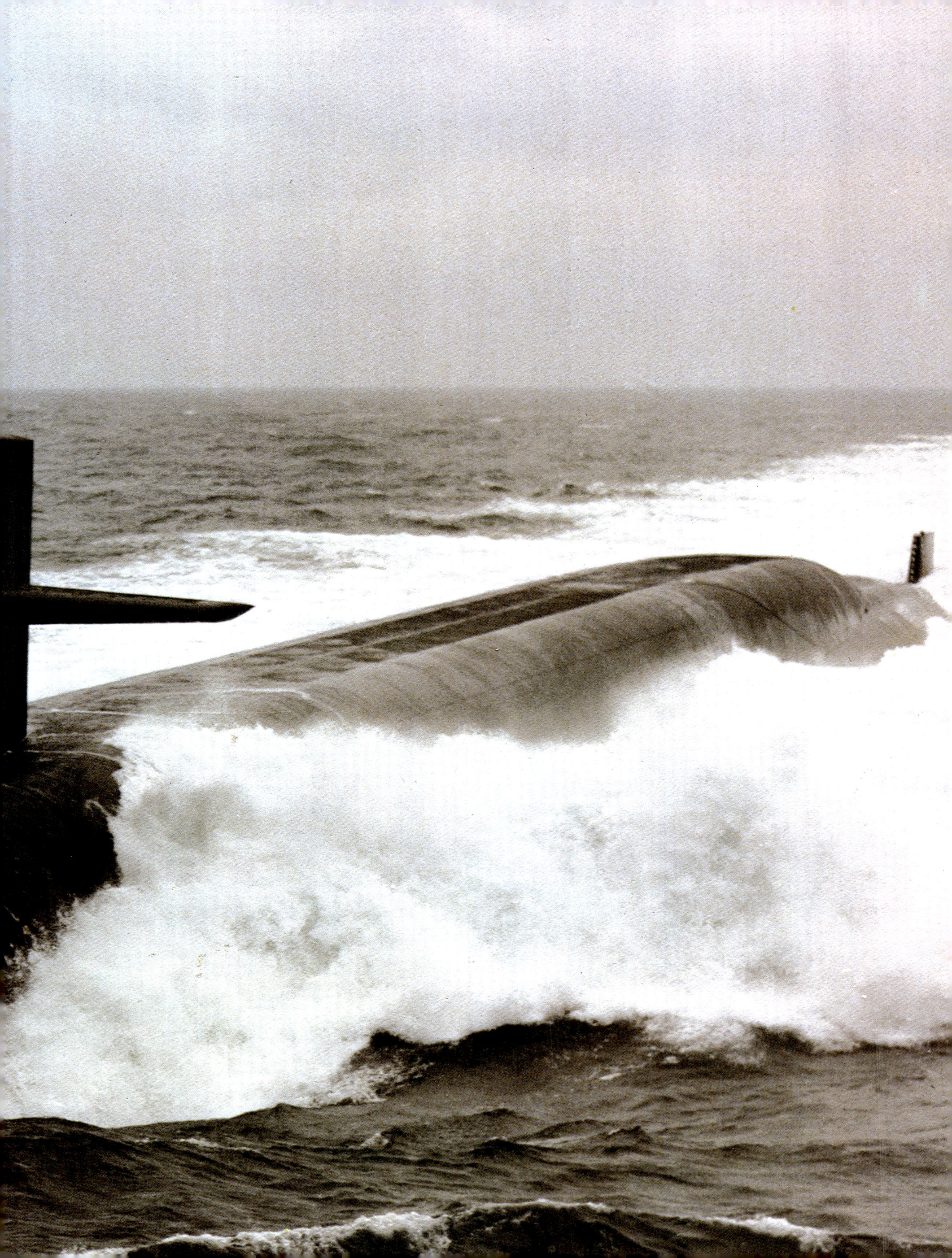

At the same time that Lockheed was developing the Trident C-4 missile, shipbuilders were gearing up for a series of eight (later increased to eleven) USS *Ohio* class Trident submarines. Each Trident/USS *Ohio* class submarine is 560 feet long, more than double the size of the USS *Ethan Allen* class Polaris submarines. They are designed to accommodate 24 Trident C4s with enough built-in growth allowance to permit them to carry the 20 percent longer Trident D5 (Trident II) missile when it comes on-line.

While the Navy was awaiting delivery of the large USS *Ohio* class subs, some of the earlier USS *Lafayette* class ships were retrofitted to each accommodate 16 Trident C4s. By 1981 four such submarines had been retrofitted. By the following year when the USS *Ohio*, harbinger of the class of the same name joined the fleet, 12 of the Navy's 31 Poseidon-carrying subs had converted to Trident C4. In 1986 the US Navy had 19 submarines, with a total of 304 Lockheed Poseidon missiles; 12 USS *Lafayette* class subs, with a total of 192 Lockheed Trident C4s; six USS *Ohio* class submarines in service with 168 Lockheed Trident C4s; and five more such submarines under construction. This gave the US Navy a total of 664 Fleet Ballistic—or Submarine Launched—Ballistic Missiles.

OTHER LMSC PROGRAMS

One of the most important products of the LMSC Space Systems Division (SSD) has been the Agena upper stage rocket. Since it was first used successfully on 28 February 1959, the Agena has served as the upper stage to Atlas, Titan and Thor launch vehicles in over 300 space launches, with a 90 percent success rate. In 1959 Agena was used on the first polar orbital launch and the first 3-axis stabilized flights. In 1966, during the Gemini manned space program, the Agena upper stage was used as the rendezvous and docking target for the Gemini manned spacecraft. The procedures developed during the Gemini-Agena docking experiments were an important step in the development of the techniques that made possible a manned lunar landing.

The technology developed by the Agena program led to the Seasat oceanographic observation satellite, which was built by Lockheed for NASA. Seasat was launched from Vandenberg AFB and placed in a near-polar orbit on 26 June 1978. The Lockheed Agena stage of the Atlas/Agena launch vehicle served as the satellite 'bus' (container) for Seasat, and provided altitude control, power, guidance, telemetry and command functions. Attached to the Agena was a sensor module with four microwave sensors and a visible spectrum/infrared spectrum radiometer. Together the two modules that constituted Seasat were 68 feet long, five feet in diameter and weighed 5060 pounds when the Agena's fuel expanded. During its 106 days of operation the spacecraft completed 1502 orbits covering 95 percent of the world's oceans every 36 hours. The project returned a great deal of data on the importance of oceans to atmospheric weather conditions.

Another important part of LMSC is the Advanced Systems Division and its diversified laboratories. The Electronic Sciences Laboratory conducts research in communications, signal processing, electro-optics and advanced computer systems. The Electronic Sciences Laboratory was instrumental in the development of the information retrieval system known as DIALOG. DIALOG originated with a 1966 government contract for the

Upper right: Lockheed's Agena D (aka the 'Standard Air Force Agena') is shown here in orbit during a Gemini Agena Target Vehicle rendezvous series in the mid-1960s. Agena upper stage rockets have been part of the US Space Program since 1959.

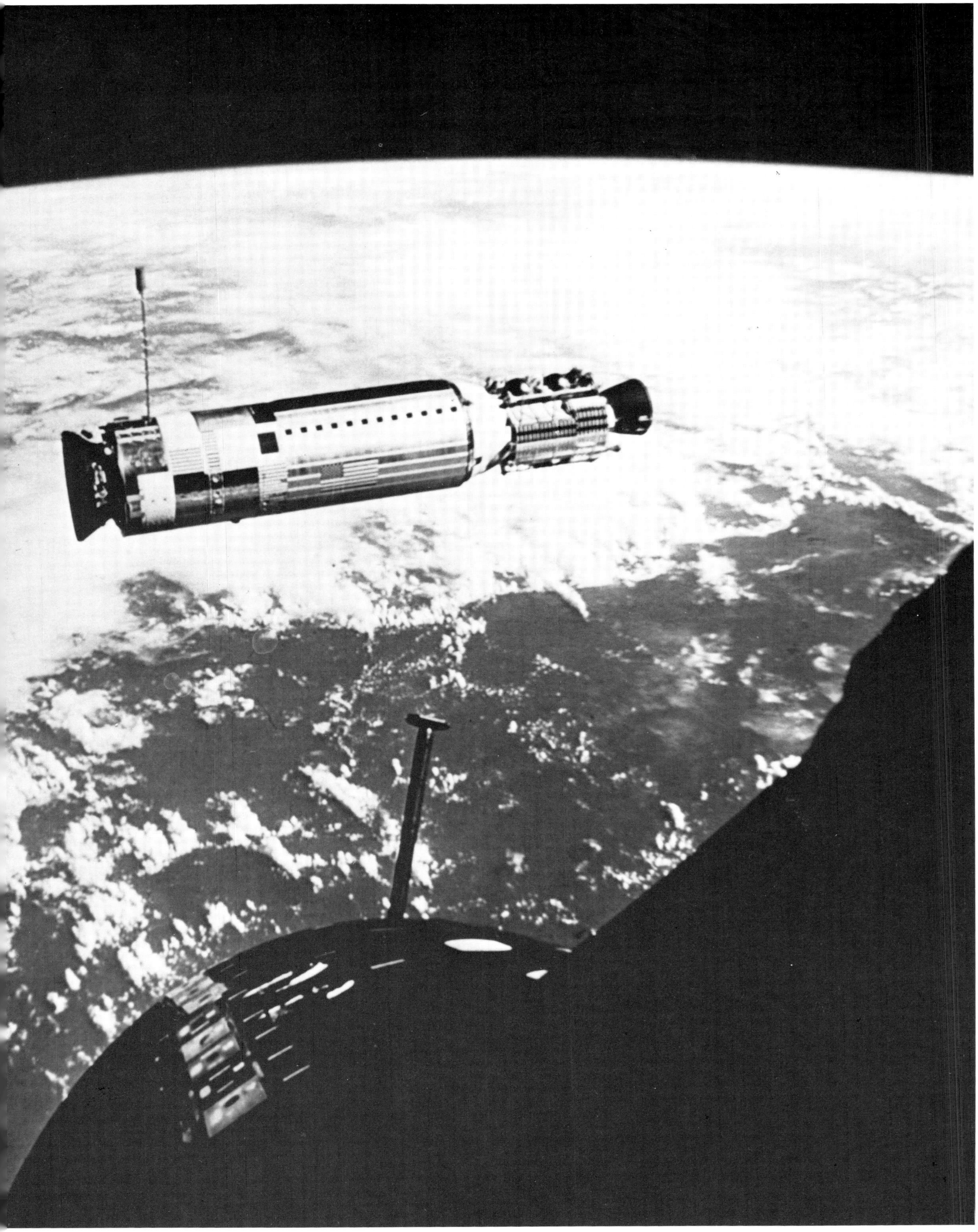

The Seasat oceanographic observation satellite (*above*), built by Lockheed for NASA, was launched from Vandenberg AFB on 26 June 1978, and rode to its near-polar orbit in a Lockheed Agena upper stage 'bus' atop an Atlas launch vehicle. *At right:* Lockheed's Materials Sciences Laboratory developed the heat-resistant ceramic tiles—aka 'bricks'—for NASA's Space Shuttle Orbiters—aka 'flying brickyards.' Each contoured tile had its place, and fit to the shape of each Shuttle Orbiter like a giant jigsaw puzzle.

establishment of a filing system for 160,000 aerospace-related documents. This in turn evolved into a system that was first commercially marketed in 1972. By 1981 DIALOG was the world's largest on-line information retrieval system, and it became a separate Lockheed Company, no longer part of LMSC.

The Materials Science Laboratory is involved with research and development in such areas as acoustics, electrochemistry, fluid mechanics, structures and related physics. It was the Materials Sciences Laboratory that developed the heat-absorbing silica tiles that are used to shield the undersides and leading edges of the Space Shuttle Orbiting Vehicle. The tiles are the result of experiments at Lockheed that date back to 1957. After 1961 the Space Systems Division began development of the all-silica material that evolved into the tiles that were used when construction began on the orbiters *Enterprise* (OV-101), *Columbia* (OV-102) and *Challenger* (OV-99) in 1974 and 1975. The silica tiles also were used in the construction of *Discovery* (OV-103) and *Atlantis* (OV-104), and were first flown in space during April 1981 aboard *Columbia*.

There are 30,757 silica tiles used on each orbiter. They are manufactured in two densities, which are designated LI-900 and LI-2000; the latter (22 pounds per cubic foot) is installed in areas subject to greater mechanical wear. Each tile is individually machined to precise standards and they are capable of protecting the spacecraft from temperatures of 2300 degrees Fahrenheit.

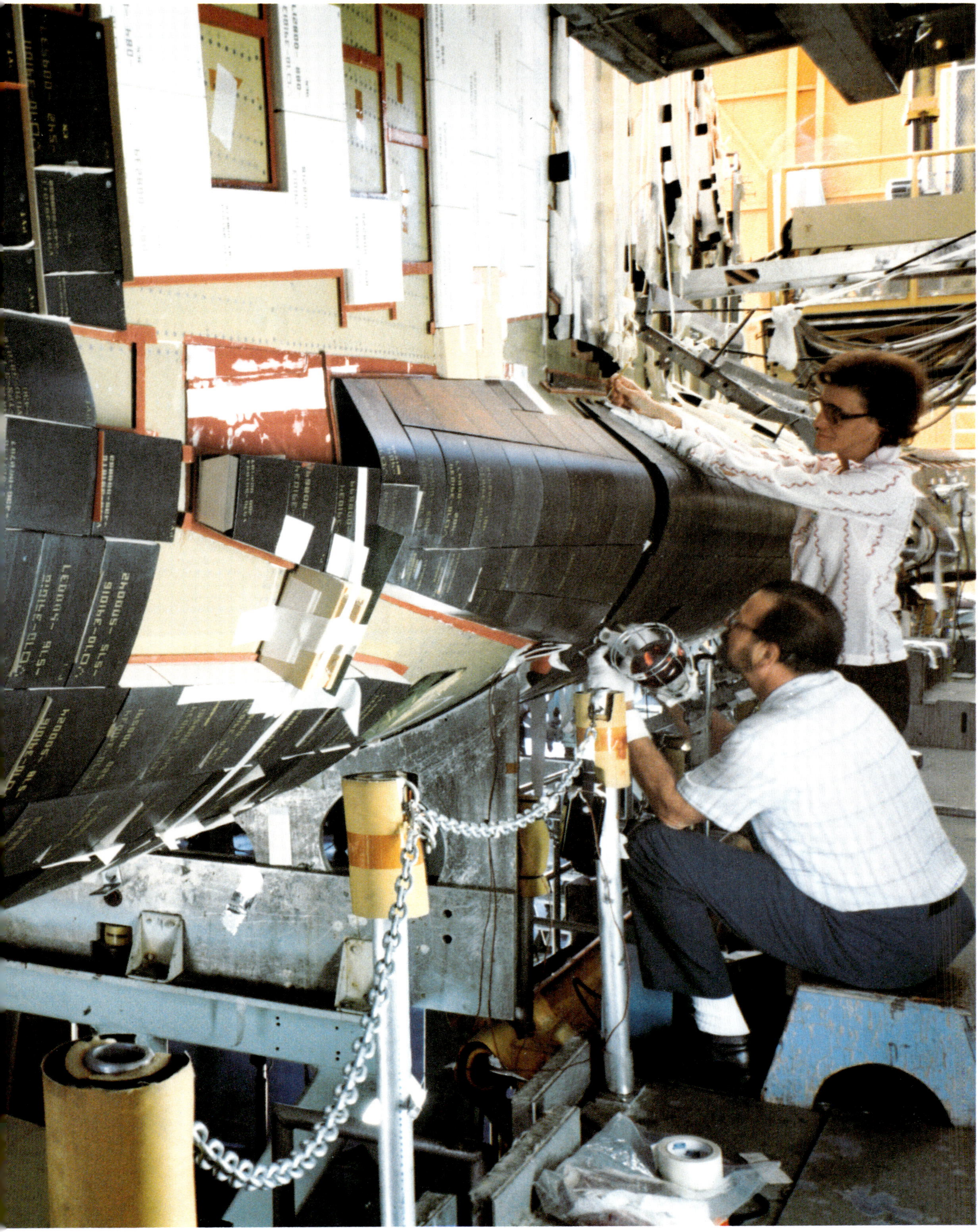

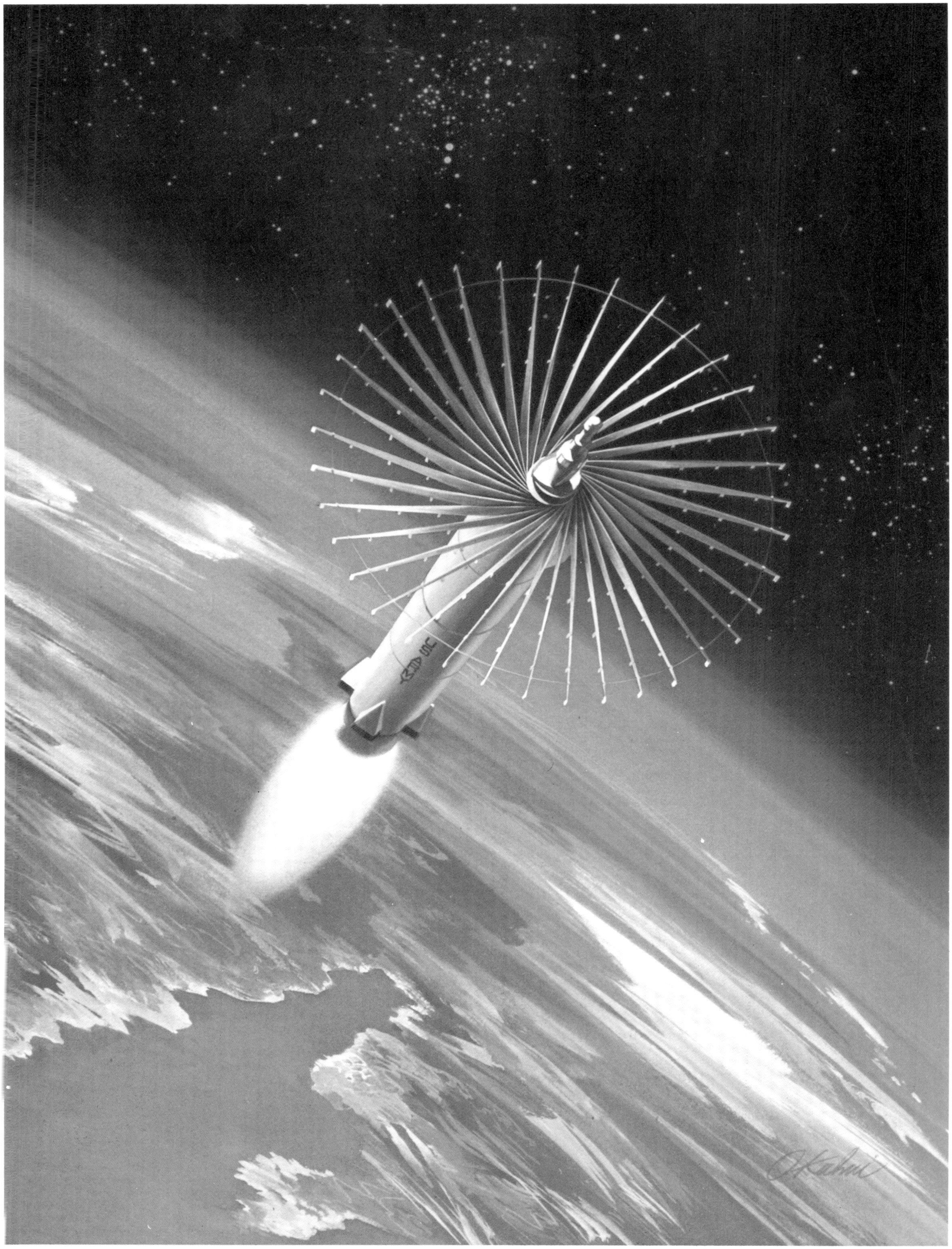

The Materials Sciences Laboratory also developed a series of unique lithium batteries, ranging from a five-kilowatt, lithium-hydrogen type to a 180-kilowatt lithium-silver oxide pile type battery. Other efforts of the laboratory have gone toward solid cryogen coolers for use in space-based detection systems. These were flown operationally aboard NASA's Nimbus 6 and Nimbus 7 spacecraft, launched in 1975 and 1978 respectively. In 1980 the laboratory developed HERTIS (High Energy Real Time Inspection System), which performs electro-optical inspection of motors, such as those of the Navy's Lockheed Fleet Ballistic Missiles.

The Physical Sciences Laboratory is involved with research in the areas of atomic and molecular physics, astronomy, nuclear physics, nuclear weapons effects, plasma physics and reentry physics. Specific projects have included the Van Allen radiation belt studies by Project Argus in 1958; the Orbiting Geophysical Observatory (OGO-5) in 1966; the Advanced Technology Satellite (ATS-5) in 1969; the International Sun-Earth Explorer in 1977; the Dynamics Explorer in 1981 and the Orbiting Solar Observatory (OSO-8) in 1975; and the Solar Maximum Mission (solar Max) launched in 1980.

The LMSC Ground Vehicle Systems line was begun in 1964. The line evolved into a family of fully-articulated, multibodied, multiwheeled vehicles. Called *Twister*, this series developed under the theory that articulated wheeled vehicles would be faster on very rough terrain than tracked vehicles. The US Army tested various members of the *Twister* family such as the XM-808 and the Scout, but rejected *Twister* technology in favor of tried and true tracked vehicle technology. Between 1973 and 1975, Lockheed built 15 *Twister* commercial prototypes, but in 1979 the manufacturing license was sold to the Oshkosh Truck Company.

In 1964 LMSC organized its Oceans Systems Division, and in 1966 the Lockheed Ocean Laboratory was established at San Diego, California. In 1966 LMSC was given the contract to build the US Navy's first Deep Submergence Rescue Vehicle (DSRV) to rescue crews from crippled submarines. The prototype research submersible that preceded the two DSRVs was named *Deep Quest*, and was launched at San Diego in 1967. *Deep Quest* and her two sister ships are tiny submarines designed to be airlifted by Lockheed's C-5A Galaxy.

In 1968 LMSC set up its Ocean Mining component to support the activities of Howard Hughes' Summa Corporation. The Hughes Mining Barge, built by LMSC, was the world's largest submersible and was used in studies aimed at developing a practical means of mining manganese nodules from the ocean floor. A follow-on to this technology was the *Glomar Explorer*. Built under the guise of a prototype ocean mining platform, the *Glomar Explorer* was actually a US government-funded ocean recovery ship used to salvage a Soviet Navy submarine from the floor of the Pacific Ocean near Hawaii. The *Glomar Explorer* was used in 1979 for successful ocean mining experiments but is now in mothballs in California's Suisun Bay. Ocean mining experiments have been suspended by those companies originally involved, pending resolution of the interpretation of the Law of the Sea Treaty.

The LMSC Advanced Tactical Systems component has been involved since 1969 in the development of battlefield technology. Its achievements have included: Radiometric Area Correlation Guidance (RACG) systems, Clustered Airfield Defeat Munitions (CADM) and the Ballistic Offensive Suppression System (formerly BOSS, redesignated AXE in 1980). Both CADM and AXE are non-nuclear airfield destruction systems.

As part of the Department of Defense Strategic Defense Initiative program, LMSC developed the Homing Overlay Experiment (HOE) system, a US Army system designed to defend against incoming ICBMs. The HOE missile operates by unfurling a ribbed, umbrellalike array and ramming an incoming ICBM. On 10 June 1984 a HOE interceptor missile was successfully tested from the Kwajalein Missile Range against a target ICBM launched from Vandenberg AFB, California.

Lockheed Missiles and Space Company's SDI Homing Overlay Experiment vehicle (*at left*) tested sucessfully on 10 June 1984. Shuttle Orbiter *Discovery's* maiden flight on 30 August 1984 carried a Lockheed-designed solar power system—seen unfolding in *Discovery's* payload bay (*overleaf*) and in the factory, fully extended (*above*).

In March 1986 a team headed by the US Army Strategic Defense Command and Lockheed Missiles & Space Company won the 1986 Strategic Defense Technical Achievement Award of the American Defense Preparedness Association (ADPA) in recognition of the successful HOE program. The Award description reads in part:

'The interception and destruction of an incoming reentry vehicle at an altitude of more than 100 miles above the earth by a ground-launched interceptor dramatically demonstrated the technical feasibility of a non-nuclear strategic defense. The totally ground-launched interceptor missile with an on-board optical guidance system (able to detect heat equivalent to that of a human body more than 1000 miles away) and a non-nuclear kill mechanism can demolish an incoming nuclear warhead, rendering it harmless.'

Termed a 'major breakthrough' by the Department of Defense, the collision in space at 10,000 miles an hour relative velocity was '. . . like hitting a bullet with a bullet.'

The interception marked the end of the six-year HOE program, but its concepts are being carried into a follow-on Army/Lockheed program called ERIS (Exoatmospheric Reentry-vehicle Interceptor Subsystem)—a program to further validate the functional technology for an operation non-nuclear, low-cost, lightweight interceptor.

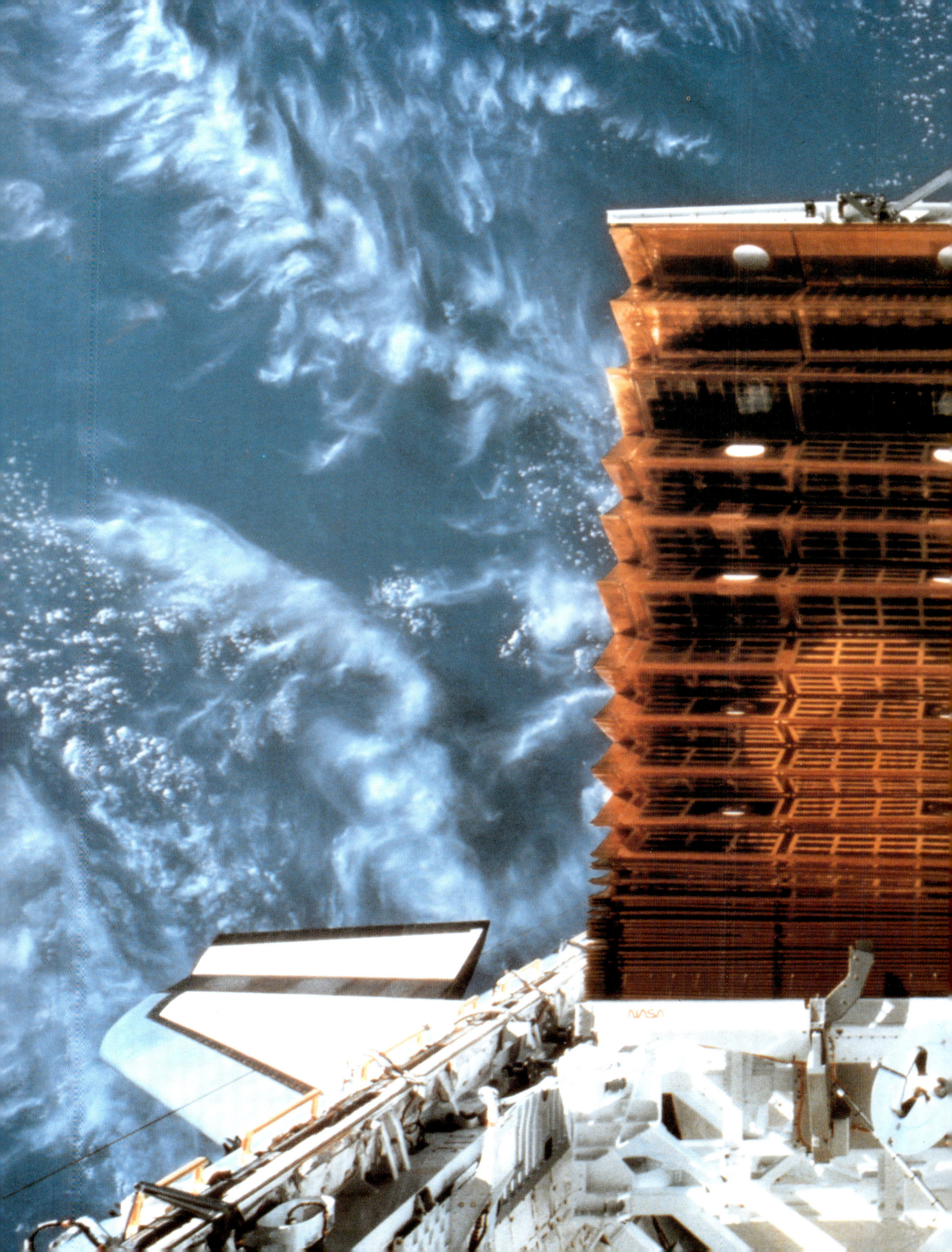
NASA

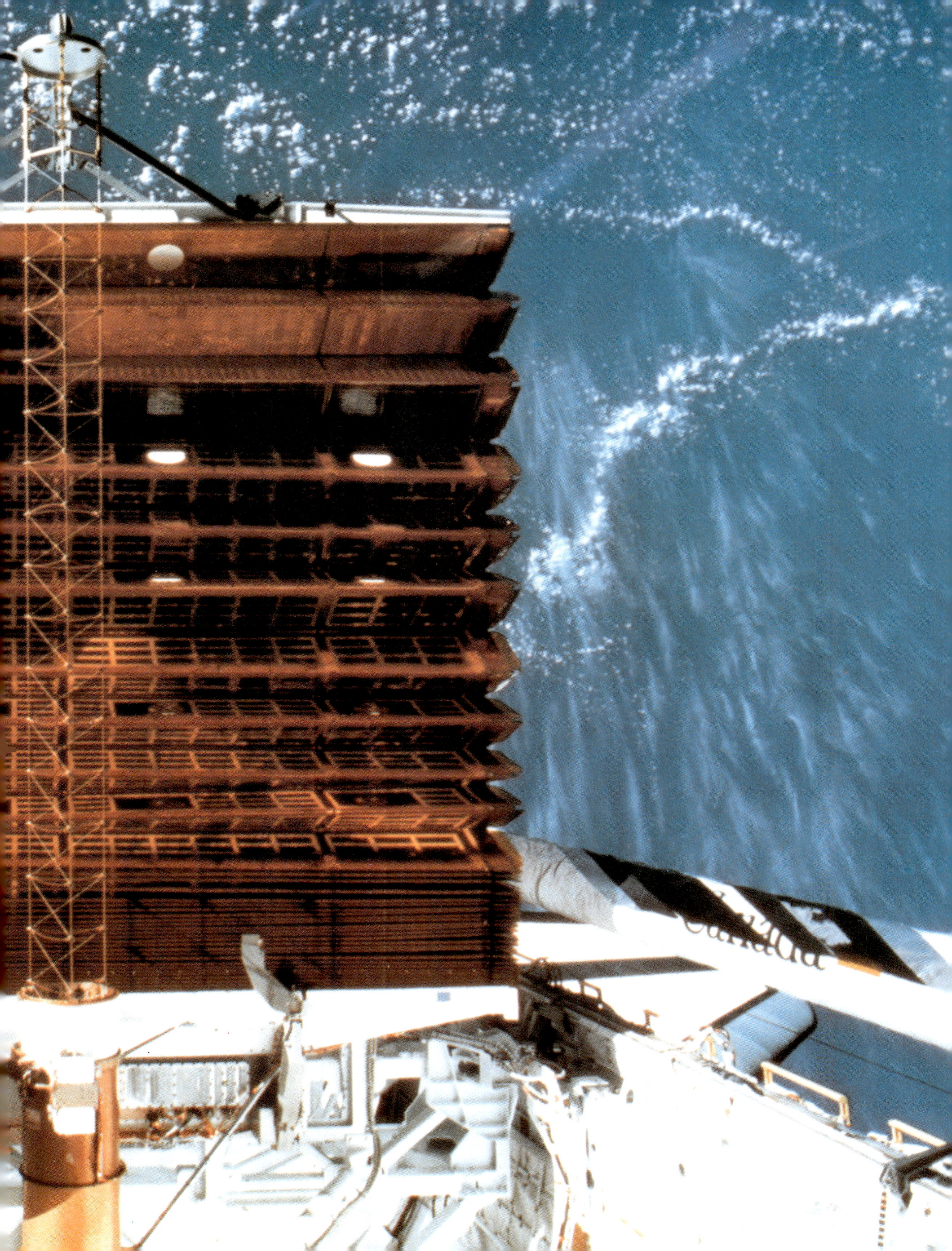

LMSC AIRCRAFT

Seemingly the most versatile of all Lockheed's components, Lockheed Missiles & Space Company not only has produced missiles and spacecraft as its name implies but, as we've seen, it also has produced a diverse range of projects—from ships to miniature submarines to multiwheeled land vehicles. Not to be left out of the specialty of its brother companies in Burbank and Marietta, LMSC has also built a few airplanes.

In 1967 LMSC had formed its Tactical Systems group to develop remote electronic sensors for use in Vietnam. During the course of the deployment of these sensors, LMSC and the US Army identified the need for an ultra-quiet, propeller-driven aircraft which could perform reconnaissance missions over enemy territory. The first of these, flown in 1968, was the Q-Star. Originally designated QT2 (Quiet Thrust, two-place), the Q-Star was actually a powered glider based on the Schweizer SGS.2-32 sailplane. The Q-Star prototype, a mid wing monoplane with fixed gear, eroded into the YO-3A, a low wing monoplane with retractable gear. A total of eleven YO-3As were built for use in Vietnam, but their use was not disclosed until 1971. They were taken out of service three years later.

In 1976 LMSC successfully demonstrated the technology for a small, unmanned reconnaissance aircraft. In 1979 the US Army gave Lockheed the go-ahead to develop this Remotely-Piloted Vehicle (RPV) under the name Aquila. Aquila flight testing was successfully completed in 1982 and work began on a production series. Although Aquila is the Spanish or Latin word for 'eagle,' it is also a constellation in the northern sky whose brightest star is Altair. Thus, the naming of the Lockheed RPV brings old and new together in one of Lockheed's oldest traditions.

Lockheed Missile and Space Company's YO-3A quiet reconnaissance aircraft (in three views, *below*) was powered by a six-cylinder air cooled engine which turned a six-bladed wooden propeller. The YO-3A was developed for the US Army Aviation Systems Command, and was used in the Vietnam War. Its predecessor, the Q-Star (*at right*), featured an unusual propeller drive system and flew with several variant many-bladed propellers, which were essential for its quietness.

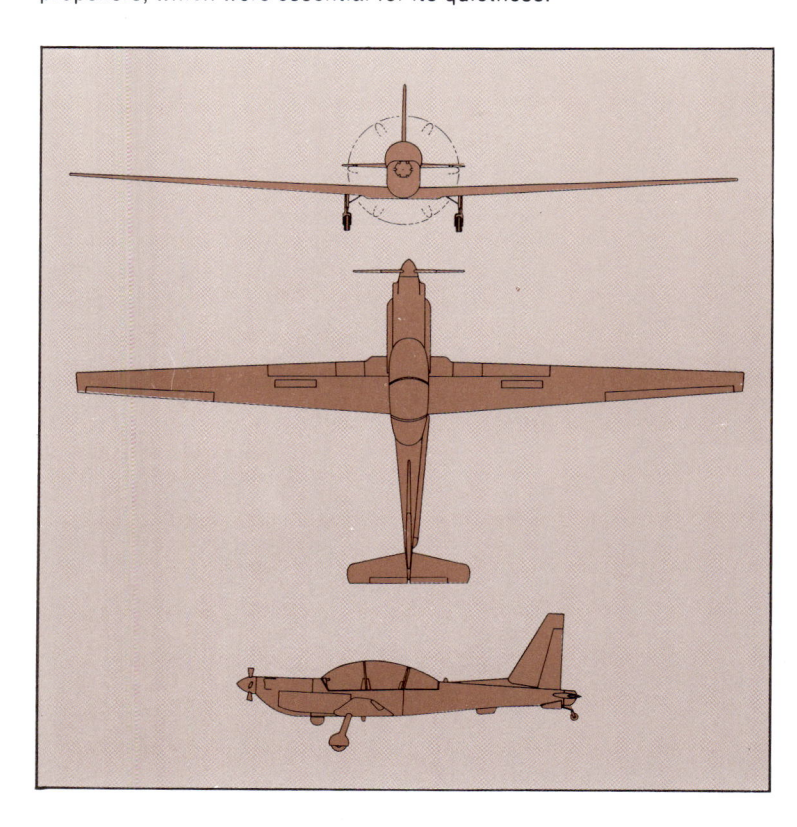

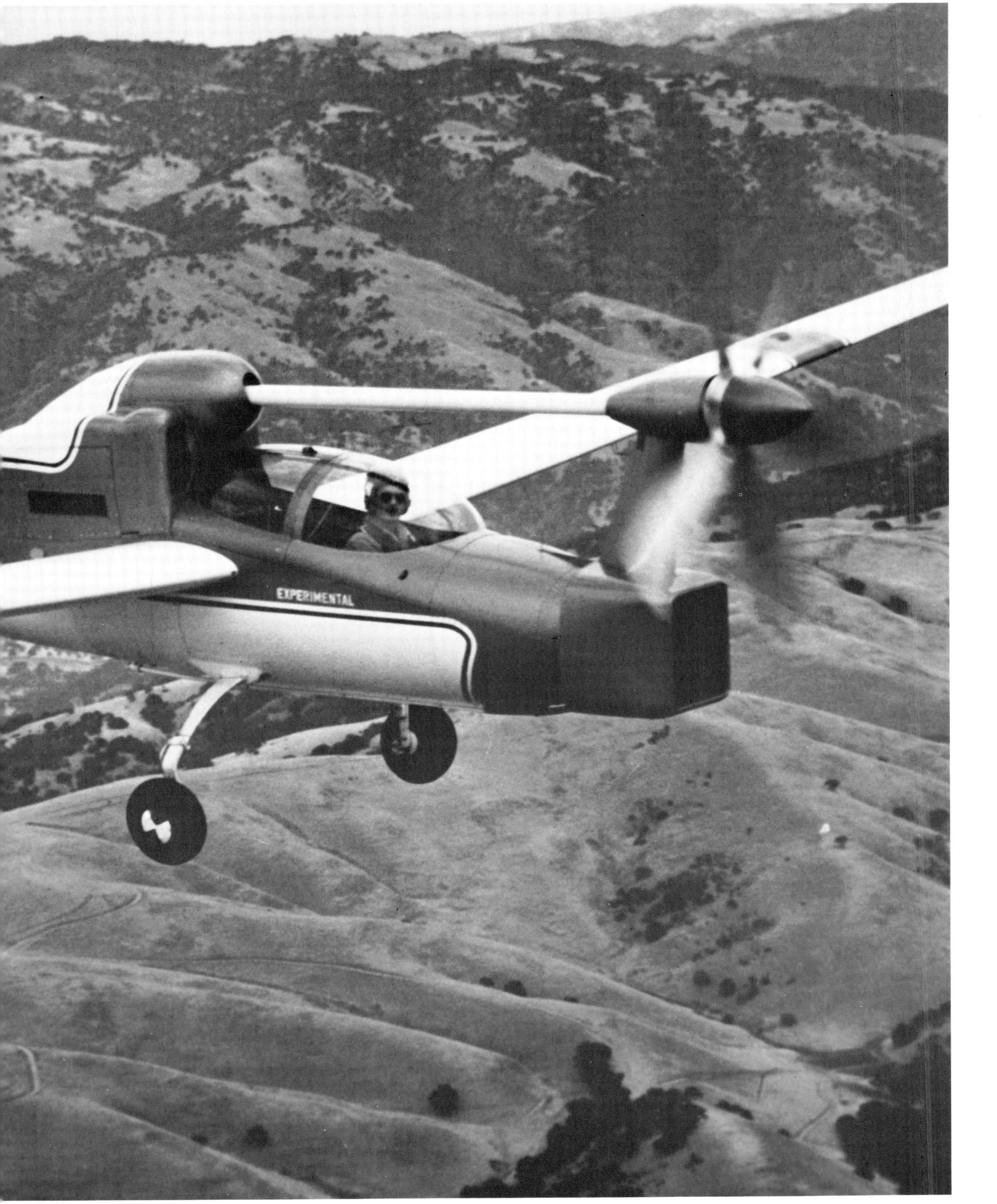
EXPERIMENTAL

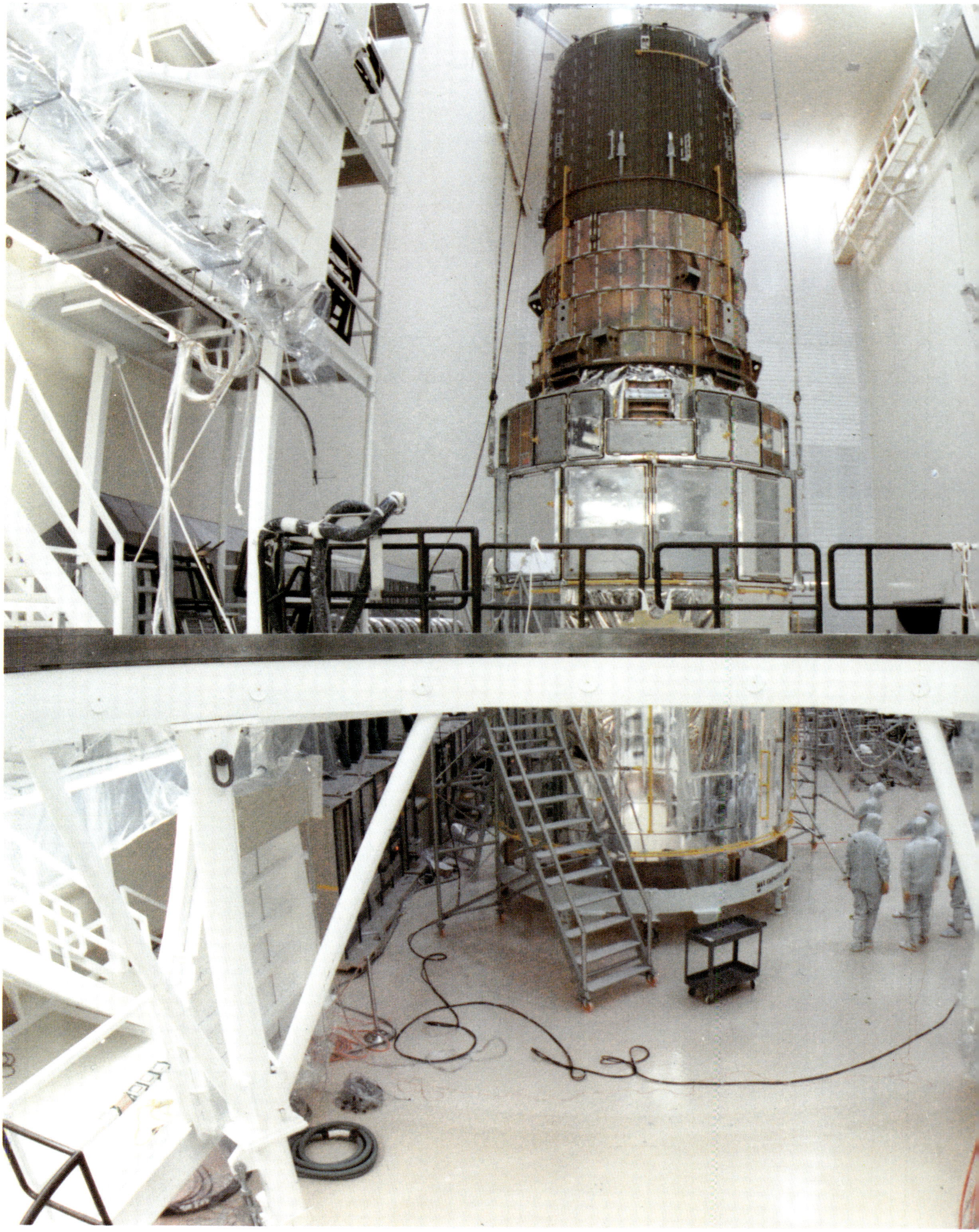

THE HUBBLE SPACE TELESCOPE

In 1977 LMSC began developing NASA's space telescope. Named for the famous American astronomer Edwin P Hubble, the new telescope was to be one of the most important steps in the history of astronomy. A 94.5-inch optical telescope, the Hubble incorporates the most perfect reflecting mirror ever ground.

While it is not the largest optical telescope ever built, the Hubble will be able to see fainter objects father away than any other because it will be 320 nautical miles above the earth—high above the atmospheric disturbances that, even on the clearest nights, cloud the view of earth-based telescopes. Resolution of fine details will be *ten times* better than that which is now available from the best earth-based telescopes.

Under the most perfect conditions, the human eye can see objects which are 600,000 light years distant from earth. With the largest, most advanced earth-based telescopes, such as the one at Mt Palomar in California, astronomers can see objects that are two billion light years away. With the Hubble, astronomers will be able to see *14 billion* light years into the distant reaches of the universe. The Hubble will do more than just open new frontiers, it will allow mankind to see 350 times more of the universe than ever before. Objects fifty times fainter than those now visible will be open to study.

At left: The Hubble Space Telescope in Lockheed's Sunnyvale Clean Room. *Above:* A high decibel sound variation test of the HST.

Not only will we be able to look at objects 14 billion light years away, but we also will be able to see light reflected from objects as they existed 14 billion *years* ago. In other words, if the universe was born *less* than 14 billion years ago—as some scientists have speculated—the Hubble Space Telescope will allow us to literally *see* the birth of the universe!

In 1984 Lockheed began the assembly of the Hubble in the world's largest 'clean room', which the company constructed at its LMSC facility near Sunnyvale, California. The original plan called for the Hubble to be launched on a NASA Space Shuttle flight in the summer of 1986 but scheduling slippage in the Shuttle program pushed the date back to October 1986. After the orbiter *Challenger* (OV-99) was destroyed in a disastrous launch failure in January 1986, the entire Space Shuttle program was temporarily suspended and the launch of the Hubble Space Telescope was postponed until 1988.

NASA's specifications for the Hubble Space Telescope call for it to remain functional for 15 years, with periodic manned missions to provide routine maintenance. It could also be returned to earth in the Space Shuttle orbiter cargo bay if a major overhaul were to be necessary.

The centerpiece of the Hubble is the 94.5-inch Ritchey-Chretien Optical Telescope Assembly (OTA), manufactured by the Perkin-Elmer Corporation of Danbury, Connecticut. In addition to the super-smooth 94.5-inch primary mirror, the OTA has a 12-inch secondary mirror located 16 feet away.

If the OTA is the heart and eyes of the Hubble, the Support Systems Module (SSM) is the backbone, ribcage and spine. Built by Lockheed, the SSM contains and protects the rest of the Hubble Telescope system and provides communications, power and directional control. The SSM also includes the light shield on the front of the telescope that operates like an eyelid if the sun comes into view.

The Fine Guidance Sensors (FGS) provide the control and balance for the system, operating the 40-pound wheels that aim the telescope. The FGS is assigned to provide the stability that will keep the Hubble focused on a single object for as long as 24 hours within a tolerance of 0.007 arc seconds. This accuracy translates to the equivalent of focusing on a twenty-five cent piece in Los Angeles from a vantage point in San Francisco.

The Hubble SSM aft shroud contains four scientific instruments: the Faint Object Camera (FOC), which is capable of focusing on objects as faint as the 29th magnitude; the Faint Object Spectrograph (FOS), which uses the visible light spectrum to determine the temperature, motion, physical characteristics and chemical composition of distant objects; the High Resolution Spectrograph (HRS), which is similar to the FOS but is capable of observing the ultraviolet portions of the spectrum not visible from earth; and the High Speed Photometer (HSP), which will help measure the intensity of light from distant objects to help determine their distance. A fifth scientific experiment, the Wide Field/Planetary Camera (WF/PC), is a set of two cameras located on the circumference of the OTA. The Wide Field portion of the system will view wide areas and star fields in deep space, while the Planetary portion will be used to obtain photographs of the planets in our solar system similar to the kind obtained on spacecraft flyby missions.

When the Hubble telescope was assembled, Lockheed subjected it to rigorous acoustic vibration tests that simulated launch conditions, as well as temperature tests that simulated the environment of outer space. Even though temperatures in space can drop to a chilly −300 degrees F, the Hubble's mylar blankets and built-in heaters are designed to keep the systems at a constant toasty +70 degree F.

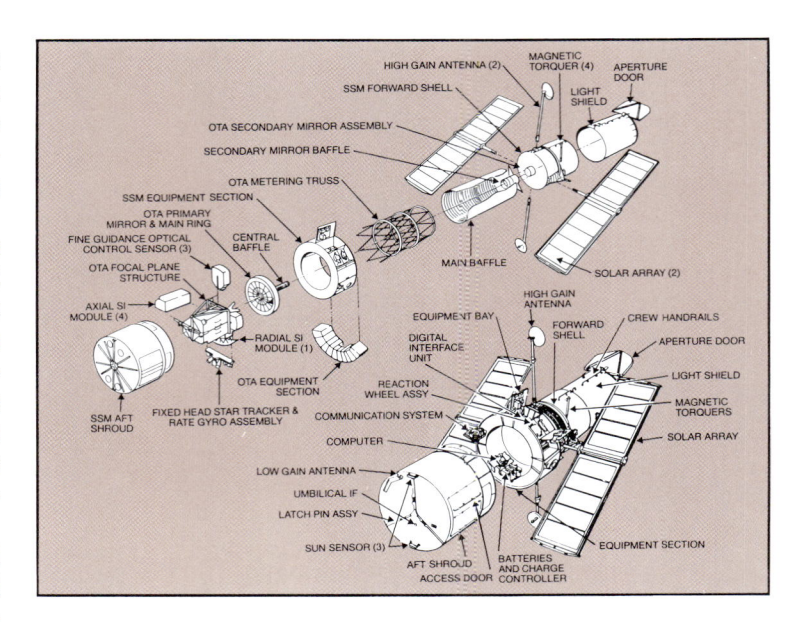

Above: Explanatory views of the Hubble Space Telescope, and *right,* an artist's conception of the HST in orbit. The super-secret 'Keyhole' series Air Force reconnaissance satellites, reportedly resemble the Hubble Space Telescope. The newest 'Keyhole,' the KH-12, which was launched in 1987, represented an advance over the previous satellite in the Keyhole series, the KH-11 (in orbital service since the 1970s). The KH-12 reportedly features near-instantaneous color television pictures of Earthbound events, extremely high resolution and almost 'spaceplane-like' maneuverability.

The Edwin P Hubble Space Telescope	
Telescope Type:	Ritchey-Chretien
Overall Length:	43.5 feet
Overall Diameter:	14.0 feet
Weight:	25,200 pounds
Primary Mirror (diameter):	94.5 inches
Secondary Mirror (diameter):	12.2 inches
Orbital Altitude:	320 nautical miles
Inclination to the Equatorial Plane:	28.5 degrees
Stability Tolerance:	.007 arc seconds
Primary Contractors:	
Systems Integration:	Lockheed Missiles & Space Company
Optical Telescope Assembly:	Perkin-Elmer Corporation
Support Systems Module:	Lockheed Missiles & Space Company
Faint Object Spectrograph:	Martin Marietta
Faint Object Camera:	European Space Agency (Dornier/Matra/British Aerospace)
High Resolution Spectrograph:	Ball Brothers
Wide Field/Planetary Camera:	NASA Jet Propulsion Laboratory
High Speed Photometer:	University of Wisconsin
Solar Arrays:	European Space Agency (British Aerospace)
Science Instrument Control and Data Handling:	Fairchild/IBM/NASA Goddard Space Flight Center

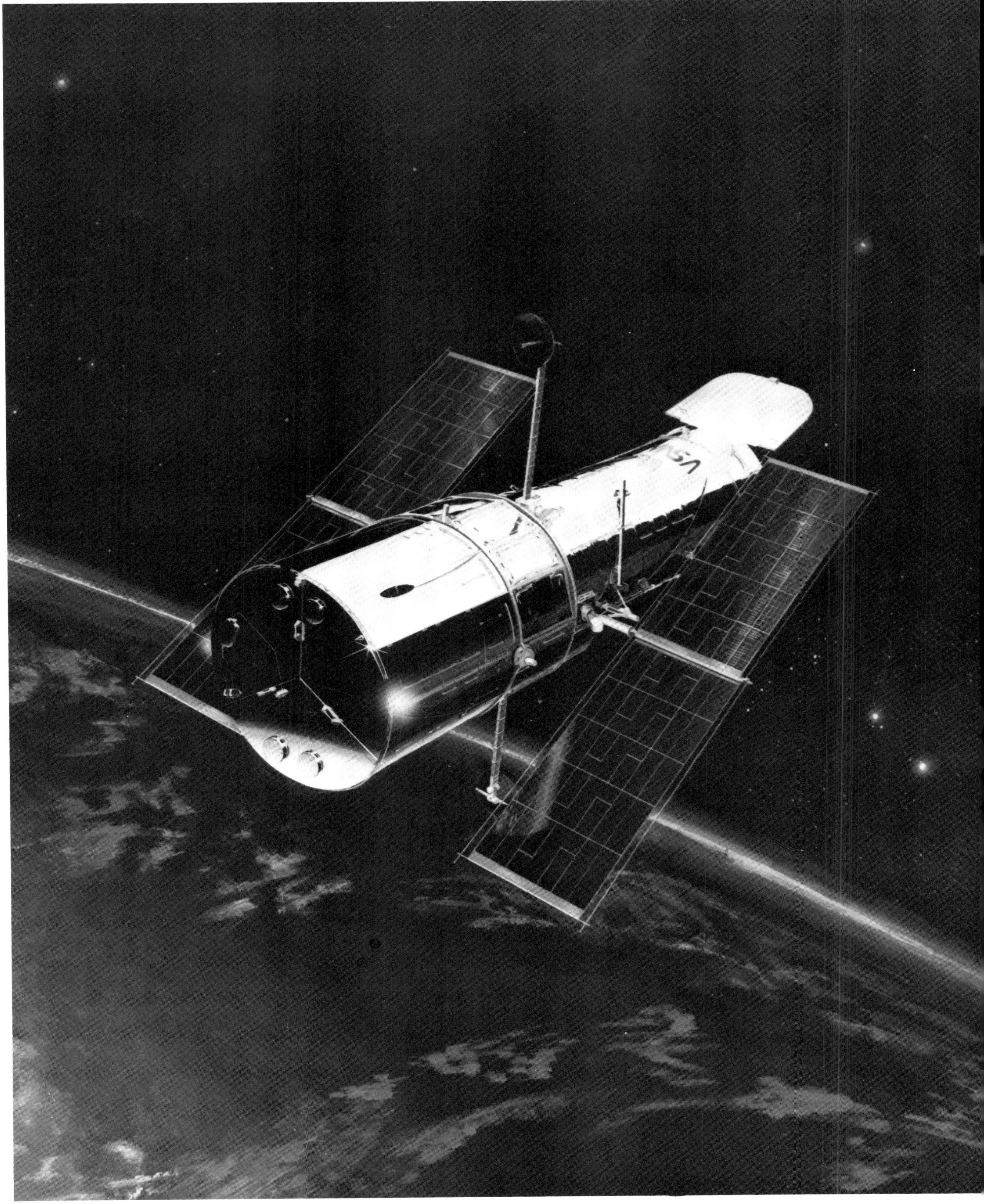

REACHING FOR THE STARS

A PORTRAIT OF LOCKHEED

Among the forty largest industrials in the United States, the Lockheed Corporation is the fifth largest aircraft company in the world after Soviet State Industries, United Technologies (Sikorsky, Pratt & Whitney, etc), Boeing and McDonnell Douglas. Lockheed is larger in terms of sales than the two largest non-US aerospace firms (Aerospatiale and British Aerospace) combined. With nearly 35,000 aircraft to its credit since 1913, it is second only to Douglas Aircraft (now a component of McDonnell Douglas Corporation) in terms of the number of aircraft that it has produced in its history.

The corporation traces its heritage to the Alco Hydro-Aeroplane Company of San Francisco that was founded by Allan and Malcolm Loughead in 1912, which built a single aircraft in its one year of existence. The two brothers later started the Loughead Aircraft Manufacturing Company that existed in Santa Barbara, California from 1916 to 1921, and resurfaced in Hollywood in 1926 as the Lockheed Aircraft Company. This company in turn became a division of the Detroit Aircraft Corporation in 1929. When the latter went bankrupt in 1931, the Lockheed component also went into receivership. The Lockheed Aircraft Corporation was resurrected as an independent entity in 1932, and it has been in operation continuously ever since, although the name was changed in 1977 from Lockheed Aircraft Corporation to simply Lockheed Corporation. Lockheed maintained its headquarters in Burbank, California from 1928 (when the ancestor Lockheed Aircraft company moved there from Hollywood) until 1986. In the latter year the Lockheed corporate headquarters was moved to Calabasas, California—roughly 20 miles from the old headquarters in Burbank.

The Lockheed Corporation employs roughly 97,000 personnel, including 23,000 scientists and engineers, at sites worldwide. The corporation activities are divided into five major 'Groups.'

Predictably, the largest Group is the Aeronautical Systems Group with about half of Lockheed's total employment. The

Then and now: This advertisement (*above*), from the Air Service Journal of 25 July 1928, proclaims the efficacy of the Hall-Scott motor as applied to the Loughead brothers' F-1; and some 60 years later, a TR-1 jockey (*at right*) stands in front of his high-flying steed.

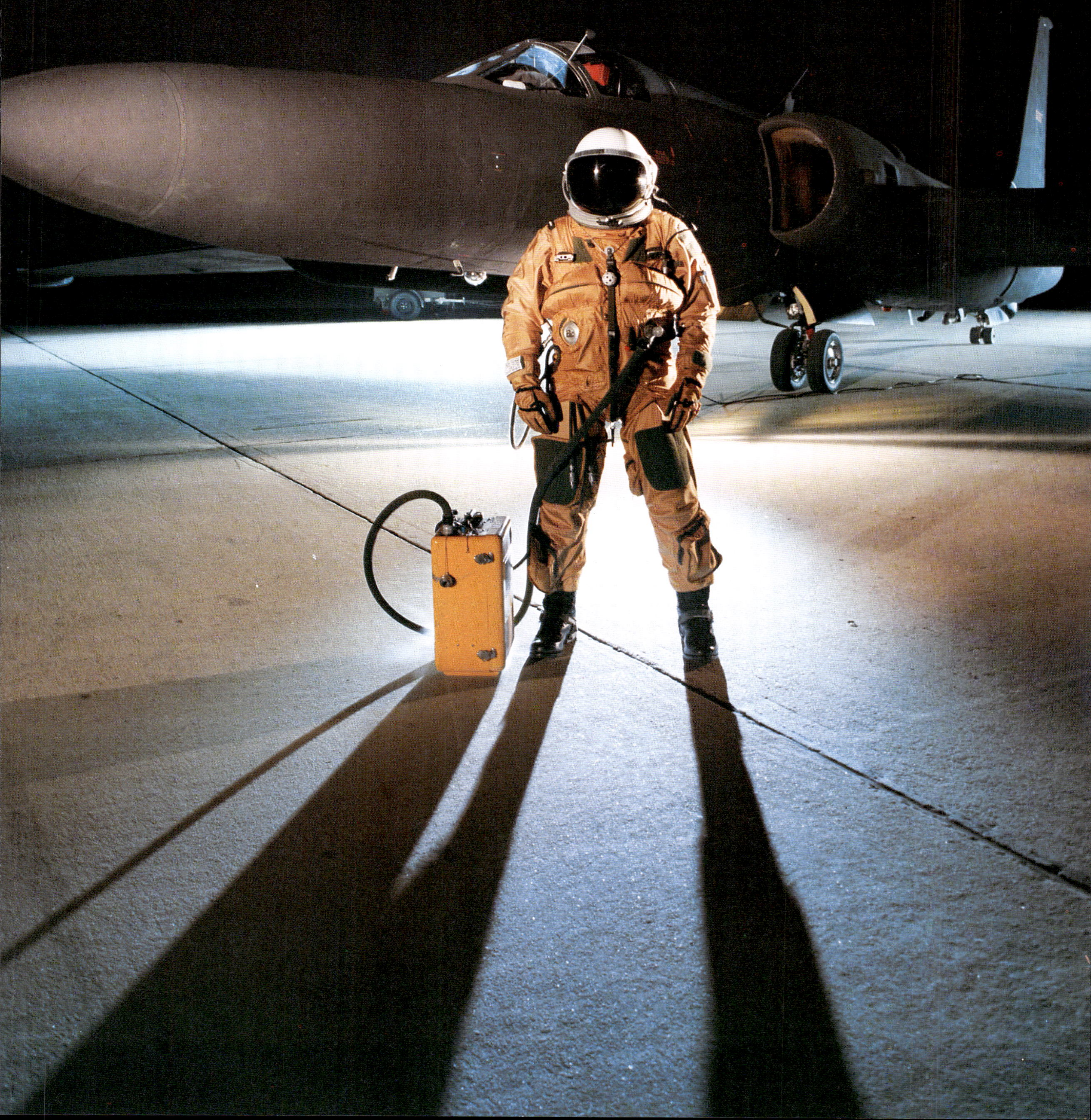

Allan Loughead shown in his later years *at left,* founded the Loughead Aircraft Manufacturing Company in 1916 and helped guide it through various permutations in the 1920s before selling out to the Detroit Aircraft Corporation in 1929. The new firm, however, collapsed under the weight of the stock market crash and Allan Loughead found himself with his entire worth tied up in valueless stock.

When Robert Gross resurrected Lockheed in 1932, there was no place for Allan, so he started over with the Allan Loughead Corp (Alcor), which never quite got off the ground. He sold real estate in Arizona and Southern California for a few years, and during World War II, he managed an aircraft factory, though not for Lockheed. Loughead returned to the real estate business after the war but did very poorly. At last, and almost destitute, he became an historical consultant to Lockheed, on a $100 per month retainer, in the late 1950s. A legendary milestone in the always intriguing Lockheed saga was sealed for posterity when Allan Loughead died in 1969.

Below left, left to right: Al Menasco, who designed the special in-line engines for Loughead's one and only Alcor airplane; movie pilot Frank Clark; flying ace Art Goebel; Allan Loughead; and Allan's daughter Beth, who is shown here as she christens the Alcor airplane, which showed promise when introduced in 1934, but which failed commercially.

At right, left to right: Hall Hibbard and Robert Gross are seen here circa 1950 against the backdrop of Lockheed Constellation's distinctive tail. Bob Gross became a Lockheed fan while helping Lloyd Stearman and Walter T Varney run Varney Speed Lanes, which flew the speedy Lockheed Orions. In 1932 when Lockheed's parent company went bankrupt, Gross, Stearman and Carl Squier showed at the bankruptcy court in Los Angeles with the deposit necessary to buy Lockheed's assets.

As chairman of the board and treasurer of the post-1932 Lockheed, Gross brought the company back to life with the Model 10 Electra, and 25 years of ups and downs, general success and excitement followed from this association. Gross died in August of 1961. Hall Hibbard was Lockheed's chief engineer and engineering vice president from 1933 to 1956, and became senior vice president from 1956 to 1963, when he retired.

229

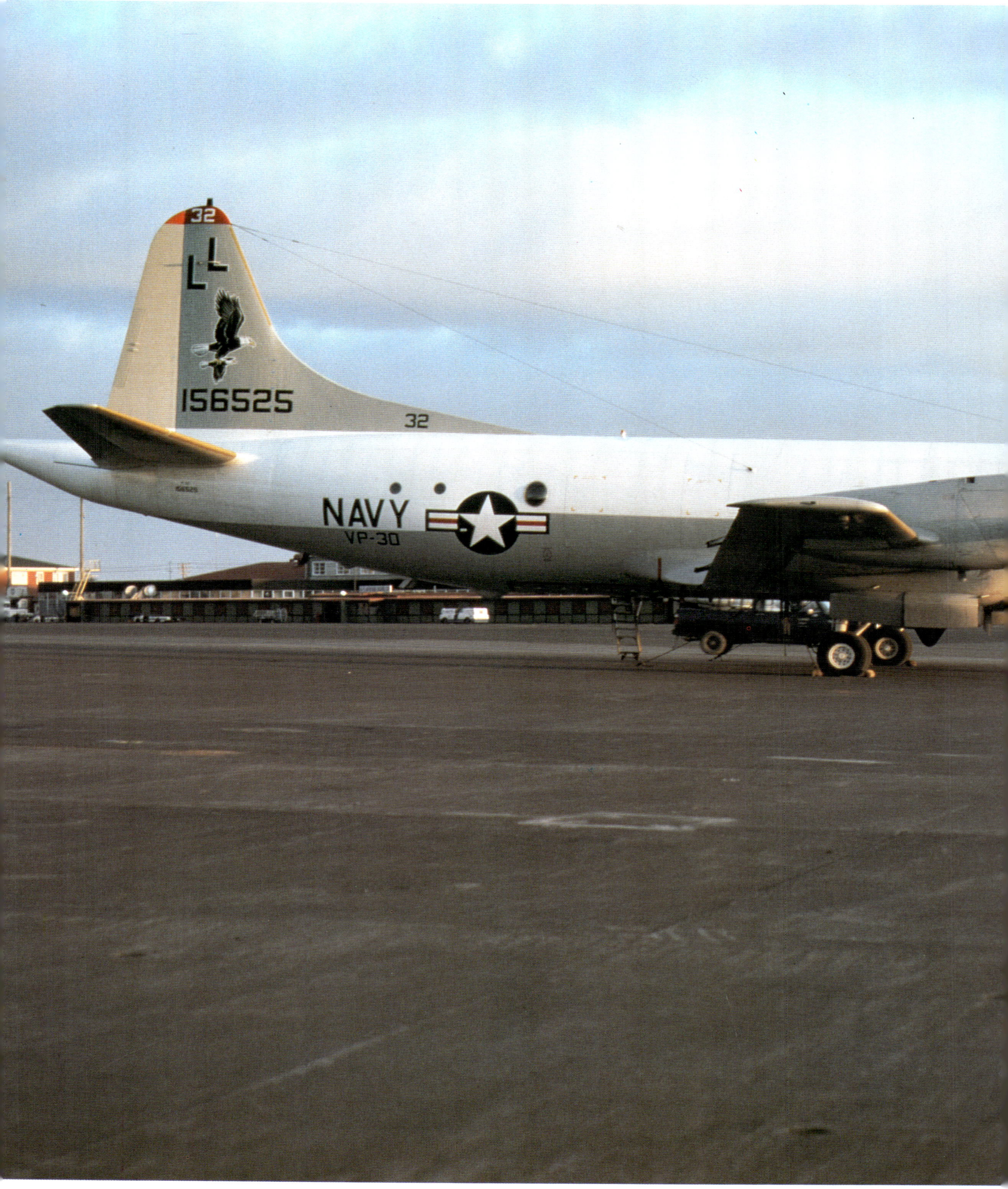
32
LL
156525
32
NAVY
VP-30

The Lockheed California P-3 Orion (*above and left*) is an important part of the Aeronautics Systems Group repertoire in the 1980s.

other four Groups are the Missiles & Space Systems Group, the Electronic Systems Group, the Marine Systems Group, and the Information Systems Group.

THE AERONAUTICAL SYSTEMS GROUP

The major Operating Companies within the Aeronautical Systems Group are the Lockheed California Company (Calac), with 17 percent of the total corporate employees, and the Lockheed Georgia Company (Gelac), which employs roughly 20 percent of the total.

Headquartered in Burbank, Lockheed California can be said to be Lockheed's oldest component because, when the corporation became divisionalized in the early 1950s, Lockheed California inherited the aircraft production facilities that had been administered directly by the corporation since 1932. The Lockheed Georgia Division was established in 1951 at Marietta, Georgia in facilities acquired from the US government. The Lockheed California Division was created the following year as a parallel organization. The two Divisions, which became 'Companies' in 1961, operate largely independently of one another and have been responsible for most of the Lockheed aircraft produced since 1952.

Lockheed California's current activities include P-3 Orion and TR-1 production, as well as ongoing development and support for recent Lockheed California products such as the S-3 Viking and L-1011 TriStar. The Advanced Development Projects office (the *Skunk Works*) is also a part of Lockheed California.

Lockheed Georgia's current activities include C-5B Galaxy, C-130 Hercules and L-100 Hercules production, as well as the C-5A Galaxy modernization project.

Other Aeronautical Systems Group components include the Lockheed Aeromod Center in Greenville, South Carolina (formed in 1984); the Murdock Engineering Company in Irving, Texas (acquired in 1973); Lockheed Support Systems in Arlington, Texas (acquired in 1975) and Lockheed Aircraft Services Company (established in 1946) headquartered in Ontario, California.

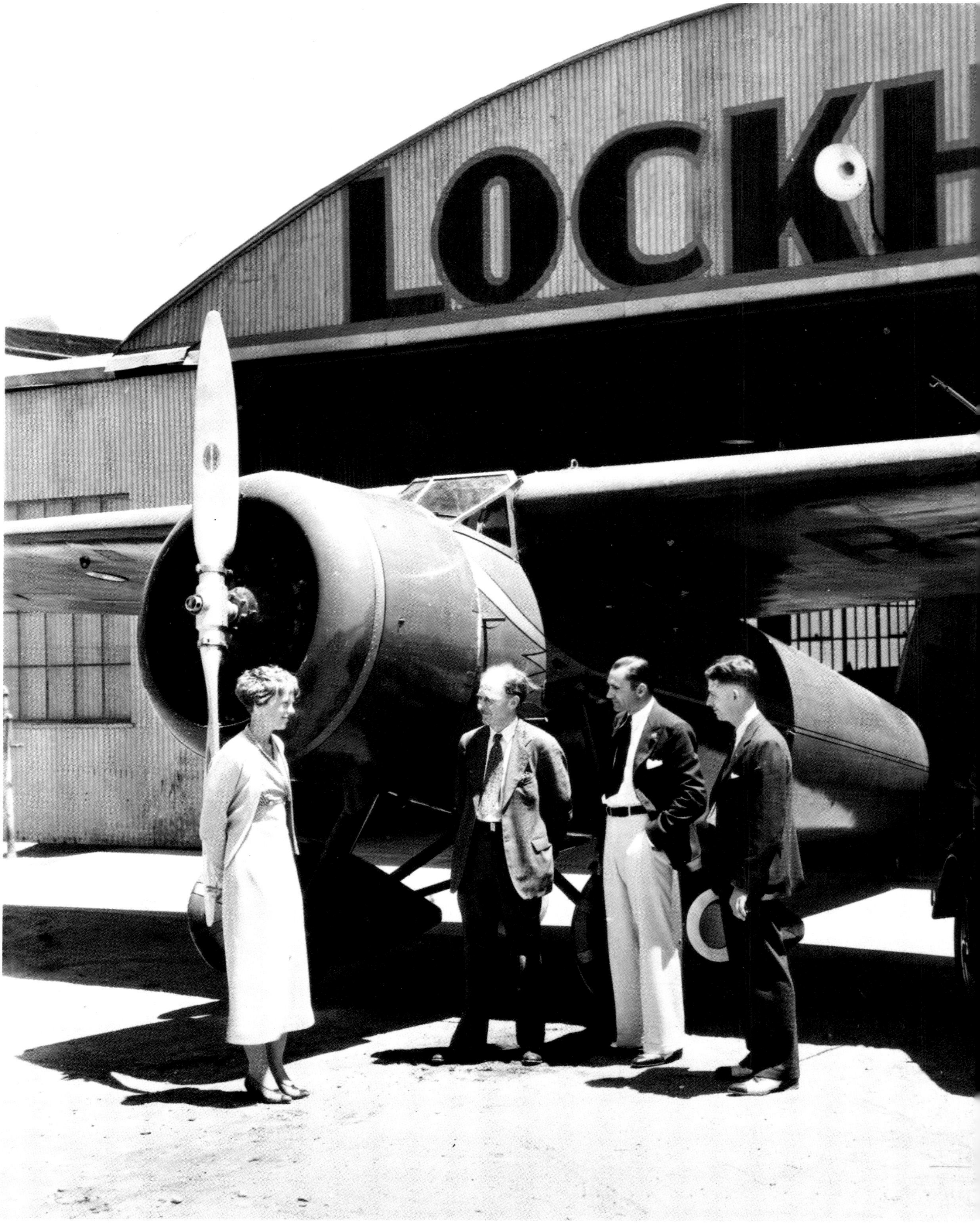
LOCKH

THE MISSILES & SPACE SYSTEMS GROUP

The largest component in this Group, and indeed in all of the Lockheed Corporation, is the Lockheed Missiles & Space Company (LMSC), based in Sunnyvale, California, which employs 35 percent of the Lockheed work force. LMSC was formed in 1954 as the Missile Systems Division and became the Lockheed Missiles & Space Company in 1961. LMSC's principal activities are: the development and production of Fleet Ballistic Missiles for the US Navy; development and production of spacecraft and space systems for the US Air Force and NASA; and a variety of government research and development projects.

The other components of the Group include the Lockheed Engineering & Management Services Company (established in 1979) in Houston, Texas. Also in the Group is the Lockheed Space Operations Company (established in 1982 at Titusville, Florida), which provides spacecraft launch support services at Kennedy Space Center, Florida and Vandenberg AFB, California. The other component of the Missiles & Space Systems Group is the newly formed Advanced Marine Systems of Santa Clara, California, which inherited the marine activities born of the advanced research activities at nearby LMSC, but which was for a time part of Lockheed's Marine Systems Group. Its activities include ongoing projects such as Manned Deep Submergence Vehicles, unmanned underwater vehicles and other underwater electronic and hardware systems.

THE INFORMATION SYSTEMS GROUP

Lockheed's smallest systems group (formed since 1981) includes CADAM, Incorporated in Burbank, California; Datacom Systems Corporation in New York City; Lockheed DataPlan, Incorporated in Los Gatos, California; DIALOG Information Services, Incorporated in Palo Alto, California; CalComp in Anaheim, California; and Metier Management Systems, a group of five computer companies with offices in Europe and the Far East. Lockheed's oldest component, Lockheed Air Terminal (established in 1940 to manage the company-owned airport in Burbank, California) was for many years a member of the Aeronautical Systems Group, but was moved to the Information Systems Group at the end of 1986.

THE MARINE SYSTEMS GROUP

The centerpiece of the Marine Systems Group is the Lockheed Shipbuilding Company of Seattle, Washington. Lockheed Shipbuilding is active in ship design, engineering, construction, overhaul, repair and logistical support. With one percent of Lockheed Corporation's total work force, the Shipbuilding component is the seventh largest Operating Company. Born in 1889 as the Seattle Division of the San Francisco Bridge Company, this component operated for 60 years from 1899 until 1959, as the independent Puget Sound Bridge and Dredging Company. It was then acquired by Lockheed as the Puget Sound Bridge & Drydock Company, and the name was changed to Lockheed Shipbuilding. Since 1898 when the company began building ships, it has produced nearly 200, including 34 during World War II. Almost fifty of these ships have been produced since the company became part of Lockheed in 1959.

At left: Lockheed Air Terminal in Burbank, the oldest operating group in the company, as it appeared in 1932. *Left to right* are Amelia Earhart, one of the company's celebrity customers; Allan Loughead, who still hung around his former company; Carl Squier, the post-1932 Lockheed vice president; and Lloyd Stearman, the resurrected company's president.

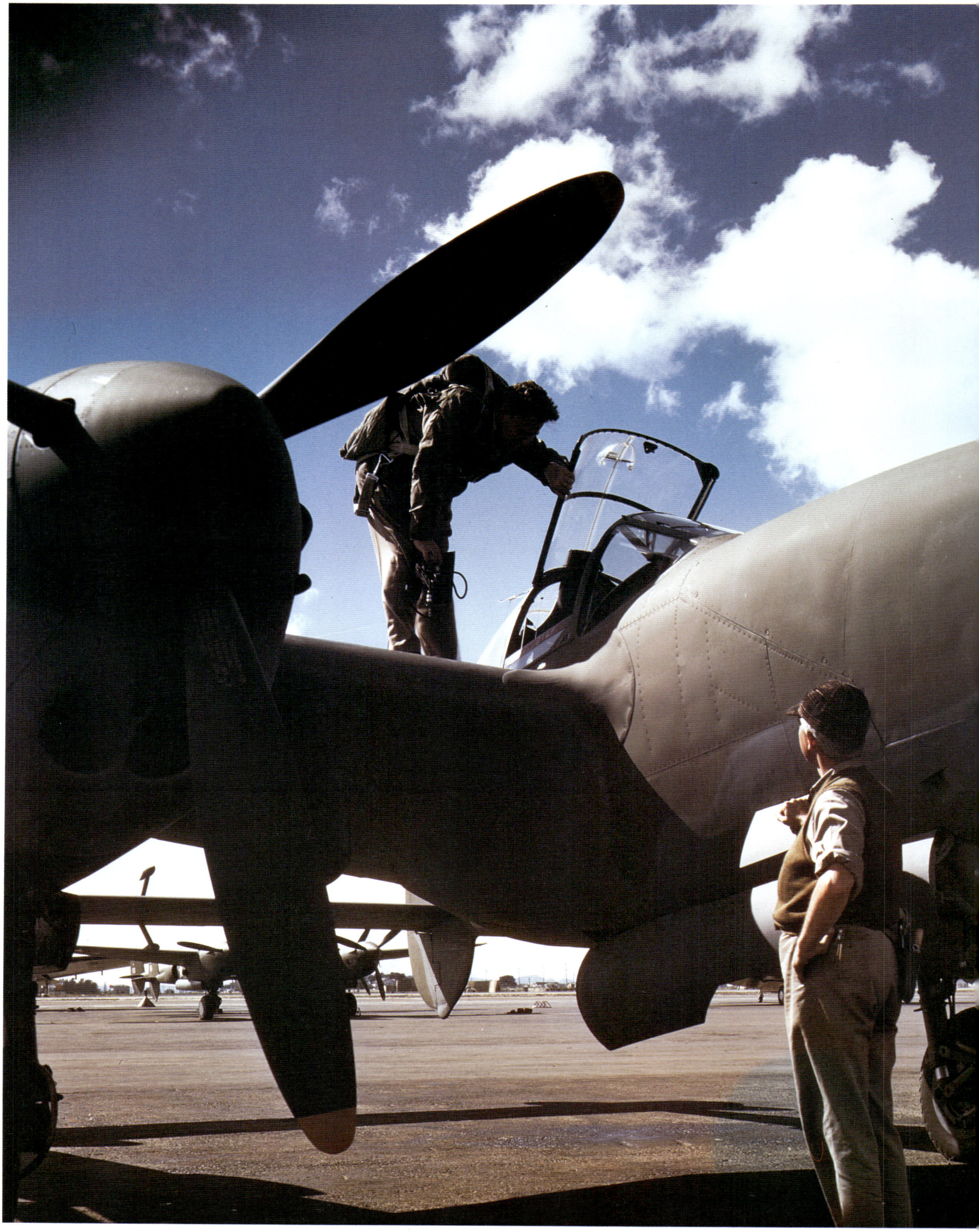

THE ELECTRONICS SYSTEMS GROUP

Lockheed's newest group was formed in 1986 with the acquisition of Sanders Associates, Incorporated (formed in 1951) of Nashua, New Hampshire. Sanders develops and manufactures advanced electronic systems for the military and commercial markets. In addition to Sanders, this group includes the Lockheed Electronics Company which was formed in 1959 through a merger of Lockheed Electronics and Avionics Division and Stavid Engineering. Prior to 1986, it had been part of the Missiles & Space Systems Group which was then known as the Missiles, Space & Electronics Group.

CORPORATE COMPONENTS NOT ASSIGNED TO GROUPS

The category includes Lockheed Finance Corporation, formed in 1977 at Burbank to help customers finance the purchase of Lockheed products and services. Lockheed-Arabia, of Riyadh, Saudi Arabia is a joint venture with Saudi Arabian interests that has as its primary concern, installation, operation, maintenance and training related to aircraft, aerospace equipment, electronic systems, communication systems, environmental projects and security projects. Lockheed Corporation International was established at Burbank in 1984 to provide international marketing and support services for all of the Lockheed Corporation's operating companies.

A CONCISE FINANCIAL HISTORY OF LOCKHEED

Since its birth in 1932, Lockheed has enjoyed a generally steady growth in sales and employment with the exception of the World War II years and the early 1970s. During World War II Lockheed, like so many aircraft manufacturers, experienced fantastic growth. In four years from 1939 to 1943 Lockheed's employment rose from 7000 to 94,329, while sales rose from $35.3 million to $697.4 million. Except for a $190,891 loss in 1934, Lockheed's net income also grew fairly steadily in the prewar years and very rapidly during the war. From $24,692 in 1933, net income rose to $442,111 for 1938, then exploded through the roof to $8.2 million for 1942.

In the five years 1941-45, Lockheed (and Lockheed-Vega) factories produced more aircraft than in *all* the rest of its history before *and* since. Lockheed built over 18,000 individual aircraft during those five years, compared to the 1215 that had been produced during seventeen years of active production by all the Lockheed and Loughead companies prior to 1941. In more than forty years of aircraft production, since 1945 Lockheed has built only about 15,000 aircraft.

The biggest-selling Lockheed airplane was the P-38 Lightning (Model 22 series), of which 9925 were built between 1939 and 1945. More than one out of every four Lockheed planes ever made were Lightnings. The second place in sales was Lockheed's biggest selling jet, the T-33 T-Bird, of which 5691 were built between 1948 and 1959. The total for all aircraft types derived from the P-80 Shooting Star (including the T-33, F-80, T2V and F-94) was 8426.

With the postwar demobilization, government orders for airplanes suddenly disappeared. Many aircraft companies folded and those that survived found themselves much smaller than

Shown *at left* being readied for a checkout flight at Burbank in 1943, the Model P-38 Lightning was Lockheed's biggest seller ever.

N4190M

Below: A Lockheed C-130 Hercules wears Saudia colors. This Saudi Arabian government-owned airline performs both civilian and paramilitary functions.

The corporation has a separate operating component called Lockheed Saudi Arabia, which is a Lockheed Finance Corporation/Saudi Arabian government joint purchasing-assistance program. Headquartered in the Saudi capital of Riyadh, the C-130 shown here is typical of what might be included. The main aims of the component are installation, operation, maintenance and training related to aircraft, as well as aerospace and security-related systems.

they had been. Lockheed's work force fell to a postwar low of 14,555 in 1947, just 15 percent of the 1943 level. Sales bottomed out at $112.7 million in 1946, down to 16 percent of the 1943 peak. Net income fell to a $2.5 million loss in 1947.

As defense contracts returned in the 1950s, Lockheed gradually began to grow again. Major factors contributing to growth included the series of fighter aircraft produced by Lockheed California; the Fleet Ballistic Missiles of the Missiles Systems Division; and Lockheed Georgia's C-130 and C-141 programs.

In terms of inflation-adjusted dollars, Lockheed regained its wartime levels in both sales and net income by the mid-1950s, and in 1968 and 1969 employment exceeded the 1943 peak. In 1969, however, Lockheed reached the most critical period in its history. A number of factors unexpectedly combined to produce the worst crisis in Lockheed history. Each of the misfortunes that precipitated the crisis would have each been bad enough by itself, but their simultaneous occurrence very nearly destroyed the corporation:

(1) First there was the AH-56 Cheyenne helicopter program, which had been canceled after Lockheed had spent millions on its development.

(2) Second, there was the C-5A Galaxy and its whole set of problems. The Galaxy should have a good project for Lockheed, but the corporation had underestimated the cost and engineering problems, and so had signed a Total Package Procurement (TPP) contract with the Air Force. The Galaxy program was further complicated—by accusations in Congress that Lockheed had mismanaged the program, and the failure of the Galaxy to develop a commercial market. As a final blow the government canceled 34 of the 115 Galaxies it had ordered, forcing Lockheed

At right: Commercial Constellations (*at rear*) and military Model 49 aircraft line the flightline at Burbank in the early 1950s.

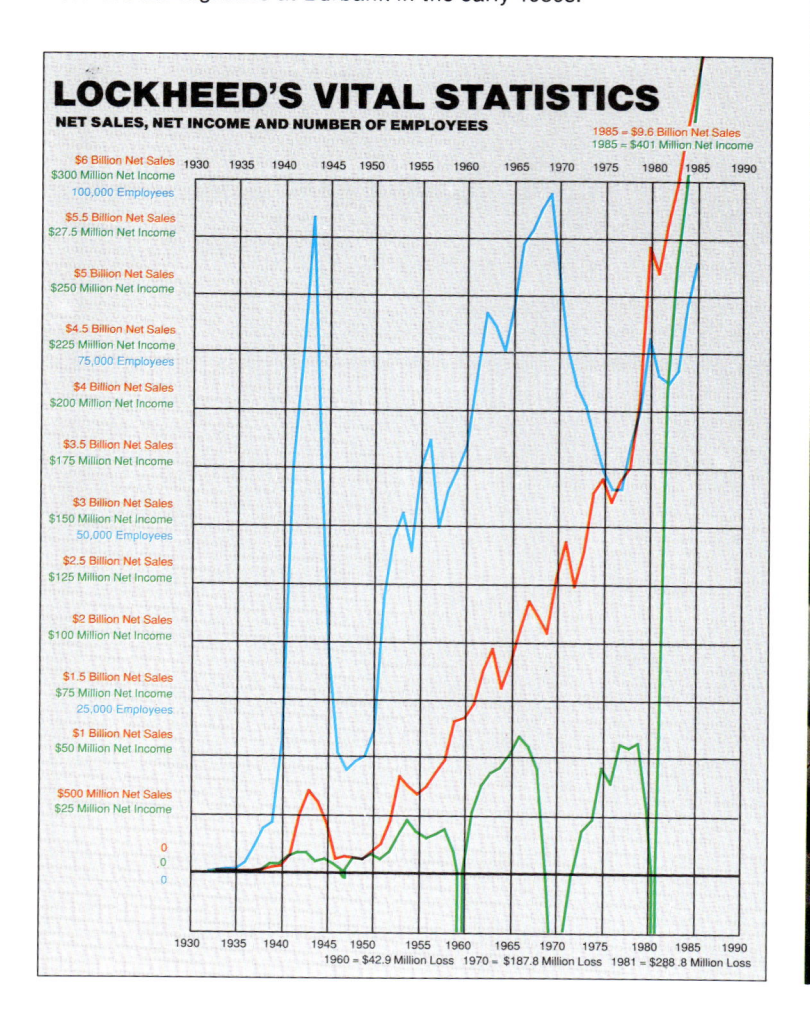

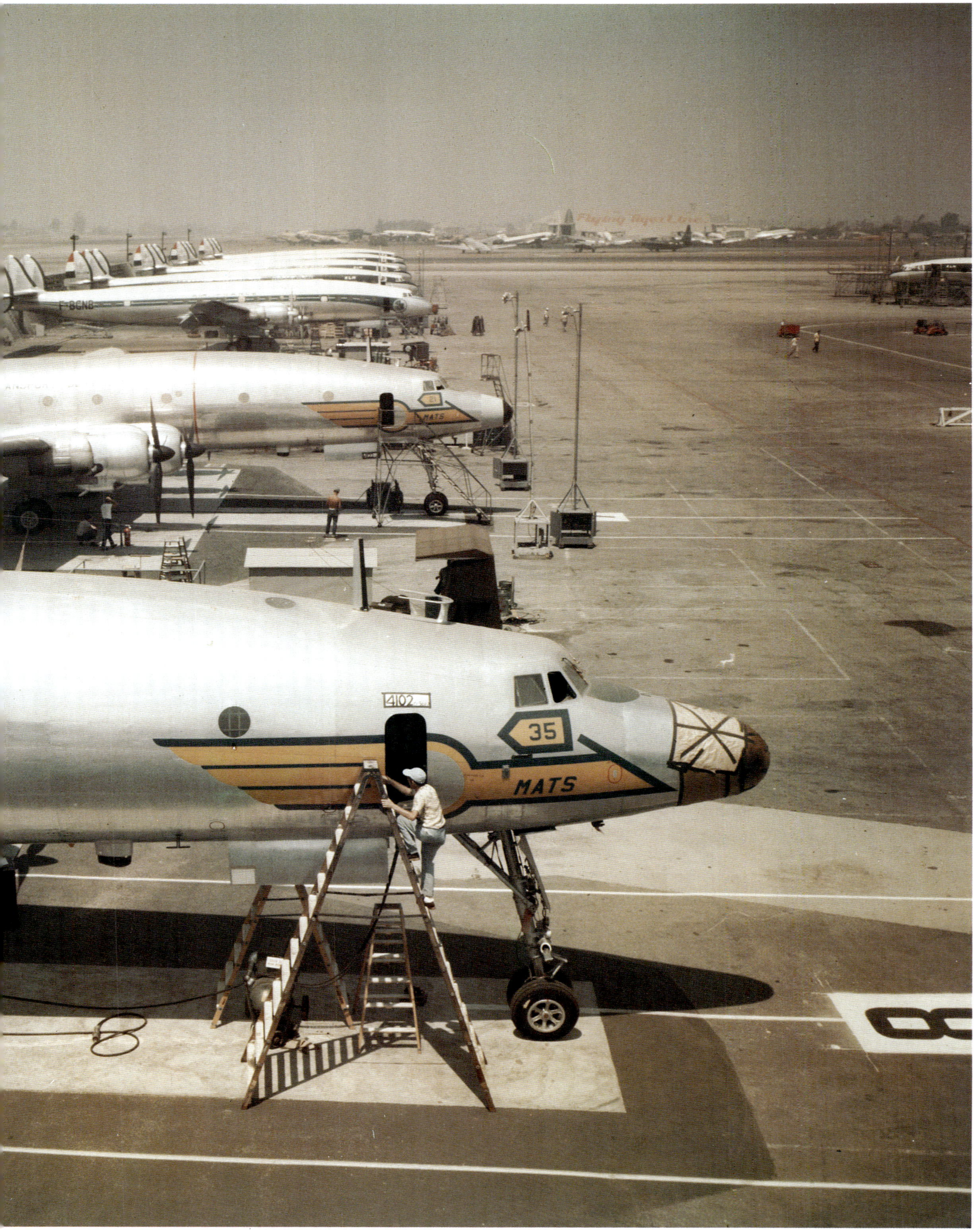
F-BGNB
4102
35
MATS

Above: The L-1011 prototype, reworked as a test aircraft in the 1980s, takes to the air over Lockheed's Palmdale factory. *Right: A* TR-1 poises for a dawn patrol. The TR-1 has been an important Lockheed California product in the 1980s.

to go to court and seek a settlement from them at a time when the government accounted for nearly 90 percent of the company's business.

(3) At the same time that Lockheed faced the difficulties with the Cheyenne and the Galaxy, the corporation was deeply committed to the development of a costly wide-body jetliner, the L-1011 TriStar. Lockheed had never built a jetliner, and even under the best of circumstances such an undertaking would have been hugely complex and expensive. As timing would have it, Lockheed's L-1011 TriStar would be facing *direct* competition from the McDonnell Douglas DC-10, which was in *exactly* the same size and weight class. In the early days of the competition, the L-1011 outsold the DC-10, but the Rolls Royce bankruptcy forced delays and forced Lockheed to have to lay off many skilled and experienced workers.

(4) The tremendous financial strain faced by Lockheed in the face of the problems with these three programs came against the backdrop of a serious crisis of public confidence in Lockheed itself. At home there were accusations of waste and mismanagement in the Galaxy program, a fire whose flames were fanned by the press—which in the midst of the interminable Vietnam war, was vociferously antimilitary. In Europe there were growing concerns expressed loudly in the media, about Lockheed Starfighters that seemed to be involved in fatal crashes on a monthly basis. And finally as the mid-seventies approached, the energy crisis of 1974 crippled the sales of the L-1011, and worldwide accusations of Lockheed bribes paid to foreign government officials resulted in congressional investigations that the press dubbed the 'Lockheed bribery scandal.' All of these events only served to further tarnish Lockheed's public image.

In 1969 Lockheed lost $32.6 million, and in 1970 the losses had ballooned to a record $187.8 million. By 1972 the corporation had posted losses for four straight years totaling $267 million. On 30 July 1971 the US Congress passed a loan guarantee package calling for the Federal Government to serve as co-signer with Lockheed for $250 million in loans from commercial banks. For this service, the US Government charged Lockheed $30 million, which was paid in addition to the interest and loan repayment to the private banks.

In the end Lockheed not only survived, but posted record, or near-record, profits by the end of the decade of the seventies. With the C-5A and L-1011, Lockheed had been in the unfortunate position of having to develop two of the world's four largest transports at a time of serious strain from other quarters. However, both of these two aircraft went on to find themselves well received by the people whom they served, and by the crews that flew them.

The TriStar, despite its critical success, was not a financial success and production closed in 1985 after 250 airplanes had been made. The only loss posted by Lockheed since 1972 was $288.8 million in 1981 because of the final write-off of the L-1011 program. The Galaxy vindicated itself after predictions that it would be a white elephant, and in 1982 the US government gave Lockheed a contract to build 50 C-5B Galaxies.

With the exception of the mysterious activities of the *Skunk Works*, Lockheed had introduced no new aircraft types since the TriStar in 1970 and the Viking in 1972. This is in marked contrast to the previous years when an average of almost ten new types were introduced in each decade. In the mid-1980s production consisted of the Hercules (introduced in 1959), the Galaxy (introduced in 1969), the TR-1 (introduced with the U-2 in 1954) and the Orion, which was introduced in 1959.

After the write-off of the L-1011 in 1981, net income began to increase again. From $207.3 million in 1982, net income nearly doubled in three years to $401 million, while sales increased from $5.6 billion to $9.5 billion in the same period.

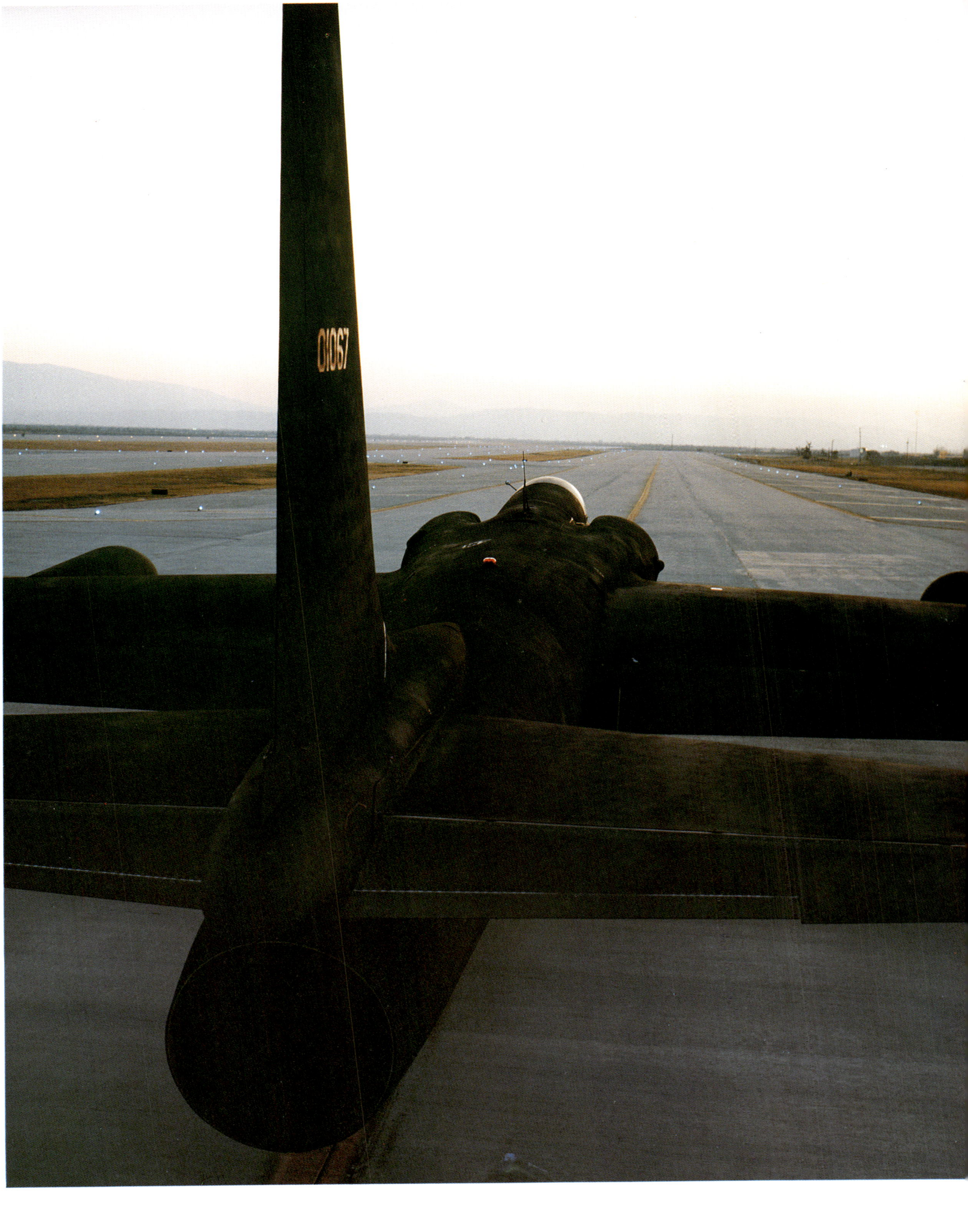
01067

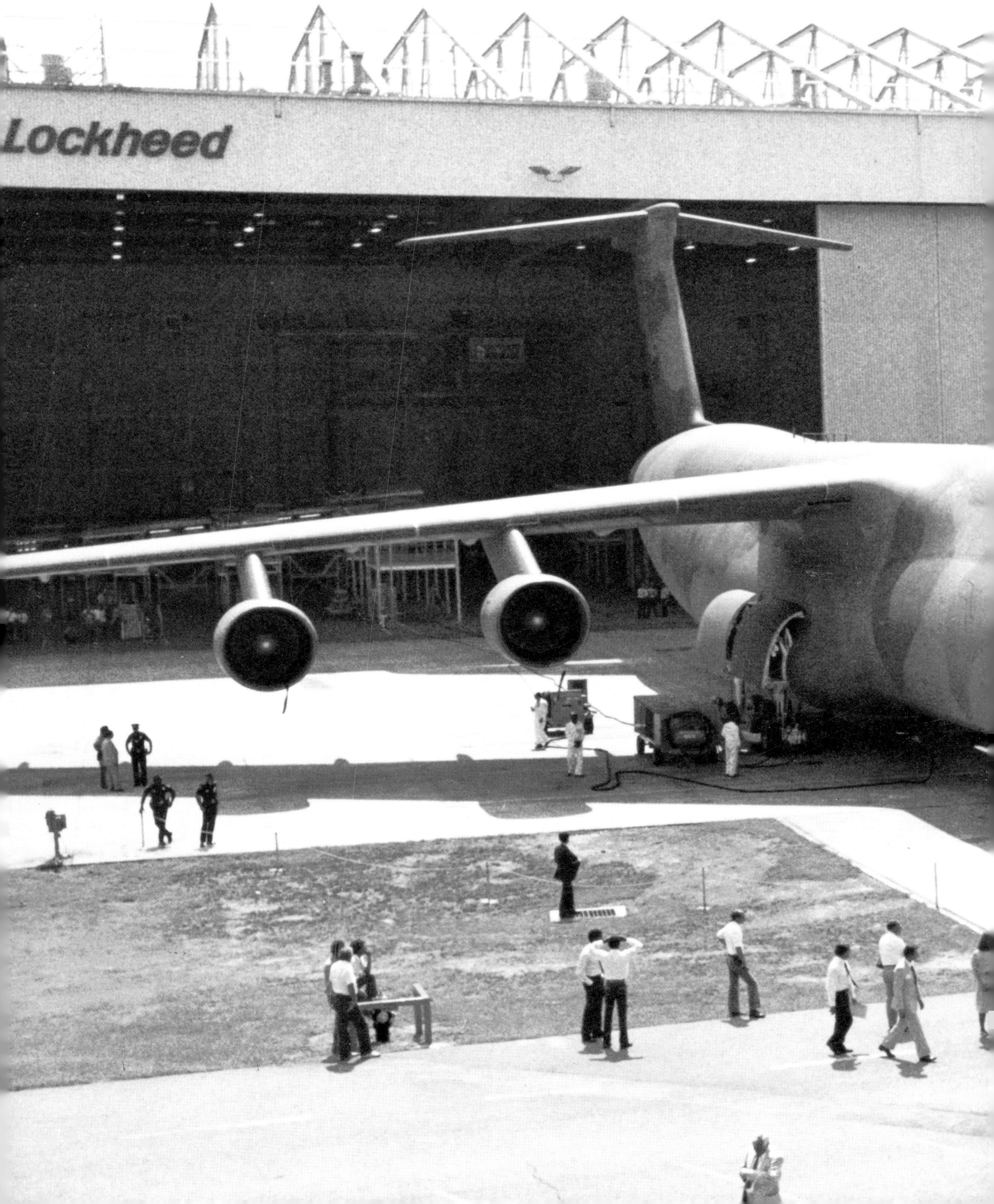
Lockheed

Lower left: The first of 50 C-5B military transport planes, manufactured by Lockheed for the US Air Force, is shown *here* being rolled out of the factory, with attendant celebration. This plane took to the air for the first C-5B flight 10 September 1985.

THE BIRTH OF THE F-22 PROGRAM

On 31 October 1986, the US Air Force announced the award of parallel $691 million contracts to Lockheed Corporation and Northrop Corporation to build service test demonstration fighters under its Advanced Tactical Fighter (ATF) program. Lockheed and Northrop would each build a pair of aircraft under the service test designations YF-22 and YF-23 respectively. The Air Force contract called for the four aircraft to be ready for testing in 1993, with the winning entrant being given a production contract for upwards of 750 of the high tech fighters. Ultimately, the winning entrant would replace the F-15 as the Air Force's first-line air superiority fighter. In the development of the YF-22 Lockheed would be supported by Boeing and General Dynamics as major subcontractors, while Northrop's partner in the YF-23 program would be McDonnell Douglas, with whom it was teamed on the earlier F-18 program.

'This is a major target for new business,' said Lockheed Aeronautical Systems Group president Robert Ormsby, Jr. 'We have been developing new advanced tactical fighter concepts at Lockheed for ten years. We have the experience, know-how and technical resources to deliver an ATF that will meet or exceed all of the Air Force requirements.'

Lockheed was one of seven aerospace contractors that submitted Air Force-funded studies for ATF concept development in 1984. Under the direction of R Richard Heppe, an expanded team of Lockheed experts had used company funds prior to the Air Force selection of Lockheed and Northrop to continue development work under contract. The resulting YF-22 and YF-23 demonstrators will help refine the ATF weapon system design through a comprehensive test and evaluation program prior to full-scale development.

'The ATF must give the Air Force superior performance and maximum operational readiness at an affordable cost,' said Heppe. 'Concentrating on these factors, Lockheed's design is evolving rapidly as our engineering, logistics support and manufacturing planning teams gather momentum,' Heppe said. 'The aircraft that is emerging will incorporate new technologies that will put it generations beyond the fighters in service today. Efficient supersonic cruise performance coupled with advanced low-observables technologies will make the Lockheed ATF both lethal and survivable well into the twenty-first century.'

Extensive use of advanced composites and advanced metallic structures will save 20 percent in weight. Advanced avionics, armament, propulsion and flight controls will be integrated into a highly automated crew station to achieve major improvements in both beyond-visual-range and close-in combat performance.

'In addition to performance capability, major drivers in our design are cost, reliability and ease of maintenance. By engineering our ATF for automated, low-cost production, we will ensure that the Air Force can afford to buy this top quality aircraft in the large quantities needed to offset the growing Soviet threat,' said Heppe. 'To sustain the highest possible sortie rates, our ATF design will incorporate highly reliable subsystems and the most advanced on-board diagnostics and maintenance, reducing requirements for spares, support equipment and manpower. Coupled with its rapid-deployment capability, this will enable the ATF to quickly achieve air superiority in all regions of a potential conflict.'

Paralleling Lockheed's ATF development program is an aggressive facility expansion effort to provide the most advanced development and manufacturing capabilities in the industry, according to Ormsby.

'A major addition is under way at our Helendale, California, unit, already the world's most sophisticated privately-owned radar test range. Also, a $55 million state-of-the-art weapons

The rather glorious-looking ATF concepts that have evolved from Lockheed California between 1985 (*right*) and 1986 (*above*) have combined the design features of the SR-71 with open bubble canopies, canard wing arrangements and 'stealth' technology.

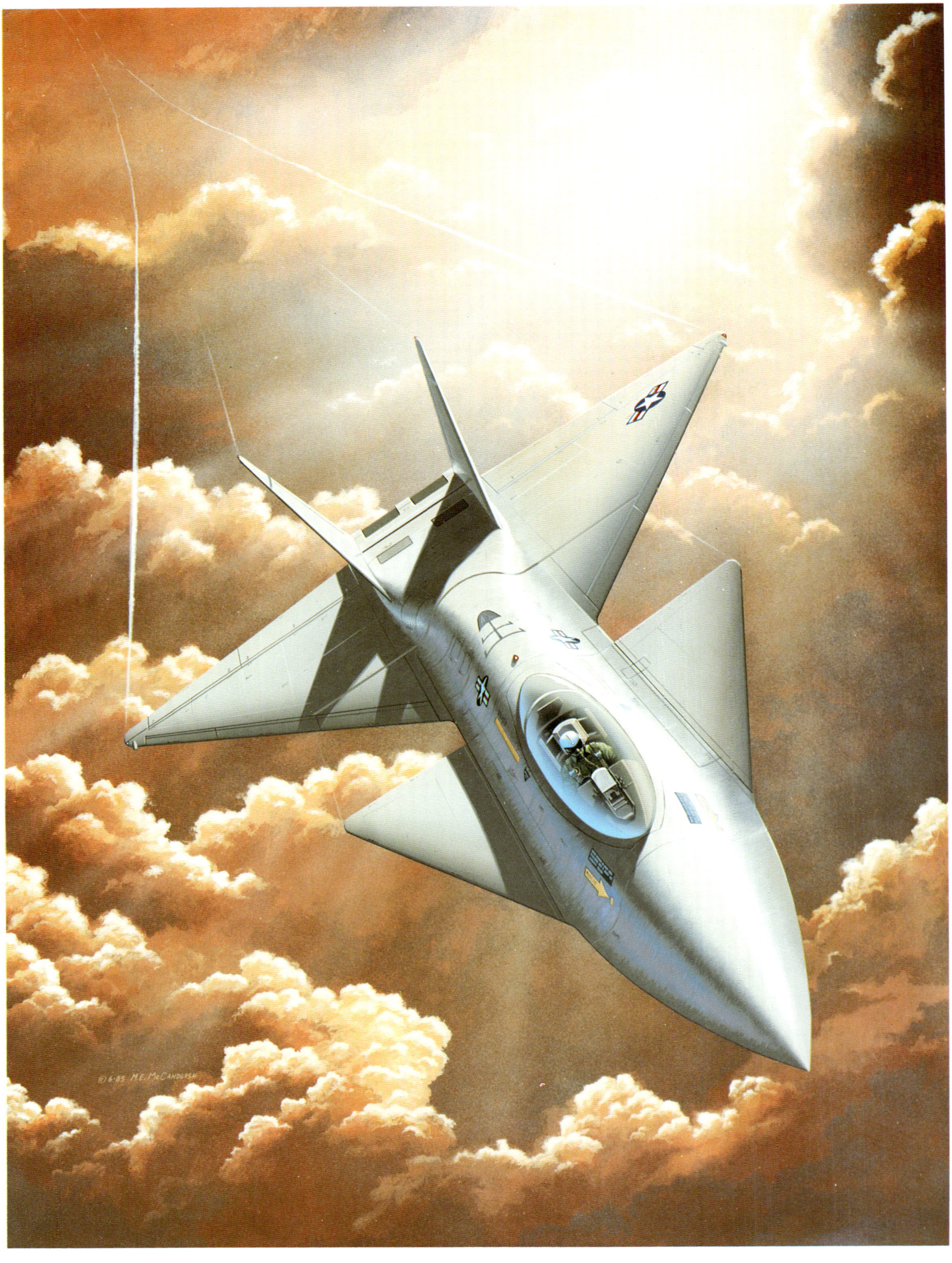
©6-85 M.E. McCANDLISH

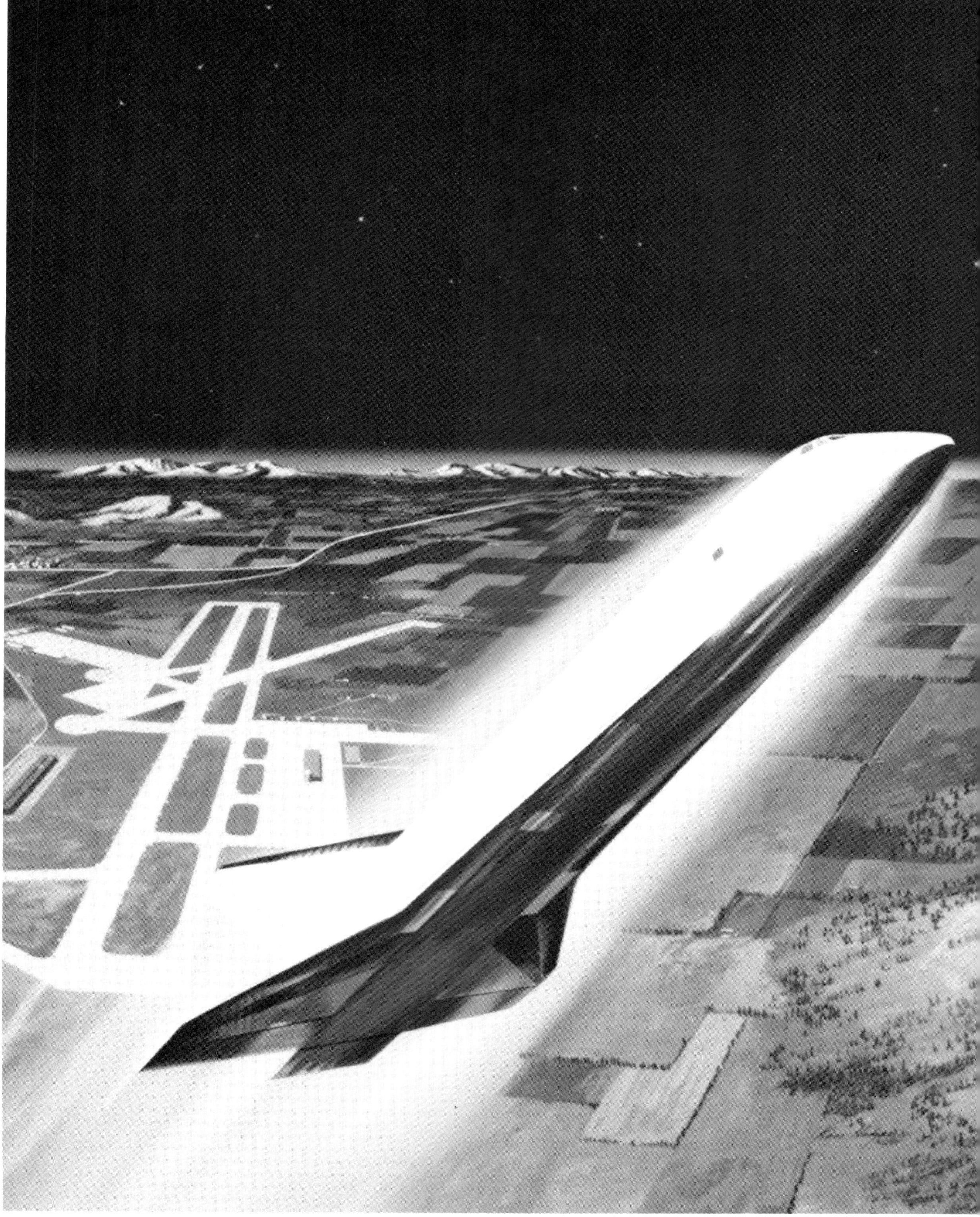

system simulation and integration complex is being built at Lockheed's Kelly Johnson Research and Development Center at Rye Canyon, California. This is all part of an investment in advanced aircraft technology that will include a "factory of tomorrow." Computer-controlled, this production facility will make extensive use of robotics; automated fabrication and assembly, and management systems that will improve quality control, avoid waste and reduce man hours,' Ormsby said.

'Lockheed developed America's first production jet fighter —the P-80—while we were still fighting World War II,' said Heppe. 'In the 1950s we built the first Mach 2 fighter in the F-104, followed in the 1960s by the first Mach 3 aircraft—the SR-71. With over 15,000 hours at or above Mach 3 we have the only true body of knowledge on supersonic cruising flight in US industry today. Lockheed has specialized in exactly the type of pioneering effort that is going on now. The ATF program is an opportunity to do what we do best . . . create innovative solutions to meet the cost, supportability and performance needs of our customers.'

REACHING FOR THE STARS

Since Wiley Post used his Lockheed Vega *Winnie Mae* to reach for new altitude records in 1934, pilots have been reaching for the stars with airplanes marked by the winged star logo. In the 1960s it was the Lockheed SR-71 Blackbird that could fly higher and faster than any other operational aircraft on *(or above)* the earth. With the Lockheed-built Hubble Space Telescope, astronomers will be able to view stars seven times more distant than have ever been seen by mankind before.

As Lockheed enters the 1990s, a vast number of new and exciting projects are on the drawing boards at Lockheed offices from Sunnyvale to Marietta. On the commercial aircraft front there is the possibility of a new Supersonic Transport, or even a role for Lockheed in the development of the *hypersonic* National Aerospace Plane (NASP), which grew out of the Trans Atmospheric Vehicle (TAV) program of the mid-1980s. At the same time, Lockheed engineers are exploring new airlifters with cargo capacities that exceed that of today's C-5 Galaxy.

In the area of military applications there is the well-publicized YF-22 Advanced Tactical Fighter program, but one can be assured that it is 'the tip of the iceberg' of the wonders that push the 'edge of the envelope' on *Skunk Works* drawing boards. While the *Skunk Works* engineers are designing the aircraft that will defend American airspace in the twenty-first century, other Lockheed engineers are working on elements of the Strategic Defense Initiative, such as ERIS, which perhaps one day will be able to defend American 'high ground' from hostile ICBMs.

On other technological fronts, Lockheed engineers continue to explore new means of aircraft propulsion ranging from Propfan engines to Liquid Hydrogen fuel. Meanwhile at Sunnyvale, as the Hubble Space Telescope moves out of the world's largest clean room for launch into space, Lockheed will be ready to start work on a new generation of space telescopes that will bring into mankind's view stars which Allan Lougheed, Robert Gross, Hall Hibbard and Kelly Johnson could only barely imagine—but toward which they reached.

As Robert Gross, Lockheed's chief executive from 1932 to 1967 is frequently quoted, '*Look ahead where the horizons are absolutely unlimited.*'

Left: Lockheed's conceptual National Aerospace Plane (NASP) would take off like an airliner and carry paying passengers on orbital and suborbital space flights. *Overleaf:* A summer 1986 conception of a proposed YF-22 Advanced Tactical Fighter in action.

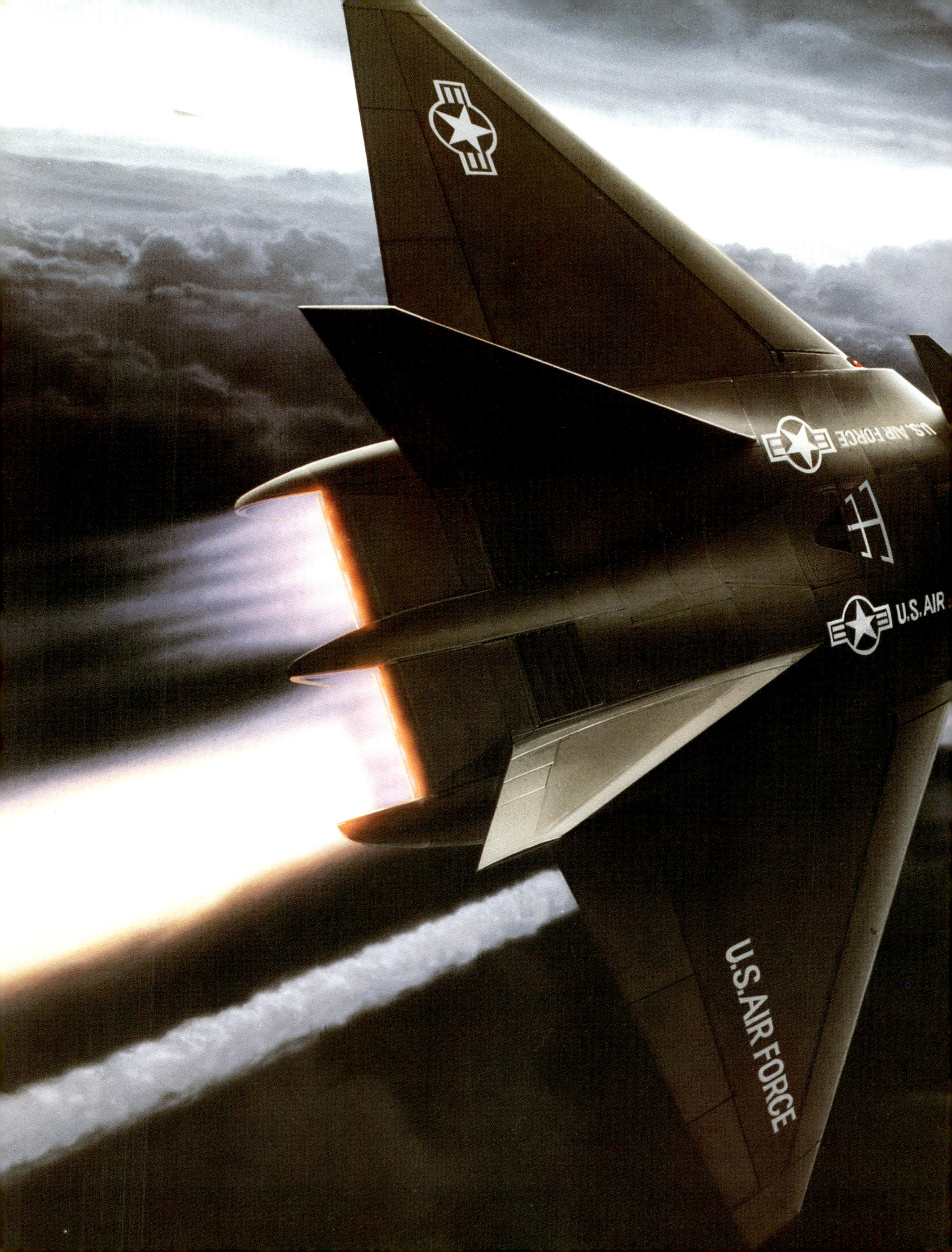
U.S. AIR FORCE
U.S. AIR
U.S.AIR FORCE

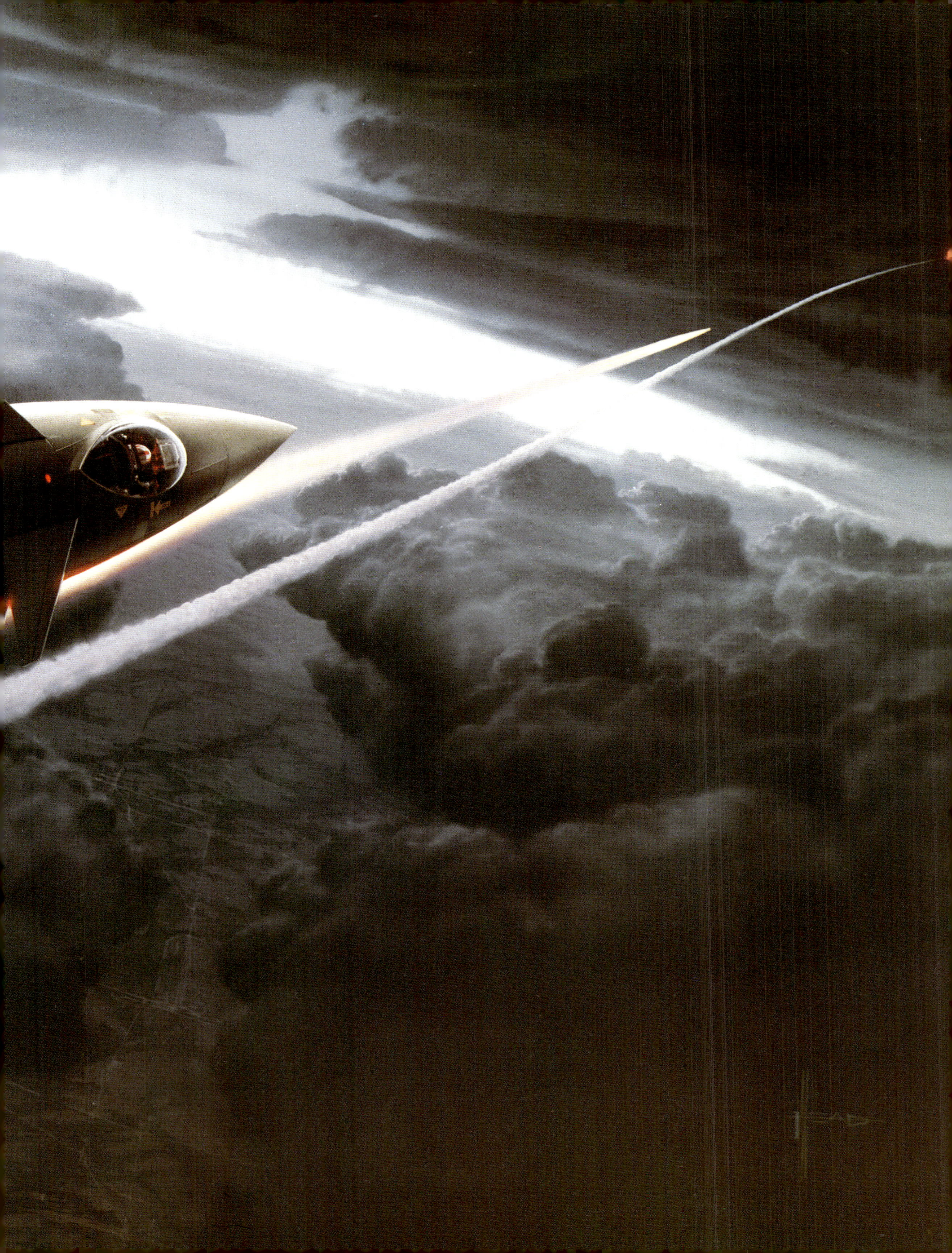

INDEX

A-11 (see also A-12) 132
A-12 reconnaissance Aircraft 132, 133, 136
A-28 and A-29 Hudson 34
AAFS program (see Advanced Aerial Fire Support Program) 147
AC-130 (see Hercules)
Acoustic Communication System (IACS) 89
Advanced Aerial Fire Support Program 147
Advanced Development Projects Office (ADP—see Skunk Works) 124, 125, 231
Advanced Tactical Fighter (ATF) 144, 244, *244*, 147
Advanced Technology Satellite (ATS-5) 217
Advanced TriStar (see TriStar)
Aer Lingus 30
Aerogyro (see Model 186/286 series) 146-147, *146-147*

Aeronautical Systems Group 226, 233
Agena upper stage rocket (see also Gemini-Agena) 212
AH-56 (see Cheyenne)
AH-64 Apache (McDonnell Douglas) 149
AIM-47A missile system 132
Air Botswana *160*
Air Canada 183, 186, 187, 193, 196
Air Express *22*, 22
Air France 46, 52
Air Gabon 161
Air India 52
Air Lanka 196
Air Lease Management 196
'Airlift Center of the World' (see Lockheed Georgia)
Air Portugal *197*
AiRover Company 42
Airtrooper (see Little Dipper)
Alaskan Star Airlines 15, 35
Albatros Werke 12

Albert, King of Belgium 10, *11*
Alco Hydro-Aeroplane Company of San Francisco 6-7, 226
Alcor Aircraft Corporation 18, 226 *226*
Alia (Jordanian airline) 196
Allen, Eddie 45, 46
Allison engines 42, 60, 65, *67,* 77, 98, *102,* 113
All Nippon Airlines 189, 196
Altair *18,* 19, 22, 23, *23,* 42, 220
American Airlines 22, 82, 189
American Defense Preparedness Association (ADPA) 217
American Overseas (airline) 46
American Transair (airline) 196
A-NEW Advanced ASW avionic system (see YP-3C)
Ansett Airlines 82
Apollo lunar landing program 116
APR-4 Electronic Countermeasure System (ECM) 82
Aquila 220
Arnold, Chief of Staff General Henry 'Hap' 96
ASG-18 radar 132
AT-18 40
AT-33A (see T-33A)
Atalanta (see P-38)
Atlantis OV-104 (see also Shuttle Orbiter) 214
Atlas launch vehicle 212, 214

Aurora (Canadian version of P-3 Orion, designated CP-140) 89
Australian Navy 90
Aviolanda 123
Avion Corporation 18
Avions Fairey 123

B-1 (Rockwell) 144
B-17 (Boeing and Lockheed) 42, *43,* 74, 76, 78
B-29 (Boeing) 108, 150, 204
B-30 (see Constellation)
B-34 Lexington 37, 41, 42
B-36 (Consolidated) 108, 113, 129
B-37 Ventura 37, 42
B-38 42
B-40 42
B-47 (Boeing and Lockheed) 150
B-52 (Boeing) 79, 133, 136, 144
B-70 (Rockwell) Valkyrie 136
Ballistic Offensive Suppression (AXE—also BOSS) 217
Barber, Lieutenant Rex 71, 76
Beale AFB 129, 136, 140, *142-143*
Bell aircraft and helicopters 96, 147, 149, 150
Beta B-120 (titanium) 140
Big Dipper (Model 34) 94, *94*
Blackbird (SR-71) 132, 133, *134-135,* 136, *136-137, 138-139,* 140, *140-141, 142-143,* 144, *145,* 244, *247*

Lower right: The legendary Jimmy Doolittle stands next to his bright red-and-orange *Shellightning* Orion. The Lockheed Orion was one of the fastest planes in the world in its day. Along with other epochal Lockheed designs it helped to pave the path for mankind's 'reach for the stars.'

Bledsoe, Major Adolphus 136
Bly, Nellie 16
Boeing 24, 44, 45, 56, 150, 200, 244
Boeing aircraft, miscellaneous 24, 44, 56, 140, 167, 171, 186, 200
Bong, Major Dick *72-73*, 76, 98
Borman, Frank 116
Boyd, Col Albert 98
Braniff Airways 82, *194*, 196
British Air Ministry 32
British Airways 30
British Orpheus jet engines 166
British Overseas Airways 46
British Royal Air Force (see Royal Air Force)
British Royal Navy 208
British West Indies Airline 196
Brown, Lieutenant Russell 101
Bullock, William 161
Burbank, California 23, 24, 32, 45, 46, *55*, 58, *62-63*, 144
Burcham, Milo 45, 97, 98

C-5 Galaxy *151*, 171-180, *171, 172*, 173, *174, 176, 178, 180, 181*, 186, 193, 231, 238, 240, *243*, 247
C-12 Vega 22
C-23 Altair 22
C-25 Altair 22
C-35 Electra (see XC-35)
C-36 Electra 28, 40

C-40 Electra 28, 40
C-47 Skytrain (Douglas) 95
C-56 Lodestar 41
C-57 Lodestar 41
C-59 Lodestar 41
C-60 Lodestar 41
C-66 Lodestar 41
C-69 (see Constellation)
C-85 Orion 22
C-101 Vega 22
C-104 Electra 40
C-111 Electra 40
C-121 (see Constellation)
C-130 Hercules (see Hercules)
C-140 Jetstar (see Jetstar)
C-141 Starlifter 166-169, *166-169*, 171, 238
Cabot, Samuel 74
CADAM, Incorporated 233
CalComp 233
Canadair 105, 119, 123
Canadian Armed Forces 89
Carter Administration 144
Cathay Pacific 193, 196
Central Intelligence Agency (CIA) 124, 132, 133
CF-104 (see F-104)
CH-47 helicopter 178
Chain Lightning (see P-58)
Challenger OV-99 214
Charleston AFB 178

Cheyenne helicopter (AH-56) 147, 149, *149*, 175, 238
City of Tacoma 18
Civil Aeronautics Authority 25
Chamberlain, Neville 29, 31, 32
Clark, Frank *228*
Cleaves, Prentice (Lockheed test pilot) 95
Clean Room (Lockheed Sunnyvale) *223*, 224
Clustered Airfield Defeat Munitions (CADM) 217
Coleman, Bob 6
Collier Trophy 28
Columbia OV-102 214
Columbine 50, *51*
Columbine III 50, 52
Combat Talon (see Hercules)
Commercial Aircraft Priority Committee 44
Concorde 200
Consolidate Aircraft 23, 108, 113, 129
Constellation *2-3*, 40, 44, 45, 46, *45, 47, 47*, 48, *48, 50, 51*, 52, *52*, 53, *53, 54, 55*, 56-57, *56-57*, 58, *59*, 76-77, *82*, 238, *238*, (see also Starliner, Super Constellation)
Constitution 58, *59*, 78
Convair (see Consolidated)
Corbin (automobiles) 6
Cotton, Sidney 30

Council, Col William 98
Covert Survivable In-weather Reconnaissance Strike Aircraft (CSIRS) 144
CP-140 (see Aurora)
Culver, C 146
Curtiss aircraft 6, 10
Curtiss engines 6, 23
Curtiss, Glenn 6, 7
Curtiss HS-2L *8*, 10, 22
CX-4 171

Datacom Systems Corporation 233
Davies, Cdr Thomas 78
Daughters, Wynn 161
DC-10 (McDonnell Douglas) 186, *189*, 194, 240
Dead Man's Island 15
Deep Quest 217
Deep Submergence Rescue Vehicle (DSRV) 217
DeHavilland Goblin engine 96
Delta Airlines 161, 193, 196, *197*
Department of Defense 207, 217
Detroit Aircraft Co 18, 24, 226
DIALOG Information Services, Inc. 212, 214, 233
DIFAR 89
Digital Magnetic Tape Set (DMTS) 89
Discovery OV-103 214, *217*
Dole, James D 13

Dole Race 13, 15
Doolittle, Jimmy 21, 25, 250
Dornier flying boat 34
Douglas Aircraft 10, 13, 16, 24, 44, 56, 133, 150, 167, 226 (see also DC-10, McDonnell Douglas)
'Droopsnoot' Lightning (see P-38) 68, 72
Dufay film 30
Dunkirk 34
Dvorscak, Bernie 178, 179, 243
Dynamics Explorer 217

E-3A Sentry Airborne Warning & Control System (AWACS) 90
E-5 fire control system 107
EAG-154 Observation Island 208
Eaker, General Ira 19
Earhart, Amelia 16, 20, 28, 28, 233
Eastern Airlines 24, 46, 82, 186, 189, 193, 196
EC-121 52, 55, 57
EC-130Q flying radio relay station 156
Edwards Air Force Base 45, 116, 124
Eilson, Ben 15
Eisenhower, Dwight 50, 51, 52, 124, 126
Electra (Model 10) 24-32, 24-29, 35, 37, 40, 41, 253
Electra (Model 188) 82, 83, 84, 84, 85
Electra Junior 28-30, 29, 31, 40
Electronic Sciences Laboratory 212
Electronic Support Measures (ESM) 90
Elizabeth, Queen of Belgium 10, 11

Elliot, Major Larry 136
Enigma code machine 35
Enterprise OV-101 214
ER-2 (see also TR-1) 129
ESM signal sorting 89
Estes, Major Thomas 136
Excalibur (see also Constellation) 40, 44, 44
Exoatmospheric Reentry-vehicle Interceptor Subsystem (ERIS) 217, 247
Explorer (see also Vega) 16, 18, 22

F-1 flying boat 10, 10-11, 22, 226
F-4 (P-38) 65, 68, 74, 74
F-5 (P-38) 65, 68, 74
F-12 (see YF-12)
F-14 (Grumman) 136
F-15 (McDonnell Douglas) 136
F-16 (General Dynamics) 123, 136
F-19 Specter (see Stealth fighter)
F-38 (P-38) 77
F-80 series (see Shooting Star)
F-86 Sabre Jet (North American) 101, 108
F-89 Scorpion (Northrop) 106, 108
F-90 108, 109, 111, 141
F-94/F-97 Starfire (Models 780/Model 880) 106-109, 107-109, 141, 256
F-101 (McDonnell Douglas) 108
F-102 (Convair) 108
F-104 Starfighter (Models 83-683) 114-123, 114-123
F-106 (Convair) 108
Fabre, Henri 7

Farnborough International Air Show 136
Federal Aviation Administration (FAA) 161, 166
Faint Object Camera (FOC) 224
Falklands Islands 156
FB-1 (see F-1)
Fiat Aerfer 123
Fighter Bomber Squadron, 7th 101
Fighter Interceptor Wing, 51st 101
Fighter Interceptor Squadrons, 106, 108, 114
Fighter Squadron, 70th 71-77
Fighter Weapons Meet, 1962 114
Fleet Ballistic Missile (FBM) 207, 212, 233, 238
Fine Guidance Sensors (FGS) 224
Flight Test Vehicles (FTV) 206, 207
Flying Fortress (see B-17)
Flying Test Stand 42
Focke-Wulf aircraft 112, 113, 119
Fokker aircraft 123
Forward Looking Infared (FLIR) system 90, 92
Fry, Jack 44, 45, 46
FTV 206
Fuller, Major John 136

G-AFGN 31
Galaxy (see C-5)
Garret AiResearch TFE-731 166
Garuda Airlines (Indonesia) 82
Gatty, Harold 17
Gemini 4 191
Gemini-Agena 212, 212
Gemini manned space program 212

General Dynamics aircraft 132 (see also F-16)
General Dynamics Kingfisher 132
General Electric 60 (AN/AAPS-138 radar antenna) 90, (J33 turbojet engine) 98, (J79 engine) 114, (J79-GE-3A) engine) 120, (TF39 engine) 175, (TF39-1C engine) 177, (engines) 144, (turbofan engines) 186
George AFB 123
German Defense Ministry 119
Gibraltar 76
Glomar Explorer 217
GMKI Hercules (see Hercules)
Goebel, Arthur 16, 228
Golden Eagle 15
Goudy, Ray 146
Graf Zeppelin 17
Graham, Terry 161
Gray Ghost 97
Great Silver Fleet 46
Groom Lake, Nevada 124, 144
Gross, Courtlandt 32, 37, 42
Gross, Robert 24, 42, 94, 151, 229
Grumman E-2C (Hawkeye AWACS) aircraft 90
Guadalcanal 71
Gulf Air 193, 196

H-51 Helicopter (see Model 186/286 series)
Hadden, Frank 161
Hall, F C 16
Hall, Norman 9
Hall-Scott (aircraft) engines 10

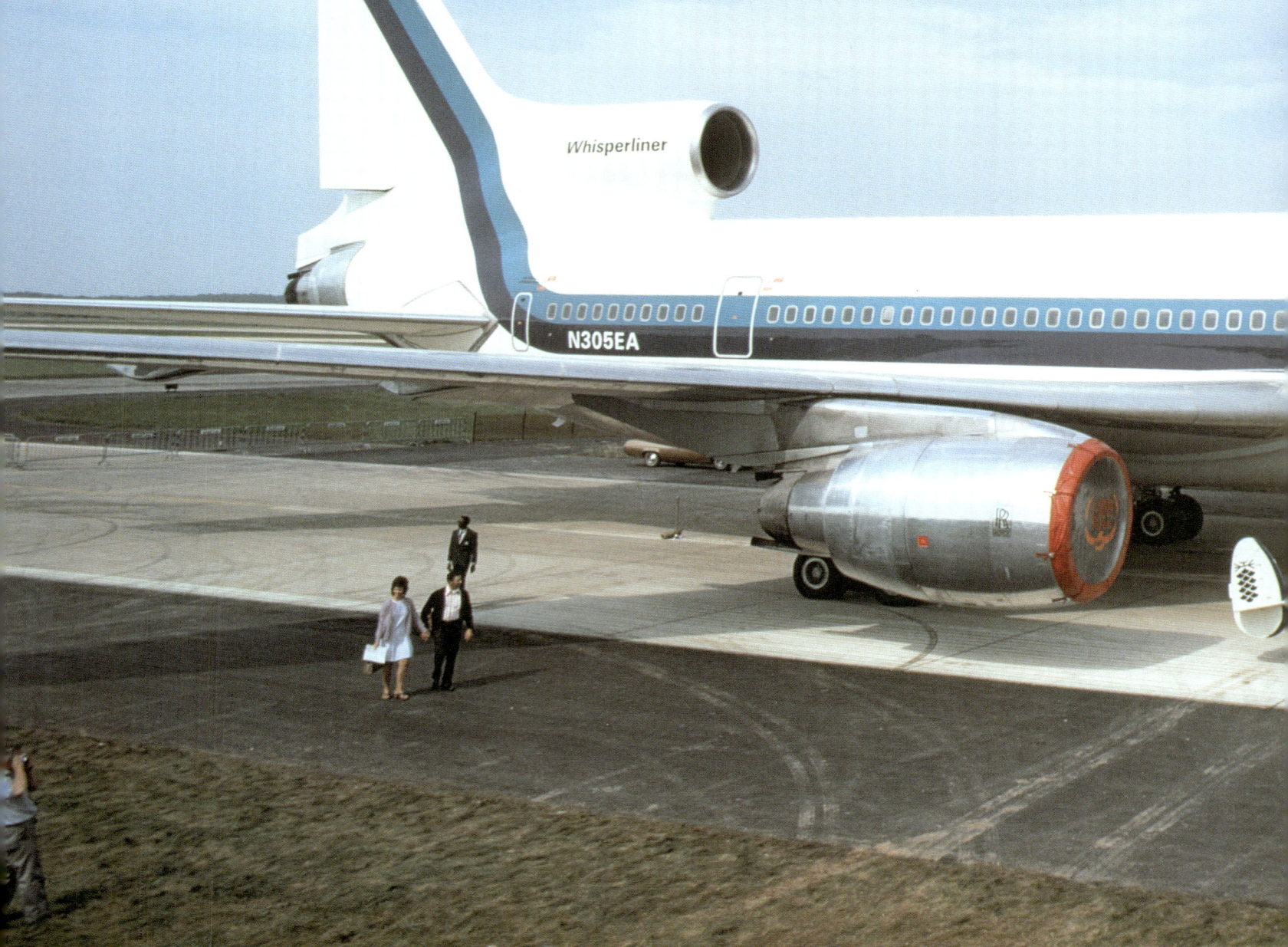

Hamilton AFB 114, *116*
Harmon International Trophy 16, 136
Harper's Dry Lake 178
Harpoon (Model 15, PV-2) *36-37*, 37, 41
HASPU-2 (see U-2) 127
Haas-Turner Airlines 196
Haughton, Daniel 175, 186
Have Blue (program) 144
Hawkes, Captain Frank *15*, 16, *16*
Hawkeye AWACS aircraft (Grumman E-2C) 90
Hawkins, Willis 58
Haze Paint 74, *74*
HC-130 Hercules (see Hercules)
Head Up Display (HUD) 161
Headle, Marshall 25
Hearst, George Jr 13, 15
Heinkel aircraft 96, 98, 119
Heinkel, Dr Ernst 96
Heit, Captain Robert 136
Henderson Army Air Field 71
Heppe, Richard 244
Hercules (Lockheed military Model 82 series and commercial Model 100 series) 150-163, 231, 238, *150-165, 237*
Hibbard, Hall 44, 60, 79, 96, *100, 228*
High Altitude Sampling Program (see HASPU-2)
High Energy Real Time Inspection System (HERTIS) 217
High Technology Test Bed (HTTB) 161, *161, 164-165*
High Revolution Spectrograph (HRS) 224
High Speed Photometer (HSP) 224

Hind (Soviet helicopter gunship) 149
Hitler, Adolf 31
HMS *Hermes* 19
Holzer, Judge Harry 24
Homing Overlay Experiment (HOE) 217, *217*
Howland Island 28
HS-2L (see Curtiss HS-2L)
HTTB aircraft *161*, 161, *164-165*
Hubble Space Telescope (HST) 223, *223-224*, 247
HUD 161
Hudson 31-35, *32-35*, 40, *41*, 42, *63*
Hughes, Howard 30-31, *31*, 44, 46, 171, *217*
Hughes Mining Barge 217 (see also *Glomar Explorer*)
Hughes Tool Co 44, 149
Hunter, Ben 15

ICBM 178, 207, 247
Ilyushin Il-10 bomber 101
Imperial Iranian Air Force 89
Imperial Japanese Navy 68
Infrared Detection System (IRDS) 89
Ingalls, Laura 20
Initial Polaris Program 207
International Air Conference (Chicago 1944) 95
International Aviation of Chicago 6
International Sun-Earth Explorer 217
Iraqi Airways 167
IRBM 207
Israel Air Force 156
Italian Air Force (see also F-104) 123
Itazuki Air Base, Japan 106

Japan 28, 31, 35, 69-77, 82, 119
Japanese Marine Self Defense Forces 90, *91*
Jet Assisted Take Off (JATO) *156*
JetStar (Model 329) 166, 167, 171, *166*
JO-1 28
JO-3 28, 29
Joerz, Captain Eldon 136
Jones, General David 127
Johnson, Clarence 'Kelly' 24, 25, *25*, 30, 32, 37, 44, 45, 60, 79, 96, 114, 124, *125*, 127, 132, 136, 144, 166
Johnson, Frank 95
Johnson, President Lyndon 132, *136*
JP-4 fuel 140
JP-7 fuel 140
Jupiter IRBM 207

Kadena AFB 136, 144
Kawasaki 82, 105
Keeler, Fred 13
Kelly Johnson Research and Development Center 247
Kelsey, Ben 60, 63
Kennedy, President John 127, 200
'Keyhole' satellites 224
KH-11 224
KH-12 224
Kiska (Aleutian Islands) 76
KLM (airlines) 30, 46, 82, 152

Koblenz, West Germany 119
Konincklijk Marine (Netherlands Navy) 90
Korean War 98, 108, 114, 150
Kruschev, Nikita *126*, 127
KS-3A aerial refueling tanker (Viking) 92
Kuiper Airborne Observatory 169
Kurile Islands 37

L-100 Hercules (see Hercules)
L-188 Electra (see Electra, Model 188)
L-500 (see C-5)
L-1000 jet engine 96
L-1011, L-1011-1, L-1011-100, L-1011-200, L-1011-500 (see Tristar)
La-9 fighter 108
LADS 161, 165
Lady Southern Cross 19
Lamphier, Captain Thomas 71, 76
LC-130 (see Hercules)
LeVier, Tony 58, 105, 114, 125
Lexington (see B-34, B-37)
Lindbergh, Anne Morrow 19, *19*
Lindbergh, Charles 13, 15, 17, 19, *19*
Link communications equipment 90
Lightning (see P-38)
Liquid hydrogen fueled aircraft *201, 203*, 247

Lower left: What differences the years make: the Lockheed Model 12 Electra (*foreground*) and the Model L-1011 TriStar differ in size but have played equally large parts in the continuing Lockheed story.

Little Dipper (Model 33) 94
Lockheed Advanced Maritime Systems Group 231, 233
Lockheed Advanced Tactical Systems 217
Lockheed Aermod Center 231
Lockheed Aeronautical Systems Group 244
Lockheed Airborne Data System (see LADS)
Lockheed Aircraft Services Co 231
Lockheed Air Terminal 233, *233*
Lockheed-Arabia 235
Lockheed Calabasas headquarters 226
Lockheed California (Calac) 231, 238 (see also Burbank, California and Palmdale, California)
Lockheed Corporation International 235
Lockheed DataPlan, Inc 233
Lockheed Electronics Company 235
Lockheed Electronic Systems Group 231
Lockheed Engineering & Management Services Co 233
Lockheed Finance Corp 235, 237
Lockheed Flying Stabilizer *188*
Lockheed Georgia (Gelac) 150, *151*, (see also Marietta, Georgia) 231, 238, *240*
Lockheed Hydraulic Brake Co 13
Lockheed Information Systems Group 231, 233
Lockheed Missile Systems Division (LSMD) 204, 205, 231, 233, 235
Lockheed Missiles & Space Co (LMSC) 209, 233; LMSC Space Systems Division (SSD) 212, 217; LMSC Advanced Systems Division 212, 214; LMSC Ground Vehicles Systems 217; LMSC Ocean Systems Division 217
Lockheed Missile & Space Systems Group 231, 235
Lockheed Ocean Laboratory 217
Lockheed Shipbuilding Co 233
Lockheed Space Operations Co 233
Lockheed Support Systems 231
Lockheed Vital Statistics 238
Lodestar *35*, 35, 37, 40, 41, *41*, 42, 44, 78
London-to-Melbourne Race (1934) 19
Los Angeles 13, 15
Los Angeles International Airport 15
LOT Airlines (Poland) 30
Loughead Aircraft Manufacturing Co 7-13, 18
Loughead, Allan 6, 7, *9*, 12, 13, *15*, 18, 206, 226, *228*, 233
Loughead, Beth *228*
Loughead brothers 6, 7, 13
Loughead, Malcolm 6, 7, *9*, 13, *15*, 18, 206, 226
Loughead, Victor 6
Low Altitude Parachute Extraction System (LAPES) *159*
Low Wing Special (see Explorer)
LTV (Ling/Temco/Vaught) 92
Lufthansa Airlines 29, 52
Lufttransport Unternehmen (LTU) 193, 196
Luftwaffe 68, 77, 98, 113, 119, 123, *123*
Lulu Belle *96*, 97
Luke AFB 119, 123

M-3 Machine guns 98
Macchi 123
Magnetic Anomaly Detector (MAD) sensor 84, 92
Manned Deep Submergence Vehicles 233
Manned Orbital Laboratory (MOL) 119
Marquardt aircraft engines 133
Marshall of Cambridge 194, 196
Marietta, Georgia (Lockheed plant at) 150, *151*, *164-165*, 167, 172
Marquardt aircraft engines 133
Mason, Tim 196
Materials Sciences Laboratory (Lockheed) 214, 217
MC-130E Combat Talon (see Hercules)
McCarty, General Chester E 151
McDivitt, James 116
McDonnell Aircraft 108
McDonnell-Douglas 149, *188*, 194, 244, 226 (see also DC-10)
Menasco, Al 42, *226*, 228

Messerschmitt aircraft 96, 119, 123
Messerschmitt, Dr Willy 96
Metier Management Systems (Lockheed Systems Group) 233
Mid-Continent Airlines 35
'Mighty Mouse' rockets *109*
Military Air Transport Service 52, 150
Military Airlift Command (MAC) 150, 167, 169, 171, 175, 178
Military Airlift Wing (MAW) 167, *180-181*
Milliken, Dr 60
Mil Mi-24 (see Hind)
Minuteman ICBM (see ICBM)
Mitchell, Major John 71
Mitsubishi aircraft 119, 123, (A6M 'Zero') 76, (G4M 'Betty') 71
Model F (see F-1)
Model G float plane 6, *7, 9*, 22
Model S (see S-1)
Model 1 (see Vega)
Model 2 (see Vega)
Model 3 Air Express 16
Model 4 low wing special (see Explorer)
Model 5 (see Vega)
Model 6 (see Vega)
Model 7 (see Explorer)
Model 8 (see Altair)
Model 9 (see Orion)
Model 10 (see Electra)
Model 12 (see Electra Junior)
Model 14 (see Super Electra)
Model 15 (see Harpoon)
Model 17 (see B-17)
Model 18 (see Lodestar)
Model 20 (see P-58)
Model 22 (see P-38)
Model 26 (see P2V)
Model 30 100
Model 33 Little Dipper 94, *94*
Model 34 Big Dipper 94, *94*
Model 37 (see Ventura)
Model 40 42
Model 44 (see Excaliber)
Model 49 (see Constellation)
Model 75 (see Saturn)
Model 80 (see Shooting Star)
Model 82 (see Hercules)
Model 83 Starfighter (see F-104)
Model 89 (see Constitution)
Model 100 Hercules (see Hercules)
Model 100-20 Hercules (see Hercules)
Model 100-30 Hercules (see Hercules)
Model 122 (see P-38)
Model 126 (see P2V)
Model 133 96, *96*, 100, *100*
Model 134 (see B-38)
Model 135 (see B-40)
Model 139 jetliner 166
Model 177 (see X-7)
Model 182 Hercules (see Hercules)
Model 186 Orion (see P-3)
Model 186/286 series helicopters 146-147, *146-148*, 149
Model 188 Electra (see Electra)
Model 212 (see Electra Junior)
Model 214 (see Hudson)
Model 222 Lightning (see P-38)
Model 245 (see SeaStar)
Model 249 (see Constellation)
Model 282 Hercules (see Hercules)
Model 283 Starfighter (see F-104)
Model 300 167, 171
Model 314 (see Hudson)
Model 322 (see P-38)
Model 325 129, 132
Model 326 (see P2V)
Model 329 (see JetStar)
Model 349 (see Constellation)
Model 382 Hercules (see Hercules)
Model 400 129, 132
Model 414 (see Hudson)
Model 422 (see P-38)
Model 426 (see P2V)
Model 437 (see O-56)
Model 475 146, *146*
Model 500 (see C-5)
Model 522 (see P-38) 65
Model 526 (see P2V)
Model 580/T-33 'T-Bird' 102
Model 622 (see P-38)
Model 626 (see P2V)
Model 649 (see Constellation)
Model 683 Starfighter, export version (see F-104)

Model 726 (see P2V)
Model 749 (see Constellation)
Model 780 Starfire (see F-94)
Model 849 (see Constellation)
Model 880 Starfire (see F-94)
Model 900 (see YP-900)
Model 949 (see Constellation)
Model 1011 (see Tristar)
Model 1049 (see Super Constellation)
Model 1249 (see Super Constellation)
Model 1329 166
Model 1449 (see Constellation)
Model 1559 56
Model 1649 (see Constellation)
Model 2000 200, 201
Moffett Naval Air Station 58, 79, 129
Mojave Desert Lockheed facility at Palmdale 124
Montgomery glider 6
Morgan, Major George 136
Multiple Independently-targeted Re-entry Vehicles (MIRV) 208
Murdock Engineering Company (Lockheed Operating Company) 231
Muroc Army Air Field (now Edwards AFB) 45, 96, 97, *97*

Narlesky, Major Ray *243*
National Aerospace Plane (NASP) *247*
National Airlines 82
NATO Starfighter Management Organization 119
Naval Air Systems Command 92
Navigational/Tactical (NT) central digit computer 90
NC-130 (see Hercules)
Neptune (see P2V series)
Netherlands Air Force 28
NF-104A (see F-104)
Nichols, Ruth 16
Nimbus 6 217
Nimbus 7 217
Noonan, Fred 28
Normandy Invasion 35, 77
North American Aviation 42, 76, 98, 108, 132, 136, 200
North Atlantic Treaty Organization (NATO) 119, 149
Northrop aircraft 10, 44, 106, 108
Norhtrop Corporation 244
Northrop, John 7-10, *9*, 13, 18
North to the Orient 19
Northwest Airlines *25-27*
Northwest Orient Airlines 25, 50, 82, 83

O-3 (see Q-Star)
O-56 (Lockheed Model 437) 37
Olympic Duo-Four 18
OMEGA worldwide navigation system 89
Operation *Frigate Bird* 208
Optical Telescope Assembly (OTA) 224
Orbiting Geophysical Observatory (OGO-5) 217
Orbiting Solar Observatory (OSO-8) 217
Orion (Model 9) *22-23*, 22-24, 25, 37
Orion, Model 186 (see P-3 series aircraft, also Aurora)
Ormsby, Roger Jr 244
Orpheus jet engines 166
Oxcart 132

P-2 (retroactively assigned designation for P2V, which see)
P2V Neptune (Model 26 series) 78-83, *78-83*
P-3 Airborne Early Warning & Control (AEW&C) aircraft 84, *84*, 85
P-3 Orion Anti Submarine Warfare (ASW) aircraft 84-91, *84-91*, 231, *250*
P3V-1 (original designation for P-3, which see)
P-16 23
P-24 (see YP-24, YP-900)
P-38 Lightning *1, 4-5*, 32, 45, 60, *62-63*, 63, *64-65*, 65, *66-67*, 68, *68-69*, *70-71*, 71, 72, *72-73*, 74, *74-75*, *76-77*, *76-77*, 78, *238*
P-49 (see XP-49)
P-58 Chain Lightning 77, *77*
P-80 (see Shooting Star)
Pacific Southwest Airlines (PSA) 82, 196
Packard, David (Deputy Secretary of Defense) 209
Palmdale, California (Lockheed facility) 132, 133, *134-135*, 136, 144, *240*
Panama-Pacific Exposition 7
Pan American Airways *2-3*, 16, 19, 25, 40, 44, 45, 46, 58, 196, 200
Parachute Low-Altitude Delivery System (PLADS) *159*
'Paradise Ranch' 124, 132, 144
Parr, Captain Ralph 101, *101*
PBO-1 34
Pearl Harbor, Hawaii 58, 68, 78
Plew, James 6
Pogo (see XFV-1)
Polaris series Fleet Ballistic Missiles (FBM), later Polaris Submarine Launched Ballistic Missiles (SLBM) 206, *207*, *206-208*, *207-210*
Poseidon Submarine Launched Ballistic Missiles 208, 209, *210*
Post, Wiley *16-17*, 17, *20*, 21, 247
Powers, Francis Gary 125, *126*
Pratt & Whitney engines 34, 52, 58, 77, 108, 127, 129, 132, 140, 146, 166, 186, *188*
Price, Nathan 96
Princess Margaret 194
Project Argus 206, 217
Propfan concept *202*, 247
PROTEUS analyzer unit 89
Pulver, Dick 58
PV-1 (see Ventura)
PV-2 (see Harpoon)

Quantas Airlines 52, 82
Q-Star 220, *220*
QT2 220
Queen Mary 33
Quesada, Elwood 205

R6V (see XR6V)
R7V (see Constellation)
R20-1 28
R50 35, 41
Raborn, Admiral WF 'Red' 207
Radiometric Area Correlation System (RACG) 217
Rankin, Commander EP 78
RC-121 (see Constellation)
RC-130 (see Hercules)
Reid, Commander WS 78
Relaxed Static Stability *189*
Remotely-Piloted Vehicle (RPV) 220 (see also Model 40)
Rex engines 129
RF-104G (see F-104)
Rich, Ben 144
Ritchie, Willie 6
Rivers Joe 6
Rocket Assisted Take-off (RATO) 79
Rocketdyne AR-2 rocket motors 116, *118*
Rockwell International (see also North American Aviation, Space Shuttle orbiters) 136
Rodman, Berton 7, *9*
Rolls Royce 186, 189, 240
Rolls Royce jet engines *186-187*, *188-189*, 194
Royal Air Force (United Kingdom) (RAF) 34-35, 37, 42, 65, 75, 129, 156, 161, 194, 196, *197*
Royal Australian Air Force 34
Royal New Zealand Air Force 37
Royal Norwegian Air Force *123*
RS-70 (see B-70)
RS-71 (see Blackbird)
RT-33 (see T-33)

S-1 Sport Biplane *12*, 12, 13, 22
S-3 Viking 90, 92-94, *92-94*, 231, 240
SABCA 123
Safair Freighters Pty Ltd 161
Salmon, Herman 'Fish' 113
San Francisco Air Show (1919) *12*, 13
Saturn 78, 95, *95*
Saudia 196, 237, *237*
Saudi Arabia 235, 237
Saudi Arabian Air Force 167
SCV Study concept 201, *201*
Seasat 212, *214*, 224
Sea Star (T2V-1) 103
Seally, MM 72, *73*
Sagner, Donald 146

SH-51 (see Model 186/286 series)
Shellightning 250
Shooting Star (F-80, P-80 series) 96-102, *96-102, 111,* 235 (see also T-33)
Silica tiles on Space Shuttle Orbiters 214, *214*
Short Mac 42, 78, 94
Short Takeoff and Landing (STOL) 161
Side-Looking Airborne Radar (SLAR) 90
Sidewinder heat-seeking missiles 115
Siebel Aircraft Co 119
Sikorsky Co 149
Silver Star (see T-33)
Sirius 18, 19, *19,* 22, 23
Skunk Works 96, 114, 124, 125, 132, 133, *134, 135,* 136, 144, 166, 204, 231, 240
Smith, General Joseph 150
Smith, Major General Wayne 151
Solar Maximum Mission (Solar Max) 217
Sonabuoy Reference System (SRS) 89
Southern Air Transport 161
Soviet Union 106, 125, 127, 133, 136, 149
Space Shuttle Orbiters 214, *214,* (see also *Atlantis, Challenger, Columbia* and *Enterprise*)
Span loader concept *202*
Sparrow missile 123
Special Operations Executive (SOE) 35
Specter (as AC-130 gunship, see Hercules; as F-19, see Stealth fighter)
Spruce Goose 171
Squier, Carl 24, 28, 32, 37, *233*
SR-71 (see Blackbird)
Stadlman, Anthony 7, 12, 13
Stafford, Tom 116
Starfighter (see F-104)
Starfire (see F-94)
Starlifter (see C-141)
Starliner, Lockheed (see Constellation)
Starliner, Vega 42, *42*
Stealth fighter 74, 141, 144
Stearman, Lloyd 24, 228, 233
STOL (Short Take-off and Landing) 161
Strategic Air Command 108, 129, 136, 140, 171
Strategic Defense Initiative (SDI) 217
Strategic Reconnaissance (see Blackbird)
Stratocruiser (see Boeing)
Submarine Launched Ballistic Missiles (SLBM) (see Polaris, Poseidon, Trident)
Sullivan, Major James 136
Summa Corporation 217
Sunnyvale, California (Headquarters of Lockheed Missiles & Space Co, which see) (see also Hubble Space Telescope and Lockheed Missiles & Space Division)
Suntan liquid hydrogen aircraft program 132
Super Constellation (see Constellation) 48, *48, 50, 51, 52, 53,* 56, 57
Super Electra 30, *30-31,* 32, 37, 40, 42
Super Hercules 161, *162, 163*
Supersonic Commercial Air Transport (SCAT) 200
Supersonic Cruise Vehicle (SCV) 201
Supersonic transports (SST) 200, 201, *201, 203*
Swissair 22
Synthetic Haze Paint 74

T-1A 105
T2V SeaStar (Model 245) 103, *104,* 235
T-33 T-Bird 32, 103, 105, 106, 235
TAA Airline (Australia) 82

Tabeling, Lt Cmdr R A 78
Tactical Coordinator IRDS display 89
TAP (see Air Portugal)
Tarling, Canadian Captain William M 105
TF-80C trainer (see Shooting Star, T-33)
TF-104G trainer (see F-104)
Thiokol XM-19 Recruit rocket 206
Thompson, Squad Leader James 34
Thompson trophy 16
Thor 212
Thores, Rudy 45
Tingmissartoq 19
Tinker AFB 167
Titan launch vehicle 212
Title Insurance & Trust Co of Los Angeles 24
TO-1 103
Total Air 196
Total Package Procurement (TPP) 238
TR-1 127, *128,* 129, 140, *227,* 231, 240, *241*
Trans-Atmospheric Vehicle (TAV) 247, *247*
Trans-Canada Airlines 30
Transparent Logic Unit 89
Trans World Airlines 186-188
Travis AFB, CA 167, *180, 181*
Trident Submarine Launched Ballistic Missile (SLBM) 209-212, *210*
Triebfluegel (see Focke-Wolf)
Tri-Star (L-1011 series) 182-203, *182-203,* 231, *241, 253* (L-1011-500) 193-197, *193-197,* (TriStar US RAF refueling tanker) 196-197, *196-197*
Truculant Turtle 78-79, *78-79*
Tupolev Tu-22M (TU-26) bomber 133, 136
Turkish Air Force 123
Turner, Colonel Roscoe 16, *20*
TV-1 102, 103
Trans World Airways (TWA) 16, 22, 44, 45, 46, 52, 55, 57, 193, 196
Twister 217

U-2 124-127, *125-127,* 140, 240
UCX utility transport 166
Ugaki, Vice Admiral Matome 72
Undersea Long Range Missile System (ULMS) 209
Union Air Terminal 25
United Airlines 189, 196
Unitwin engine 42, 43
Univac 1832 general purpose digital computer 92
US-3 modified Viking (see S-3)
US Airborne troops *169*
US Air Force (USAF) 46, 48, 52, 57, 77, 82, 127-129, 132, 136, 140, 144, 150, 151, 194, 206, 233, *255,* 238, *243,* 244
USAF Aerospace Research Pilots School 116
USAF Air Defense Command (ADC) 114, 116
USAF Blackbird fleet 136
USAF Special Operations Squadron (SOS) 153
USAF Tactical Air Command (TAC) 116, 123, 151
USAF Museum 136
US Air National Guard 116
US Army 16, 23, 68, 82, 147, 149
US Army Air Corps (USAAC) 19, 23, 28, 35, 42, 60, 63, 65, 74, 77, 96
US Army Air Forces (USAAF) 34, 35, 37, 42, 44-46, 60, 65, 68, 71-77, 150, 204
US Army Air Force Plant Six 150
US Coast Guard 28
US Congress 240
US Department of Agriculture 27

US Marine Corps 82, *156*
US Military Assistance Program (MAP) 123
US Navy 19, 28, 35, 42, 48, 52, 58, 77, 78, 79, 82, 129, 132, 151, 152, 156, 207, 209, 233, 255
US Navy Blue Angels *156*
US Navy Special Projects Office 207
US Neutrality Act 32
USS *Chopper* 89
USS *Coral Sea* 79
USS *Enterprise* 93
USS *Ethan Allen* 208, *209*
USS *Ethan Allen* class submarines 212
USS *Forrestal* 156
USS *Francis Scott Key* 209
USS *Franklin D Roosevelt* 79
USS *George Washington* 207, 208
USS *James Madison* 209
USS *John F Kennedy* 92
USS *Lafayette* class submarines 212
USS *Lexington* 29
USS *Ohio* class submarines *210,* 212
USS *Patrick Henry* 208
USSR (see Soviet Union)

Varney Speed Lanes 22
Varney, Walter 228
Vega (Lockheed Models 1, 2, 5) *13, 13-15, 14-17,* 16, 17, 18, 22-24, 28, 42, 94
Vega Aircraft Company (later Corporation), a Lockheed subsidiary 37, 40-42, 56, 78, 235
Ventura Model 137, PV-1 37, *38-41,* 40, 41, 42, 78, *255*
Vick, Major Dewain 136
Vietnam 52, 57, 82, 136, 147, 169, 178, 220
Viking (see S-3)
von Halem, Heinz 112
Von Karman, Dr 60
Vulcan electric cannon 115, *120*
Vultee Aircraft Co 65

WC-121 (see Constellation)
WC-130 (see Hercules)
Weaver, Bill 196
Western Airlines 16, 22, 82
Westinghouse XJ 34 engines 108
White Steam Car Co 6
Wide Field Planetary Camera (WF/PC) 224
Widdlefield, Major Noel 136
Wilkins, Captain Sir George Hubert 15, 16, 18
Winnie Mae 16-17, *17,* 247
Wood, Robert 23
World Airways 196
World War I 10, 32
World War II 28, *31,* 32, 37, 40, 42, 63, 65, 77, 78, 113, 150, 235, 247
Worlds Fair 1939 31
Wright Army Air Field 23, 65
Wright brothers 6, 167
Wright aircraft engines 19, 34, 37, 42, 48, 77, 114
Wright, Orville 46
Wright Patterson AFB 136
WV (see Constellation)

X-6 *206*
X-7 204, 206, *206*
X-7A3 206, *206*
X-17 206
XA-938 23
XC-35 *27,* 28, 40

Overleaf: Darkness is falling, but like the onrushing darkness of the Cold War, it was no hinderance for the sturdy all-weather, night-flying F-94 Starfire interceptor that Lockheed built for the Air Force in the early 1950s.

XF-90 prototypes 108, 109
XF-104 114, *116,* 124
XFO-1 113
XFV-1 (Pogo) 112-113, *112-113*
XFY-1 (Convair) 113
XH-51A (see Model 186/286 series)
XJO-3 28
XL-1 engine 12
XP-38 (see P-38)
XP-80 (see P-80)
XP-900 23
XP-49 65
XRJ-37-MN-1 206
XR6V (see Constitution)

YAH-56 (see Cheyenne) 149
Yamamoto, Admiral Isoraku 68, 76
Yankee Doodle 16
Y1A-9 23
Y1P-24 23
Y1P-25 23
YC-121 (see Constellation)
YC-130 (see Hercules)
YC-141 (see Starfighter)
Yeager, Colonel Chuck 116, 119
YF-22 244, 247
YF-23 244
YF-12 132, 133, *133-135,* 136, *141*
YF-94 (see Starfire)
YF-97 (see Starfire)
YF-104 (see Starfighter)
YO-3A (see Q-Star)
Yom Kippur War 169, 178
YP-80 (see Shooting Star)
YP-3C (see P-3)
YP3V-1 (see P-3)
YP-24 22, *22,* 23
YP-38 (see P-38)
YP-80 (see P-80)
YS-3 (see S-3)

Zero (see Mitsubishi)

Photo Credits

All photos courtesy of the **Lockheed Corporation** except:

George W Hamlin: 164-165, 236-237

Donnie Head: 156-157 (right), 160 (top), 188-189

National Archives: 69 (top right), 72-73 (bottom right)

Marion Pyles: 189 (top right)

US Air Force: 56-57 (bottom left), 152 (bottom left), 153 (bottom right), 169 (top)

© **Bill Yenne:** 22 (bottom left), 40 (top and bottom left), 41 (top and bottom right), 85 (top right), 119 (bottom right), 76 (bottom left), 81 (top right), 85 (top right), 119 (bottom right), 140 (bottom left), 140-141 (top and bottom center), 141 (bottom right), 142-143, 144, 154, 156, 156 (bottom left), 179-171, 174, 180-181, 196 (bottom left), 208 238 (bottom left)

Designed by Bill Yenne

Edited by Timothy Jacobs and John Kirk

The author would like to extend his thanks and deep appreciation to Roy Blay of Lockheed Corporate Headquarters for reviewing the manuscript; Joe Dabney at Lockheed Georgia for supplying background information and for reviewing the manuscript; Don Fitts at Lockheed Georgia for reviewing the manuscript; Jack Gudgel of Lockheed Missiles & Space for arranging my close-up inspection of the Hubble Space Telescope; Hal Hurlocker at Lockheed Corporate Headquarters for reviewing the manuscript; Dick Martin at Lockheed Georgia for supplying background information and photos; Gail Rolka for typing the manuscript; Eric Schulzinger at Lockheed California for his generous assistance in my marathon search through the Lockheed photo archives and for supplying many of his own photos; Bob Slayman at Lockheed Corporate Headquarters for reviewing the manuscript and Richard Stadler at Lockheed California for supplying background information, for reviewing the manuscript and for his continued generous assistance throughout the project.

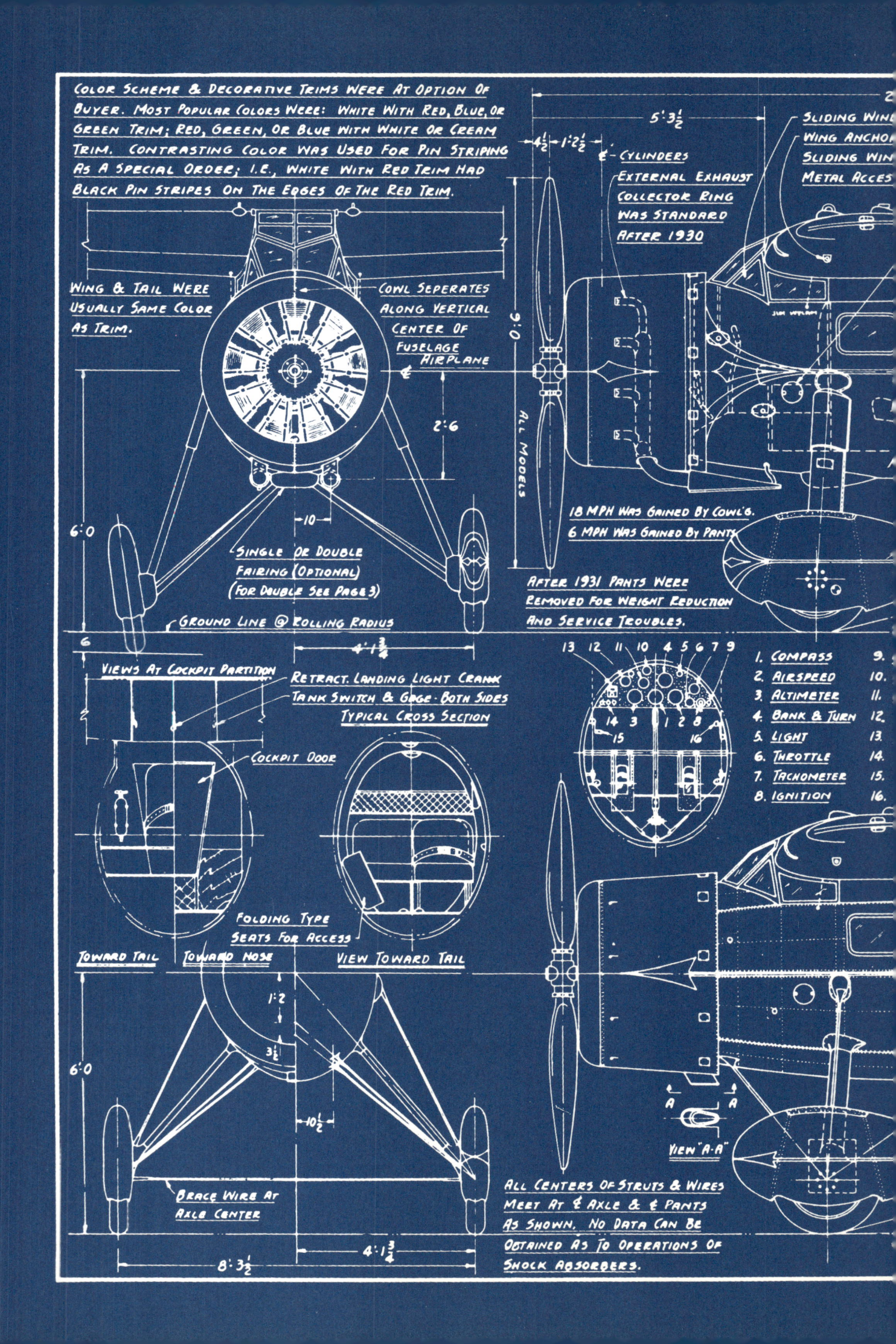

Color Scheme & Decorative Trims Were At Option Of Buyer. Most Popular Colors Were: White With Red, Blue, Or Green Trim; Red, Green, Or Blue With White Or Cream Trim. Contrasting Color Was Used For Pin Striping As A Special Order; I.E., White With Red Trim Had Black Pin Stripes On The Edges Of The Red Trim.

Wing & Tail Were Usually Same Color As Trim.

Cowl Seperates Along Vertical Center Of Fuselage Airplane

Sliding Wind
Wing Anchor
Sliding Win
Metal Acces

Cylinders External Exhaust Collector Ring Was Standard After 1930

Single Or Double Fairing (Optional) (For Double See Page 3)

Ground Line @ Rolling Radius

18 MPH Was Gained By Cowl'g.
6 MPH Was Gained By Pants

After 1931 Pants Were Removed For Weight Reduction And Service Troubles.

Views At Cockpit Partition

Retract. Landing Light Crank
Tank Switch & Gage - Both Sides
Typical Cross Section

Cockpit Door

Folding Type Seats For Access

Toward Tail   Toward Nose   View Toward Tail

1. Compass   9.
2. Airspeed   10.
3. Altimeter   11.
4. Bank & Turn 12.
5. Light   13.
6. Throttle   14.
7. Tachometer 15.
8. Ignition   16.

Brace Wire At Axle Center

View "A-A"

All Centers Of Struts & Wires Meet At ℄ Axle & ℄ Pants As Shown. No Data Can Be Obtained As To Operations Of Shock Absorbers.